DEER & DEER HUN
Book 2

DEER & DEER HUNTING

Book 2

Strategies and Tactics
for the Advanced Hunter

Robert Wegner

Stackpole Books

Published by
STACKPOLE BOOKS
Cameron and Kelker Streets
P.O. Box 1831
Harrisburg, PA 17105

First paperback printing, May 1992

Printed in the United States of America

10 9 8 7 6 5 4 3

Chapters 1-3, 6-15, and 17-21 of this book originally appeared in
Deer & Deer Hunting magazine. They are published here in revised
form with the permission of the Publisher and the Editors of *Deer &
Deer Hunting* magazine.

Library of Congress Cataloging-in-Publication Data
(Revised for vol. 2)

Wegner, Robert.
    Deer & deer hunting.

    Bibliography: p.
    Includes indexes.
    Contents: v. [1] The serious hunter's guide —
v. 2. Strategies and tactics for the advanced hunter.
    1. Deer hunting — Collected works. 2. Deer —
Collected works. I. Deer and deer hunting. II. Title.
SK301.W35   1984   799.2′77357   84-2413
ISBN 0-8117-2586-3

The sportsman studies and observes all of the characteristics of
deer, not alone because they interest him and furnish him
with food for thought while on the hunt and for discussion by
the campfire, but because he is aware that he must know
all the resources of the game in order to hunt it successfully.

— John Dean Caton, 1890

Dedication

To *Odocoileus virginianus* ♂ and ♀, which have
survived to this day despite dogs, predators, disease,
bows and arrows, guns and rifles, snares, nets, modern
farming practices and poisonous chemicals, and acid
rain, and which, I suspect, will outlive us all.

Contents

Part III   **THE DEER HUNTING MYSTIQUE**

Part IV   **THE DEER HUNTER**

Part V   **WHERE TO FIND MORE INFORMATION**

Acknowledgments

I would like to thank my colleague and friend Al Hofacker, the managing editor of *Deer & Deer Hunting* magazine, for editing my prose throughout the years and for constructing charts, graphs, figures and tables for purposes of illustrating technical information and for keeping me up to date on the newest research findings on white-tailed deer and the hunting of them. I would also like to thank my wife, Maren Lea, for being an excellent in-house critic, copy editor, typist, secretary, camp cook and outstanding deer hunting partner. Without the spirited enthusiasm and help of these two people, *Deer & Deer Hunting* (original volume and Book 2) would not have been possible. I thank you both.

Robert Wegner
Deer Foot Road
March 9, 1987

PART I

GIANTS AMONG DEER HUNTERS

Chapter 1

Judge Caton: Deer Hunter, Naturalist

The pleasure of the sportsman in the chase is measured by the intelligence of the game and its capacity to elude pursuit and in the labor involved in the capture. It is a contest with sharp wits where satisfaction is mingled with admiration for the object overcome.

— John Dean Caton, 1877

Some people who hunt the white-tailed deer study it seriously. Quite a few even make a life of it — not in the sense of becoming a "professional deer hunter," for there is no such thing despite all the claims to the contrary by the cult heroes on the lecture circuit — but in the sense that deer hunting becomes a lifetime study combining the sport of hunting with the science of natural history.

No serious student of the white-tailed deer begins his study of the natural history of this animal or the hunting of them without first consulting the life and work of John Dean Caton (1812–1895), that prominent Chief Justice of the Supreme Court of Illinois and one of the most distinguished "deer doctors" that America ever produced. Setting the tradition followed by such modern-day deer Ph.Ds as Aaron Moen, Larry Marchinton, and Valerius Geist, Caton systematically studied the natural history of the whitetail and made the hunting of them his favorite leisure-time diversion. Although Judge Caton claimed to be an amateur naturalist, he nevertheless maintained that severe and systematic study and discipline so indispensable to the professional scientist.

Although trained as a jurist, he studied the whitetail throughout his life not only in dust-covered books, but in the grandest school of all — the realm of nature, where he pursued his quarry with gun and pen in hand. Like his contemporaries Theodore Roosevelt, T. S. Van Dyke, and Carl Rungius, Caton participated in the stirring excitement of the chase so that he could

John Dean Caton (1812–1895). *Photo credit Robert Wegner*

learn even more about the whitetail's habits, especially its breeding characteristics during the rut. Like his contemporaries, Caton believed that the deer hunter, even more than the scientist, has the greatest opportunity to study the whitetail's habits, ways, and capabilities, for he spends more time in the deer forest.

Throughout his life, this famous sportsman/naturalist combined with great religiosity the study of the natural history of the white-tailed deer with the thrilling incidents encountered in the hunting of them. As his great and lasting contribution to the study of deer and deer hunting, he not only published the first scientific treatise on the subject, *The Antelope and Deer of America* (1877), but also created America's first deer park in 1858, a 300-acre enclosure established solely for observing and studying the various kinds of deer he held in captivity with special pref-

erence for his favorite species, *Odocoileus virginianus.* His enthusiasm for deer remained infectious; at the conclusion of reading his work and studying his life, you wonder why everybody does not turn to keeping deer and studying their habits.

Caton was born on a small farm near the Hudson River in Orange County, New York, in 1812. By the time he was four years old, his mother became a widow struggling to feed and clothe her four small children. The young boy spent most of his youth as an apprentice to farmers and harness makers while continuously striving to get an education. He was aided by persons who befriended him, admiring his ability and perseverance. However, his mother was able to keep the boy in the district school only with the greatest of difficulty, for he maintained a reputation for being a mischievous boy. "I preferred," Caton later wrote in his unpublished memoirs, "an active outdoor life, running, jumping, wrestling, and hunting."

The farmers he worked for never wearied of relating their deer hunting experiences to him, and the boy never wearied of listening to them. "Their hunting experiences when deer, bear, and wild turkeys were so abundant as to be almost nuisances, fairly transported me to the wild woods and wild scenes and the exciting chases which they so graphically described; and I longed for the time to come when I should be old enough to carry a rifle, and when I might wend my way to a new country such as they described, where I too might revel among game which had scarcely ever been alarmed by civilized man."

After studying at Grosvenor High School in Rome, New York, and spending an apprenticeship in the law offices of

Beardsley and Matteson in Utica, young Caton finally managed to secure a legal education in the spring of 1833; but not without a great deal of difficulty. While the young lad never claimed to be a rail-splitter, to maintain himself he cut a cord a day of second-growth white beech for twenty-five cents a cord. As an expert rifleman, Caton sometimes added wild fowl to his boarding house menu of fat pork and corned beef by shooting off the heads of wild turkeys.

Tales of the daring life in the great wild West, heard from the lips of a Dutchman named Detmore, fired Caton's burning de-sire to emigrate to the western country in search of his fortune. His bold start for the West was spontaneous; his precise destination quite unfixed. The Erie Canal took him to Buffalo; a steamer called the "Sheldon Thompson," to Detroit; a stage-coach, to Ann Arbor; and a horse-drawn wagon, to White Pigeon, Michigan, where he began to live off the land on grouse, wild turkeys, and venison.

In June of 1833, the six-foot, well-proportioned outdoorsman arrived in the small hamlet of Chicago with his cherished rifle called "Old Hemlock" in hand and fourteen dollars and some odd cents

Throughout his life, Judge Caton religiously combined the study of the natural history of the white-tailed deer with the thrilling incidents encountered in the hunting of them. *Photo credit Chicago Historical Society*

in his pocket. The young, boyish, enthusiastic lawyer from Monroe, New York, who was destined to become one of the great deer men of the nineteenth century, stopped for the first night at a log tavern at Wolf Point kept by W. W. Wattles—thoroughly prepared to set his stake and commence the business of life. By February of 1834, he had opened the first law office in Old Chicago and as an "old resident" of nine months, the twenty-one-year-old backwoodsman with a heavy black beard stood before 250 inhabitants and then proceeded to authorize a village incorporation under the general laws of the State of Illinois.

Chicago, at that time, consisted of merely a few log houses clustered around Fort Dearborn, a range of sand hills along the shoreline of Lake Michigan covered with cedars and willows, and—to the south and west—an endless stretch of prairie. Virgin pines bordered the lake north of the Chicago River. Dense shrubbery forests clothed the east sides of both branches of the river. According to Caton, "wolves stole from these coverts by night and prowled through the hamlet, hunting for garbage around the back doors of our cabins. Late in 1833, when a bear was reported in the skirt of timber along the South Branch, George White's loud voice and bell—he was as black as night in a cavern, his voice had the volume of a foghorn, and he was recognized as the town-crier—summoned all to the chase. All the curs and hounds, of high and low degree, were mustered, with abundance of firearms of the best quality in the hands of those who knew well how to use them. Soon Bruin was treed and dispatched very near to where the Rock Island depot now stands."

When Caton arrived in Chicago, he found the whole area occupied as the deer hunting grounds of the Pottawatomie Indians. He soon formed the acquaintance of many of their chiefs, acquaintances that ripened into cordial friendships. He found they possessed a great deal of information resulting from their careful observations of deer, and he traveled with them over the prairies in pursuit of deer. "I hunted and fished with them, I camped with them in the groves, I drank with them at the native springs of which they were never at a loss to find, and I partook of their hospitality around their campfires."

All of Caton's deer hunts became exercises in acquiring and recording practical information about the whitetail's senses and habits, whether group-hunting them with the Pottawatomie Indians, coursing deer with greyhounds, floating the waterways, or still-hunting.

On one of his earliest recorded still-hunts in December of 1847, Caton followed a large, antlered buck from daylight until around four o'clock in the afternoon over the bluffs of the Vermilion River near his farm in Ottawa. After tramping through six inches of dry, hard snow all day—"as difficult to walk in as dry cornmeal"—he stopped on a bluff. Too fatigued to track much farther, he rested his gun against a tree, feeling deeply chagrined at the dimming chance of getting the deer. Suddenly he heard the brush crack and the buck stopped not more than thirty feet from him, but the brush was too thick for a shot. Caton tells us what happened:

"The buck stared at me some seconds, as if something told him of danger; but at length he seemed to become reassured and bounded along in his original course as if he was in somewhat of a hurry, but not in manifest alarm. As I anticipated, on his third or fourth bound he gave me a chance, and I fired as he was descending. His heels flew into the air with a snap as if his hoofs would fly off, and he fell all in a heap. There was something in the size of the deer and his antlers, the way in which his hind legs, as quick as lightning, stretched almost perpendicularly in the air, and the mode of his falling, which produced a thrill of delight which I have never before or since experienced."

Although the deer's nose sensed danger, it did not see the least motion, and was unable to make Caton out, even though the hunter was in full view with a dog standing at his feet. This incident and others led Caton to believe that deer do not readily recognize objects by sight alone and that the whitetail's sight represents the animal's greatest weakness, something to be borne in mind by the successful hunter. Caton suspected, as modern-day deer researchers conclude, that deer depend strongly on motion and depth perception to locate and identify an object by sight alone. While Caton doubted the whitetail's ability to see color—a question that remains unanswered to this day—he considered one general conclusion indisputable. Deer quickly detect moving objects by sight, causing alertness and flight behavior.

But like many of us, he observed that on some days, with the wind in your favor, you can more readily approach deer than others. An explanation for this variance in their threshold of responses to visual stimuli eluded him. Cornell's deer biologist, Aaron Moen, also concludes that "on some days the slightest movement some distance away triggers flight behavior, while on other days the animals can be approached much more closely. I do not know why this apparent difference exists.

It may be related to both daily physiological rhythms and to transient environmental conditions."

While Caton perhaps overestimated the defective vision of whitetails, I do know that during the first thirty minutes and the last thirty minutes of the legal hunting hours the camouflaged deer hunter in a tree stand frequently has the edge; but, don't count on it.

Despite a busy career as a jurist and businessman, Caton tramped the broad prairies of Illinois in search of whitetails during every free day he could spare, thus making the study of these animals and the hunting of them his main recreational activity. In 1853, the state of Illinois passed its first deer law establishing a six-month deer hunting season. Caton made the most of it. Although he enjoyed hunting various species of deer in California, Wisconsin, Michigan, Canada, and the Adirondacks of New York, among other places, and participated in almost every mode of deer hunting imaginable, including jacklighting on the waterways, he always returned with great joy to the Grand Prairie of Illinois to hunt whitetails on horseback. This type of deer hunting afforded him the most varied and exciting experiences. The white-tailed deer, he once remarked, "has an intelligence which enables it to resort to expedients to baffle its pursuer, and it possesses a vitality which enables it to escape with wounds which would prostrate the other species at once."

Caton found the prairies of Illinois the proper theater for coursing, for running deer with greyhounds by sight, not scent. In commenting on this exhilarating mode of chasing deer, he classified it as by far the most dangerous, especially for the in-

"The Virginia Deer is not only the most abundant and hence the most useful of all the American species, but its capture affords the most varied and the most exciting exercise to the sportsmen. Its sight is fully equal if not superior to that of any of the other species. It has an intelligence which enables it to resort to expedients to baffle its pursuer, and it possesses a vitality which enables it to escape with wounds which would prostrate some other species at once. If its actual endurance is inferior to some others, in fleetness it surpasses all of them." — John Dean Caton, 1877. *Photo credit Charles J. Alsheimer*

experienced rider, for if he returns with a sound horse and a sound body, he may consider himself fortunate. With a lunch of bread and cold venison steak in his pocket and a double-barreled gun in hand — one barrel a rifle and the other for buckshot — Caton raced across the prairies urging his steed to the utmost to keep up with the expert greyhounds as they drew near to their quarry. "To be the foremost in such a chase," Caton admitted, "to keep

even with the leading hound, and see that each stride lessens the intervening space between the pursuers and the pursued, is the culmination of excitement only known to the ardent sportsman."

Although Caton preferred coursing deer to all other modes of hunting, like his friend, T. S. Van Dyke, he also loved to still-hunt in the pine woods north of Chicago, but with the added element of the silent and sagacious deer dog. "The best dog I ever owned for the still hunt was a pointer. Though not so fleet or so powerful as the greyhound, his fine nose and great sagacity compensated for all else. He would take the track of the deer and follow it by the scent just as fast or slow as directed, and as still as a cat. When he brought a wounded deer to bay, he would give tongue as furiously as one could desire, and hold him at bay with great pertinacity; but, of course, he never seized the animal."

Throughout his lifetime the great debate raged on over hounding deer versus still-hunting them. Caton took the unusual position of doing both with equal fervor. On the one hand, he understood and loved the great excitement of hunting deer with dogs: "Rifles are cocked, not a whisper is breathed, not a twig is broken, not a leaf is stirred. Every wandering thought is summoned back and absorbed in the excitement of the moment. The course of the hounds may be traced by their voices, each listener calculating the chances of their arriving at his stand."

Yet, he also understood the avid still-hunter who argued, "What business has a man got in the woods who can't take home a piece of venison to his shantee without scaring all the deer for ten miles around before he gets at it? The flesh of the poor creature is worth nothing neither, after their blood is heated by being driven to death with dogs!"

Even though Caton loved to hunt deer with dogs as well as the silent still-hunt, he readily acknowledged that "the sublime stillness of silent nature in the solitude of the dark forest is broken by the noisy bay of great packs of hounds as the timid deer goes rushing through the woods frightened out of his native gracefulness."

The controversial debate over hounding deer versus still-hunting them rages on to this very day with as much fire as it reached during Caton's time, especially in the Southeast, where the long tradition of hounding deer still lives on, if ever so dimly. In the Caesar Kleberg Wildlife Research Institute's book, *Game Harvest Management* (1985), deer researchers from the University of Georgia conclude that changes do occur in the herd age structure, sex ratios, and genetic characteristics of white-tailed deer depending upon whether they are hunted with dogs or still-hunted.

In a paper entitled, "Demographic and Genetic Characteristics of White-tailed Deer Populations Subjected to Still or Dog Hunting," researchers argue that "deer populations subjected to different harvest methodology (still-hunting or dog hunting) exhibit strong genetic differences in population characteristics." But these researchers remain reluctant to assess a positive or negative value to these genetic differences, thus adding little if any fuel to either side of the debate. But one thing is certain: Their "chi-square analysis of the differences in allelic frequency, estimates of heterozygosity, and the mean number of alleles/locus" would have dazzled the mind of John Dean Caton as much as it does the mind of this deer hunter.

Most of Caton's deer hunts, regardless of where he hunted or his mode of deer hunting—whether still-hunting or dog hunting—ended in camp by aging and weighing the harvested deer and preparing the skins and other parts of the skeleton for mounting and research purposes. "After our camp work was done," he wrote in his journal while deer hunting in the secluded valleys of California's Gaviota Pass, "we enjoyed a most leisurely feast of venison prepared in all the different modes most approved of in camp, sweetened by long absence and hard toil."

The incidents of the day were then recounted in Caton's deer camp with such extravagant embellishments as were deemed necessary to enable each companion to outwit the other with his own dazzling stories. The soothing influence of the burned herb and a dash of good old Port eased the disappointments and heightened the accomplishments. But before turning in on beds formed by rank, wild oats, all comrades agreed with the Judge when he insisted that "an old buck is as cunning as a fox, but if you understand his ways, it is possible to circumvent him, and to do so is the very essence of sport."

Caton not only studied deer while hunting them in the wild and sharing the experiences of others in his deer camp, but by way of daily contact with them in his 300-acre deer park he carefully observed and documented their social behavior and physiology, especially the nature and function of antlers and glands. At his deer park he kept fifty to sixty deer in captivity, including all of the American deer except the moose and caribou. Here he measured, drew, photographed, studied, and collected deer antlers with all the obsession and furor of the current American antler craze. Indeed, he was perhaps the first American deer hunter to "romance the antler." In his numerous writings he described their system of nutrition, mode of growth, maturity, decay and rejection, the effects of castration and, finally, their uses.

One question dealing with white-tailed deer antlers, in particular, preoccupied Caton—an answer for which he searched in vain: why the great irregularity in the time of "casting" their antlers? Whereas deer hunters usually refer to the "shedding" of velvet or antlers, deer researchers differentiate between deer "shedding their velvet" and "casting their antlers." In any event, in his deer park Caton observed that a four-year-old buck once cast his antlers in April; the following year he cast them in November. In his *Sporting Notebook,* he wrote: "This does not seem to depend on the conditions of the animal, the character of their food, the temperature of the weather, nor indeed upon any assignable cause which I have been able to discover."

Modern-day deer researchers, however, tell us that declining levels of testosterone adjusted by the photoperiod cycles regulate antler casting and that deer maintained under similar environmental conditions tend to cast their antlers on almost the same day annually. Diseased deer, on the other hand, and deer in poor nutritional condition cast their antlers at an earlier date than they would if living under the best of nutritional conditions. Some researchers believe that reports of earlier antler casting by large-antlered bucks or older deer may be explained by their high social rank during the rut and the higher energy costs involved in maintaining that rank. Captive deer seem to cast their antlers earlier as they grow older, which may in part explain Caton's unusual observation.

Caton was undoubtedly the first researcher to stage an authentic buck fight. His description of that terrific battle has remained in the literature on deer and deer hunting to this very day:

"The battle was joined by a rush together like rams, their faces bowed down nearly to a level with the ground, when the clash of horns could have been heard at a great distance; but they did not again fall back to repeat the shock, as is usual with rams, but the battle was continued by pushing, guarding, and attempting to break each other's guard, and goading whenever a chance could be got, which was very rare. It was a trial of strength and endurance, assisted by skill in fencing and activity. The contest lasted for two hours without the animals being once separated, during which they fought over perhaps half an acre of ground. Almost from the beginning, both fought with their mouths open, for they do not protrude the tongue prominently, like the ox, when breathing through the mouth. So evenly matched were they that both were nearly exhausted, when one at last suddenly turned tail to and fled; his adversary pursued him but a little way. I could not detect a scratch upon either sufficient to scrape off the hair, and the only punishment suffered was fatigue and a consciousness of defeat by the vanquished."

In dealing with antlers and deer physiology in general, Caton urged hunters to record all observations to the smallest detail. "If hunters would provide themselves with notebooks and tape measure and whenever they kill an interesting specimen would make careful measurements and minute notes of them, they would soon educate themselves into excellent naturalists, and would add vastly to our fund of reliable zoological knowledge, and I trust the time is coming when sportsmen will generally adopt this course. In this way, they will double the pleasures of the chase, and when they meet in the camp or at the club house to recount their triumphs and compare their observations, they will enjoy an intellectual treat far surpassing the story of the simple score or the skillful shot."

At his deer park in Ottawa, his detailed observations and experimentation shed much light on the deer's capacity for domestication. With the death of one of his gamekeepers — gored to death by a rutting, white-tailed buck — America learned of the inherent dangers of keeping deer in captivity.

Not content to merely study and examine the American species, in both captivity and the wild, he traveled to Norway to study red deer and reindeer for comparative purposes. When visiting Europe a second time, he studied the deer of England, Ireland, and Scotland as well. He also went to China and Japan to learn about the unique deer of China, Pere David's deer, and the Japanese Sika deer. In the fall of 1872, he hunted and studied the habitat of wild animals in Nova Scotia. In our country, he hunted and traveled through every state of the Union except Montana and Idaho, extending his hunting tramps into Manitoba and British Columbia.

From these foreign excursions and vast tramps across America, he brought home to his farm in Ottawa a remarkable collection of deer prints, photographs, antlers, deer droppings, tails, glands, skins, ears, hoofs, plus sundry deer memorabilia, and constantly received specimens in the mail from deer hunters around the world.

From Scotland he returned with a copy of Sir Edwin Landseer's "The Monarch of the Glen," which he considered the most famous deer painting in the world. In return, he shipped various species of American deer to Scotland, France, Belgium, and Germany. In his billiard room he hung the heads of the trophy bucks he shot while on these excursions — "the greatest sporting events of my life."

The final outcome of his sporting events, his patient and industrious study of deer in captivity, and his vast travels to foreign countries resulted in the publication of *The Antelope and Deer of America* (1877), a book dealing with the life history of these animals and the various methods of hunting them. It took a deer hunter to write that great book, for in it Caton brought to life the world of deer in general and the whitetail in particular, with the same vitality and enthusiasm which prompted him to carry his rifle in daily pursuit of them.

The book became an immediate success. *Forest and Stream,* the leading sportsmen's magazine of its time, called it "the most important publication ever printed on the subject; indeed it is so comprehensive in its scope and exhaustive in detail that it may justly be termed the only one. Some works (too many) on themes of this nature are the ground-out products of gullible scribes who are content to put into a book and sell to the public what they may have absorbed from the gossip of old hunters matching yarns. You will find nothing of this kind in Judge Caton's book."

The *New York Times* highly recommended it for sportsmen because it "contained the exact experiences of a deer hunter who has a direct interest and a practical acquaintance with the subject he

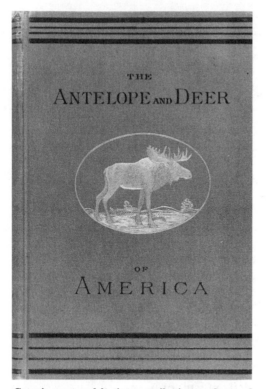

Caton's great and lasting contribution to deer and deer hunting. *Photo credit Robert Wegner*

exhaustively treats." All of the reviews in the scientific journals and the newspapers praised the book without reservation, thus making it the standard authority of its day on the subject.

The *American Naturalist* summarized it best of all when they wrote: "It is not too much to say that in the present state of zoological science in this country the technical scientists, full of their skulls and teeth and dry hides and their taxonomic refinements, are turning eager eyes toward the sportsmen and practical field naturalists in the hope of learning what they now most need to know. Judge Caton illustrates the honorable capacity of the amateur naturalist to supplement museum-acquired learning with other information

of equal scientific importance, of greater practical utility and much more general interest."

The *Atlantic Monthly* called his deer book "the best work upon the subject . . . in many respects, a model for all writers upon natural history."

Forest and Stream seized an opportunity to buy the rights and issued a second edition in 1884; in 1974, almost one century later, Salem House of Salem, New Hampshire, reprinted the classic. Although presently out of print again, the 1974 reprint frequently turns up in used bookstores and in the catalogues of out-of-print booksellers specializing in outdoor literature. If you can locate a copy, borrow it or buy it, and read it; it's the first blue-chip deer book America produced. Given the dismal nature of American outdoor publishing today, we will probably never see another one like it.

As an amateur naturalist with a refining disregard for the dry technicalities of the professional scientists, Caton presented his facts in eloquent prose that lends charm to science, especially for the general reader who takes an interest in the habits and peculiarities of the white-tailed deer. In a letter to the editor of the *American Sportsman* dated December 5, 1874, he commented on the sporting press of his time in this regard: "It is exceedingly gratifying to me to see the sporting papers putting on the garb of the scientific. This speaks quite as well for the readers as for the managers of the paper, for while a journal must and will instruct its readers, it must also conform to their tastes and reflect their general views. Who can doubt that the sportsmen of today are much better students of nature than those of a former time, and that they now enjoy the study of the natural history of the deer which they pursue with such supreme satisfaction, rendered more complete by a knowledge of their natural history."

A complete knowledge of natural history and woodcraft meant many things to Judge Caton. It entailed knowing in an intimate way the habits and movements of deer, being skillful in whatever weapon you choose to use, being able to prepare shelters along the trail and hearty venison meals in the field, and in general creating and maintaining a deer camp as a school for the young beginner where he or she may learn many things besides just the mode of pursuing and capturing the animal. The hunter, above all others, Caton believed, can study the habits of the animals he pursues and captures, and in the process, gather a fund of knowledge that he can pass along to the novice that will also be of untold value to the scientist as well, who frequently studies deer only in the laboratory, library, and penned enclosures. "The hunter, who seeks and takes the game in its native fastness, may thus, I say, give the scientist valuable assistance."

But above all else, woodcraft for Caton revolved around ethics in the field. Shortly before his death, he published a classic essay entitled, "The Ethics of Field Sports," in which he urged us to go to the deer forest with partners whose tastes are congenial with our own, for companionship remains indispensable for the full enjoyment of life in deer camp. Indeed, friendship and good feelings always prevailed in Caton's deer camp. "Between us there at once grew up a fraternal feeling; a cord of sympathy was drawn out between us which made us brothers and would have prompted us to make great sacrifices for each other, if need had been."

Caton only shot deer when he needed venison, or when others needed it or when he needed the animal for research purposes. He rightly argued that we must associate utility with the sport of deer hunting. "If the deer cannot be utilized, a pang of regret takes the place of gratification in the breast of the true sportsman." If you don't utilize the animal to the fullest—eat the venison, tan the hides, and mount the antlers—don't hunt. In conclusion he wrote: "Let me beseech all sportsmen to maintain the dignity of the craft to which they belong and to exert all their influence to elevate the standing of that craft and to preserve our game."

Like his contemporary, T. S. Van Dyke, another lawyer, deer hunter, and avid student of the whitetail, Judge Caton loved to leave the noise and legal hassles of city life to set his face toward the green wildwood where whitetails and nature reign supreme. He went to the deer forest with men whose tastes were congenial to his own. His deer camp became a school of learning where he instructed many a tenderfoot about the ways of the whitetail and the marvels of natural history. He loved to pitch his tent deep in the forest "beside a fountain gushing from the living rock as if some Moses in former times had touched it with his wand," as he so eloquently described it. There the music of its waters would sooth the Judge to sleep after a hard day's chase of great-antlered bucks. Before falling into the deepest repose, he would think to himself, "Oh, how delightful are such scenes! Their very remembrance is a joy renewed."

When the Judge shot a deer, he examined it with tremendous vitality, as he would a book full of knowledge and information. As an amateur naturalist with a vivid imagination and profound persistence, he selected and solved many of the earliest scientific natural-history problems dealing with deer. As he examined his downed quarry, a vibrant thrill flashed through every fiber of his massive, rugged, 240-pound frame. We have no finer guide and mentor than this all-time giant among American deer hunters. As long as the white-tailed deer roams the forests of this country and man pursues this marvelous and unique creature, we will always remember Judge Caton's measure of what a deer hunt is all about: "The pleasure of the sportsman in the chase is measured by the intelligence of the game and its capacity to elude pursuit and in the labor involved in the capture. It is a contest with sharp wits where satisfaction is mingled with admiration for the object overcome."

For the American deer hunter who carries a firearm in pursuit of the white-tailed deer, the name John Dean Caton lingers in the back of our mind like the afterglow of a magnificent sunset. He lived a life full of honors and accomplishments; his life reads like a Horatio Alger story. Beginning life as an impoverished farmhand, he later corresponded with such dignitaries as Charles Darwin and Abraham Lincoln. After retiring from the Illinois Supreme Court, he presided over the Illinois & Mississippi Telegraph company as its president, controlling all of the telegraph lines in the state of Illinois and amassing a colossal fortune in the process, listed at more than $2 million at the time of his death. When this pioneer lawyer, judge, deer hunter, and naturalist died on July 30, 1895, the editor of *Forest and Stream* wrote the final tribute:

"Judge Caton was in his day a tireless sportsman, a fine shot and a most observing student of all things afield. His *Antelope and Deer of America* would alone have assured him recognition, and we believe that it was in matters of sportsmanship and of natural history that he took his chief pride and main enjoyment."

Chapter 2

William Monypeny Newsom

One Shot—No Cripples!
—William Monypeny Newsom, 1931

Judge Caton always insisted that the first requisite of a white-tailed deer hunter should be a full appreciation for the charm and nobility of his quarry and a real love of wilderness. No one appreciated the nobility of the white-tailed deer and the charm of the deer forest more than William Monypeny Newsom (1887–1942). Born in Columbus, Ohio, this thoroughbred sportsman began his deer hunting adventures at the early age of ten in the deer forests of New Hampshire, where he armed himself with a well-worn 44–40 rifle and a screwdriver that he used to assist the ejector when it refused to work—as it usually did.

As the years went by, the young Newsom learned "that deer hunting, to be successful, must be intelligent as well as energetic," as he so aptly put it in his classic text entitled *White-Tailed Deer* (1926). Thus, the young hunter studied the ways

and habits of the white-tailed deer. "Out of season," the author wrote in an autobiographical sketch, "I continued to study the subject and experiment, going into the hills with a pack on my back, sometimes alone, sometimes with a companion, in pursuit of trout and more information about my friend the deer. I owe a great deal to T. S. Van Dyke, that great sportsman who pioneered the way." Indeed, Newsom read and studied the works of Judge Caton and Van Dyke; their ideas shaped Newsom's thoughts on deer and deer hunting for the rest of his life.

The young deer hunter, however, read other books besides those on the subject of deer and deer hunting, for he received his Ph.D. from Yale University in 1909, at the ripe age of twenty-two. Shortly thereafter he went on to become a highly successful Wall Street broker. But during the 1920s, he preoccupied himself more and

William Monypeny Newsom (1887–1942), a saint among deer hunters. *Photo credit Robert Wegner*

more with the great American outdoors and with writing about his deer hunting adventures for such popular magazines as *Outdoor Life, Field and Stream, Forest and Stream,* and *The Saturday Evening Post,* as well as for such technical journals as the *Journal of Mammalogy, Natural History,* and *American Game.* Throughout his life he remained an active Fellow of the Royal Geographic Society and a member of the American Society of Mammalogists and the Explorers Club. He is perhaps best known for his analysis of the mammals on Anticosti Island (at the mouth of the St. Lawrence River), his work on whitetail anatomy, and shooting skills culminating in that popular phrase

"One Shot—No Cripples!" as well as his blue-chip deer book, *White-Tailed Deer.*

Being born with that restless spirit of exploration that kept him constantly wanting to look over the next horizon, Newsom, typically enough, preferred still-hunting the white-tailed deer to all other methods of deer hunting. According to his theory of still-hunting, every hunter ought to possess four essential qualities: perseverance, patience, common sense, and enthusiasm for the out-of-doors. Without these basic qualities, Newsom tells us, "you will never learn still-hunting and unless you understand it you will never care for it."

Beyond these basic qualities, however, Newsom also denoted one essential ingredient that the still-hunter cannot do without: proper analysis of the wind. How well we shoot a rifle becomes mere detail as compared to this major ingredient. Think about the wind, Newsom insists, and study it constantly. The white-tailed deer may sometimes err in its sight and hearing, "but of the sense of smell no, not our modern educated deer." Yes, even a bath in this regard is an excellent aid to still-hunting.

It goes without saying that since whitetails can scent a human at more than a quarter of a mile away, if the wind is favorable and atmospheric conditions right, we should always try to hunt into or across the wind. Newsom's own preference in this regard is for a strong, steady breeze that carries our scent in one known direction. Beyond the fact that whitetails are frequently nervous and fidgety in high wind, windy days are usually excellent days to still-hunt, since there are plenty of natural noises in the woods to help overcome the noises we make. However, the wind is obviously a handicap to our hearing as well.

Like any other game, still-hunting takes concentration: The still-hunter's greatest priority is to keep thinking about whitetails and nothing *but* them. Newsom's advice is simple and to the point: "Keep your mind on your work every minute and don't dream. Never mind what goes on in the business you left at home. It is right here that the Indian wins out, for he has no thought but deer."

During our normal day-to-day routines, almost all of us are strapped to time schedules. While still-hunting, however, we need to disregard time and leave our watches at home. Or better yet, throw them out! Time pieces only make us miserable while hunting, and that's where the deer has the advantage. "Now that we know the sun is keeping the right time," Newsom insists, "why not let the sun do all of it and stop trying to keep those millions of clocks and watches running exactly alike; and then struggling to keep up to them." After all, it's really those deer that get away from us while still-hunting that teach us about deer, not the ones we kill. So why the fixation with time?

Still-hunting, Newsom argues while quoting William Hornaday, represents "the true method of outwitting the deer, which for genuine keenness of ear, eye and nose have, I believe, no superior in the whole Deer Family. One fine old whitetailed buck killed by fair and square trailing and stalking is equal to two mule deer and three elk. When first alarmed, the mule deer and elk are prone to bolt from curiosity and stare at the hunter for that fatal ten seconds which so often ends with a ringing bang and a fatal bullet. But not the whitetail. Time after time the trailing still-hunter, stealing forward ever so cau-

tiously, sees ahead of him and far beyond fair rifle-shot, a sudden flash of white, a pillar of cloud swaying from side to side between the tree trunks and the vanishing-point of a scurrying whitetail. This creature knows quite well that, as a discourager of cervine curiosity, nothing in the world equals a breechloading rifle."

While Newsom considered himself a fairly good deer stalker, he still-hunted many a whitetail in the months of November and December when for days on end he found it utterly impossible to come within fair rifle shot of a buck worth keeping. I think many deer hunters would agree with Newsom that still-hunting and watching the white-tailed deer represent the fairest hunting any man can ever hope for. As every still-hunter knows, it takes white-tailed deer to make scenery. Indeed, Newsom acknowledges that he goes into the woods because he feels more comfortable there than in the city. Going into a woods filled with whitetails and becoming a part of the natural scenery remained at the heart of a Newsom deer hunt. When Newsom found man denigrating the natural scenery, he reacted sharply and noted that in these days of automatic weaponry shot by "rattle-brained snap-shooters" from campsites filled with all kinds of dangerous chemical compounds, we need to recall from time to time an old Idaho State Forest sign: "This Is God's Country, Don't Set It On Fire And Make It Look Like Hell!"

As an active member of the Explorers Club, Newsom loved trophy animals and serious exploratory endeavors. Enticed by the frontiers of scientific knowledge and the great challenges of hunting expeditions, he willingly sought out physical discomfort in the tradition of that bully explorer Teddy Roosevelt, another member of the Club. Fascinated and intrigued with the natural history, mystery, and misinformation of Anticosti Island, Newsom set out on an expedition in the fall of 1936 to study white-tailed deer development on the island for the American Museum of Natural History.

Contrary to the popular myth of Anticostian whitetails being small in weight, averaging from ninety to 100 pounds, the first buck he killed on the Newsom-Watson expedition weighed 240 pounds. He found their weights very comparable to the largest Adirondack bucks he shot in his home turf of New York. Only in antler development did Newsom find an unusual feature: Regardless of the size of the antlers, the largest racks never varied from the typical eight-point formation.

In an article in the *Journal of Mammalogy,* Newsom reported that an eccentric millionaire named Henri Menier, one of the richest sportsmen in France and owner of Menier's Chocolate, first released whitetails on the island in June 1896. On the first day of his deer hunt in 1936, Newsom counted sixty-five deer. He estimated the deer population at about fifteen deer per square mile. He also checked the speed of deer on the open fields near Baie St. Clair by means of a stopwatch, a steel tape, and a motorized handcar on a lumber railroad. He estimated their average speed while running from danger at eighteen miles per hour and their top speed at thirty miles per hour.

Canada's incredible isle of the whitetail captured Newsom's imagination; it provided a quality deer hunting experience in a quality environment, and still does. Its spectacular sights and trophy whitetails amidst the thick spruce forests overwhelmed Newsom in the same way its does trophy hunters of the 1980s. If New-

som were to revisit this prime whitetail hunting ground today, he would find a trophy hunter's paradise with a deer density of one deer for every twenty-seven acres or twenty-four deer per square mile. In 1985, the total kill was 6456 whitetails consisting of 3387 bucks, 2105 does, and 964 fawns — resulting in a remarkable success ratio of 1.72 deer per hunter.

Newsom always considered buck hunting as a "separate proposition" from merely going deer hunting. Fascinated with big bucks and their antlers, he roamed the high country of British Columbia, Pike County in Pennsylvania, northern Maine, and the Adirondack Mountains of New York in pursuit of magnificent heads. He always considered trophy bucks as a distinct species from does, fawns, and yearling bucks, a species that maintains very different habits and mental traits. Still-hunting bedding areas in rugged terrain and still-hunting along lines of scrapes and rubs on beech ridges with plenty of cover at hand remained his favorite tactic.

One day while buck hunting in the Adirondacks, he left an old tote road and decided to cover every inch of a favorite beech ridge. In his deer hunting journal, he describes what happened: "Very slowly, I poked along—not because of the noise but because I must see a buck in thick cover before he sees me. For perhaps an hour this went on. Then a grayish-white stick caught my eye. Then another beside it. I raised the little binoculars slowly. With their help I could make out the outline of a deer through the brush and now the grayish-white tips of his antlers showed clearly. One jump and he would be gone. When I put down the glasses, knowing what to look for now, I could see the body outline distinctly. Slowly I raised the rifle and fired. Yes, he was a fine buck. Nine points, heavy beams, wide spread, fat, weight 212 pounds dressed."

Newsom shot many of his heavy-antlered bucks in the limestone country of New York State. In his obsession with antlers, he traveled the state, searching out and photographing the record heads. Many trophy heads and photos of others decorated the walls of his study. One evening after the deer season closed, Newsom sat in his study with several of his deer hunting partners. Newsom noticed that Roy Chapman Andrews, a naturalist and fellow member of the Explorers Club, continuously looked, perhaps unconsciously, at a heavy-antlered whitetail hanging over the mantel. Their deer talk focused on antlers.

"This talk of hunting deer," Andrews remarked after a while, "may have been all right in pioneer days, when a deer meant meat and a dry doe was something to talk about. But with the buck law and our modern ideas of conservation—well, it has come to be a sex problem now."

Marshall McLean, another hunting partner and Wall Street broker, who was looking over Newsom's old 35–55, smiled.

"You're trying to say," said McLean, "that this isn't a deer rifle at all. It's for buck exclusively, and what every hunter has in the back of his head when he says 'deer' is really a whale of an old buck, like that head up there—heavy beam and plenty of horn growth."

"Exactly," said Andrews. "I wish I knew how to pick a territory where those big ones grow." Turning to Newsom he said, "Do you know the answer to that one?"

"I'm not sure I do," said Newsom, "but I have an idea that I've been working on for some time. It's dead sure some localities produce larger heads than other localities, sometimes only a few miles away. It's amazing that we haven't paid more attention to the why and wherefore of large heads in this country, because that's what we are all looking for."

"I hope you can solve the riddle of where the big ones grow," said McLean. "There are several million deer hunters in this country who would like to know the answer. If you start an investigation maybe they could help. At least it would start them thinking."

Realizing that he could learn little about whitetails and their antler development while sitting around his study in New York, Newsom left for the Adirondacks in an attempt to solve this riddle. In Essex County, one of New York's top trophy counties, he located some of the outstanding heads and pinpointed on a soil map the exact location of where the hunters shot them. He took bone samples from skulls for analysis. After a careful examination of more than 200 trophy antlers and skull plates, he noted that the largest antlers all came from ranges containing limestone; these antlers also contained a higher percentage of ash than did the antlers from nonlimestone country. Obviously, you don't need to be a geologist, Newsom rightly insists, to find limestone areas. Stop at the nearest office of the Soil Conservation Service and study soil survey maps. "Given limestone country with an abundance of deer food," Newsom argues, "it will be your own fault if you don't find that perfect head with long points and heavy beams—the one we are all looking for."

Like Caton and Van Dyke before him, Newsom continuously formulated questions about white-tailed deer behavior and the hunting of them, questions that have mesmerized generations of deer hunters.

This classic of wilderness lore stands as a giant amidst the vast array of white-tailed deer books. *Photo credit Robert Wegner*

Wildlife ecologist Aldo Leopold cut apart the dust jacket of Newsom's book, containing Newsom's favorite questions, and affixed it to his own hunting journal. Deer hunters still ask these questions today. How can we distinguish the track of a buck from that of a doe, not considering the shape of the track? When in plain sight of a deer, how can we remain invisible to him? How do deer recognize each other? Are the footprints of the fore feet larger than those of the hind feet? How far can a deer scent you? Hear you? How can you outwit a skulking deer in thick cover? How does cold weather affect the sound of your footsteps? Do you really know the exact location of a deer's heart? What shots will drop him instantly in his tracks? How can you tell, when you shoot at a deer, whether or not you have hit him? How long should you wait before following a deer wounded in the lungs? If struck in the liver?

Newsom attempted to answer these questions in his classic deer book, *White-Tailed Deer,* published in 1926. To this day, it stands as a giant amidst the vast array of white-tailed deer books. The work engages the reader, like Van Dyke's *The Still Hunter,* in an imaginary deer hunt accompanied with everything from the successful bagging of trophy whitetails to stimulating dialogue on deer hunting methodology. It accomplishes this with high-level prose, delightful humor, more than fifty superb black-and-white photos, and numerous illustrations of white-tailed deer nostalgia. As a classic of wilderness lore, it remains today as instructive and invaluable as when it was first written. Indeed, sportsmen and naturalists will find practical hints in this book; animal lovers at large will rejoice in the magnificent photo engravings and drawings; and the general reader will enjoy the hunting adventures and delightful narration.

The author states his thesis in the preface: "Because I believe that more hunters are disappointed through lack of care and preparation rather than because of the lack of deer, it is my earnest desire to assist still-hunting to a plane higher than a mere endurance contest for the hunter; and for the deer, to do what I can to assure clean kills, with fewer maimed and mutilated cripples; for I owe the deer my thanks for many enjoyable days."

This aspect of assuring a quick, clean, and humane kill represents Newsom's greatest contribution to our sport. In this regard, the book contains detailed diagrams and illustrations of deer skeletons, as well as descriptive photographs of the internal anatomy of the whitetail. One entire chapter is devoted to trailing and finding wounded deer and to a complete analysis of the sportsman's duty of completing the work quickly, no matter what hardship it entails. Prior to this point in the literature on deer and deer hunting, this subject never really received the attention it deserved.

Striving to assure quick, clean, and humane kills, Newsom became amazed at the hunter's general ignorance of whitetailed deer anatomy. "The more I discussed the subject with hunters, the more I realized that many deer that get away from us do so because *we actually hit the spot we shoot at*. That spot of ours is nearly always placed too far back and too high. Many wounded deer result, causing hours of endless toil to the hunters and, far worse, more hours of intense, silent agony to the deer that are lost."

In interviewing explorers, guides, and sportsmen in various states, Newsom found that few hunters could locate exactly the center of a deer's heart on a broadside sketch regardless of their previous field experiences. Worse, few of them could accurately locate the shoulderbones. Hunters capable of instructing others, "good hunters" with more than average experience and men who had hunted but relied on the instruction of others, all failed Newsom's anatomy quizzes. I wonder how many of us would pass his anatomy tests today?

Quick, clean kills became Newsom's pet hobby. In his study, he drew sketches of deer skeletons and photographed the internal organs of the animal in the lab. His illustrations and anatomy photos of whitetails appeared in the popular hunting magazines across the country. After reading them, various hunters told Newsom that their wrong guesses as to the exact location of the heart were immaterial, that they would not mistake the location of the heart on a living deer. Newsom's reply: "To locate the heart accurately on a living deer is obviously even more difficult, as under hunting conditions he is usually in poor light and in a hurry." After tracing a white line around the heart of the dissected young deer Newsom photographed, he found that it measured three by five inches. As you can see from his pioneering anatomy photos, the lungs take up a great deal of the room in the chest cavity, nearly surrounding the heart. Only in the photo with the lungs deflated and pinned back is the heart completely visible.

Every fall around the evening fires in deer camps all across America, that old question surfaces: "How did that buck run 200 yards after a bullet perforated his heart?" Most of us know that their run following a heart shot usually consists of a frenzied, low-to-the-ground dash at the end of which the deer falls in a heap. Yet, we all know that deer sometimes manage to run as far as 200 yards with a heart shot. Indeed, Roy Chapman Andrews, Newsom's hunting partner, tells us that after shooting more than 1000 deer as specimens for the American Museum of Natural History, he recalls that on only two occasions did deer immediately drop after a heart shot. But no one ever explained this phenomenon before Newsom. In an article entitled "Deer Shots" in the *Pennsylvania Game News* (December, 1940), Newsom attempted to set forth a plausible explanation.

"On October 31, 1938, murderer John W. Deering was placed before a stone wall in the Utah State Prison with an electrocardiograph attached to his person. He

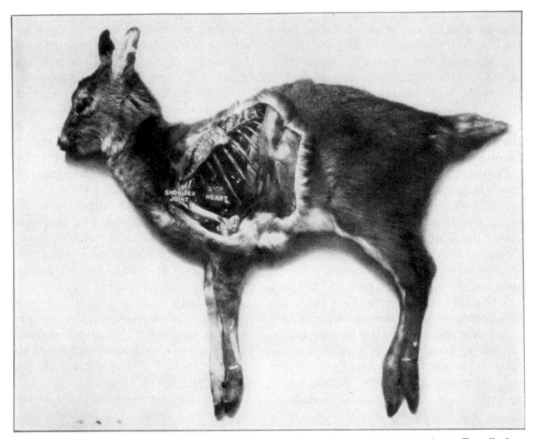

A young white-tailed deer with lungs deflated. Note the position of the shoulder and the heart. Two ribs have been cut off to show the location of the heart. *Photo credit William Monypeny Newsom*

was outwardly calm. The prison doctor placed a target over his heart. Five picked riflemen fired at the target at short range and four bullets simultaneously pierced his heart. Yet Deering's heart did not stop when pierced by four bullets but continued to beat for 15.6 seconds thereafter. The cardiograph record also showed that a few moments before the shots were fired, through fear, Deering's heart beats, normally seventy-two per minute, were increased to 180 per minute.

"Now I cannot say that the effect of a heart shot on a deer and a man are in any way similar. But let us see what would happen if we suppose this might have a bearing on the deer question. If the deer is frightened before the shot, his heart beats would increase tremendously, also increasing circulation of blood to the brain and muscles. And how far would he run in the 15.6 seconds before his heart stopped? At Anticosti Island I timed a mature white-tailed deer over a measured course with a stop watch. It was shot at but purposely missed. Its speed was eighteen miles per hour. The highest speed when another deer was fully extended and had to run, was about thirty miles per hour. At eighteen miles per hour, the deer could travel

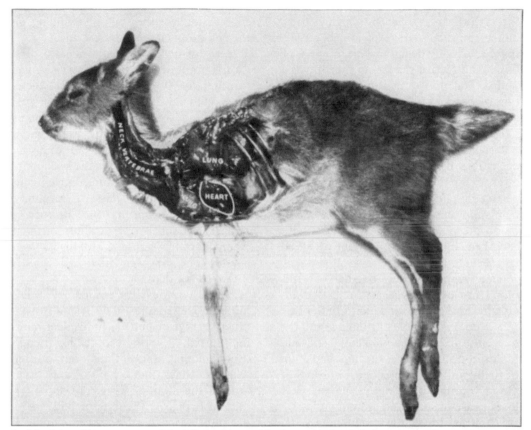

In this picture, Newsom removed the left shoulder and foreleg and inflated the lungs except the rear lobe on the left side. He pinned back the lung to show all of the heart; outlined in white, it measures three by five inches. He then covered the neck vertebrae with black tape to show their location. *Photo credit William Monypeny Newsom*

137 yards in 15.6 seconds. At twenty-five miles per hour the deer could travel about 152 yards. At thirty miles per hour the deer could travel about 229 yards. Doesn't it sound to you a little bit as if John Deering may have solved the riddle and that the deer's heart does not stop when perforated?"

At first glance, the execution of John Deering in Utah may seem a long leap from bagging a buck behind the barn. But actually there is a very direct connection. That connection became even clearer in a letter I received from William Campbell, a medical doctor at the East Wood Clinic in Paris, Tennessee, after he read Newsom's comments about John Deering and wounded deer behavior.

"I read with interest the article entitled 'How Far Will A Deer Travel When Hit Through The Heart?' by William Monypeny Newsom in your August 1985 issue of *Deer & Deer Hunting* magazine. I would like to add the following comments.

"There is a great deal of difference in the electrical activity of the heart as measured on an electrocardiogram and the effectiveness of the heart muscle as a pump. When the heart is struck by a high velocity bullet (especially an expandable missile that has already penetrated muscle and/or bone), it effectively ceases to function as a pump. There not only is massive destruction of heart muscle, but gaping entrance and exit wounds from which blood is able to escape. There may still be electrical depolarization of the heart muscle which is detectable by electrocardiogram, but in essence the output of the heart to the peripheral circulation is zero. In a human being approximately sixty to eighty cc's of blood are pumped out of the heart with each beat but the total amount of blood in the vascular system is approximately 3600cc. Approximately one-half of this blood has been oxygenated and is available to serve muscle and brain. In the case of a deer, it is capable of running until the oxygen supply is exhausted and lactic acid build-up occurs (either through depletion of the blood in the vascular tree or loss of blood through bleeding). Then the deer loses consciousness and promptly dies.

"Contrary to what is seen in movies and on television, a human being with a mortal wound does not always promptly collapse stone cold dead; neither does a deer. A deer is programmed by nature to usually run when injured, and that it does."

While interviewing hunters, one "well-known expert" told Newsom that it was quite useless to shoot at the heart because it swung back and forth precisely like a tin can on a string eighteen inches long. He drew a diagram; it indicated how the heart moved back and forth over twice its own diameter! No, the heart merely contracts and expands and does not move back and forth and around the chest area. "It is not like a piston in a cylinder," Newsom insists. "Its action is muscular contraction and expansion and the movement is very slight — not like the tin can swinging on the end of an eighteen-inch string."

Newsom observed that when the first shot is not a deadly, paralyzing shot, you can literally fill the deer with lead thereafter, with no apparent effect. The first shot, if not effective, seems to merely deaden the nerves. Newsom experienced an excellent example of this kind of a situation while deer hunting in the backcountry of Maine. While in camp, smoking his pipe and drinking a glass of burgundy, Newsom's hunting partner jumped a scraggly old buck only a short distance from camp. He shot at it with his 33 Winchester. The shot went high and he only wounded the deer.

Thereafter, the battle ensued. Every few minutes, Newsom heard his friend fire another barrage of bullets. In his deer hunting journal, Newsom recorded his friend's overwhelming, concentrated outpouring. "Several times they chased each other around the swamp, with constant intermittent firing. By the time he had fired a hatful of cartridges I began to wonder if he was chasing the deer, or the deer perhaps was chasing him. When I was beginning to chuckle out loud he came puffing into camp." The dialogue went something like this:

"Didn't you hear me shooting?" he asked Newsom in an exasperated manner.

"I thought I did hear a shot," Newsom said casually. "Were you shooting?"

"Was I?" he exploded. "I've been shooting for ages. I'm all worn out pumping lead into him. Why the devil didn't you come and help me?"

"Why," Newsom said, "I thought you only had one buck to shoot at."

"One buck or what's left of him. Let's go into the swamp and look at the wreck."

Newsom followed his partner back into the swamp and found the buck nearly shot to pieces. His friend hit the deer nine times; nearly every one of those shots, Newsom believed, would have been deadly at once, if the first shot had not rendered the animal insensible to further shock.

They returned to camp, but before turning to their pipes of tobacco and high-grade burgundy, they sat down and drew up a very detailed and intricate map of the behavior of the wounded deer for future reference.

Millions of hunters follow the tracks of white-tailed deer, but not all of those hunters are as well-versed in the habits of the game they are pursuing or in the practical methods of the chase as they should be. Newsom's book can do much for all

A Puzzle in Tracking Wounded Deer.

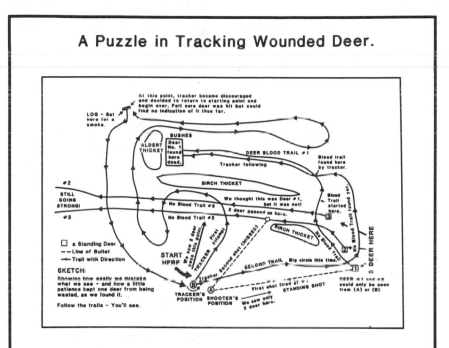

Deer hunters standing at points A and B, saw two deer, standing at your right at position 1 and 2. They shot and hit deer #1. Deer #3 was not seen until he passed in front of them at the center of the diagram where they mistook #3 for #1. The hunter could not see through the birch thicket. To work this puzzle in tracking wounded deer out, start at position B.

Reprinted from William Monypeny Newsom. 1926.
White-Tailed Deer.

such disciples of Nimrod. It provides a great deal of information about the whitetail's way of living. If its ethical injunctions are heeded, the lingering deaths of these magnificent creatures, now too common because of the hunter's failure to take correct aim when firing and to rigorously pursue fallen game, will be substantially decreased. After reading the book, one veteran deer stalker wrote as follows in *The Springfield Republican:* "If every would-be deerslayer were compelled to read this book e'vr venturing into the woods with his gun, there would be more kills and fewer wounded deer that get away to suffer long; and likewise, fewer accidents." Amen!

The editor of *Outdoor Life* called the work "a splendid contribution to American natural history." The book won praise from the scientific community as well. Writing in the *Journal of Mammalogy,* Hartley H. T. Jackson, an internationally-known mammalogist, noted that the deer hunter should welcome this book, for in it you will find scattered nuggets of original information on the habit and life history of the whitetail. In an unpublished letter to Newsom, Dr. F. A. Lucas, an honorary director of the American Museum of Natural History, wrote that "besides adding to our knowledge of the Virginia deer, your book may diminish the number of lingering deaths due to ignorance of where to aim, and possibly actually lessen the number of deer killed, while increasing the hunter's bag . . . A deer hit on the spot indicated on some of the diagrams might escape apparently unhurt, only to die a lingering death. Let us hope that a study of your book may lessen the number of such deaths."

Like its predecessor, *The Still Hunter* by Van Dyke, Newsom's book represents an intelligent and energetic treatise on the game of wits called still-hunting. Indeed, we owe both Van Dyke and Newsom a great debt for their pioneering information on the art of still-hunting today's "educated" whitetail. Despite some of the traditional myths—such as the rut starting because of the first heavy frost and despite the rather sexist language of its time—the work represents one of the first major books on the white-tailed deer to be published in this century. It ultimately examines the animal from almost every angle, including favorite foods, daily habits, senses of smell, sight, and hearing, as well as the hunting of this fascinating species.

While the book is currently out of print, it can be readily located by a reliable out-of-print bookseller. It maintains a value of approximately $30. The author's sense of humor should carry the reader from beginning to end in one setting. Consider, for example, the following recipe: "The head can be baked in a hole with the skin on. When done, peel off and skin. I have never tried it, but I'd have to be pretty hungry to tackle it; and if I were, I doubt if I could wait a half-day for it to cook. You can also try baking it in clay— providing you can find the proper clay, which is more difficult than getting the deer."

The book remained an all-time favorite of Aldo Leopold, a Yale classmate of Newsom's. Although Newsom's rifle has been laid aside forever, those hunters who enjoy still-hunting the whitetail can only follow in his footsteps. I cannot agree with Newsom more than when he writes that "you can hunt the world over for trophies—far back of beyond you may go; but one day you'll come back to follow the track of the white-tailed deer in the snow."

Chapter 3

Deerslayers of Yesteryear

I never wantonly killed a deer when I could gain nothing by its destruction. With the true hunter it is not the destruction of life which affords the pleasure of the chase; it is the excitement attendant upon the very uncertainty of it which induces men even to leave luxurious homes and expose themselves to the hardships and perils of the wilderness.

—Philip Tome, 1854

Many early American deerslayers followed the track of the white-tailed deer well before William Monypeny Newsom. Indeed, throughout the pioneer stage of American history, following the track of the white-tailed deer was not merely a pleasure, but a business — and often a very important business. At various times many men who rose to great distinction in our history took part in it, men such as Andrew Jackson and Sam Houston. But aside from these pioneers who won distinction purely as statesmen and soldiers, other members of the class of professional hunters rose to national fame and left their mark on American history because of their life in the vast wilderness. In this class of hunters we think of course of Daniel Boone, Davy Crockett, and Kit Carson; men renowned in every quarter of the Union for their skill as deer hunters,

Indian fighters, and wilderness explorers whose deeds still remain stock themes in the legendary lore of American deer hunting. These men, as Theodore Roosevelt once said, "stand for all time as types of the pioneer settlers who won our land: the bridge-builders, the road-makers, the forest-fellers, the explorers, the land-tillers, the mighty men of their hands, who laid the foundation of this commonwealth."

But another class of deer hunters existed from the very foundation of the Republic, men who found the deer hunt not merely a business but the most exhilarating and health-giving of all pastimes. While these hunters never became eminent in the complex life of civilization, they always remained deer hunters and glorified the title. Many of these deer hunters were frontier farmers who depended as much upon venison for their existence as on their cultivated crops and livestock. Historically, every pioneer farmer became a deer hunter and trapper; they had to, for the whitetail supplied them with deer skins which they used to barter for the supplies they needed. Some of these pioneer farmers so enjoyed the deer hunt that they became "professional" deer hunters, ultimately saying farewell to the plow.

The literature about these colorful pioneer farmers turned diehard deerslayers remains sparse and hidden in the special collections of state archives throughout the country. Fortunately, for the American deer hunter, Col. Henry W. Shoemaker (1880–1958), that prominent chronicler of America's deer hunting legends, tales and folklore, and a naturalist and conservationist in his own right, preserved their words, collected their songs and ballads as sung in their backwoods deer hunt-

This rustic volume of nostalgic stories provides us with a composite sketch of the early American deerslayer. *Photo credit Robert Wegner*

ing cabins, described their methods of hunting, cataloged their equipment, and documented their hair-splitting adventures as well as the spiritual side of their deer hunts.

In his numerous volumes and articles on outdoor folklore, Shoemaker captures the old-time charm and romance of deer hunting better than anyone. Indeed, his work best expresses the soul of the American deer hunter who tramped the mountains of central Pennsylvania. In his thorough and extensive study of Pennsylvania's deer hunters, we can visualize the American deerslayer of yesteryear whether he be found in the Alleghenies or somewhere else in the land—the Adirondacks, the great Plains or the land of Hiawatha. In his writings, especially *Pennsylvania Deer and Their Horns* (1915), Shoemaker creates the living deer hunter and tells us how he went forth to slay his quarry. His nostalgic stories, based on fact not fiction, provide us with a composite sketch of what the early American deerslayer was like.

Interviewing many of the last deer hunters of the 1800s, Shoemaker followed the furrows of the deer hunting legends to the very end; as he traveled through the Pennsylvania mountains on foot and horseback, he listened to their deer hunting stories after supper in lumber camps, farmhouses, and backwoods taverns and recorded them in more than 200 books, pamphlets, and magazine articles. These deerslayers were actually historians without knowing it. While on the watch for the whitetail, they dreamed of the glorious past; in their deer camps they kept alive the tales of their glorious age. Shoemaker preserves this oral history in his books and pamphlets. These early deerslayers, Shoemaker recalls, "were like the bards of long ago, men who were of the types made familiar by Sobieski and Stuart's *Lays of the Deer Forest* (1848) — bearded men, hoary-headed men, with keen, deep eyes, long thin noses and high cheek bones, men of action, probity and decision. Simple as the day God made the first man!"

Indeed, no one did more to preserve the record of the lives and deeds of our early pioneer deer hunters than Henry W. Shoemaker. Although his biographical sketches are brief, thanks to this dean of deer hunting folklore we meet some of the all-time greats of yesteryear and relive their adventures of the chase while reviving old memories of our deer hunting past: men such as Philip Tome, the almighty Allegheny elk hunter; Seth Iredell Nelson, slayer of more than 3500 whitetails; John Q. Dyce, the famous Clinton County deer hunter who killed three deer with one shot; and E. N. Woodcock, the famous Black Forest deer hunter. In reliving the adventures of these deer hunters and in studying the persons and places of our deer hunting past, we do not merely yearn for yesteryear, but we bestow a special meaning upon the persons and places of our deer hunting present, and to some degree our future.

The first and perhaps most famous of these backwoods, pioneer deerslayers was Philip Tome (1782–1855), the almighty elk hunter of the Alleghenies, whose memory Shoemaker preserved for us by keeping Tome's classic autobiography, *Pioneer Life; or Thirty Years a Hunter* (1854), in print. This indomitable, Indian-looking hunter whose prowess in the deer forest will never be forgotten, seemingly had but one ambition: to challenge the brute force of Nature — and to challenge it in such a way that every hazard favored his adver-

Philip Tome (1782–1855), one of the greatest American deerslayers of his time. This indomitable, Indian-looking Nimrod, whose prowess in the deer forest will never be forgotten, seemingly had but one ambition: to challenge the brute force of Nature — and to challenge it in such a way that every hazard favored his adversary. *Photo credit Warren County Historical Society*

sary. Like his pioneer predecessors, this pioneer farmer turned deerslayer viewed deer and elk hunts as arduous, military campaigns to be waged, campaigns that often entailed blazing trails through dense, virgin underbrush for miles at a time only to be interrupted by short catnaps in hollow trees or in the skins of freshly killed bears. These Homeric deer hunts literally lasted for months at a time, frequently terminating only when the snow melted and the deer tracks could no longer be followed.

From his earliest boyhood, Philip Tome was accustomed to the rugged life of the frontiersman. He shot deer with his father at the early age of twelve and quickly learned the ways of the whitetail and the Indian secrets of hunting them, as well as the language of the Seneca Indians. He rattled antlers to attract bucks, snorted to stop them in their tracks, and grunted to lure them into the vicinity of his shooting platforms. Like his Indian comrades, he loved living in quickly improvised hemlock shanties and regaled himself at the campfire while eating trout and venison steak. But above all, he took great pride in the moment when he nailed a trophy skull to the top of his lean-to.

Like most deer hunters, Tome served an apprenticeship with his father but he also learned his first lessons in deer hunting from an old hunter named John Mills, a pioneer farmer who became so enamored with hunting that he quit farming and left for the Canadian wilderness. Before doing so, he offered to sell Tome one of his cherished deerhounds and to teach the young lad all he knew about deer and deer hunting for $15; Tome accepted. By the first decade of the nineteenth century, the Tomes established their deer hunting grounds near the headwaters of the Kettle, Pine, Sinnemahoning and Allegheny rivers. In this area they killed large numbers of deer, bears, and elk. They used part of the meat for their own purposes but most of it they salted, cured, and rafted downstream to be sold in the settlements along the river.

Never conquered by man or beast, Tome by the age of eighteen was clearly more conversant with the howl of the wolves and the snort of deer than with the tones of civilized oratory. While hunting deer and elk in October of 1800 along the banks of Pine Creek in the east-central part of Pennsylvania's Potter County, the wolves flocked around him in droves. "Their unearthly howling," Tome recalls in his autobiography, "mingled with the dismal screeching of the owls overhead made a concert of sounds that banished sleep from my eyes the greater part of the night. I sat in my shanty, with my gun in one hand, a tomahawk in the other, and a knife by my side. When the wolves became unusually uproarious, I would send the dog out to drive them away, and if they drove him back in, I would fire in among them. At length, toward morning, I fell asleep from sheer exhaustion and slept until daylight, when I arose, ate my breakfast and started again on the elk track."

While hunting and tracking deer, Tome actually used the wolves to his advantage, for they followed him for the entrails of the deer. "We could hear the wolves and foxes howling and barking in our rear, guided by our fires . . . We encouraged them in pursuing the deer . . . The wolves and our dogs hunted together, sometimes one and sometimes the other obtained the deer, and if it fell into our hands we always left the wolves their portion to keep them near, for we considered them of great assistance to us in deer hunting."

Tome employed various modes of deer hunting: fire hunting, stalking, hounding, and stand hunting in elevated platforms over salt licks. Fire hunting, however, remained his most successful mode of killing deer from the first of June to the last of September. He describes this mode of deer hunting in his autobiography:

"The deer would come to the river after dark to eat the moss which grew on the bottom and collect together about the ripples in groups of from three to ten. The hunters would build a fire of yellow pitch pine in the middle of a canoe and station a man in the stern to steer and one or two more in front to fire at the deer. When there were no deer in sight they could push and paddle the canoe along. When they came within sight of the deer the canoe was allowed to float down with the current, and the steersman laid it in a position the most advantageous for those who were in the bow with guns. The deer would generally raise their heads and stand looking at the fire until the canoe came within a few yards of them.

"The hunters could judge by their movements whether they would make a break or stand still until they came near them, and fired or not according to the movements of the deer. When the deer attempted to run out of the water where the bank was bluff and steep, they would see their own shadows and thinking it was a dog or a wolf, would utter a snort and spring back into the water, sometimes coming near enough to the canoe to give the hunters two or three more shots at them.

"In this manner they would kill from one to four deer in one place. Having dressed and laid out the meat on the shore, they would proceed down the river in search of another group. If the night was favorable, from three to ten deer were killed in this manner. On their return they would fish for eels, salmon and other fish, and take in their venison as they came along. Their canoes were capable of carrying from 2000 to 4000 pounds with safety. With a five-tine spear they would take from twenty to sixty eels and a large quantity of salmon; and in the morning return home with fish and venison sufficient to supply an ordinary family for two months."

On one occasion, while fire hunting for deer along the banks of Pine Creek in northwestern Pennsylvania with a hunter named Clark, Tome got one deer without even firing a shot:

"Pushing up the stream about seven miles, we turned and commenced floating down at nine o'clock. After proceeding about a mile, Clark, who sat forward, saw a large buck, a short distance ahead. He fired and wounded the animal, when it wheeled and attempted to plunge over the canoe. Clark held up his hand to protect himself, which frightened the buck still more; he sprang across the canoe giving Clark a blow between the eyes with its hind feet, knocking him prostrate. I asked him if he was hurt, and he replied that he was nearly killed. I pushed ashore as soon as possible, and took him out of the canoe. His face was bathed in blood and presented a ghastly appearance. Upon washing away the blood I discovered that he was not as badly injured as I had feared. There was a severe contusion in the spot where he was struck, but the skin was not broken; the blood had dropped from the wounded deer.

"I then went after the deer which I found lying down, badly wounded but not dead. I finished it with a ball through the head and dragged it to the canoe. We floated down a mile, when we saw a buck and doe eating moss. Clark fired, killing the buck, and the doe ran ashore, when, becoming frightened at her shadow, she leaped back toward the canoe. As she raised to spring over, I hit her on the nose with a paddle, and she fell back into the canoe, when I cut her throat. We then floated down, picked up our buck, and proceeded homeward with three deer, one of which had not cost us even a shot."

On another occasion, it seemed that even an infinite supply of gunpowder and lead could not down the deer. Tome recalls what happened:

"About the middle of July in 1805, Morrison, Francis and myself were out on a hunt. Going up the creek about five miles, we commenced floating down, and soon shot a deer, which we stowed away in our canoe. When we had gone a short distance farther, two of us saw a deer in the stream and both fired at the same time but neither appeared to hit it. We re-loaded and directed the man who was steering to run the canoe to the shore. We then stood on the shore, about thirty rods from the deer and each fired eight shots at it, as rapidly as we could load, when our guns became so hot that we were compelled to stop. The steersman had been holding up the torch for us to see by, yet the position of the animal was the same as when first observed. At each shot it seemed to spring up, each time higher and higher, then dropping into the same spot. We then threw sticks at it, to drive it away, when it gave two or three leaps and suddenly disappeared. This affair may appear somewhat strange to the reader, as it did to me, but the facts are as I have stated, and always appeared to me unaccountable."

Most of us would probably attribute this unaccountable affair to that vicious malady, buck fever.

Expecting his deer hunting campaigns to last about six weeks at a time, Tome always took along an abundant supply of provisions. For four hunters they consisted of flour, potatoes, sugar, chocolate, corn, and a good quantity of salt with which to cure the venison. They also equipped themselves with six empty barrels for the meat, an iron pot holding about six gallons, a camp kettle, four axes, a broad axe, a chalk line, a canoe howel (an instrument for scooping water out of canoes), a drawing knife, two augers, six tomahawks, and three to four

pounds of gunpowder and lead. Each hunter took a rifle and a musket, two knives, a quart cup, four shirts, two blankets, and a good supply of soap. Thus equipped and accompanied by four deerhounds, Tome and his comrades pushed upstream with their canoe; two hunters stayed in the canoe, while the other two hunted along the shore.

The augers that Tome carried with him were used to bore holes in black oak logs, into which he poured three pints of salt and a small quantity of saltpeter. He would then insert a plug in each hole. He found that when the wood became saturated with the salt, the deer would come and gnaw at it. When deer started to respond to his salt lick, he immediately built a scaffold within three to four rods of the salt; he would then wait for the deer to become accustomed to the sight of the scaffold before he would make any attempt to hunt from it.

Tome also enjoyed hunting deer with hounds. He kept two large deerhounds for this purpose and believed that the best dog for deer hunting was "half bloodhound, a quarter cur and the other quarter greyhound." He took great pride in his deerhounds.

"When they were once in chase of a deer, they would not lose one in ten. So famous did they become for their prowess, that if any of the neighbors saw them running, they would exclaim, 'There are Tome's dogs; the deer cannot be far off.' The deer could never baffle them by any of their usual stratagems, and they would often run them down before they reached the water. Those wishing to deer hunt successfully should always procure at any cost, the largest and best dogs to be found."

Between deer hunts, Tome conducted a

profitable business of capturing live elk, exhibiting them to all interested spectators, and later selling them alive for as much as $500 a head. Laying his musket and rifle called "Sure Kill" aside, but with the aid of his dog and an Indian named Billy Fox, he caught several live, full-grown elk by hand along the banks of the Susquehanna. These deer hunting conquests eventually led Chief Cornplanter, a distinguished Chief of the Seneca tribe for whom Tome served as an interpreter, to bestow upon him the title "The Allegheny Elk Hunter." With regard to the size of the elk he caught, Tome proudly boasted, "I did not care how large—the larger the better."

In his hunting memoirs, Tome tells us that in one deer season that lasted from June until mid-January he killed forty-seven deer. He usually averaged 130 bears, elk, and deer per season. These figures seem almost incomprehensible given the rules and regulations of today. Indeed, his yearly deer kill statistics surpass the lifetime expectations of the modern deer hunter. Yet, like James Fenimore Cooper and Frank Forester, contemporary writers on sporting ethics, Tome maintained a strong ethical code with respect to his deer hunting. His code of ethics could have been penned by Cooper or Forester; it stands as a classic model for today's deer hunters:

"I never wantonly killed a deer, when I could gain nothing by its destruction. With the true hunter it is not the destruction of life which affords the pleasure of the chase; it is the excitement attendant upon the very uncertainty of it which induces men even to leave luxurious homes and expose themselves to the hardships and perils of the wilderness. Even when, after a weary chase, the game is brought down, he cannot, after the first thrill of triumph, look without a pang of remorse, upon the form which was so beautifully adapted to its situation, and which his hand has reduced to a mere lump of flesh."

Tome wrote these words at the age of seventy-two. Perhaps the flow of time soothed some of the fiery enthusiasm of youth; but nevertheless the sentiment and ethic ring true, thus giving Tome a spiritual kinship across two centuries with the sportsman/deer hunter of today. Not surprisingly, the *Saturday Review of Literature* viewed his autobiography as "a source book for the mores of the fringe of the first American frontier."

Philip Tome was no crude, backwoods barbarian. In reading his *Pioneer Life,* a rare book of interest to the American deer hunter, we learn that he read extensively and enjoyed a good command of the English language. He was also an interpreter for Cornplanter and Governor Blacksnake, two Seneca Indian chiefs of the Allegheny River, and commanded great respect from their tribes. We recognize the names of those who hunted with him as well-to-do gentlemen, business men, and others who stood out in a prominent way in the early pioneer days.

Historians of hunting recognize Tome as more than an ordinary deer hunter. Charles Sheldon, a collector and curator of one of the finest libraries ever assembled on North American big-game hunting, classifies Tome's *Pioneer Life* as "remarkable and accurate and one of the prize books of my library." Theodore Roosevelt believed that no matter how thrilling a deer hunting narrative might be, it did not appeal to him unless it was also great literature. Tome's deer hunting narrative lives up to Roosevelt's exacting standards. As a work of literature, Shoe-maker unhesitatingly recommended it "as the great, outstanding contemporary narrative of the Pennsylvania big game fields." All lovers of the hunt will enjoy reading about his exciting deer hunting episodes in the hills of Warren County, Pennsylvania. John Howard, a collector of North American hunting lore, calls it "one of the more interesting chronicles of nineteenth century big game hunting."

Few copies, if any, exist of the 1854 edition. If found, an original edition will probably cost $800 or more. In 1928, a second edition appeared, thanks to the editorial efforts of Shoemaker. This 1928 edition, limited to 500 signed copies, if found, sells for approximately $100. In 1971, Arno Press and the *New York Times* reprinted the original 1854 edition as part of their First American Frontier series from a rare copy owned by the Wisconsin State Historical Society. Unfortunately, that inexpensive edition is now out of print as well. While obviously not in great supply, systematic hunting through out-of-print book catalogs specializing in outdoor literature can still uncover either the 1928 or the 1971 edition of this great chronicle of deer hunting nostalgia.

On his final deer hunt, a lengthy trip down the Allegheny River in company with three friends and four dogs, Tome killed sixty-seven deer. He died in 1855, a time when venison was still placed on the free lunch counters of the better saloons in Pittsburgh and Philadelphia. It was due to deerslayers such as Philip Tome and Seth Iredell Nelson that those free lunch counters remained well stocked with venison loin.

Historically, we must undoubtedly consider Seth Iredell Nelson (1809–1905),

slayer of more than 3500 whitetails, 500 elk, and 500 bears as one of America's longest-living heroes of our deer hunting past. According to Nelson's gamebook, he killed his last white-tailed buck at the age of eighty-four in Clinton County, Pennsylvania in 1895, at a time of their greatest rarity. In an interview with Shoemaker, Nelson noted that when he first came to Portville, Pennsylvania in 1851, every woodshed along the one-mile Main Street stood decorated with trophy antlers. Every man, Nelson reported, seemed to be a trophy deer hunter and sought to outdo his neighbor with a record head nailed to his woodshed—the apparent historic beginnings of the American antler craze of the 1980s.

During his lifetime, Nelson and his son, Seth, Jr., were regarded as two of the most renowned and resourceful deer hunters and armorers of central Pennsylvania. While deer hunting some of the same terrain covered by Philip Tome, Nelson was given the title "King Hunter of the Sinnemahoning" by the Seneca Indians. At his deer hunting lodge on the Sinnemahoning at the foot of Altar Rock, famed in Indian lore, Nelson maintained a gunshop, making and repairing guns, knives, and ammunition. We still find many of his choice weapons in the museums of Pennsylvania. When Nelson died at the age of ninety-five in 1905, he was still helping his son, Seth, Jr., turn out guns for deer hunting—lock, stock, and barrel. They buried him on top of Karthaus Mountain, overlooking the one-time deer hunting paradise where for nearly a half century he roamed as the supreme ruler.

Nelson's gunshop near Round Island in Clinton County instilled the love of buck hunting and arms in several generations of mountain boys. Arms-loving pilgrims of note and diehard deerslayers came from all over Pennsylvania to learn about the dying secrets of the Kentucky rifles, which despite their name mainly came from Pennsylvania. According to Shoemaker, many of these pilgrims camped out near Nelson's gunshop "until a specially ordered weapon was begun and finished, so as to supervise every detail of its fabrication. Quaint and full of historic lore was this mystic wayside shire of arms."

In an interview with Nelson, Shoemaker learned that many of these backwoods deerslayers would often "insist that the shutters be closed and the smith's work carried on by candle-light, lest a passing hex cast a glance upon the barrel, which would ever afterward be deprived of the power to kill. The proud owner of a cherished gun would never leave it near a hex, lest she run her cold trembling hand along the barrel and forever destroy its accuracy. There were also spells or powwowing to make a gun shoot perfectly, and these were put on before a foe was to be removed, and more especially with the heavy rifles used at shooting matches. Needles and papers written full of incantations were slipped under the barrels where they joined the stocks to keep away the witches."

Famous guns frequently passed through Nelson's shop. Robert Covenhoven's rifle, for example, with thirteen notches on the underside of the stock as well as his scalping knife with seven notches, where this merciless scalp hunter enumerated his red victims prior to collecting the scalp bounty at Harris' Ferry, came in for repairs while owned by an old deer hunter named Miller Day.

When Shoemaker first visited Nelson's deer hunting lodge in August 1899, he noticed a medium-sized set of moose antlers

Seth Iredell Nelson (1809–1905), slayer of more than 3500 whitetails, instilled the love of buck hunting and arms in several generations of mountain boys. *Photo credit Robert Wegner*

hanging on the wall of the great Nimrod's living room. Having heard stories of the occasional appearance of moose in Pennsylvania, he asked Nelson where the antlers came from. "The magnificent old hunter replied that they were Canadian antlers sent to him some years before by a party who had once hunted with him in Pennsylvania. 'But,' added the old Nimrod, 'there once were moose in Pennsylvania.' Asked if he had ever seen any, he replied that he never had, that the last moose were gone long before his day, but that he had killed at least 500 elk, sometimes called 'grey moose' in the Pennsylvania forests."

During his lifetime, Nelson also killed more than one hundred wolves, nearly a hundred panthers, and Pennsylvania's last wolverine while on a deer hunting expedition in the autumn of 1863. The hide of this wolverine he exhibited in the Maxwell collection of stuffed animals at the Centennial Exposition in 1876.

Throughout his life, he accompanied many parties of deer hunters as their trusted guide. Governors and naturalists from around the country headed the list of prominent men who hunted deer with this grand old hunter with the long, black beard and the piercing blue eyes; eyes that reflected the endless deer trails of trackless

John Q. Dyce (1830–1904), the famous Clinton County deerslayer who killed three deer with one shot. *Photo credit Robert Wegner*

forests, Indians, panthers, wolves, and unbridled romance.

No one captured the romance of the early deerslayer more than the celebrated "Poet Hunter" of the Bald Eagle Mountains, John Q. Dyce. Born in 1830 near McElhattan, Pennsylvania, Dyce came from a prominent family in the Highlands of Scotland, a family of famed soldiers, artists, surgeons, and scientists. Educated in an old log schoolhouse, Dyce later went to the Dickinson Seminary at Williamsport to be educated as a Methodist preacher. Feeling at variance with the theological dogma of his day and more interested in pursuing deer, Dyce retired from the Seminary to become a professional deerslayer and backwoods poet. Standing more than six feet tall with long, raven-black hair and a beard, he more closely resembled an ancient philosopher of Greece and Rome than an early American deerslayer.

Nevertheless, his greatest deer hunting exploit occurred in Clinton County in 1870, when he killed three deer with a single shot. After sighting a buck, doe and fawn standing along Spring Run Ridge, he fired. The bullet pierced the brain of the buck, the throat of the doe, and lodged itself in the heart of the fawn. According to Shoemaker, this incident remains the only case of this kind recorded in the annals of Pennsylvania deer hunting.

Dyce frequently shot as many as nine deer in a single day and as many as ninety-eight in one season. In conversations with Shoemaker, Dyce, whom Shoemaker considered the most intelligent and informed deer hunter of his generation, reported shooting a good number of antlered does, bucks in the velvet as late as October and November, and a good number of atypical racks which he always believed had more points on the left antler than on the right.

Dyce's deer hunting shack contained a violin, a mouth-organ, an accordion, and a few dulcimers. Indeed, no deer hunting shack in those olden days was complete without musical instruments. In the evening after a day's hunt, Dyce would sing old-time ballads while the camp musician accompanied him on violin, mouth-organ, or dulcimer. His favorite ballad was entitled "All is Vanity, Saith the Preacher." This ballad tells the story of what happened at a small country church at Welcombe when a deer hunter interrupted the parson while reading the second lesson by opening the church door and shouting, "I've got um!" All of the men in the congregation arose at once and followed the deer hunter in eager pursuit of the wounded deer. The ballad describes what happened:

The hounds, astonished, howled and
    thund'red,
Until the forest shook with dread.
The singing o'er, the prayer was said,
But scarcely had the text been read
When, panting with fatigue and fear,
Rushed past the door a hunted deer.
Prayer, hymn and text were all forgot,
And for the sermon mattered not —
Forth dashed the dogs — not one was mute —
Men, women, children followed suit.
The men prepared the deer to slaughter,
The girls to head it to the water.
None staid but lame old Billy Tench,
Who sat unwilling on his bench.
Nor for the sake of hymn or prayer
Did Billy keep his station there,
But, as he said, with rueful phiz:
"For a damned spell of roomatiz!"
The parson groaned with inward pain,
And lifting up his hands amain,
Cried dolefully: "Tis all in vain!"
Up starting nimbly from his bench,
"Tis not in vain," cried old Billy Tench,
"When my good hound, old Never-Fail,

E. N. Woodcock (1844–1917), the famous Black Forest deer hunter who hunted deer in the mountains of Pennsylvania for more than fifty years. *Photo credit Robert Wegner*

Once gets his nose upon the trail,
There's not a spike buck anywhere
Can get away from him, I'll swear."

Although crippled with "a damned spell of roomatiz," by the age of sixty-nine after fifty years of deer hunting in the mountains of Pennsylvania, E. N. Woodcock (1844–1917), like Billy Tench, continued to dream of white-tailed bucks and the endless miles of deer trails he tramped while hunting deer in the Black Forest of Potter County. Historians of hunting, such as Shoemaker, rightly consider Woodcock to be one of the truest and best sportsmen/deer hunters to ever shoulder a rifle. Not even that "damned spell of roomatiz" could dampen Woodcock's deer hunting spirit. Indeed, like Tome, Nelson, and Dyce, his enthusiasm for deer and deer hunting ran high to the day he died. His greatest desire always remained to get into the Black Forest for just one more deer hunt before the end of the trail of life's journey. In his autobiography *Fifty Years a Hunter and Trapper* (1913), Woodcock proudly boasted that he could lay claim to one thing that few deer hunters could: In fifty years of deer hunting he only lost two seasons from the deer trail, both times being detained by rheumatism, the only affliction that could ever stop these diehard deerslayers.

Born in Potter County, a deer hunting mecca to this very day, Woodcock traveled the entire country to hunt deer in such states as California, Oregon, Washington, Michigan, Indiana, Oklahoma, Missouri, and New York. But he always returned to his favorite deer hunting terrain, "The Black Forest," located in the extreme southeastern part of Potter County, Pennsylvania.

"It was here," Woodcock recalls in his autobiography, "that I made my first bed in a foot or more of snow with a fire against a fallen tree and a few boughs thrown on the ground for a bed. At other times perhaps a bear skin just removed from the bear for covering, or I might have no covering other than to remove my coat and spread it over me. This I have often done when belated on the trail so that I was unable to reach the cabin and was happy and contented."

Like Philip Tome, Woodcock shot whitetails and bears at the early age of nine and frequently tramped back to deer camp in the black wilderness with a tallow candle in an old tin lantern, which gave him about as much light as a lightning bug. Back then, he would beg or steal, if need be, his father's old double-barrel flintlock shotgun called "Sudden Death" and escape to the nearest salt lick to watch for deer. He describes his early experiences in this regard:

"I would beg father to let me take the gun and watch the lick. As I was only nine years old, they would not allow me to have the gun, so I was obliged to steal it out when no one was in sight, carry it to the barn and then watch my opportunity and 'skipper' from the barn to the lick. All worked smoothly and I got to the lick all right. It was toward sundown and I had scarcely poked the gun through the hole in the blind and looked out when I saw two or three deer coming toward the lick. I cocked the old gun and made ready but about this time I was taken with the worst chill that any boy ever had and I shook so that I could scarcely hold the gun to the peep hole. It was only a moment when two of the deer stepped into the lick, and I took the best aim I could under the condition, and pulled the trigger. Well of all the bawling a deer ever made, I think this one did the worst, but I did not stop to see what I had done but took across the field to the house at a lively gait, leaving the gun in the blind.

"The folks heard the shot and saw me running for the house at break-neck speed (this of course was the first they knew I was out with the gun). My older brother came to meet me and see what the trouble was. When I told him what I had done, he went with me to the lick and there we found a fair sized buck wallowing in the lick with his back broken, one buckshot (or rather one slug, for the gun was loaded with pieces cut from a bar of lead); one slug had struck and broken the spine and this was the cause of the deer bawling so loud as this was the only one that hit.

"The old shotgun was now taken from

its usual corner in the kitchen and hung up over the mantlepiece above the big fire place and well out of my reach. This did not stop my hunting."

This turn of events only encouraged the boy to hang around gunshops like Seth Nelson's, where the lad heard infamous tales of deer and deer shooting while constantly looking at and dreaming about guns. By the age of twelve, he convinced his father to have the local gunsmith, Mr. Goodsil, make him a double-barrel shotgun. He now began gunning for deer in earnest; he received fifteen cents for the saddles and ten cents for the whole deer.

Like every backwoods deer hunter and trapper, Nimrod Woodcock longed for taller timber and tried to get farther and farther from the "ting-tong of the cow bells." In saying farewell to the plow, his trail and trapline excursions became longer and longer. Jerking venison and feasting on trout highlighted his deer hunting campaigns, which by the age of seventeen lasted for three months at a time. He usually returned home for Christmas.

Like most deerslayers of his time, he used the railroad, a team of horses, and a bobsled to travel farther and farther into the heart of the deer forest, where the business of deer hunting became serious. On a deer hunting campaign in the fall of 1868, with his partner, William Earl, a deer hunter from Vermont, Woodcock recalled that "we were seldom in camp until after dark, and we were up early and had breakfast over and our lunch packed in our knapsacks. The lunch usually consisted of a good hunk of boiled venison and a couple of doughnuts and a few crackers, occasionally the breast of a partridge, fried in coon or bear oil. Sometimes the lunch would freeze in the knapsacks and it would be necessary to gather a little paper bark from a yellow birch and a little rosin from a hemlock, black birch or hard maple tree and build a little fire to thaw the lunch. This, however, was quickly done, and was a pleasure rather than a hardship. I have delighted in eating the lunch in this manner for many a winter on the trap line or trail, as have many other hunters and trappers."

The first peep of day usually found them in hot pursuit of a certain large buck they generally called "Old Golden." Once on a buck's trail, they followed him to the end, no matter how long the trail continued. They often passed through several counties, traveling more than fifteen miles at a time. After killing the deer, they frequently sold it to a lumber camp for $10 and a night's lodging. "We hustled from early morning until long after dark . . . hardly a day passed that we did not kill at least one deer and some days two or three between us." When they ended their one-month campaign, they gave their hemlock shanty to a hunter named Ball and returned to civilization with some thirty-odd deer.

Unlike Tome, Woodcock preferred to still-hunt whitetails rather than to drive them. "I wish to say right here," he wrote in his autobiography, "that I do not like driving deer any better than I do the hounding and running of deer with dogs. The dog is all right but I want no dogging of deer for me." During the latter half of Woodcock's life Pennsylvania, like many other states, banned using dogs for running deer as well as shooting deer at salt licks.

Although prejudiced against dogs in the deer forest, on one occasion a dog greatly assisted the old Nimrod while doing battle with a white-tailed buck. After following a deer trail along a creek, Woodcock suddenly stopped and prepared to climb over a fallen tree across the trail. In his *Fifty Years a Hunter and Trapper,* he details the battle:

"I was just in the act of climbing this log when a good-sized buck went to jump the log also and we met, head on. I had no gun and if I had would have had no time to use it. I seized the deer by the horns and forced him back from the log with a startled cry at the same time. The deer, instead of trying to get away, seemed bound to come over the log to where I was, so I held to the deer's horns, not daring to let loose.

"I could keep him from raising over the log and after he tried several times to jump the log, he then tried to break loose from me, but I had the advantage of the deer owing to the log being so high that the deer could not pull me over, neither could the deer get in shape to strike me with his feet under the log. I think that I was so badly frightened at the sudden meeting with the deer, that I did not know what to do so I hung tight to the buck's horns and called as loud as I could for help, thinking that someone might possibly be passing along the road, which was not so far away, hear my call and come to my assistance, but no one came.

"A man by the name of Nelson lived about a fourth of a mile away, who had a large bulldog. The dog's name was Turk. This dog would follow me at every chance that he could get. As no assistance came, I had about made up my mind to release my hold on the deer as my strength was fast leaving me, when I thought to call for Turk. I began calling as loud as I could and it seemed that the dog had heard my calling before I began, for almost before I was aware of his presence the dog sprang over the log and seized the deer by the hind leg, but the dog had barely grabbed the deer when the deer kicked him away from the path into the laurel.

"In an instant the dog, with an angry yelp, jumped and seized the deer by the throat and in a moment the deer ceased to struggle and began to settle to the ground. As soon as I dared to release my hold on the deer's horns I got my pocket knife out and sprang over the log and ran the knife blade into the deer's throat. The deer did not seem to notice the knife. I think that the dog had choked the life out of him. The battle was over and it was only a few minutes but it was the hardest battle that I ever had and the dog came to my assistance none too soon for I could not have held on much longer."

During the heyday of market hunting the value of an individual deer, the value of the natural resource itself, remained quite different from today. The deer population for these old-time deerslayers such as Woodcock and his cohorts seemed limitless. Consequently, their trigger-itch and shooting behavior sometimes reflected this notion of an unlimited deer supply, a notion and its subsequent shooting behavior no longer acceptable in this day and age. An example of this trigger-itch behavior comes to light in a chapter of his autobiography entitled "Hits and Misses on the Trail," where he relates what happened when a group of deer ("a bunch of five or six") made its way past him at breakneck speed:

"I opened fire on the bunch without taking aim at any particular deer, as it was too dark to get down to real business and the deer were in too much of a hurry to change their feeding grounds to give me very much of a shot. I was not stingy of my ammunition and pumped lead at the bunch as long as I could guess where the deer were. As soon as I had ceased to waste ammunition I heard my brother calling for me. When I got to him he was at work taking the entrails out of a good sized buck. We dragged the deer down to where the deer were when I began shooting to see if I had chanced to hit one of the bunch. It was too dark to see much but we found a little blood on the snow in one place but concluded that I had not done much damage." This unacceptable behavior still occurs too often in the deer forest.

It is interesting to note that as early as the 1860s, Woodcock used skunk scent to disguise his human odor while hunting deer. But after fifty years of deer hunting, he reached negative conclusions with regard to the use of scents while hunting and trapping. "I have experimented with scents for years and have found scents of no particular benefit . . . I do not wish to insinuate upon those that do use scent, but for me, I would not give a cent for a barrel of so-called fox decoy . . . No boys, no scent for me, the animal soon learns to associate the scent business with man, then you are up against it. With me there is nothing mysterious about hunting and trapping. It is simply practical ways . . . learned from many years of deer hunting."

Woodcock always maintained an open invitation to his fellow deer hunters to come to his deer camp and enjoy the wilderness at large: "Brothers, I will tell you where my camp is and you will always find the latchstring out. My camp stands at the very head of the Allegheny River, 1700 feet above sea level. From the cabin door you can throw a stone over the divide to where the water flows into the west branch of the Susquehanna. In a half hour a person can from my camp, catch trout from the waters of the Allegheny and the Susquehanna . . . Yes, boys take your camp outfit and go out into the woods among the hills, streams and lakes. There you will find one of the most competent doctors and nurses that ever treated the ills of the human family."

Each of these deerslayers remained local heroes in their respective deer hunting turfs. Indeed, these pioneer farmers turned deerslayers remain in a class of their own. As long as we tramp the back forty in pursuit of the white-tailed deer, nostalgic memories of their daring feats will linger on: memories of their endless pursuits of mammoth bucks, their victorious conflicts with "hooves and horns" of their wounded quarry and the shattering effect of their deer kill statistics.

Although these early American deerslayers killed thousands of deer, as the white-tailed deer became scarcer by the end of the nineteenth century they began to react against the savage tendencies of the market hunting prevalent in their day. They now emphasized respect and esthetic appreciation for nature. Combining nostalgia for what they considered the wilder hunting of the past with the moral imperatives of gentlemanly conduct, they championed the general code of sporting ethics called sportsmanship. While they did not regret their commercial hunting exploits of the past, they overwhelmingly proposed a wiser usage of the natural resource toward the end of their lives.

In their writings and discussions with Shoemaker, they strongly emphasized combining the study of nature with the hunting experience and sought to restrain hunting methods and appetites. The added dimension of communing with nature and scientific curiosity gradually replaced their trigger-itch; while their notions of conservation remained hazy, the blazing-away mentality subsided.

In changing their attitudes, Tome and Woodcock in particular de-emphasized the importance of the kill, or the number of kills, and underscored instead the tonic quality of the outdoor experience and the redemptive and educational aspects of the deer hunting ceremony and ritual. Deer hunting must become an art, they insisted, an ennobling and instructive ceremony in which the hunter confirms his manhood and self-mastery in the deer forest but not at the expense of the natural resource. By 1900, an idealistic type of deer hunter emerged in America called the hunter-naturalist who viewed hunting as the best possible mode of environmental perception. While Tome, Nelson, Dyce, and Woodcock did not see the development of this movement, they abandoned their market gunning in favor of a firm commitment to conservation, the hunter-naturalist ideal, and the attendant code of sportsmanship. Had they lived longer, they probably would have wandered the deer forest for science and sport like their hunter-naturalist descendants.

Chapter 4

The Father of Deer Photography

Looking back to that period, many years ago, when the finger eagerly pulled the trigger and the eye anxiously sought to pierce the momentary veil of smoke between the gun and its intended victim, and then to that later period, when the simple pressing of a button captured, for all time, the graceful image of the hunted quarry, one becomes conscious of a peculiar mental evolution.

—George Shiras III, 1906

The hunter-naturalist ideal most clearly manifested itself in the life and hunting adventures of George Shiras III (1859–1942), the father of modern deer photography and one of America's most widely known and appreciated field naturalists. Following in the tradition of the hunter-naturalist, the most significant aspect of Shiras's approach to deer hunting focused on an active, participatory role in nature; the goal revolved around an intense involvement with deer in their natural habitat. The deer hunt allowed Shiras to become an integral part of nature. It forced him into an awareness of natural phenomena being organized into a coherent and unified framework. He perceived the deer as an object of great respect and strong affection. Yet, he participated in that ancient and mysterious contradiction of the hunter's soul, the ultimate paradox: He killed the thing he loved. In the deer hunt, he saw the creature at its best—when it's being hunted.

Although born in Pittsburgh, Pennsylvania's great industrial center, and educated in the eastern Ivy League tradition—Phillips Academy, Cornell and Yale—Shiras hunted deer, first with the gun and later with the camera, over virtually every part of the Lake Superior region. From his famous Whitefish Lake deer camp near Marquette, Michigan, he tramped into the wilderness to hunt, study, and observe deer and to photograph their everyday existence. Like Judge

"Hark!" One of a group of ten nighttime photos winning extraordinary honors at the Paris (1900) and St. Louis (1904) exhibitions. George Shiras III. © *National Geographic Society*

Caton and T. S. Van Dyke, he pursued deer in one way or another for more than sixty years, whether elk, moose, caribou, mulies, blacktails, or whitetails. In 1900, his classic photos entitled "A Doe and her Twin Fawns Feeding on a Lake in Northern Michigan" and "Hark!," a unique and superb photo of a white-tailed buck, received the Gold Medal at the Paris Exposition; in 1904 they again received the Grand Prize at the World's Fair in St. Louis.

His deer photos first attracted attention throughout the world to the possibility of wildlife photography at night. A French sportsman put into words the worldwide enthusiasm Shiras's deer photos evoked: "The stag that is coming out of the reeds, how beautiful and majestic he is! And the doe! And the little family! I was quite

stricken with amazement at them. This is not mere photography—it is high art! How happy I would be to place these splendid pieces in my hunting castle." These classic deer photos, together with Shiras's in-depth field studies of the whitetail, have had a far-reaching influence in developing in others a love for the great out-of-doors and for deer, especially the white-tailed deer, thus making this man a true giant among American deer hunters.

Arriving in the deer forests of Michigan in 1870, at the age of eleven, the young Shiras, like his father and grandfather before him, became an early devotee of the rod and gun and tramped the banks of little-known streams and lakelets in search

The hunter-naturalist ideal most clearly manifests itself in the life and hunting adventures of George Shiras III (1859–1942), the father of wildlife photography. *Photo credit Marquette County Historical Society*

This picture, entitled "A Doe and Her Twin Fawns Feeding on a Lake in Northern Michigan," received the Gold Medal at the Paris Exposition in 1900 and attracted worldwide attention to the deer photography of George Shiras III. George Shiras III. © *National Geographic Society*

of deer. In 1882, Shiras located his first permanent deer camp in the pristine wilderness about twenty miles east of Marquette on a small secluded lake which the young Nimrod named Whitefish Lake. In an essay published in *National Geographic Magazine,* he described his first encounter with this magical place: "A glance to the north disclosed a narrow lake about a mile long, heavily forested along shore with pine and hemlock, except at the end, where a growth of reeds, backed by cedars and black ash, indicated the outlet stream. To the south a beautiful bay, or slough, lay between high hills, with reeds, water lilies, and sandy beaches at the end, through which the inlet stream issued from a gorge filled, as far as vision reached, with stately elms. This was the center of fine deer country." Shiras returned to this secluded hideaway for more than sixty consecutive years in his never-ending pursuit of the white-tailed deer. Deer camp aficionados will find his brilliant autobiographical account of this remarkable deer camp and his romantic adventures with whitetails at this location in his classic two-volume work entitled *Hunting Wild Life with Camera and Flashlight* (1935).

Shiras's first permanent deer camp, 1882. Jake Brown, his deer hunting guide, sits at the table. Several wild pigeons hang from the ridgepole. George Shiras III. © *National Geographic Society*

From that account, we learn that Shiras's early deer hunting adventures revolved around jacklighting deer on Whitefish Lake, a method of deer hunting generally considered a legitimate form of sport during the 1870s and 1880s. On his first adventure in jacklighting, or fire hunting as they commonly referred to it, the young Shiras sat in a dugout canoe, made from a white pine log. With his hunting guide, Jake Brown, maintaining a fire in an old frying pan containing a

handful of pine knots to which he added strips of burning birch bark as more light was needed, the two backwoods deerslayers followed the shoreline of Whitefish Lake. Suddenly, Jake Brown whispered to his young tenderfoot, "Put up your rifle, there's a deer ahead." Shiras tells us what happened.

"At first I could neither see nor hear one, but after passing some reeds bordering a little bay, I saw, standing within less than thirty yards, a small buck, intently feeding on the succulent water plants growing a few inches below the surface.

"Silently I raised my gun and aimed for the shoulder. As the black smoke and heavy report evidenced the pulling of the trigger, the deer gave a spasmodic whirl and rushed toward the shore at an extraordinary speed, the water flying in all directions. Once more I fired, just as the animal, in a single leap, cleared the first bushes and disappeared.

"Reverberating echoes from the high ground across the lake did not drown Jake's chuckle; but he gave assurance of another shot within an hour.

"ANOTHER SHOT!! What a mockery this seemed to one who felt sure that this first-time effort had been successful. If not, what chance would there ever be of doing better?

"With assumed confidence, therefore, I insisted that we should find the deer dead within a short distance. But Jake only laughed and steered the canoe toward the opposite shore. It was evidently his opinion that buck fever had given my prey a further lease on life."

That night the disappointed Shiras resolved to rise at daybreak with the vague hope of finding it. The next morning he pushed his canoe off without disturbing the others in camp, and headed for the marsh where he had shot at the deer. The dry mud soon gave evidence of where the buck had gone ashore. Pushing his canoe into the brush, he leaped clear of the muddy shoreline and grabbed a protruding snag for support. To his utter surprise the protruding snag turned out to be the hind leg of his dead buck. He sank to the ground trembling with emotion. Thorough examination of the deer indicated that nine buckshot passed entirely through the body, piercing the heart and lungs. This instance clearly demonstrated to the young deer hunter how far a deer will run even when mortally wounded. That most deer indicate by their actions the effect of a shot remained an unknown fact for the jacklighters of the 1880s.

Shiras, however, soon began to view jacklighting as deadly unfair and consequently abandoned the practice well before Michigan outlawed jacklighting deer in 1887. As a result of his jacklighting experiences, he acquired a dramatic fascination with the romantic adventures of surprising deer in their natural haunts by a sudden glare of direct and revealing light. He eventually devised a flashlight apparatus that enabled him to photograph deer that he encountered on his nightly canoe trips. After several years of experimentation, mishaps, and personal frustrations, he successfully developed and patented a hand-held mechanism that photographed deer at night and fired like a pistol. His nighttime photographs of deer taken on his evening cruises around Whitefish Lake remain world-famous.

To his flashlight apparatus, Shiras added a cord—either baited or stretched across a deer trail—that resulted in deer taking their own pictures. He also developed a startling innovation consisting of two flash cameras—one taking a picture of a deer at ease, the other photographing the animal in motion a split-second later as it spooked in alarm from the initial flash. Shiras was the first to employ two lenses to achieve a stereoscopic three-dimensional effect and originated a special camera to "shoot" birds flying at high speeds. He liked to think that his deer photographs, aside from their permanent scientific value, were instrumental in promoting a greater interest in the animal. Indeed, many of his deer photographs

Shiras in the bow of his deer hunting skiff in 1893 holding a flashlight used in taking night photos of deer on the shores of Whitefish Lake. The box on the revolving table in the bow holds two cameras. The jacklight used to locate deer was mounted on top of the camera box. George Shiras III. © *National Geographic Society*

taken in the 1890s cannot be topped today, even with our most sophisticated modern equipment.

Shiras's first camera consisted of a 4 x 5 outfit called the "Schmidt Detective Camera," having a high-grade, rectilinear lens and a fairly rapid shutter that Shiras could set and release by a string and button on the exterior of the box. Using this camera, Shiras obtained remarkably fine pictures of deer. The lens, however, as Shiras complained, "was of short focus, and it was necessary to get within about twenty-five feet of a deer for satisfactory results—a difficult feat in bright sunlight." Shiras

obviously accustomed himself to keen and exciting sport. Such difficulties led Jake Brown, Shiras's backwoods guide, to exclaim that "if the camera must be used, the best thing to do was to shoot the deer first and photograph it afterward."

Shiras tried sitting in blinds near runways, but shifting air currents usually betrayed his presence. The difficulty underscored the difference between shooting deer at great distances with the rifle and photographing them within a few yards. To overcome the difficulty and since daylight photography of deer requires direct sunlight with the animal standing clear of dense brush, Shiras chose the canoe as an aid in surprising deer at short bends in streams, believing that the best deer pictures can be obtained in the early summer months when the animal tries to escape flies and insects and seeks its preferred aquatic plants along the waterways.

It seems ironic that Shiras selected as the object of his first camera hunts the most cunning and elusive of all animals, the white-tailed deer. The explanation, as Shiras acknowledges, "lies in the fact that I simply wished to hunt deer and the camera afforded the means of gratifying this desire (regardless of the season.)"

But camera hunting deer often entailed dangers far exceeding those of gun hunting or what the father of deer photography aptly called "unexpected pyrotechnics." In his autobiography, Shiras explains this peculiar phrase by telling us what happened on the first dark of the moon in July of 1890:

"I left camp in a canoe with the new outfit in the bow and the ever-faithful Jake astern, going downstream from camp to avoid the winds of the open lake. My plan was to use the jacklight to locate the deer; then, on approaching it, to cover the jack and utilize the three lamps and a reflector when discharging the flashlight powder.

Jake Brown, a Michigan backwoods deerslayer and one of Shiras's deer hunting guides, sitting in front of his classy deer hunting abode, 1883. George Shiras III. © *National Geographic Society*

"In one place it was necessary to lift the canoe over half-submerged rocks; but, since we both wore gum boots, this was easily done. Shortly afterward it was realized that this little portage had probably saved the flashlight hunter from severe injuries.

"After we rounded the next bend, a pair of glowing eyes attracted our attention, and in a moment the jack was covered and the three lamps were ablaze. As we approached, the deer jumped to one side, making it necessary to change the course of the canoe, for I had not then devised a revolving table capable of covering any quick movement of an animal.

"As I turned to whisper instructions to Jake, my elbow caught on the rubber tubing, and toppled the entire apparatus into the canoe. The cap of the reservoir became detached, permitting the escape of all the powder, part of which clung to the wet surface of my rubber boots, the remainder going into the bow, where it caught fire from the overturned lamps.

"At once came a tremendous explosion of the drier powder, and the damper portion gave forth a brilliant sputtering flame with a cloud of stifling smoke, compelling me to leap overboard in order to extinguish the blaze on my boots and later that in the boat.

"Since I was facing the paddler when the mishap occurred, and because much of the powder was wet, my eyes were protected, but the incident gave a timely warning of the caution necessary in handling such an explosive.

"When Jake learned that no particular harm had been done by the explosion beyond the puncturing of a chimerical scheme, he gave vent to unrestrained mirth. Standing waist deep in the slowly moving current, my hands smarting from the touch of the flames, and the little camera floating about in the murky waters, I was in no mood to appreciate the humor of the situation.

"I uncovered the jacklight and turned its rays toward the stern, and the sight of Jake's hilarity, with its superabundance expressed by his whacking the paddle on the water in rhythm with each outburst, caused me to give an upward lift to the already elevated bow of the canoe. Down went the stern until only Jake's eyes showed above the surface. Every sound was stifled except a little sputtering.

"As Jake struggled to his feet, a grinning countenace showed his willingness to take good-naturedly this somewhat rude form of reprisal. In a few minutes the boat was ashore, the water removed, and the camera found on a near-by sand bar. While returning to camp, my now sympathetic assistant attempted a diversion by pointing out in vivid language how surprised the deer must have been 'when the moon blew up,' but his monologue was not interrupted."

Shiras soon learned that nighttime deer hunting with the camera possessed a greater attraction for an experienced sportsman like himself than did deer hunting with a gun, and he conveyed this information to others through the columns of *Forest and Stream* edited by his friend George Bird Grinnell. The dark, warm nights, the smell of magnesium powder in the flashlight apparatus, the gentle ripple of the canoe paddle, the wooded banks wrapped in haunting shadows with only the skyline dimly revealing the hunter's course—all served to enhance the romance and mystique of the whole adventure. Hoof stomps, snorts, deer struggling and plunging toward the brush—all mesmerized these camera hunters. Suddenly, the form of a majestic buck would appear and the tension mounted. Suddenly, as Shiras writes in his diary, "There is a click, and a white wave of light breaks out from the bow of the boat—deer, hills, trees—everything stands out for an instant in the white glare of noonday. A dull report, and then a veil of inkly darkness descends. What a strange phenomenon! Nothing like it has ever been seen on the lake during the days of its deerhood."

As the real and lasting merits of the camera as an integral part of the sportsman's equipment became more and more apparent to Shiras, he gradually formulated a profound hunting creed that won the immediate approval and appreciation of President Theodore Roosevelt, for the peep sights of the rifle never circumscribed the vision of George Shiras III. When his deer camp was generously supplied with venison, the camera offered a further means of exercising even greater hunting skill than did rifle hunting—for skill, not kill, became the primary motive in Shiras's deer hunts. While the word "skill" includes the word "kill," Shiras interpreted the latter word in a subordinate sense: The method becomes more important than the purely material results.

In his view, Shiras considered the taking of an animal's life as "an unavoidable incident in the gratification of desires existing wholly apart from the shedding of blood." In following the ideals of the hunter-naturalist, that grand tradition that stretches from Melville to Hemingway, Shiras found in the hunt not only a journey into the heart of nature but a journey that promises to reveal the mysteries of nature itself, the secrets of the human soul as well as the mysteries of white-tailed deer behavior.

The all-inspiring motive of every deer hunter, Shiras argued, should be fair play in the deer forest: Each hunter should give the animal a fair chance. Gamebags must exist; the open season must be but a small fraction of the year, and the harvest must not be converted into cash. A deer hunter's life must consist of three basic elements: anticipation, realization, and reminiscence. Shiras realized that the real enjoyment of the deer hunting experience arises from the freedom it grants us from business cares and social artificiality. He underscores the point in his hunting diary: "We hopefully sit for hours shivering on the limb of a mountain oak and contentedly return empty-handed."

While Shiras never indiscriminately decried the man with the gun, he experienced a gradual and personal evolution toward a higher stage of hunting. Although an eager deer hunter from early youth, one who pursued his quarry in the most relentless way, the longer he hunted and the greater his success, the more inept he became at vividly recalling his deer hunting scenes with clarity and distinctness. He took so many mental photographs of deer and his deer hunting experiences that the "gray film" of his mind failed to permanently record individual events. But not so for the camera hunter, Shiras hastened to add: "Each year adds value to his successful shots, and when he departs for the happy hunting grounds, his works live on forever."

Shiras's hunting code evolved simultaneously with the emergence of the scientific fly fisherman and the clay pigeon shooter; his sporting ethics lent a helping hand to elevating the standards and broadening the scope of outdoor recreation in this country. While his deer hunting expeditions, whether with gun or camera, took him to most of the wildest spots on the North American continent, from Hudson Bay to Mexico, his concern for sporting ethics and game conservation ultimately took him to Washington where, in 1902, he became a member of the United States Congress as an avowed Republican.

As a Congressman, Shiras found a unique opportunity to wage his battle for wildlife. In 1904, he successfully introduced the Act to Protect Migratory Game Birds of the United States, which put waterfowl hunting on a realistic basis by bringing all migratory game birds under federal control. The Migratory Bird Bill stands as a lasting tribute to his perception and determination in wildlife conservation. In 1925, he sponsored in Michigan the so-called Shiras Gun Law, prohibiting the carrying of a gun in any hunting area in the state during the closed season—a statute enabling game wardens to convict poachers who slaughtered thousands of deer illegally.

After hearing a rumor that several moose were seen near the southern boundary of Yellowstone National Park, Shiras set out with his eternal cigar and his insatiable curiosity to investigate the rumor, since no moose were ever reported in the Rockies south of Canada. He ascended the Upper Yellowstone by canoe during three successive seasons and, to the astonishment of sportsmen and naturalists, found a population of moose estimated by him at more than 2000 animals. Dr. Edward W. Nelson, Chief of the United States Biological Survey, later pronounced these animals to be a new subspecies of moose and named them for their discoverer—*Alces americana shirasi*. Upon learning of the new name given to the moose of Yellowstone, Roosevelt wrote

Shiras and expressed his approval that such a noble animal be named after a great hunter-naturalist. In 1918, Roosevelt and Shiras met at Trinity College in Hartford, Connecticut. There, both of these men received honorary Doctor of Science degrees for their distinguished accomplishments as field naturalists.

Like Roosevelt, Shiras belonged to the leading sportsmen's organizations of his time: the Explorers' Club of New York, the Boone and Crockett Club, and the American Game Protective Association. He was also a leading member of the Huron Mountain Club, a famous midwestern hunting club whose lofty ideals set the tone for sporting ethics across America.

After reading Shiras's profusely illustrated articles and studying his magnificent deer photos as they continually appeared in *National Geographic* magazine, Roosevelt wrote Shiras a letter urging him "to write a big book—a book of bulk as well as worth." Roosevelt concluded his letter by saying, "I feel strongly that this country stands much more in need of the work of a great faunal naturalist than of the work of any number of closet specialists and microscopic tissue-cutters." Roosevelt was especially interested in having Shiras complete a manuscript based on his white-tailed deer studies. As a consequence of Roosevelt's insistence, Shiras assured the Colonel that he would prepare for publication in book form the results of his work as a field naturalist, especially his work dealing with the natural history of the white-tailed deer.

Shiras completed his outstanding two-volume work in 1935. Published by the National Geographic Society, dedicated to the memory of Theodore Roosevelt, and entitled *Hunting Wild Life with Camera and Flashlight,* this noble and beautiful work stands as a monument to Shiras's devoted labors for the preservation of the wilderness and its native creatures, especially the white-tailed deer. In its teachings on the natural history of deer and in its preachings on sporting ethics, it encourages its reader to a higher appreciation of both. The breadth of his interest and the universality of his observations and deductions remind us of those of Judge Caton. His pioneering genius in the field of wildlife photography elicit comparison with that of Audubon in the realm of bird painting and with that of Ned Smith in the realm of deer painting. His kindly humor reminds us of T. S. Van Dyke, a humor that enlivens the pages of his blue-chip deer book with a wealth of human anecdotes ultimately revealing his deep concern for man, bird, and beast.

Since the white-tailed deer had been Shiras's favorite quarry with the rifle in his youth, he set out to acquire an in-depth knowledge of the animal's daily habits; he spent a lifetime doing so. In trying to get deer to take their own pictures, he quickly learned that whitetails have an extremely delicate sense of touch in their front legs and that even making contact with a small, black, silk thread often set them into immediate flight. When fleeing, Shiras observed that their reactions to alarm vary with individuals but that does frequently take flight with their tails up, whereas bucks often react to alarm by fleeing with their tails tucked in the down position.

One night well before the enactment of modern game laws, just as the full moon arose, Shiras visited an artificial salt lick near an abandoned lumber camp. After climbing a steep bank, he looked carefully over the top toward the lick and saw a gray body with its head down. The deer suddenly dashed off, but then stopped and looked up, its eyes glowing from the reflection of the brilliant light of the moon. Shiras fired his rifle, but the brilliant orbs continued to glow. He fired again. After firing a third shot, he became convinced that no live deer could withstand such a bombardment. Closer investigation revealed that he had killed an unusually large buck with his first shot, but that the buck's spreading antlers had wedged themselves in the branches of a dead cedar tree, thus preventing the body from falling to the ground. The head had locked itself into the cedar tree in such a way that the eyes continued to face the hunter; they continued to glow as well. Shiras speculated that a deer's eyes will probably continue to glow after death until rigor mortis sets in.

According to my friend Robert Jackson, a professor of psychology at the University of Wisconsin—La Crosse, most hunters pass through various stages of hunting, one of which he calls the shooter-stage, a stage in which the Nimrod finds it difficult to restrain himself from burning an overwhelming amount of gunpowder or, as Shiras calls it, "scaring deer to death by a fusillade of misses." Shiras himself passed through this stage of wanderlust and trigger-itch, and in his autobiography he gives us a classic example of this behavior.

While deer hunting in a canoe on Sixteen-Mile Lake in northern Michigan with his trusted guide, Jake Brown, Shiras spotted a buck feeding in the shallow water along a wooded point. He left the canoe to begin stalking the buck along the shoreline. Jake soon shouted, "The deer has gone into the water on the other side." Shiras ran across the point with another hunting companion and saw the buck within easy rifle shot, swimming through a bay, but a bay filled with thick mud.

Shots from their repeating rifles began at once. Bullets ricocheted around the swimming buck but to no avail, given the hasty shooting. Shiras soon heard his colleague's rifle click, indicating an empty chamber. While hastily looking for more shells himself, he remarked, "Just watch me knock that old boy over!" His rifle barked and barked; the buck's head gradually sank into the water.

"This shows the difference when you take accurate aim!" Shiras remarked.

When this dilentante fusillade ended, old Jake took the young hunters in the canoe and headed for the sinking buck. After pulling the buck to shore, Shiras examined the buck's head, the only part of the body that had been exposed to the heated barrage of bullets.

"There's not a mark on it other than two bullet holes through the ears," he hollered with a frown on his brow.

On shore the two hunters and their guide cleaned the mud from the carcass and carefully examined the entire body without finding another mark. While in a state of amazement and bewilderment, Jake opened the body cavity and remarked, "I know what did this buck in, it died of fright." He proceeded to show the two deer shooters the deer's stomach filled with blood and indicated that in its struggles with the thick mud, the buck had ruptured a major blood vessel. The old guide added to the chagrin of the two young deer shooters, "Next time use blank cartridges, the more powder in them the better."

In a brief portrait of his uncle, Winfield Shiras tells us that George Shiras III continued to hunt with both gun and camera almost to the day he died. Although he preferred camera hunting, he certainly never forgot his youthful enthusiasm for buck hunting, as the following passage from an article in the *New York Sun*, dated August 25, 1895, vividly illustrates:

"One beautiful autumn afternoon when but a mere lad, I took my place in the bow of a dugout and was silently paddled along the shore of a little lake sequestered in an almost unbroken wilderness. An aged Sioux hunter acted as my guide and mentor. Soon the quick ear of the Indian detected the indescribable swish-swash-swish of a deer as it waded leisurely through the high reeds on the opposite shore. In a few minutes the declining sun broke out with startling distinctness the half submerged body of a handsome buck as he energetically floundered about in the shallow water in quest of lily pads and succulent water grasses.

"Steadily the canoe drew high across the placid bay without one interrupting glance from the pronged target so soon to be deprived of the vital spark we treasure so ourselves. The buck fever raged madly in the forecastle of that tiny craft . . . True to the Indian custom, the word 'shoot' never came until the raising head gave notice that we might be seen, so close at hand was the boat. The right barrel belched forth a noisy cloud of gray smoke, concealing from the eager eyes the transverse rain of leaden hail, but the other senses plainly told that few had gone astray. Two dying leaps and the struggling beast fell in a mass of fair white lilies with the life bereft before the echoes of that deadly blast had traversed back to me.

"In my boyish enthusiasm the name of that buck was mud, literally and figuratively. The numerous bullet holes were evi-

This deer hunting camp in Alger County in the Upper Peninsula, 1884, belonged to Peter White, one of Michigan's foremost pioneers and Shiras's father-in-law. These boys obviously enjoyed roughing it; notice how they built the roof over the table in front of their lean-to. George Shiras III. © *National Geographic Society*

dence of marksmanship and skill; the blood-stained reeds and lilies, the streamers and rosettes of victory."

Born a sportsman of Scotch descent, Shiras sprang from a long line of deer hunters and anglers; it's not difficult to picture his forbears stalking stags in the Scottish Highlands. Throughout his life, Shiras maintained a deep and abiding love for the north country. Citizens of Michigan's Upper Peninsula remember Shiras as

a "live wire" and many natives called him the "lone fisherman," because of his fishing prowess. As an active gunner to the end, George Shiras III still shot ducks and geese on his beloved Whitefish Lake in the last November of his life.

Old-time Michigan deer hunters remember Shiras as one of the first and principal supporters of that state's "one buck" law, a law that remained sacred in Michigan from its inception in 1921 until the first "any deer" season in 1952. Shiras

Shiras bringing two large whitetails back to his deer camp, 1898. George Shiras III. © *National Geographic Society*

looked upon that law as a commonsense approach to deer herd management and argued that "if a farmer had as many roosters as hens, or as many bulls as cows and killed the same regardless of sex he would be regarded as one lacking in common sense as to raise suspicion of his sanity." But Shiras, as a man ahead of his time, foresaw the effects of a "bucks only" policy and wrote: "So well does the buck law, when efficiently enforced, build up deer and elk herds that the increasing total sometimes threatens starvation in limited areas and necessitates a regulated kill of the females as the only practical method of keeping the animals within reasonable limits."

George Shiras's rare sense of humor seemed limitless; he played many a prank on wilderness guides and deer hunting companions, and likewise had many a prank played on himself. He once spent a mosquito-haunted night in a tree stand waiting for a shot at a deer. After returning to camp without a deer, he encouraged a friend of his to take up the vigil for the rest of the night. The friend asked Shiras if there were any mosquitoes about. Shiras told his friend, "mosquitoes are seldom bad at this season of the year." The friend returned to camp the next morning without a deer and with his hands and face badly swollen. The friend made no comment.

Some years later in Marquette, Michigan, the same friend persuaded Shiras to get on his hands and knees over deep water where Shiras's friend exclaimed, "I have seen several four pound trout." When Shiras leaned over to inspect the water for the fish, his victim of that mosquito-infested deer hunt promptly pushed him into the water.

"You'll not be bothered with mosquitoes down there," his friend said as the father of deer photography spluttered to the surface.

Chapter 5

Painter of the Whitetail

It would be less than honest to maintain that all hunters are upright gentle-men, or even true sportsmen. But I'll bet that if all boys were taught the joys of hunting and appreciation of the out-of-doors half our psychiatrists, social workers, policemen and prison guards would be out of work when the next generation takes over.

— Ned Smith, 1971

A signed and numbered print of Ned Smith's original acrylic, entitled "Through the Pines," hangs on the wall in my study next to George Shiras's classic photo of a white-tailed doe and her twin fawns feeding on a lake. Every time I look at these two treasured artifacts of whitetail memorabilia, I long to get into the hardwoods to take up the track of the whitetail. Although working in different mediums, these two deer hunting artists in their photos and prints capture the essence of the white-tailed deer in a way most of us often overlook or fail to see. Shiras's photos and Smith's paintings not only enhance the excitement of seeing deer, but they crystalize the image of the animal and its habitat in our mind in an unforgettable way. The white-tailed deer remained

the favorite animal for both of these wild life artists. Ned Smith (1919–1985) considered the very word "whitetail" as the most thrilling and enhancing word in the outdoorsman's vocabulary.

In 1919, the year of Ned Smith's birth, Pennsylvania deer hunters shot 2939 white-tailed bucks during a buck-only season. In 1984, the year of Ned's last deer hunt, Pennsylvania deer hunters harvested 140,180 white-tailed deer in an either-sex season. In 1959, Smith witnessed Governor Lawrence sign into law a bill adopting the white-tailed deer as the Commonwealth's official State animal. In 1981, Ned designed the official logo for the Pennsylvania Deer Association and became its first honorary lifetime member. When one thinks of white-tailed deer and

Ned Smith, a meticulous worker, examined, sketched, and filled countless notebooks in his tireless effort to capture the essence of the white-tailed deer in his paintings. *Photo credit Marie Smith*

deer hunting in Pennsylvania or elsewhere, one thinks of Ned Smith, that great painter of the whitetail.

Born and raised in Millersburg, Pennsylvania, Ned Smith lived in that area all his life. In an unpublished letter to a magazine editor, he explained: "I loved the fields, mountains and the Susquehanna River and saw no reason to leave them." His friend Chuck Fergus, a columnist for the *Pennsylvania Game News,* remarked that Ned was "an unashamed stay-at-home." Ned's father, an avid botanist and "woods snooper," introduced the boy into the natural world of the Susquehanna Valley and the surrounding fields and mountains by carrying the three-year-old on his back as he tramped the deer forests in the land of Philip Tome and E. N.

Woodcock. As a result, Ned Smith acquired a love for the sights, sounds, and smells of the outdoors. By age ten, Ned took full advantage of central Pennsylvania's rich bounty of mammal, bird, plant, and aquatic life by making his own field trips around the quaint village of Millersburg. Taking to drawing in his preschool years, he learned to document on paper the memories of his early outdoor excursions.

Ned's career as a wildlife artist took off when Tom Samworth, an outdoor publishing baron, discovered Smith's drawings and offered him a job as an illustrator for books on outdoor subjects. After a year of illustrating books, he accepted a full-time job as a staff artist with the *Pennsylvania Game News* in 1948. For twenty years his realistic deer paintings, noted for their accuracy and originality, graced the cover of this magazine while his numerous pen-and-ink sketches of deer with their lifelike quality illustrated the stories inside. The scores of cover paintings, the thousands of illustrations, and his monthly column entitled "Gone for the Day" matured steadily. No one has ever put more life into the white-tailed deer on paper or canvas than Ned Smith.

In 1971, the Pennsylvania Game Commission published Ned's regular columns in a volume with the same title, *Gone for the Day*. Based on Ned's field journals, this collection of wildlife sketches reveals and documents the man's adventures with deer and his profound love for the sport of deer hunting. Although Ned hunted and killed elk, moose, and bear during his lifetime, the whitetail topped his list of favored big game. Much of the credit for the popularity of white-tailed deer hunting, Ned gave to the quarry itself:

"There's not a game animal in North America, or anywhere else that I know of, that can hold a candle to the whitetail. In the first place, with reasonable protection it can live almost anywhere. The elk needs extensive forests, the bighorn almost in-

While Ned Smith worked in many mediums—water color, acrylic, pen and ink, pencil, and oils—the whitetail remained his favorite subject matter.

accessible mountain ranges, the prong-horn unbroken prairies and foothills. But the whitetail can manage very nicely in either a northern mountain vastness or a five-acre farm woodlot. Instead of suffering from civilization's changes it often-times profits by them—enjoying the browse produced by man's lumbering operations, the food plants encouraged by his pipeline and powerline clearings, and his crops.

"In addition, the whitetail can take care of its hide remarkably well. An old white-tailed buck, veteran of several seasons, has got to be one of the smartest animals alive. His native alertness, backed up with phenomenal hearing and the sense of smell, make him exasperatingly difficult to stalk, and even when surprised he usually does the right thing. When he must, he can cover the roughest ground at break-neck speed and clear the highest windfall with soaring grace. But given a choice, he neither panics nor stares in disbelief. In-stead, he slips from sight as silently as a puff of smoke. By the time the hunter realizes his quarry is no longer behind that nearby oak where he last saw the flick of his tail, the cagey old buck has put an-other ridge between himself and the man with the gun.

"To qualify as a great game animal, a species must present a challenge to the hunter. The animal need not be colossal in stature or ferocious in disposition. He need not be beautifully colored or propor-tioned, or wear trophy horns or antlers. It is not even essential that he be edible. But to be worth hunting he must be alert enough to sense danger, smart enough to get out of it, and adaptable enough to thrive in the midst of it. These things our whitetail does to perfection—and lots more."

Lots of people claim they hunted white-tails with Ned Smith, but few did, for Ned Smith, like George Mattis, preferred to deer hunt alone. Both Smith and Mattis witnessed a steady decline in the popular-ity of gang hunting for deer throughout much of the whitetail's range after World War II. Instead of gangs of thirty drivers combing entire mountains, solitary deer hunters such as Ned Smith slowly moved through the deer forest attempting to beat the whitetail at his own solitary game. Like Mattis, Ned strongly believed as he wrote in an article entitled "The Lone Deer Hunter" that "no other hunting method puts the man with the gun in closer touch with his quarry, nor provides more personal satisfaction when a kill is made." The inconveniences, difficulties, and hazards of hunting alone never changed Ned's opinion in this regard. Ned Smith in his deer hunting adventures pre-ferred solitude to deer camp camaraderie.

The historic record indicates that "Ned-ley Dedley" Smith deer hunted only sev-eral times in the traditional group setting, one such hunt being the great *Game News* deer hunt of 1971. In that particular deer hunt, Ned joined his friends from the *Pennsylvania Game News* magazine: Jim Bashline, Bob Bell, George Harrison, and Will Johns. Despite his love for solo deer hunting, Ned obviously enjoyed the steak, grouse, and Chateau Latour at Harrison's Hidden Valley Camp in Pennsylvania's northeastern Huntingdon County.

At 8:30 a.m., on the opening day of that particular hunt, Ned shot a five-pointer in the lungs with a single shot from his old 300 Savage, a rifle going back to the 1930s with a unique sliding tang safety made by Ned himself well before it was offered on the Model 99s. As a con-noisseur of venison, Ned fretted about a previous hunter's gunshot in the right ham of his five-pointer. While that shot had not disabled the deer, it did destroy several steaks.

Unlike the opening day success of this 1971 deer hunt, Ned tagged many white-tailed bucks on or very near the closing bell of the season, at a weary time when most hunters think that all bucks hang on meat poles. Indeed, Ned always considered a "last day buck" as something special and he shot a good number of them on the south side of Peter's Mountain, his cherished deer hunting spot. Even when he missed a beautiful buck on the last day of the season, Ned viewed it as a great moment of excitement given to him by the Red Gods of the outdoors. On the last afternoon of one season, after a frustrating week of few deer sightings and poor weather, Ned spotted a classic eight-pointer with a tremendous spread about 100 yards away standing in thick, leafy oak brush. In his dog-eared field diary, Ned recalls what happened when the Red Gods smiled.

I couldn't seem to get a clear shot from where I stood. A nearby jumble of rocks offered a better vantage point, but when I attempted to climb them their crusted coating broke with a resounding crash and a tinkle of falling fragments. The buck's head went up and for several breathless minutes he stared in my direction while I attempted to balance motionless on one foot. Finally, when I thought I could endure the pose no longer, he waggled his tail and resumed browsing.

Though it initially seemed impossible to get a clear shot, shorten the range, find a rest for my Savage M99, or anything else to swing the odds slightly in my favor, I did finally locate an opening that seemed *reasonably clear of brush. The scope showed the buck still browsing contentedly. It was pretty far for an offhand shot in my stooped position, but I had to try it before he moved away from the opening. The post reticle swung to a point just behind his shoulder and settled there. No problem. The footing was precarious but the sight picture seemed steady, which was surprising in the light of my eagerness to have that buck. 'Ease it off,' I told myself.*

At the rifle's roar the great buck simply left the ground and cleared the ledge in a couple of flowing leaps, dropping from sight on the downhill side. I sprinted to the ledge but he was gone. Half running and half sliding, I followed the tracks down the mountainside and west all the way to the pipeline. No blood, no hair, no drag marks. Nothing but shattered snow crust and churned-up leaves. He had escaped unscathed.

The cause of the miss is not really that important. What is important is that the Red Gods had placed a beautiful buck in my sights on the last day of the season, and in doing so taught me that as long as a minute of the hunting season remains there is still an opportunity for success. The experience has become as vital a part of the hunt as my knife and rope. Many times when the season grows old and the chances of meeting up with a buck seem slim, the memory of that scene returns to mind. Once again I see that handsome fellow standing in the sunshine, his wide rack swaying as he feeds, and I take heart. He's the inspiration I need to imagine a buck around the next bend in the trail, to hunt just as diligently, just as carefully and just as hopefully on the last day as the first.

In his deer and deer hunting adventures, Ned Smith touched a chord that lures all of us into the forest. As we read his diaries and articles and study his prints and illustrations, we find an American deer hunter who spent most of his wakeful hours with the sky above him, the deer forest beneath his well-oiled boots, and the prevailing wind in his face. Like George Shiras III before him, Ned followed the trail of the hunter-naturalist regardless of the season.

While climbing Berry's Mountain in the whitened landscape of one January day, Smith observed a clever old white-tailed doe add spice to his snow-time outing. From a hilltop he could see down into a wooded hollow at the base of Berry's Mountain. There he saw three persimmon trees and in the tallest one ten wintering robins. While observing the robins, the incurable nature snooper caught a rare glimpse of bird-deer interaction. In his journal he recorded the event:

The wintering robins busily pecked the sweet pulp from the blackened fruit still clinging to the branches. At frequent intervals a pummelled persimmon would drop to the snowy ground practically into the jaws of a lanky old doe waiting there. Between falling persimmons she would smell around in the snow for others but each muffled plop brought her on the run.

I must confess that the thought of those delicious orange-fleshed fruits got the better of my sense of fair play, and I eased down the slope toward the trees. The doe trotted into the woods at my approach, as I knew she would, but the robins fled, too, darn the luck. Try as I would, I couldn't find more than a single shrivelled persimmon in the snow, and though I stood quietly to one side and looked pathetically hungry the robins refused to come back and work for me.

In early spring, Ned tramped the barren hills and mud-soaked valleys in search of shed antlers. When June turned the Pennsylvania outdoors into a veritable nursery, he searched, located, and photographed newly born fawns. Each July he continued to follow deer trails to observe "ghostlike tails dancing through the woods." Deer looked at him, snorted at him, and stamped their hooves at him. Despite the humidity and heat of August, Ned Smith amusingly watched playful deer abruptly change direction, kicking out their heels like spirited colts, running, stopping, and bucking—galloping, romping, and dashing around in circles "with legs spread and nostrils aquiver."

One of his diary entries for September recalls how he spied on a buck while the deer rubbed his antlers one late afternoon along the edge of a field. Before the buck slipped back into the shadows of the deer woods, Smith studied the pink-looking, newly exposed antlers through his binoculars. Blood dripped from the buck's forehead. Ned thought to himself: "He's done a thorough job. A few fringes around the antler burrs were all that remained of the fuzzy covering." Smith observed that white-tailed bucks in his deer hunting turf near Berry's Mountain preferred to rub their antlers on red maples, aspens, and pines.

When not looking for buck rubs in the woods, Ned crisscrossed cornfields and peered down the endless rows, looking for white-tailed bucks between the rows of the leafy stalks. Ned took up bowhunting with great enthusiasm, but after a marathon tracking session and a frustrating experience of not being able to retrieve a wounded eight-pointer, his bow remained in the storage closet of his studio next to innumerable boxes of antlers. Ned Smith preferred the rifle and the muzzleloader.

For fifty years the gray, somber sky of November and December enticed Ned Smith into the woods to look for the swollen necks and glassy eyes of rutting bucks. Whether still hunting Nine-O'clock Run or sitting along a well-worn deer trail in the hollow of Berry's Mountain, Ned's thoughts always focused on rutting bucks and their behavior. But Ned always found another by-product of the annual deer hunt: an informal course in nature study, a course Ned considered as an inescapable part of every still-hunter's or stump-sitter's day. In his December journal for 1968, Ned explained this by-product of the deer hunt:

The stump-sitter, especially, is usually in an excellent position to see the shiest forest denizens without being seen. Because he is perfectly still, the slightest movement catches his eye, and because he makes no sound he hears the first suspicious rustle. His own stillness shields him against detection by wild ears and eyes. Only the wind can give him away. Whether the result is the appearance of a new bird or animal or an old familiar species doing a new thing, it is a deer hunting bonus that can save the day when that buck fails to show up.

Ned found it hard to believe that more deer hunters do not return to the forest after deer season. He wondered where all those so-called "nature-hunters" are after the season closes. I have often asked the same question.

Whether white-tailed bucks failed to show up or not, Ned Smith hunted them with all the persistence and tenacity of his great deer hunting predecessors, Philip Tome and E. N. Woodcock. Regardless of the weather—rain, snow, or fog—Smith prowled the oaks and wooded hillsides until he hit a fresh track of a buck. He would follow it until the deer exploded unexpectedly from the brush. On the last day of the 1968 buck season, at 4:50 p.m., with ten minutes before closing, he jumped a four-pointer fifty feet away. His pet 300 Savage cracked and the buck plunged dead to the runway. "A quitting-time buck if ever there was one," he wrote in his field notes while watching the buck swing from his catalpa tree.

In the mind of Ned Smith, the white-tailed buck represented the personification of a vigorous, healthy, ideal quarry. He loved to chase them, study them, photograph them, illustrate them, paint them, talk about them, write about them, dream about them, shoot and eat them; a more enthusiastic buck hunter never prowled the deer forest. The month of December meant one thing for Ned Smith: buck season, prowling the deer forest and "dry-gulching a big buck." The opening day for bucks never arrived soon enough for him. While stump-sitting on Peter's Mountain, Ned often thought to himself: "There's nothing so suspenseful as those last few minutes before the magic opening hour on opening day. You scarcely breathe, straining to catch the first sound or glimpse of moving deer. Each faint rustle is analyzed, each flicker of movement scrutinized. Nothing is taken for granted."

On one opening day in December just as the sun cleared the top of Third Mountain, Ned Smith caught a dandy eight-pointer pussyfooting through a small scrub oak flat. Slowly threading his way along a deer trail through the natural openings, the buck suddenly stopped before emerging from the scrub oak. Ned quickly put the unwrapped chocolate bar he was fiddling with back into his pocket, and raised his Model 99 Savage ever so slowly. As man and buck stood frozen in time—that eternal moment of truth for the hunter—Ned heard the sound of pounding hooves and cracking brush behind the buck as three does broke from cover. The buck stood still, silhouetted against the scrub oak flat with only his head and neck visible. The antlerless deer kept moving. The buck stood ghostlike in the same position as Ned squeezed off a shot. At the crack of the rifle the eight-pointer bolted from the scrub oak and plunged down the side of mountain. Ned shot again; the buck disappeared and all was silent. Ned ran down slope, hoping for another shot. But no more shots were needed. As he crossed the oak flat, he found the buck lying dead in the snow, a big-bodied deer with an almost perfect eight-point rack with one shot in the neck.

For more than thirty years Ned Smith started the deer season by walking unerringly through nearly a half-mile woods in the pre-dawn darkness to reach his rocky-ledge deer stand on Peter's Mountain. As he walked through the darkness he experienced all kinds of weather, everything from clear, quiet, starry nights with the moon just beginning to set to windy, noisy nights with drizzling rain, snow, or pea-soup fog. His thoughts often turned to the early Pennsylvania Nimrods who preceded him, and their annual treks to deer hunting camps in Centre and Clinton counties when those dedicated deerslayers of yesteryear made their way in Model Ts. He would often recall how he would traipse from one end of Millersburg to another as a young lad when these deerslayers returned to civilization so that he could gawk at their storybook bucks hanging in the various trees around town and dream of shooting bucks like that someday.

As he walked to his deer stand, he often

thought of the one million Pennsylvania deer hunters and the men of all ages he encountered in the deer forest. "These are the hunters of Pennsylvania," he thought to himself, "a million strong, but no two alike. And yet, they all share certain characteristics—faces made ruddy by wind and cold, legs kept strong and agile by rough footing, bright eyes, discerning ears, disregard for discomfort, and a love of winter woods and the challenge of the hunt.

"A cross-section of our society? Hardly. I see no hippies or beatnik types, nor hear a single protest song. No thug relieves me of my wallet as I wait; no young punk mugs the old man in the woods. The natural outdoor world is wondrous enough for all without the stimulation of booze, glue or pot."

Some bucks came easy while he was deer hunting on Peter's Mountain, some hard. On one December opening he scarcely settled down on his rocky ledge when a buck with high, symmetrical antlers stared at him from behind a big tree trunk. When the buck stepped out into the opening, Ned squeezed the trigger. At the report of the rifle, the deer wheeled and plunged out of sight. Hearing him crash to the ground, Ned soon found the buck piled against a windfall. When he filled his tag so early in the season, Ned would spend the rest of the deer season hiking around his deer hunting grounds and studying deer trails in order to learn which ones the deer used most heavily during hunting season.

Other bucks, however, came only after days of frustration, bad weather, and hard hunting. In his last "Gone For The Day" column, Ned tells us about one deer season when everything seemed to go wrong. On the opening day he could not find his rocky seat due to fog and heavy rain. Consequently, he settled down where he found himself to wait for the light of dawn. As the opening hour approached, he saw flickers of flashlights from other hunters intruding in "his" domain. When he finally reached his cherished spot, all he saw were antlerless deer passing like specters in the night. More hunters passed him than deer. Indeed, no bucks passed him at all; the opening day ended as did several more days in a row with a bloodless close. Only after several arduous days of still-hunting, stump-sitting, and woods snooping did Ned manage to drop a spike buck for the pot.

His unpublished notebooks remind me of the unpublished hunting journals of Aldo Leopold, for like Leopold, Smith summarized the hunting events of each day afield with great specificity. Out of these hunting experiences, like Leopold, he carved his creative art. In his notebooks, he recorded such information as where he hunted, often drawing detailed maps of the area; whom he deer hunted with, most often Jack "trigger finger" Miller if anyone; the weather conditions of the day and how they affected the forest floor for still-hunting; the kill, if successful, and the shot placement with great anatomical detail; each deer seen and its behavior and reaction to the hunter; the amount of hunting pressure; number of shots heard, and the behavior of the deer hunters he encountered. Some of his detailed notes he wrote out in long hand with pen and ink; other entries he typed.

At the end of each deer season, he summarized the entire experience. A typical entry in Ned Smith's unpublished hunting notebooks reads as follows:

Conclusions on the 1967 deer season: *Not many deer coming to the scrub oak stand; most of the traffic seems to be going in and out about seventy-five to 100 yards to the west near the top of the hill. Perhaps I could move that way a bit and still cover the trail to the east. That would also get me out of line of the trail through the s. oak to the north. The only disadvantage would be in the case of deer that are alarmed and moving in or out to the east. Perhaps the lack of good thermals to stop my scent drift to the south cut down on the number of deer coming up to this stand. The shifting winds did give me trouble this year. Lots of deer passing Hole-in-Hill, pushed on the first day and apparently feeding and pushed on the last. However, during the first day no deer (except the first two) came up from below that stand. Could they have seen me there? Or scented me? Doubt the latter, for deer passing below me going downhill didn't get my scent. No snorting heard, so perhaps they just weren't travelling that route. Rock seat is too far down mountain side to cover open woods around Hole-in-Hill, and is pretty exposed to deer trail below it. Perhaps moving northwest to head of rocky draw would let me cover both. With snow on ground I could possibly also see deer on flat at bottom of draw, but to cover this adequately I should probably drop down to near same level and toward Big Hollow to avoid evening thermal reversal. Old stand still sees lots of activity, but this season deer all but trampled all over it. I'd have been too close.*

Best spot for p.m. feeding on the boundary line seems to be west of Williamstown path. Shot a three-pointer about 200 yards beyond path a few years ago while other deer were heard feeding down along run. This year saw deer in mid-afternoon along trail and along run a bit farther west where fallen tree covers the boundary line. Should try to see trail and stream from same spot. Wind is often a problem here. If wind is right I should try walking north on pipeline and hunting along trail that follows stream to boundary line. Good trails come from s. oak and woods on south side of run to stream at several places. One at a bowl about two hundred yards from pipeline, another where boundary line crosses stream.

With detailed summaries of the past season's deer hunt in hand, like this one, Ned always began the next deer season without having to relearn the lessons of the past. In his notebooks he also kept very extensive notes on shot placement, cartridge performance, and wounded deer behavior following the shot. The best example of this type of information we find recorded in an entry in his unpublished hunting journal dated December 1, 1940.

On that day, Ned took his stand on the north side of Berry's Mountain about 8:00 a.m. After sitting for about an hour, the twenty-one-year-old Nimrod heard a deer coming down the mountain. When the deer approached within seventy yards of the young lad's stand, Ned saw a six-point rack and touched off his 32–40 Winchester. The first shot showed no visible effect on the buck; he merely turned about and walked back up the mountain from where he came. In doing so, he walked very slowly, but showed no sign of stumbling or staggering. This first bullet Ned later discovered pierced both shoulder blades but higher than intended. So Ned shot again. The second bullet hit the middle of the lungs and knocked the buck down. But the buck immediately gained his composure and broke into a gallop. Like William Monypeny Newsom, Ned Smith always prided himself on one shot, no cripples. But in this particular case the young deerslayer burned a considerable

amount of gunpowder, as he himself admits:

The third and fourth shots had no visible effect on the buck, although they both entered about the same place the second shot had, and made a mess of the lungs. All this time the buck had run in an arc around me, constantly staying at the same range and offering me all broadside shots. He did not raise his flag at any time. After the fourth shot he was lost from view behind some thick laurel, and I couldn't see him again until he burst out of a thicket only about twenty feet from where I stood, heading directly towards me. I fired one hasty shot and jumped to the side, barely in time to prevent my being knocked down by the buck which had fallen after this last shot and slid down the icy mountain side, his sharp hoofs flailing madly. He stopped about ten feet from where I stood, after sliding over the spot I had previously occupied, and I was forced to end his life with a bullet in the neck at the whithers. The shot before this last one had merely grazed his shoulder, side and hip, and his falling at this time was due to the damage inflicted by the previously fired shots.

In hindsight, Ned realized that the buck's walking away after the first shot in such a slow manner should have indicated a hard hit. He noted that the buck did not turn downhill even after his lungs were almost blown away. Detailed examination indicated that none of these bullets made a larger hole on exit than when they entered. The pattern for the group of three that went through the lungs Ned could cover with the palm of his hand. He rated the individual performance of the bullets from his 32–40 Winchester as extremely poor with a "minimum of upsetting action."

With the exception of this early gunpowder incident, Smith killed most of his bucks with one shot. While deer hunting on the Durleton Plantation in Georgetown, South Carolina, for example, on November 8, 1947, Ned jumped a spike buck out of a thicket near the Pee Dee River. The buck cut across the edge of a cornfield and took refuge in a live oak thicket. Ned caught a glimpse of him standing in the thicket. He fired one shot, killing him with a 257 Roberts hollow-point 100-grain bullet, broadside at fifty feet. The bullet entered the right side six inches behind the shoulder; it exited at the rear edge of the left shoulder, shredding the liver and the right portion of the lungs. The buck stumbled to his knees but leaped to his feet again and galloped off low to the ground. Ned found him about fifty feet from where he shot him. Although the bullet made a one-and-a-half-inch hole on exit and Ned could clearly see blood spray against the sun when the bullet struck, he found no blood trail. The spikes measured eight inches in length and the buck weighed approximately 110 pounds on the hoof. Not a trophy, but a buck to which many of us can relate.

As an outdoor writer, Ned Smith wrote for the common man who, as Ned acknowledged, "likes to kick around in the woods more than he really has time for." Countless young Pennsylvania deer

The quiet, unassuming artist at his desk, thinking about The Orchard Buck. *Photo credit Charles J. Alsheimer. (See color section, which precedes title page.)*

hunters picked out the *Game News* from the library rack in school and found in "The Gone For The Day" column exciting reading about Ned Smith's buck hunting adventures on Peter's Mountain in State Game Lands No. 210. One such young hunter, named Chuck Fergus, read Smith's deer hunting tales with great delight and later characterized Smith's prose in the "Thornapples" column in the *Game News* as "lean, vigorous, honest and unpretentious, with vivid descriptions that could only have come from countless hours outdoors." Ned combined his talents as an outdoor writer, photographer, deer hunter, and artist with an unique understanding of nature to become one of America's most popular wildlife portraitists, especially of the white-tailed deer.

Ned Smith breathed life into his white-tailed deer paintings, illustrations, and deer hunting tales. His deer paintings and illustrations grace the dust jackets of many of the finest deer books of the twentieth century, many of them published by Stackpole Books. His deer paintings and illustrations have appeared in such magazines as *National Wildlife, Outdoor Life, Field & Stream, South Carolina Wildlife, Sports Afield, Audubon, Deer & Deer Hunting,* and many more. Private collectors increasingly demand his deer paintings. A number of his wildlife paintings remain in the permanent collection of the Carnegie Mellon Museum. Connoisseurs of deer paintings will always remember his name, a name that ensures quality, dedication, and self-discipline, a name that symbolizes a true love of nature and a passion for preserving the leap of a white-tailed buck. Ned Smith loved guns and animals and remained a die-hard buck hunter to the day he died.

When thinking of Ned Smith, his friend and editor Bob Bell once wrote: "He was intensely efficient, but an unassuming man who smiled often and laughed a lot." Leonard Lee Rue III, a deer hunting artist with the camera, said of his friend in conversation with a field editor for *Deer & Deer Hunting* magazine: "Ned Smith is in a class by himself; nobody paints deer better than he does. I always envied him because he was such a good writer, nature photographer, and wildlife painter. Most of us could only handle one medium but he mastered all three. Ned's the best there is, period!"

On Monday, April 22, 1985, Ned Smith died at the age of sixty-five. That day Ned never got to the daily task of opening the mail. He never saw the June 1985 issue of *Deer & Deer Hunting* that arrived that same day in his mail box. Consequently he never saw the finished portrait of him, although he had read an early draft, entitled "Ned Smith: The Deer Hunter's Artist," written by my friend Charlie Alsheimer, who wrote that "Ned Smith's experiences in the deer woods give him an edge over many other painters of deer. Because so few artists are deer hunters, it's difficult to find many good deer prints. The hunter-artist in Ned Smith enables him to depict the whitetail as the avid hunter envisions it."

When I think of Ned Smith I think of white-tailed deer paintings and illustrations of the highest distinction and quality. His paintings will always hang on the walls of my study and I will always cherish his inscription to my copy of his "Gone for the Day": "To Rob Wegner with gratitude for *Deer & Deer Hunting* — my bible." Ned Smith is gone for the day, but his wildlife art will live forever.

PART II

DEER HUNTING LORE
AND
NATURAL HISTORY

Chapter 6

The Overhanging Branch

We can show the marks he made
When 'gainst the oak his antlers frayed.
— Sir Walter Scott

While sitting in an oak tree that overlooks a primary breeding scrape, I continually observe white-tailed bucks not only licking in a vigorous manner the overhanging oak branch above the scrape, but nibbling and chewing the branch; licking, sniffing, and thrashing it; grasping it with their teeth and pulling it down; twisting it and raking their antlers through it; rubbing their preorbital gland on it; and ultimately rubbing the branch against their forehead scent glands, located near the base of their antlers.

Although whitetails are not necessarily territorial animals in the traditional sense of defending a territory, they do scent mark a breeding territory. These scent-marking activities, deer biologists tell us, leave visual and olfactory signals in the deer forest that become physical extensions, as it were, of the deer itself. But

what's the function of these activities? How do we decode these seemingly mysterious gestures? What is the importance of these scent-making activities in the social organization of deer? What does this form of body language tell us? What's being communicated?

Despite our ignorance and insensitivity to the olfactory environment, to the whitetail it represents a major form of language, a language of silent communication, a language of chemical communication. To successfully hunt whitetails during the rut, we must have a basic understanding of this language of chemical communication and a knowledge of the significance of the overhanging branch. In attempting to answer these questions with regard to the overhanging branch and the language of silent communication, we must turn to the scientific

Find an intensely used overhanging branch for rubbing and licking in July and/or August and you will have found a major dominance area. Sit tight. During the summer months you will be able to view firsthand the expression of dominance—the establishment of a dominance hierarchy via rubbing, sniffing, and licking the overhanging branch. Many deer hunters overlook this pre-season scouting tool.

Michael E. Graham

community, for little if any information of substance exists in the popular press.

One of the earliest and fullest descriptions of a white-tailed buck placing scent on the overhanging branch, which we invariably find above most active scrapes, we find recorded in the February 1954 issue of the *Journal of Mammalogy* written by William Pruitt, a professor of zoology at the University of Michigan. While studying rutting whitetails in a second-

growth, oak-hickory woodlot on the E. S. George Reserve in mid-November, Pruitt observed an eight-point buck rattling his antlers on low oak limbs above scrapes and uttering low grunts.

The buck, Pruitt reported, "reached up and grasped low-hanging oak limbs in his mouth, pulled them down, and by twisting his head, raked his antlers through them. Inspection of the spot immediately after the buck had left revealed the presence of a typical pawed circle about three feet in diameter, where all the leaves had been removed and the soil torn and trampled, with hoof and antler marks plainly and deeply imprinted. Loose soil was scattered for several feet around the circle on top of the leaf litter. No evidence of fresh urine was noted. The lower limbs of the tree immediately over the circle were torn, scarred, and broken."

In his description, Pruitt compared the activities of the buck to those of a domestic bull when he smells a cow in heat. While uttering low, whining grunts the buck would wheel in a circle, flashing his flag while grunting and pawing the ground. But Pruitt did not go much beyond mere description.

While studying this phenomenon of licking, sniffing, chewing, rubbing, and thrashing the overhanging branch, William Graf, a California deer biologist, referred to the overhanging branches in the *Journal of Mammalogy* in 1956 as "signposts" of a breeding area that psychologically affect all deer entering the territory. But an in-depth explanation of this psychological effect remained elusive. He did note that scent marking on overhanging branches frequently occurs in or near bedding areas. I have frequently found this to be the case while deer hunting in southwestern Wisconsin.

Graf pointed out that this highly ritualized pattern of behavior usually starts with the careful and deliberate nosing or sniffing of the branch chosen for this operation. The deer performs this nosing with great delicacy and patient precision bordering almost on pure ecstasy. The entire sequence of actions may last from five to fifteen minutes. This behavior is not confined to the rut alone. I have observed a great deal of licking, sniffing, and rubbing of the overhanging branch by bucks

The buck's ultimate sign of chemical communication. *Photo credit Tom Edwards*

in July and August when they are determining the pecking order. The repeated use of the same overhanging branch season after season, year after year, by the same bucks as well as different bucks certainly indicates a greater importance to these acts than the immediate fulfillment of using the branch to vent surplus energy and spirit.

In 1967, George Schaller, a naturalist of first rank, emphasized in his book entitled *The Deer and the Tiger* the idea of a transfer of scent from the preorbital gland, a shallow pit in the lacrimal bone just in front of the eye, to the overhanging branch. Schaller argued that the thrashing of the overhanging branch left a visual signal enhanced by a chemical signal of the

The preorbital or lacrymal gland is located in front of the eye. Its waxy secretion is visible in this photo. Whether it plays a significant role in the transfer of scent to the overhanging branch remains a highly debatable question. Some deer biologists say no. Some wildlife photographers and deer hunters say yes. What do you say about this subject? *Photo credit Leonard Lee Rue III*

scent from the preorbital glands. He found the odor of the scent from the preorbital gland of the blackbuck of India to be musky and somewhat like acetic acid. Schaller observed that "on several occasions bucks rubbed their preorbital glands on tree trunks, then appeared to spread the scent over their antlers, head, and neck by brushing against the bark, which not only enhanced the odor of their bodies but also left evidence of their presence on the tree. It is possible that these chemical signals have an intimidatory effect on other bucks that smell them, and

thus a large number of such signs in a limited area might tend to space bucks out. On the other hand, the increased number of signals toward the peak of the rut probably also attracts the animals and through mutual stimulation influences the synchronization of sexual activity."

In 1970, Dietland Müller-Schwarze, a zoologist now working at the College of Environmental Science and Forestry at Syracuse, New York, began a long-term study of the functional capacity of various deer glands and the role they play in the chemical communication of deer. While studying black-tailed deer in California, Müller-Schwarze, unlike Schaller, doubted the functional significance of the preorbital gland. His microscopic study of the preorbital gland of blacktails convinced him that this gland remained relatively non-glandular, thus calling into question the transfer of any scent from the preorbital gland to the overhanging branch, at least in the case of blacktails.

His study of the functional significance of deer glands in 1970, however, emphasized several important ideas: (1) Overhanging branches become *"centers of social attention."* New deer entering foreign territories typically walk around and sniff these overhanging branches; (2) The overhanging branches are frequently found near bedding areas, as already mentioned; (3) Bucks seem to spend more time rubbing the overhanging branch on their forehead. Skin samples from the middle of the forehead of blacktails proved to be more glandular than the preorbital sac, suggesting that this area was capable of forcing glandular secretions outward, and thus playing a significant role in the silent communication of deer.

After observing blacktails in the field and in captivity for more than 3000 hours,

Müller-Schwarze concluded, in 1971, that deer of either sex and all ages mark their home range by rubbing the forehead against dry branch tips. In the process of marking the branches, pheromones, or chemical messages, are exchanged between the various deer in the territory. Müller-Schwarze defined these pheromones as "substances secreted to the outside by an individual deer and received by a second deer of the same species in which these substances create a specific reaction or a definite form of behavior."

After numerous observations of blacktails rubbing overhanging branches, Müller-Schwarze underscored four basic facts: (1) A branch treated by one member of the group becomes a center of attention for other group members; (2) When a new deer is introduced into a pen already inhabited by a group of deer, its first activity is to sniff the branches. The branches that have already been marked by the pen's inhabitants initiate a dramatic and sudden retreat of the newly introduced animal; (3) Forehead scent marking occurs very often near or in the bedding area, a fixed point in the home range of the animal. I have frequently seen whitetails bed down right next to an overhanging branch immediately after rubbing their forehead on it; (4) Sudoriferous glands capable of producing pheromones are found in the skin of the forehead of males, and these glands become more highly developed during the rut.

At an international conference on deer behavior at Alberta, Canada, in 1971, Müller-Schwarze correctly observed that since time immemorial deer hunters have talked about the peculiar odors emanating from the scent glands of these animals, but that we remain quite ignorant of the functions these odors play in the life of the animal. Two questions continually occupied the mind of Müller-Schwarze: (1) What information do certain scents carry in various social situations? (2) What is the nature of the scent gland product? Of the pheromone? Although his research yielded more details every month, conclusive answers to these difficult questions remained elusive.

At this conference, he seemed to suggest that bucks rub the overhanging branch more often than does, although all sexes sniff it. I have found this to be the case with regard to whitetails. He also emphasized the idea that many overhanging branches become *"shared and exclusive rubbing sites."* I have found this to also be true with regard to whitetails in the breeding area that I study and hunt. In addition, he reported that low ranking males sniff the branches most often. Females, he argued, "sniff the branches more often in fall than in spring. This may be interpreted as behavior that ensures encounters of the two sexes during the rutting season."

Most importantly, he noted that this scent-marking activity takes place throughout the entire year, although greatly increased in intensity during the fall rutting season. During July and August, I spend most of my time afield observing overhanging branches. These centers of social attention at this time of the year provide a unique opportunity to study deer behavior and to observe bucks in the process of establishing the pecking order. *Few serious deer hunters take advantage of this great opportunity.* Forget about the heat, the humidity, and the pesky mosquitoes.

At this same conference on deer behavior at Alberta, Larry Marchinton, an avid deer hunter and biologist from the School of Forest Resources at the University of Georgia, reported that whitetails identify overhanging branches by both visual and olfactory signals. After an intense study of fourteen white-tailed bucks by radio-tracking and direct observations, including more than 382 hours (264 during the rutting season), Marchinton concluded that white-tailed bucks defend areas and utilize signpost marking on overhanging branches to delineate these areas. Trained dogs could detect deer scent on the marked branches for at least four days after they had been rubbed. According to Marchinton, a buck would rub the overhanging branch by "nuzzling, licking, and pulling on the branch with his mouth and sometimes by raking it with his antlers. The branches marked were generally about antler height when the buck was walking in a normal head up position. On a few occasions, however, the branches were much higher and it was necessary for the animal to stand on his hind legs to reach them with his mouth. In every observation, after a branch was marked the buck pawed back leaves or litter directly under the branch."

Most scent-marking activity on overhanging branches seems to take place late in the afternoon after periods of bedding. Not only does it involve efficient communication between the sexes during the rut, but it apparently also plays a significant role in the establishment of dominance among bucks well before the rut. Marchinton concluded his study of rutting bucks by suggesting that "signposts such as the overhanging branch not only play a part in relating warnings but also in providing communication between the sexes to increase the probability of males locating females for mating. In addition, licking the tarsal glands may permit the

transfer of scent from these glands to the trees that are rubbed and licked and to overhanging branches that are mouthed."

With the support of a grant from the National Science Foundation, Müller-Schwarze continued to probe the questions surrounding the social significance of forehead rubbing on overhanging branches. In a very significant paper entitled "Social Significance of Forehead Rubbing in Black-Tailed Deer," published in *Animal Behavior* in 1972, he observed that forehead rubbing occurs year round; it begins at an early age and constitutes a very intricate system of social communication, a system of such chemical complexity that scientists haven't even begun to understand it. More specifically, he sought answers to the following eleven questions:

"(1) Do certain individuals rub more often than others? (2) Do certain individuals sniff more often than others? (3) Does the frequency of sniffing twigs vary with the frequency of rubbing? (4) Are the rubbing and sniffing frequencies correlated with agonistic behavior and/or with established social rank within the group? (5) What specific social relationships exist between frequent sniffers and frequent rubbers? (6) How are rubbing sites distributed within the area in which the animals live? (7) Does sniffing occur most often at the most often rubbed places? (8) Do certain individuals maintain exclusive rubbing posts, and are these respected by other group members? (9) Who sniffs whose rubbing marks most often? (10) Do certain social constellations favour rubbing, such as presence or absence of certain individuals, ongoing fights, or past and present rubbing by other individuals? (11) Do certain environmental factors facilitate or inhibit forehead rubbing?"

In researching these fascinating questions, Müller-Schwarze discovered some very unique deer behavior:

(1) Males rub the overhanging branch more often than females.

(2) Although no sex differences occur with regard to the frequency of sniffing these branches, females sniff more often in autumn than in spring, unlike the case for males. The highest frequencies of sniffing occur with individuals that rank *lower* on the social scale of dominance.

(3) With regard to the frequency between rubbing and sniffing, Müller-Schwarze concluded "that in both sexes the most dominant individual shows a tendency to sniff branches less often than other group members, but only among males does the most dominant individual rub most often."

(4) With regard to the relationship between rubbing and agonistic encounters such as fighting, chasing, striking with the forelegs, threatening, and sparring, the frequency of winning these encounters "is positively correlated with the frequency of rubbing among males. However, the average frequency per hour of rubbing increased during the observation period, while the number of fights per hour decreased. It is, therefore, assumed that rubbing replaces fighting, and serves in maintaining the relative social positions of the males." While observing overhanging branches during the months of July and August, I have noticed that the rubbing and sniffing activity not only serves to maintain the social positions but seems to play a significant role in determining the pecking order.

(5) Among bucks the rubbing frequency roughly correlates itself with the frequency of winning agonistic encounters while maintaining the social rank. The lowest ranking males tend to sniff the overhanging branch most often.

(6) Where do we find these commonly used overhanging branches or shared rubbing sites? Müller-Schwarze believes that many of them seem to be located in or very near bedding areas. I agree. In my personal observations of whitetails, I have found the most active overhanging branches along the sides of oak ridges that face the south with east-west deer trails on them.

(7) The frequency of sniffing an overhanging branch is positively correlated with the frequency of rubbing that branch.

(8) Dominant bucks at the top of the social hierarchy tend to maintain more exclusive rubbing sites than subordinate bucks.

(9) Low-ranking males exhibit a marked tendency to sniff more often than others the shared rubbing branches dominated by a male of high rank. According to Müller-Schwarze, "high ranking males did not sniff very often the shared sites rubbed most often by males ranking below them."

(10) An ongoing fight or sparring match between two bucks near an overhanging branch frequently initiates a third male, if present, to rub and thrash the overhanging branch. In this situation it is not uncommon for one of the fighting deer to suddenly turn and approach in a hostile and threatening manner the deer thrashing the branch, which usually causes the thrashing deer to beat a hasty retreat. Forehead rubbing on the branch, in other words, frequently facilitates competitive fighting. "One male after extensive forehead rubbing in the spring of 1970," Müller-Schwarze recalls, "started jumping and attacking other bucks."

(11) Bucks tend to increase their rubbing activities at overhanging branches after periods of rain and snowstorms in an attempt to replace washed-off scent marks.

Müller-Schwarze concluded his landmark essay on the social significance of forehead rubbing by noting "that the forehead rubbing of the silent genus *Odocoileus* may be the functional equivalent of the bugling and roaring in the genus *Cervus*. Both behavior patterns can be interpreted as means to advertise to males and females the presence and possibly physiological state of a particular male. . . . These rubbing sites may be one means of agonistic interaction, in addition to direct contact behavior such as threatening, chasing, and fighting. This assumption is supported by the fact that low ranking individuals most often sniffed those shared rubbing sites which were dominated by the rubbing activity of higher ranking males. In other mammals individuals which mark particularly often are also often dominant over others or are likely to win a fight."

By 1977, it became a widely held contention that white-tailed bucks scent mark overhanging branches by rubbing their foreheads on them. In an excellent monograph on the social behavior of the white-tailed deer, David Hirth, a keen observer of the whitetail, recorded for us a typical scrape sequence after watching bucks make more than twenty-nine scrapes:

"A typical scrape sequence began with a buck going to the edge of a tree, usually a large mesquite or anacqua rather than a small shrub, and pulling on a branch with his mouth. One buck was observed standing on his hindlegs to reach a branch with his mouth. While pulling on the branch, bucks stood with their hindlegs spread wide and forelegs together and swung their antlers back and forth at the upper part of the branch. This also involved rubbing the branch across their forehead and often letting the branch spring back along their forehead. Pulling ordinarily lasted from five to ten seconds. After letting go of the branch, bucks usually, but not always, pawed the ground with a foreleg. Sometimes they only pawed a few times, but more often a shallow depression in the soil was dug out. On fourteen occasions, the buck urinated onto the area he had pawed."

In 1977, Marchinton also concluded that bucks usually mark overhanging branches as a prelude to making scrapes. In a systematic study of more than seventy scrapes, he found that eighty-six percent of them had overhanging branches above them; the scrape/overhanging branch associations were obviously not due to mere chance alone. Bucks, according to Marchinton, are even highly selective in their choice of tree species and physical characteristics. "Bucks possibly make discriminations based on very subtle olfactory or taste factors, and the aromatic qualities of the tree enhance its utility as an olfactory signal." In measuring the distance from scrapes to frayed overhanging branches in the breeding area that I hunt and observe, I have found the distance to average around fifty-eight inches.

In 1978, with the aid of an artificial tree, simulated oak sticks, and gas liquid chromatography (i.e., a sensitive microchemical technique for measuring odors), Müller-Schwarze added another piece of significant information to the puzzle: These shared rubbing sites not only serve as information centers where deer of both sexes can determine what male deer are within an area and where deer can signal their presence, but more importantly, these information centers provide all deer with a knowledge of the age-class of male deer. When he presented forehead secretions on the same nylon rod, on separate rods, and blank controls, black-tailed bucks discriminated between the secretions of male yearlings and fawns. Müller-Schwarze based the discriminations on differential rates of sniffing and licking. His chemical evidence suggests that the secretions of male yearlings and fawns differ quantitatively.

In 1982, after extensive microscopic examinations of the forehead skin of white-tailed deer, Marchinton demonstrated that the forehead is a scent organ used to anoint rubs made by males and not the preorbital gland as commonly thought. His skin biopsies revealed the highest glandular activity in dominant males and the lowest in fawns. Not only did he demonstrate that the foreheads of white-tailed deer function as scent-producing organs in signpost communications, but that "the forehead pelage of mature male white-tailed deer is markedly different in color and texture from that of does. This is especially evident during the rut when the appearance of the forehead alone is sufficient for a perceptive observer to identify the sex."

Marchinton's data indicate a direct correlation between increases in forehead gland activity and greater age and higher social status in males. "Our research indicates to us," Marchinton writes, "that the position of an adult male in the hierarchy is reflected in the level of activity of his forehead glands." In his research findings, however, Marchinton cautiously warns that the hormonal mechanism underlying this entire phenomenon remains obscure—a very important point mock scrape advocates and scent manufacturers might want to take into consideration before making their wild and exaggerated claims on doing the nearly impossible in the chemically complex world of the white-tailed deer. Let's be modest; we know very little about the chemical communication of whitetails.

The point of this entire discussion is simply this: Find an intensely used overhanging branch for rubbing and licking in July and/or August and you will have found a major dominance area. Sit tight. During these summer months you will be able to view first-hand the expression of dominance—the establishment of a dominance hierarchy via rubbing, sniffing, and licking the overhanging branch *before the breeding season*. As a result, you will obviously know where to be during the peak of the breeding season. Pre-rut rubbing on overhanging branches represents a much more important component of pre-season scouting than most deer hunters realize. White-tailed bucks establish dominance *before* the rut so that they minimize contest-competition during the breeding season, thus maximizing the chances of doe insemination. The overhanging branch represents a very important overlooked deer sign. Serious deer hunters emphasize the importance of them; they rarely hunt breeding scrapes without them. This is where the action is!

Remember, forehead rubbing on overhanging branches occurs throughout the entire year. When you find one of these common rubbing posts in July and August, you will have found their *center of social attention*. Deer are continually placing scent on these overhanging branches while they establish social dominance. This situation, to reiterate, will frequently be found in or near a bedding area and that area will eventually become the main breeding area for the bucks in residence. You will be able to return to this

Photo credit Judd Cooney

White-tailed bucks approach the overhanging branch with careful deliberation and patient precision, in stark contrast to their frequent jittery and jumpy movements. They approach these centers of social activity at all times of the year, not merely during the rut.

Photo credit Leonard Lee Rue III

Photo credit Leonard Lee Rue III

spot throughout the year to observe bucks, bucks, and more bucks. The "licking branch" that I have observed for the past three years has three basic ingredients: (1) It is located near a bedding area; (2) The area in which it is found becomes the main breeding area during the rut; and (3) Bucks leave their scent on this "licking branch" throughout the year, allowing me the opportunity to observe buck behavior almost at will.

If you want to observe free-standing white-tailed bucks throughout the year, you have to find one of these shared, common rubbing posts. When you find this shared signpost, you will have reached Nirvana—the ultimate in the white-tailed deer experience. Sit back and watch bucks and their marking behavior; watch them anoint the overhanging branches with their forehead scent glands; and in the process study the whitetail story of silent, chemical communication—a story we know so little about.

Chapter 7

Deer Fences and Other Contrivances

Man has employed every conceivable contrivance to fence deer out: every-thing from New Zealand energizers to one-way deer gates, from "sniff-ometers" to peanut butter fences.

— Robert Wegner, 1985

Man's imagination seems endless when we consider the contrivances he concocts to fence out deer, to end the thrashing of overhanging branches and crop depredation. Indeed, the story of deer and fences goes back through the Middle Ages to the very beginnings of man. There have always been fences, dividing walls, stockades, hedges, or contrivances of one separating kind or another. One thinks of the Great Wall of China or Hadrian's Wall in northern England, built from coast to coast, to keep out the marauders from the north.

One also thinks of the early deer pound and the Indian deer drive as pictured in Champlain's *Voyages and Discoveries,* published in 1619, in which Indians constructed fences of rough logs with branches interwoven among the uprights. Using large bones to strike hollow trees, beaters drove deer into the pound along the fence line where the deer eventually met a bottleneck with Indians armed with spears. This crude, funnel-shaped, fenced trap into whose open end the Indians herded deer by their shouting, gesticulating, war whoops seems a far cry from the super-tech, electronic, deer-barrier fences of today that attempt to fence deer out, not in, and with a deterring blast of 5000 volts of electricity.

Millions of deer contend with fences on a daily basis. Most of the deer negotiate them quite successfully. They crawl under barbed-wire fences at ground level when not hurried; they leap over them when startled or chased; others jump through the strands of wire. Actually, they are exceedingly skillful in going between the strands of barbed-wire fences. This past deer season I watched a four-point buck being pursued by hunters pass through the strands of a common, barbed-wire fence with great ease when he could have easily jumped over the top. Deer, more often than not, tend to crawl under fences at ground level; they will crawl through any place where their head will pass. Yet, the bulkiness of antlers sometimes forces them to jump.

High, woven-wire fences, however, often prove insurmountable for many deer, particularly fawns and animals in a weakened condition. Nationwide, hundreds, perhaps thousands, of deer an-nually suffer a tragic fate of struggling with barbed-wire or fences of one kind or another until violent death eases the pain. Countless examples of deer entangled in fences come to mind.

In early January of 1971, for example, Bill Carey, a deer hunter from Vermillion, Alberta, noticed what appeared to be a dead deer in an alfalfa field. He assumed that someone had shot it and failed to re-cover it. As he approached the deer, how-ever, he suddenly realized that it was in fact two white-tailed bucks with inter-locked antlers, both temporarily entan-

Deer can push their way through any mesh fence with an opening barely large enough to admit their heads. They pass under fences with a quick flick of their head, hardly checking their speed. Because deer tend to travel along fence lines before ducking under them, taking a stand near favorite crossings can prove to be effective. *Photo credit Leonard Lee Rue III*

gled in a barbed-wire fence. One buck was still alive; the other buck was dead, partially eaten by coyotes. With the aid of his hunting partner, Carey roped and hog-tied the buck. He then sawed several inches off the main antler beam, which freed the live buck from his burden. Once released the startled buck vanished into the nearby timber, waving the traditional fond adieu.

On November 5, 1971, Edward Wesslen of Blackfalds, Ontario, found two dead bucks along his fence line, ensnared in barbed wire. In their death struggle they uprooted 100 feet of barbed-wire fence and posts, and tore up the ground around the scene of battle.

Wire and deer generally represent a bad combination. I have found whitetails twisted up in woven-wire and barbed-wire fences during the various seasons of the year. My friend, Lennie Rue, has seen deer break their antlers, jaws, and legs on fences. "There really isn't much we can do about it," he insists. "It's just one more hazard of modern civilization that deer have to contend with."

When Rue visited the Gage Holland Ranch near Big Bend, Texas, in 1961, he received a mule deer skull with twenty pounds of fencing wire wrapped around its antlers. The deer had run into a fence and torn loose hundreds of feet of wire. As the buck turned, the wires twisted into a cable. Not being able to free himself, the buck perished in a miserable way.

Near Cherry Creek, Montana, Rue recalls, "two mule deer bucks were slugging it out during the breeding season. As they shoved each other around, one of the buck's antlers got twisted up in a strand of barbed-wire fence. As the bucks continued to twist and turn, their antlers thoroughly and fatally tied together. Eventually, one buck strangled himself by a

The skeleton of a fawn caught on a fence by its hind foot. *Photo credit Leonard Lee Rue III. (See color section, which precedes title page.)*

piece of wire twisted around his neck. When James R. Martin found the two deer, he had to dispatch the live one. In the course of the fight, the deer pulled loose yards and yards of wire and broke off thirteen fence posts."

Apparently, fence posts and lines serve as natural routes of travel for deer. In fact, deer trails often run parallel with fences for great distances at a time. This explains why we frequently find shed antlers along fence lines and why we recover many wounded deer along fence lines as well. While scouting, it's a good practice to observe deer sign on and under fences, for well-worn trails going underneath fences and tufts of hair on the barbs indicate favorite deer crossings. After all, the world's largest non-typical white-tailed buck fell dead of natural causes against a fence line in St. Louis County, Missouri. Perhaps he was just following his natural route when he collapsed of old age?

Trophy bucks not only follow fence lines, but occasionally use fence posts for buck rubs. In an article entitled "The Ghost of the Fence Post Buck," Russell Thornberry, an outfitter specializing in trophy deer in Alberta, recalls how he found a unique buck rub on a corner post of a fence line that marked the junction of five major deer trails. According to Russell, the fence post was worn hard where the buck worked it over. On the ground below the fence post he found a scrape that the buck kept fresh. The buck visited the scrape and reworked the fence post during the nighttime hours. "We threw dried grass into the scrape and each morning it was pawed back down to clean black dirt. And there in the frost on the fence post were the slashes and gouges made by heavy antlers. At the mid-point of the fence post where the buck did most of his work, the post was worn down and splintered and a full fourteen inches behind the center of the post the corner brace was also worn and gouged."

Indeed, deer seem to hang around fences. Researchers in New York even found a piece of 19-gauge wire lodged in the liver of a white-tailed deer killed by a hunter on the Archer and Anna Huntington Wildlife Forest Station during an experimental hunt in 1967. While the deer lived, the wire in the liver apparently caused the deer no difficulty.

In any event, fences figure more importantly in connection with deer and deer damage. The very idea of a deer-proof fence to protect cultivated crops came prominently to the fore in California in the early 1930s, when Tracy I. Storer, a professor of zoology at the University of California, and Gordon H. True, a parasitologist at the California Division of Fish and Game, began to devise fences whereby deer and agriculture could co-exist without serious competition. Adequate fencing, they believed, represented the real solution of the deer exclusion problem.

Knowing well that deer skillfully go through and under barbed-wire fences, they proposed building a fence with a woven fabric sixty inches in height plus three strands of barbed wire spaced eight inches apart, giving the deer-proof fence a total height of eighty-four inches or seven feet. They also suggested adding barbed wire at the ground level to discourage the animals from digging beneath the fence. Did it work? Probably. The effectiveness of this early attempt to fence out deer, however, seems somewhat questionable since we know that deer can clear heights of up to nine feet or even higher starting from a standing position.

By the end of the 1930s, this country witnessed a phenomenal development in the new use of electricity: the electric fence as a means of controlling deer. The story of electric fences and deer began in Pennsylvania, where agricultural crops were being destroyed by the feeding activities of an excessive white-tailed deer population. The story revolves around the work of Richard Gerstell, a deer researcher with the Pennsylvania Game Commission.

While studying the problem of deer and cultivated crops at one of the State's Game Farms, Gerstell observed two common traits of the whitetail: (1) their intense curiosity evidenced by their general tendency to smell any new inanimate object they confront, and; (2) their usual habit when undisturbed of crawling under, rather than jumping over, objects twenty to thirty inches above the ground. Many deer hunters have reached the same conclusion in this regard. After observing more than seventy whitetails confronting an electric fence, Gerstell noted that ninety-five percent of them were shocked in the act of smelling the wire and the remainder in attempting to crawl under it.

The shock produced a distasteful effect. Without exception the deer exhibited a strong reflex reaction; they jumped high into the air and bolted. They could not be enticed into the vicinity of the wire. The full force of the current penetrated their moist, bare nasal area. Hardened antlers acted as non-conductors while antlers in the velvet served as effective electric carriers. According to Gerstell, the deer seemed "to remember their experiences" with electric fences for a period lasting as long as three weeks.

Due to the health hazards involved both to man and deer, Gerstell did not recommend the widespread use of electric fencing as a method of controlling deer. Instead, he formulated the deer-fence dilemma we still face today: "When deer become so numerous that they cause excessive property damage, it is almost without exception due to an overpopulation of their natural range. Under such conditions, 'fencing them off' one area usually means 'fencing them on to' an adjacent, or nearby tract. The basic correction of this difficulty lies solely in the reduction of the population densities involved (by way of regulated sport hunting)."

Although "care" and "caution" became the watchwords in the development of electric fences to control deer during the thirties and forties, one Milwaukee-based firm, the Prime Manufacturing Company, built a deer fence based on Gerstell's observation that ninety-five percent of all deer contacting electric fences were shocked in the act of smelling the wire. Their fence consisted of six strands of barbed wire with four strands being electrified and with danglers to attract nosing by the animals, thus quickening the deer's acquaintanceship with the properties of the fence. The designer of the fence believed that baiting the charged wires with small bundles of hay improved the efficiency of the fence because it delivered the shock directly to the sensitive nose of the animal.

After experimenting with this deer fence, Herbert Stoddard, one of America's great conservationists, wrote in his journal in 1936, that "whether this electric fence will continue to exclude deer we do not know, for they can be pestiferous creatures with regard to their choice food. Their reaction on first contact with the charged wire may be quite amusing. One made a jump of twelve feet (tracks measured on soft ground), after touching the wire with its wet nose."

These early experiments indicated that deer, contrary to popular opinion, will not jump wire fences if they can slip under them. In general, these early researchers frowned upon the widespread use of electric fences to control deer, especially after several crude outfits drawing current from high-tension power lines started forest fires and killed deer, farmers, and hunters as well. Obviously, the electric deer fence should not be a subject for amateur experimentation.

After experimenting with more than twenty electric deer fences of various kinds and in realizing their shortcomings and health hazards, Ilo Bartlett, a well-known deer biologist from Michigan who reportedly dreamt about deer problems,

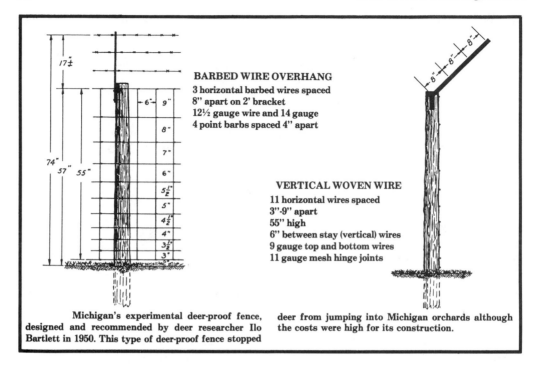

BARBED WIRE OVERHANG
3 horizontal barbed wires spaced
8" apart on 2' bracket
12½ gauge wire and 14 gauge
4 point barbs spaced 4" apart

VERTICAL WOVEN WIRE
11 horizontal wires spaced
3"-9" apart
55" high
6" between stay (vertical) wires
9 gauge top and bottom wires
11 gauge mesh hinge joints

Michigan's experimental deer-proof fence, designed and recommended by deer researcher Ilo Bartlett in 1950. This type of deer-proof fence stopped deer from jumping into Michigan orchards although the costs were high for its construction.

recommended using a vertical, woven-wire, deer-proof fence with a two-foot "overhang." While experimenting with deer and fences in Michigan in 1950, Bartlett found that an eight-foot woven-wire fence with a two-foot "overhang" composed of three barbed wires eight inches apart extending upward and outward at a forty-five degree angle stopped deer from jumping into orchards. Although the costs were high for the construction of such deer-proof fences, he recommended their use as opposed to the electric deer fence.

In the state of Vermont at this time, the Fish and Game Service apparently disagreed with Bartlett's advice and continued to wage war on the whitetail by helping farmers construct more electric deer fences and other contrivances to fence out deer. After a great deal of experimentation with electric deer fences, however, the Director of the Fish and Game Service reached conclusions similar to those of Ilo Bartlett. As the director himself admitted, "the electric deer fence didn't provide any real relief from crop damage. We just fenced deer off on another neighbor. This was not good and is admitted."

Nevertheless, some valuable observations and suggestions came out of Vermont's experimentation with deer fencing. First of all, deer biologists realized the almost total insulation of a deer's body to electric shock. Tests on freshly killed deer revealed that only a small portion of the body was affected by currents as great as 3000 volts. These areas included the ears, front of face, the nose, and the forward portion of the legs. Thus, the arrangement of the wires on the deer fence became crucial; they had to be so spaced as to ensure direct contact with these parts of the body.

Secondly, in attempting to erect a deer-proof electric fence, deer biologists in Vermont designed "the outrigger," the most important single development in the electric fence for controlling deer damage. The outrigger or extension wire lies twenty-four inches outside the main line of posts and thirty inches above the ground. This wire is fastened onto shellacked and creosoted wooden braces. Researchers discovered that deer greatly fear getting between this outrigger and the main wire fence, and do so only when they run blindly into the fence. Not only does the outrigger give depth to the fence, but apparently deters deer from jumping over this single wire and coming between it and the main fence. Deer biologists based the outrigger on the established fact that deer do not naturally jump over any type of fence, if they can crawl beneath it. Before the outrigger, fences had to be of considerable height to prevent deer from jumping over them. While the outrigger did not keep every deer out, it aided Vermonters in excluding deer from cultivated crops.

In their research, Vermont deer biologists noted that unalarmed deer in their home range repeatedly crossed common barbed-wire fences at the same places. By repeatedly ducking beneath low wires, deer wore trails several inches deep into the ground.

By the end of the 1950s, the outrigger electric deer fence of various shapes and sizes appeared in several states: Virginia, New Jersey, California, and Florida, for example, used it with high, moderate, and mixed success. The high cost of these types of deer fences prevented their wider use.

In realizing this cost limitation and in observing deer going through fences rather than jumping over them, deer researchers at the University of California's Hopland Field Station, located in the northern area of that state, designed an overhanging deer fence. The first of these experimental deer fences consisted of a two-foot vertical segment with a six-foot twenty-five degree slope extension in the direction of the deer pressure. This fence forced the approaching deer to go under the sloping wire before contacting the vertical wire. The overhanging fence was built with wire (2x4-inch mesh), and proved to be completely effective in turning back deer in several experimental situations. The overhanging deer fence, however, only worked in one direction.

Not only were deer biologists, farmers, and orchardists concerned with deer fences, but foresters also wanted to protect experimental plots and to demonstrate the effect of deer browsing on plantations and natural seedlings. Historically, the relatively high cost of deer fencing discouraged its large-scale use in forestry. Nevertheless, foresters in the Pocono Experimental Forest in Pennsylvania took an

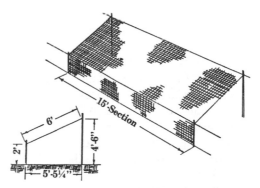

The overhanging deer-fence built with non-climbable wire (2" x 4" mesh) and redwood posts successfully excluded deer from California plots where deer grazing was not desired. This deer-fence, however, only worked in one direction.

interest in the late 1950s in constructing low-cost deer fencing for large enclosures. They found the key to reducing costs was to use live trees in place of fenceposts wherever possible. By using trees to fence enclosures, both the job of setting the posts and the costs of the posts themselves were reduced to a minimum.

During the 1960s deer biologists and wildlife managers seemed to reach a consensus with regard to deer fences: The efficiency of *electric* deer fences remained too marginal for widespread use, costly, and ineffective especially when lack of moisture in the soil prevented good grounding. The most practical method of minimizing or controlling deer damage to high-value crops, researchers argued, revolved around the well-constructed deer-proof fence of the overhanging and upright kind. Although initial costs were high and continuing maintenance necessary, they found economic justification for the protection of certain crops, orchards, vineyards, and new forest plantings with this type of deer fence. Indeed, the overhanging or slanting deer fence proved quite effective because it acted as a psychological barrier to deer. Deer usually tried to crawl under such fences; finding that impossible and with wire extended above them, they would decide against jumping. In heavy snowfall areas, however, these slanted deer fences tend to collapse under the weight of snow.

Easy access of vehicles through deer fences resulted in California researchers constructing deer guards similar to cattle guards in structure. They built these deer guards with cross members consisting of pipes, rails, or sharpened boards laid on edge. Researchers made them fifteen to twenty-five feet long. Highly motivated deer, however, merely trotted or bounded across them, thus deactivating another contrivance of modern science to the status of little or no value.

Yes, man goes through a great deal of time, effort, and money to fence out deer. In 1964, for example, deer biologists at the Stephen F. Austin Experimental Forest near Nacogdoches, Texas, constructed 5.2 miles of deer fence eight and a half feet high for a total cost of $16,429 (1964 prices). One can only imagine what that would cost today.

In the early 1970s, wildlife researchers in Colorado began to experiment with deer-proof fences to keep deer off the highways, since miles of Colorado highways bisect deer migration-movements. "Giving deer the steer" became the slogan for Dale Reed, a wildlife researcher with the Colorado Division of Wildlife, who experimented with a one-way deer gate that permitted deer to safely cross a major highway. Reed funnelled deer along a 1.5-mile, eight-foot deer fence toward an underpass under Interstate 70 at Mud Springs Gulch west of Vail. When approaching the built-in, one-way deer gate, the deer stopped, looked to either side of the gate's opening, and with ears laid back jumped through with great aggressive behavior.

Although some deer seemed reluctant to pass through the one-way deer gate, hundreds of deer soon did so and successfully went through the concrete underpass as well, thus escaping the immediate highway right-of-way. Dale Reed explains the rationale underlying the one-way deer gate: "It was hoped the structure's characteristics would take advantage of the deer's natural behavior and they would jump through the flexible tines of the gate much like they do through heavy brush.

Confined deer had been observed testing weak areas in eight-foot, deer-fences in order to escape. The one-way deer gate provides this weak area in one direction only."

In addition to this device, the Colorado State Highway Department installed animated, neon deer signs in attempting to ensure the safety of both deer and motorists. Deer researchers in north-central Colorado even constructed snow fences in such a manner as to change deer movement patterns with regard to highways and overbrowsed areas.

Of all the devices constructed to change deer patterns, the peanut butter deer fence and the deer "sniffometer" must surely be the most interesting. After experimenting with a so-called "sniffometer," a four-compartment odorant panel connected to a four-channel event recorder, and twenty-four different odorants, everything from buck lure to anise oil, from apple slices and hay oil to soybean meal, Charles Kinsey of the Minnesota Department of Natural Resources demonstrated that deer showed a marked preference for peanut butter. Although not a common deer food, the quality and intensity of its odor appealed to deer. In Kinsey's tests, "the deer's response to the same sample of peanut butter after one month of exposure showed that the odor lasted." Maybe we should leave our skunk essence in the garage?

In studying individual and group behavior of deer near electric deer fences in southern Minnesota in 1975, Kinsey concluded, like researchers before him, that unless a deer touches the electric wire with its nose, it's not likely to be affected by the shock. But a whitetail approaching a peanut butter-scented electric wire can be tricked into sniffing and licking it, thus increasing the incidence of nose-to-conductor contacts. Kinsey spread peanut butter on adhesive tape attached to small pieces of aluminum foil along the electric wire. The peanut butter deer fence worked best, Kinsey insisted, when deer were relaxed and could investigate the odor with leisure. Of all the deer Kinsey observed doing so, eighty-two percent of them received shocks and fled.

In 1983, this recent modification of the electric deer fence struck the fancy of William F. Porter, a professor of the Department of Environmental and Forest Biology at the State University of New York, who examined the effectiveness of this peanut butter deer fence in reducing summer deer depredation on apple seedlings in central New York orchards.

Porter found that the peanut butter and the aluminum foil flags provided both visual and odor stimuli that encouraged deer to make nose-to-fence contact. The peanut butter deer fence obviously does not constitute a physical barrier to deer but one predicated on behavioral conditioning instead. In Porter's experiments, the effect of the fence persisted for three successive years and greatly reduced deer depredation on young apple trees in central New York. The fence showed no decline in performance when expanded from one to five acres. The potential for excluding deer from larger areas, however, remained uncertain as did the questions concerning the effects of deer density and the related question of alternate food supplies. A benefit-cost analysis showed the peanut butter-baited deer fence to be a viable economic alternative because it cost about fifteen cents a meter as opposed to $4.10 a meter for more traditional electric deer fencing.

In searching for alternative configura-

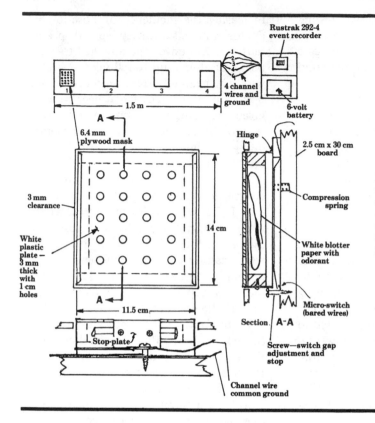

Rustrak 292-4
event recorder

4 channel
wires and
ground

6-volt
battery

1.5 m

A

6.4 mm
plywood mask

3 mm
clearance

White
plastic
plate —
3 mm
thick
with
1 cm
holes

14 cm

A

11.5 cm

Stop-plate

Hinge

2.5 cm x 30 cm
board

Compression
spring

White blotter
paper with
odorant

Section A-A

Micro-switch
(bared wires)

Screw—switch gap
adjustment and
stop

Channel wire
common ground

Left: A deer "sniffometer." This four-compartment odorant panel connected to a four-channel event recorder (Rustrak Model 292-4), measures a deer's preference for any of four odorants applied to the blotter paper.

Right: The peanut butter, electric deer-fence designed by Charles Kinsey has proven to be very effective in field situations in Minnesota and New York. It does not constitute a physical barrier to deer but rather one predicated on behavioral conditioning. It is probably the least expensive deer-fence alternative.

tions, James Kroll, a professor at the Stephen F. Austin State University in Nacogdoches, Texas, developed and tested another idea somewhat similar in configuration to the peanut-butter deer fence. Kroll's so-called "double deer fence" consists of two separate deer fences thirty-eight inches apart. The outer fence consists of one wire on fiberglass posts eighteen inches high. The inner power fence consists of two strands (twelve inches and thirty-six inches high), or up to seven strands depending on ground conditions and deer pressure. The double deer fence seemingly controls deer in two ways: (1) the outer fence with its electrical pulses turns away the majority of deer, and; (2) the two fences together impair a deer's perception so it won't jump over them. According to Snell Systems, Inc., the manufacturer of this configuration, the double deer-fence "eliminates better than ninety-five percent of deer predation."

Airport managers and pilots in Pennsylvania follow closely the experiments of these deer biologists and wildlife managers in fencing deer out and the newest deer fence configurations, for runway collisions of aircraft and white-tailed deer are of major concern in the Keystone State. Between 1967 and 1978, twenty-three collisions of aircraft with deer occurred at thirteen Pennsylvania airports. Fourteen of

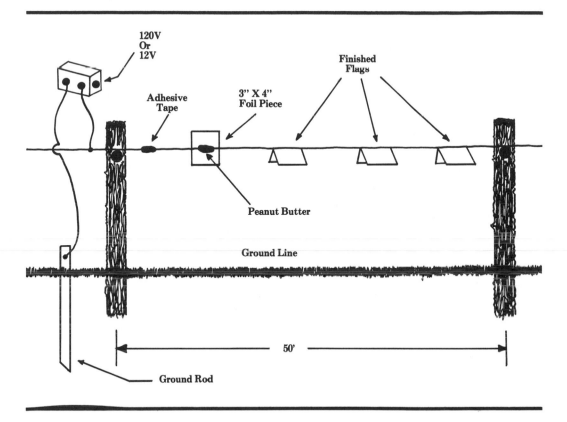

the collisions resulted in aircraft damage; two caused human injury. To date no human fatalities have been reported. During these twelve years, two of the accidents resulted in damages of more than $50,000 each. Several airport managers state that while no accidents have occurred, they have seen many near misses.

Deer become most abundant at airports in Pennsylvania and other northeastern states during the fall, especially during the deer hunting season when landing fields serve as sanctuaries. For example, in November of 1974, according to a report in the *Wildlife Society Bulletin,* "Deer on a runway at the Ebensburg Municipal Airport prevented a student pilot from land-

ing during a simulated emergency exercise. On the go-around the student lost control of the plane which subsequently crashed and burned in a nearby wooded area. Both the instructor and the student received minor injuries, and the $50,000 aircraft was destroyed. In November of 1976, a mail plane hit two deer at Mid-State Airport, Philipsburg, immediately after touching down. Both engines had to be replaced at considerable cost. Even the very large commercial airports are prone to such accidents. Between October 1978 and July 1979, Greater Pittsburgh International Airport had seven incidents involving deer, and several large, commercial passenger planes had to abort their take-offs to avoid deer on runways. It is not difficult to imagine what would happen if a Boeing 747 or DC-10 filled with passengers hit a group of deer seconds before lifting off or while landing."

On August 28, 1982, the imagined became reality when a trophy eight-pointer tested the nerves to the very breaking point of ninety passengers and the bewildered crew of a USAir DC-9 at the Greater Pittsburgh International Airport. According to the *Pittsburgh Press,* "the deer strike caused $200,000 of damage to the DC-9. The experience terrified passengers who said they felt a bump and the plane shuddering. Several reported an engine started to spark and blow flames. The plane circled the airport, swung low over the field so airport crews could look for damage and landed safely on a runway lined with emergency vehicles."

Consequently, a private contractor put up 12,400 feet of electric, Kiwi deer fencing along the main departure runway at a cost of $15,000. The deer fence made by Kiwi Fence Systems carries as much as 5000 volts of electricity. According to the *Pittsburgh Press,* "this electrified runway deer fence shoos the herd and has the airport deer finally on the run."

The deer fence story reached a climax in September 1983, when deer biologists, game managers, and deer fence entrepreneurs from all parts of the country met in New York at Cornell University as part of the First Eastern Wildlife Damage Conference to facilitate the use of the most up-to-date methods of fencing out deer.

At this conference William Porter emphasized the successful use of the peanut-butter deer fence. But others argued in favor of another new innovation. Ron Brenneman, for example, of the Hammermill Paper Company of Coudersport, Pennsylvania, reported that a five-strand vertical electric deer fence consisting of five wires, the first ten inches off the ground and the remaining four at twelve-inch intervals with a maximum of fifty-eight inches in height, successfully repelled whitetails from damaging seedling and sprout regeneration in an Allegheny hardwood forest during 1979 to 1981. He constructed this five-wire deer fence with high-tensile-strength galvanized steel wire and powered it with a Gallagher E-12 energizer with a maximum output of 5800 volts. According to Brenneman, it provided effective control of deer.

Darel Smith, of Advanced Farm Systems of Bradford, Maine, agreed and encouraged widespread use of this type of deer fencing, which has become known as the Penn State 5-Wire. According to Smith, "When such a deer fence is installed, you change deer habits. Second and third generation deer become easier to control because they have learned to live with the fence from day one. We are having excellent success with this deer fence system, going from a high percent of damage to a very low percent of damage. It is a cost-effective system and it keeps farmers, state wildlife officers, and deer hunters happy." Another deer fence entrepreneur, John Wall, of Kiwi Fence Systems of Waynesburg, Pennsylvania, told the small group of scientists present that from his experience and business contacts in all parts of the country, the Penn State 5-Wire was being widely accepted at airports and farms alike, in keeping whitetails out of areas not reserved for them.

The modern technology underlying the Penn State 5-Wire represents the first innovation in agricultural fencing since the introduction of barbed wire in the 1880s. The new technology was first developed in New Zealand and Australia for controlling sheep, cattle, and horses. Its use of high-tensile wire allows man to construct single-stranded wire fences with greater strength, lower maintenance requirements, and lower costs than conventional barbed wire. It costs approximately one-third as much as a conventional eight-foot, woven-wire fence.

In designing the Penn State 5-Wire, William Palmer of Penn State came to the conclusion after testing many designs and configurations that the bottom wire must be ten inches from the ground while the remaining wires need to be spaced at twelve-inch intervals. Electric deer fences with wider wire spacing, according to Palmer, prove to be ineffective. Spacing remains critical because deer usually try to go under or through a fence rather than jump it.

When deer attempt to penetrate the Penn State 5-Wire, Palmer insists, "the tensioned wire and high voltage ensure their getting a powerful shock. This modifies their behavior, and they become trained to avoid the fence, staying three to four feet away from the wires. This, in turn, discourages jumping since they normally come within inches of a barrier before leaping over it. Not every deer needs to be shocked, because the avoidance behavior of those that have been shocked, especially the dominant adults, is imitated by other deer in the small social groups so typical of whitetails." Be prepared for one problem when using this deer fence. One of Penn State's agronomists explains: "My neighbors are complaining that their damage has greatly increased since the erection of the university's fence. Deer that normally would have fed on Penn State land are now feeding on their land."

Fencing deer out represents a costly method to control deer damage, and in the final analysis merely means fencing them on to somebody else's property. One leading manufacturer of deer fences admits as much in its advertisement: "Remember, in spite of the power employed by Techfence energizers, deer can't be harmed. They walk away the wiser, but none the worse for it (they'll find another orchard or field down the road.)"

Indeed, man has employed every conceivable contrivance to fence out deer: the woven-wire deer-proof fence, the outrigger-type electric deer fence, the overhanging deer fence, deer guards, one-way deer gates, deer "sniffometers," peanut-butter deer fences, double deer fences, as well as Penn State 5-Wires. New deer fence configurations appear regularly in the popular press and the scientific journals. Manufacturers and advertisers encourage and stimulate interest in these new devices for fencing out deer. A recent ad for one deer-proof fence proclaims: "A fully charged fence. A partly charged fence. You can readily imagine which deer fence will leave the most lasting impression."

The Gallagher slanted 7-wire, spring-tight, high-tensile, electric deer fence with its New Zealand-styled energizer surely leaves the most lasting impression, for it shocks deer with jolts from 5000 to 7000 volts. Research at the Cary Arboretum in Millbrook, New York, under the guidance of Jay McAninch, one of the most knowledgeable researchers on deer fences, demonstrates that on large acreages with high deer pressure and under year-round conditions, this slanted 7-wire proves to be highly effective with costs ranging from twenty-five to forty cents per linear foot.

Yet regardless of the deer fence design, the wide range of variables involved, such as changes in seasonal deer pressure, changes in deer populations, the size of the area to be protected, as well as the economic value of the material to be pro-

The Gallagher spring-tight, seven-wire electric deer fence with its high-power energizer leaves a lasting impression on any deer coming in contact with it. Its sloped design forces deer to come in contact with the wire when attempting to penetrate the fence. While using this fence, researchers had excellent success in repelling deer from exotic plantings at the Cary Arboretum in Millbrook, New York. *Photo credit Brookside Industries, Inc.*

tected, still call into question the general efficiency of deer fencing as a means of control. Despite fifty years of research and development with regard to deer fences, solutions to the myriad of deer damage situations hardly seems more than satisfactory, although several designs show promise for alleviating deer damage.

In his book on how to cope with deer in forest, field, and garden entitled *Trees and Deer* (1983), Richard Prior, a deer consultant to the British Deer Society, observed that after erecting more than 3000 miles of

deer fences in Scotland at an annual erection and maintenance fee in excess of $1 million, few deer fences remained deer-proof for more than a decade. "Fencing deer out," Prior writes "is no long-term solution, for the deer fence will be breached or decay sooner or later, and a resident population will become established."

In assessing the effectiveness of electric deer fences, Prior reached the conclusion that electric deer fencing remains very much in an exploratory stage. With regard to conventional deer-proof fences, Prior underscored the classic reputation of the deer's ability of eventually pushing their way through any mesh fence with an opening large enough to admit their heads. "Even male deer with spreading antlers pass through wire fences with a quick flick of the head, hardly checking their speed."

What next? You guessed it! Regulated sport hunting; it not only proves to be less costly, but remains more effective as well. To offset costs, some state wildlife agencies have instituted cost-sharing arrangements with farmers whose crops deer repeatedly damage. But since many of these subsidized farmers still post their land for deer hunting, even though access is mandated in many cases, deer hunters take a dim view of departments of conservation spending license money in this manner.

Professor Scott Craven of the University of Wisconsin's Department of Wildlife Ecology perhaps states it best when he says that "deer, and the damage they cause, are part of the larger problem of wildlife—a public resource—on private land. Unlike moles, rats, and other species implicated in damage, deer cannot be casually eliminated when in conflict with the landowner's use of his land. But neither can the landowner be expected to bear the entire burden of support for the public resource. The solution must lie somewhere between these extremes. Deer herds must be managed to satisfy a variety of interest groups. Most landowners enjoy having some deer on their properties, despite real or potential damage problems. This fact, coupled with the deer's economic and aesthetic values, suggests that everyone's needs will be served by a combination of herd control through hunting, a conscientious and reasonable effort at damage control by landowner's, and a state program to assist landowners."

Chapter 8

Whitetails and Cornfields

Look at the stalk, sturdy, economical, efficient. It stands braced on its roots. It is of quick growth. Its long broad leaves are so arranged that they catch rain and dew and funnel it down where it is needed. As a plant, it is very near to perfection. It silks out, as we say, with vastly more silk than is needed, just so each kernel on the incipient ear can be properly fertilized. It tassels out, with a pollen-bearing apparatus that is ideal for its purpose. And it concentrates its yield, a big quantity of useful grain in compact form. It ripens and is an almost perfect storage crop. It is packed with nutriment for man or beast.

—Hal Borland, 1954

Both the white-tailed deer and corn were indigenous in America at the time of its discovery. One can scarcely imagine what the exploration and development of America would have been like without them. In fact, the corn plant and the white-tailed deer formed the bridge over which English civilization crept. As one of the leading white-tailed deer foods of this country, corn (*Zea mays*) today grows in greatest abundance in the East and the prairies.

Whitetails frequently use this distinctive American cereal in ways that do not conflict with man's interests: They eat the waste corn after the farmer harvests the fields, and they bed during the day among the cornstalks which provide them with excellent cover before the harvest. Whitetails also use corn, however, in ways that directly conflict with man's interests: They peel back the tight husk of the ear on standing corn and meticulously strip the cob, kernel by kernel, to the tune of millions and millions of dollars each year. Between October 1983 and September 1984, 47,000 Wisconsin farmers alone (fifty-five percent of Wisconsin's 86,000 farmers) reported deer damage to their cornfields. University of Wisconsin researchers estimated the value of this damage at $20.6 million, or $438 per farm.

Whitetails most frequently use cornfields when the corn reaches three to four feet in height. The most frequent damage results when they nip off the tops of the stalk and pull out the developing whorl. Wildlife biologist John Calhoun of Illinois describes what happens: "The animal usually takes one bite, drops the stalk, and moves on. Where this occurs on scattered stalks, the corn can be pollinated from surrounding plants and little permanent damage is done. If damage is over a large area and the nipping is done immediately before the tassel emerges, the corn may not form a good ear. This sort of damage is usually very local, however, and is usually caused by some unusual circumstance such as in fields near a refuge, in areas where high water has forced large numbers of deer out of the lowlands, or where farmers have allowed deer to go too long unharvested."

In Iowa, corn constitutes the most heavily utilized food item in the annual diet of the whitetail; it consists of 67.7 percent by weight, 39.7 percent by volume, and is eaten by 84.4 percent of Iowa's deer. In Kansas, corn and sorghum make up fifty-three percent of the total volume eaten by whitetails. In Ohio, corn ranks as the second principal food eaten by whitetails in frequency but first in weight. In Illinois, whitetails utilize corn in a manner that far exceeds their use of wild foods. In southern Wisconsin during the autumn months, the monthly volume of corn in the whitetail's rumen averages twenty-four percent. In west-central Minnesota, corn consists of 37.7 percent by volume of the whitetail's diet and remains the most frequently damaged field crop in that Corn-Belt state. In Nebraska, corn remains the preferred white-tailed deer food especially in the fall and winter; during the summertime corn silks provide whitetails with a tasty treat as well. In the Midwest in general, cultivated crops such as corn and soybeans represent, according to a United

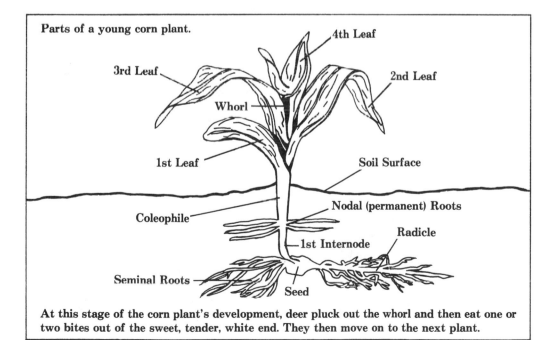

Parts of a young corn plant.

4th Leaf
3rd Leaf
2nd Leaf
Whorl
1st Leaf
Soil Surface
Coleophile
Nodal (permanent) Roots
Radicle
1st Internode
Seminal Roots
Seed

At this stage of the corn plant's development, deer pluck out the whorl and then eat one or two bites out of the sweet, tender, white end. They then move on to the next plant.

Stunted corn, the result of whitetails nipping off the stalk of the young corn plant. *Photo credit Richard P. Smith*

States Forest Service Report, forty-one to fifty-six percent of the foods eaten by the white-tailed deer on agricultural ranges.

Despite the vast amount of literature on the food habits of deer, many questions remain unanswered with regard to the whitetail's use of corn and cornfields. Do whitetails prefer waste corn to standing corn? Will they leave their home ranges to search for standing corn? If so, how far will deer move out of their normal home range? Will this movement be daily or will deer reside near the cornfield? How much waste corn will a deer consume? How much unpicked corn will a deer consume? Can we estimate corn damage caused by deer? How much corn damage will farmers tolerate? Do whitetails prefer to feed on the external limits of cornfields? Does any pattern emerge for their use of cornfields? What is the value and cost of corn as a food patch for deer? What effect do autumn tillage systems have on the whitetail's winter use of waste corn? How do the answers to these questions affect the deer hunter?

In the interest of answering some of these questions, *Deer & Deer Hunting* magazine contributed a grant-in-aid to the University of Wisconsin's Department of Wildlife Ecology for a research project entitled "Deer Use of Corn in Agricultural Areas." This chapter describes that research project and its results. I would like to thank Professor Orrin J. Rongstad and his graduate student, John S. C. Herron of the Department of Wildlife Ecology, for providing me with a copy of the Preliminary Report entitled "Deer Use of Corn in Agricultural Areas," which greatly facilitated the writing of this chapter. I greatly enjoyed my travels with these dedicated deer researchers in their heaterless, rusted-to-the-block '78 Chevy Suburban with bald tires, dead batteries, and broken windows. After a wintry day spent collecting data in this marvelous machine, one's mind turned toward "Back Woods Corn Likker." If more sportsmen saw the kinds of sacrifices these devoted researchers make in the interest of pursuing knowledge of the white-tailed deer, more funds would surely be forthcoming to support worthwhile projects of this kind.

The results of most studies on deer in the Midwest agree that agricultural crops constitute the reason these areas support such large numbers of deer. We know that both corn and alfalfa comprise the major portion of the whitetail's diet. Yet, aside from some nutritional studies of captive deer, we know very little about the quantity of corn that whitetails consume in the wild or how much of an impact deer populations create on cornfields.

Quantifying the amount of use deer make of cornfields remained our ultimate purpose. We had three primary goals in mind: (1) to determine how many deer used six different cornfields during the winter of 1984–85; (2) to monitor the amount of corn consumed by deer on a daily basis during the winter months; and (3) to follow the movements of thirty-eight deer marked with radio transmitters and to determine if any of them shifted out of their normal home range to reach a food source such as a cornfield and to measure that distance. We studied the whitetail's use of cornfields by observing one small cornfield and five corn patches planted as wildlife food plots. During the late fall and winter of 1984–85, we measured the whitetail's use of corn and cornfields by periodic observations of the study fields and by track counts after snowfalls. We estimated the amount of corn consumed by deer by sampling the corn remaining in each field during the study period.

All six field sites were located on the Badger Army Ammunition Plant (BAAP), located in Sauk County in southern Wisconsin. BAAP occupies nearly 7000 acres of rolling pasture and cropland. Ten percent of the study area consists of woody cover. Previous research on the area indicated that BAAP supported a healthy herd of between 250 to 400 whitetails, depending on the season. These deer relied heavily on both corn and alfalfa as food sources, and were especially dependent on waste corn left in harvested fields during the winter months.

During 1984, the management of BAAP planted five wildlife food patches in cooperation with the U.S. Dairy Forage Research Center. These food patches, all corn, consisted of 0.48, 0.53, 0.90, 1.61, and 2.09 acres in size. The two smallest cornfields were not included in the study since they produced no corn. Only the 0.90-acre field received fertilizer and herbicide treatment. In addition, through a cooperative agreement with the U.S. Dairy Forage Research Center and the management of the ammunition plant, 5.23 acres of an existing cornfield remained unharvested and standing until late April of 1985.

We monitored deer use of these fields by track counts after fresh snowfalls. This method yielded between fifteen and nineteen observations for each field, concentrated between December 24, 1984 and March 6, 1985. In addition, we determined the whitetail's use of the 5.23-acre cornfield by direct observation during the evening activity period. The other food patches could not be economically observed due to their distance from roads.

On March 6, we knocked down 839 ears of corn in two corners of the 5.23-acre cornfield in order to see if deer would favor these sites. Both corners of the field were on the east side of the cornfield from which most deer appeared to be coming. We counted the remaining ears of corn on April 21.

We eliminated two of the wildlife food patches (0.43 and 0.53 acres in size) from the study after initial observations revealed that these two fields produced virtually no corn due to the lack of fertilizer and herbicide.

By the time the study began in late fall, the three food patches already showed evidence of use by deer. By counting the remaining ears of corn and the fresh cobs,

Corn consumed by white-tailed deer in four cornfields in southern Wisconsin.

	The Cornfield	Field 3	Field 4	Field 5
Acres	5.23	1.61	2.09	0.90
No. Stalks	107,304	35,378	43,472	19,696
No. Ears	101,616	8,453	12,042	4,865
Ave. Ear (In.)	7.5	4.9	4.8	4.9
Percent Corn Remaining				
9/1/84	94.7	23.9	27.7	24.7
10/6/84		17.7	25.5	19.1
12/24/84	93.7	4.2	11.7	12.2
1/9/85	92.1	2.7	9.4	5.6
4/21/85	89.1	2	1	2.3
Est. Ears Remaining				
9/1/84	101,616	8,453	12,042	4,865
10/6/84		6,262	11,085	3,762
12/24/84	100,543	1,486	5,086	2,403
1/9/85	98,826	955	4,086	1,103
4/21/85	95,607	708	434	453
Total Corn Consumed				
12/24/84-4/1/85	4,936	778	4,652	1,950
Est. Deer Days	232	172	2,635	404
Ears/Deer/Day	21.3	4.5	1.8	4.8

John Herron, "Deer Use of Corn in Agricultural Areas," 1985

we estimated the amount of corn present in each field at the beginning of the fall. However, we calculated deer use from data collected after December 24. Field 4 received the heaviest use during the study with track counts indicating frequent visits by more than twenty deer per night. The 5.23-acre cornfield (hereafter referred to as "The Cornfield"), consistently received light use by deer with six out of sixteen track counts indicating no deer use the previous day.

Field 3. This 1.61-acre field received the lightest deer use of the three food plots. During most of the fall, an adult doe tagged with a radio transmitter regularly used this cornfield during the day and fre-

quently bedded in the cornfield in the evening. Located at the corner of an alfalfa field and surrounded on three sides by an abandoned field, this field existed approximately 350 yards from the nearest road, hidden from view due to terrain. Its distance from wooded cover (160 yards) probably accounts for the relatively low use it received. Deer use averaged about two deer per night and began to increase slightly in late December. It began to decrease around the middle of February, presumably due to decreasing corn; it peaked sharply during the season's last snow at the end of March.

A comparison of the amount of corn consumed and deer use for the season indicates that deer consumed a total of 7745 ears of corn during the fall. During the study period deer consumed 778 ears or 4.5 ears per deer per day. This number remains partly offset by the fact that ears of corn in Field 3 were uniformly small, averaging 4.9 inches in length.

By January 9, only stunted or deformed ears of less than three inches in length remained. Although an occasional squirrel used this cornfield, we considered corn consumption by wildlife other than deer neglible (less than fifteen visits). A covey of eleven quail, however, frequently used Field 3, due to the variety of habitat available in the surrounding area and to the

Deer use and corn yields of four cornfields in southern Wisconsin.

	Ears of Corn as of:			
	9/15/84	12/24/84	4/21/85	Deer-Days*
Field 3	8,453	1,486	708	635
Field 4	12,042	5,086	434	2,635
Field 5	4,865	1,103	453	404
The Cornfield	101,616	100,543	95,607	232

*12/24/84 to 4/21/85

John Herron, "Deer Use of Corn in Agricultural Areas," 1985.

presence of a good stand of foxtail grass in the food patch itself.

Field 4. This field received very heavy deer use with an estimated forty-five deer living within a half-mile. This field was adjacent to woody cover and a mowed field of grass that deer also heavily used. Deer use of this field started off at about eight per night at the end of December. Deer use increased steadily throughout the winter months, peaking by February 12, when sixty-eight deer visited the cornfield during the night. Undoubtedly, some of the deer tracks counted represented deer who had visited the cornfield twice during the night, once in the evening and again in the early morning. By early March, deer use dropped to around twelve deer per night. Deer use peaked once more following the snow on March 30.

Comparing the amount of corn consumed with deer use for the season indicates that deer consumed 11,608 ears of corn during the fall, or 4.4 ears per deer per day. This number is also partly offset by the small size of ears in the field, with an average size of 4.8 inches. During the study period (December 24 to March 6, 1985), deer consumed 4652 ears, or 1.8 ears per deer per day. As mentioned earlier, this number remains undoubtedly low since many deer probably visited the food plot twice an evening in late winter, so deer were probably consuming closer to 3.6 ears of corn per day. Data collected between December 24 and January 9 indicate that deer consumed 4.2 ears per deer per day. By January 9, deer consumed nearly all of the corn in the food patch; most of the ears remaining were either deformed or overgrown with fungus.

Field 4 received heavy use by squirrels who visited the field on the average of 4.9 times each day. At least two squirrels lived beside the food patch. On April 21, we counted 562 cobs under trees adjacent to the field. We could not determine whether these represented ears completely consumed by squirrels or ears they picked up after being fed on by deer. It was obvious, however, that many songbirds did most of their feeding on the corn that the squirrels discarded, gleaning the remaining kernels.

Field 5. This field, the smallest food patch studied, consisted of a fair stand of corn. It was adjacent to a small patch of woods. Tracks indicated that most of the deer using this food patch approached it from the northeast. Deer use of Field 5 showed a different pattern than the other fields. Use at the beginning of the season was rather high, averaging twelve deer per night at the end of December and increasing to about twenty deer per night during the first week of January. From then on, deer use dropped continuously to about two deer per night in March. As with the other fields, a slight and temporary increase in deer use occurred with a new snow on March 30.

In Field 5 deer consumed 4412 ears of corn during the fall. This number also remains partly offset by the small size of the ears in the field with an average size of 4.9 inches. During the study period, deer consumed 1950 ears, or 4.8 ears per deer per day. Data collected between December 24 and January 9 indicate that deer consumed 8.0 ears per deer per day. As with the other two food patches, by January 9 only deformed ears of corn remained.

Squirrels visited this food patch on the average of 5.6 times each day. At the end of the study, we found 508 cobs underneath trees adjacent to the food patch. Once again, we don't know if this represents corn completely consumed by squirrels or cobs scavenged after being fed upon by deer. Field 5 also supported a covey of seven to ten quail. When in the field, they usually stayed in an area of velvetleaf, a common cornfield weed. Quail tracks and sightings also indicated that the quail searched among the corncobs left by the squirrels.

The 5.23-Acre Cornfield. The results of this field surprised us. In spite of being the largest field studied and having an abundance of corn, it received the lightest deer use. The Cornfield was part of a larger nine-acre field with the outer rows harvested. Eighteen to twenty-four rows of harvested corn surrounded the standing corn. The harvested portion of The Cornfield showed no evidence of deer feeding during the entire study.

Daily deer use of The Cornfield fluctuated from zero to ten deer between the end of December and early February, averaging about two deer per visit. Deer use stabilized somewhat during March, averaging three deer per visit, and then declined again until early March when deer Number 8, a radio-marked doe, moved into the area with three other deer. These four deer used the field consistently until spring green-up toward the end of March. A marked increase in deer use followed the snow of March 30, with sixteen deer using The Cornfield for two nights.

During the study, deer consumed 4936 ears of corn, averaging 21.3 ears per deer per day. These were full-sized ears, nine to ten inches in length. This result appears alarmingly high; we are uncertain where the error lies. A count of stripped and partially consumed ears of corn (rather than ears remaining) also indicates that deer consumed about 5000 ears of corn during the fall and winter. Deer use of The Cornfield was so low that repeated track counts between December 24 and March 6

showed no deer tracks other than those counted on previous days. We felt that track counts during this period represented an absolute count of deer use, not an estimate.

Apparently any error in estimating deer use would have to be an underestimate of deer use between April 1, when most field observations stopped, and April 21 when we sampled the remaining corn. During the month of April we only saw one radio-marked doe and three other deer; we assumed no other deer were in the area. Possibly the high deer use noted for March 31 and April 1 does not represent temporary peaks in deer use during the snow, but represents continued high use by deer during the early spring. If this were the case, then The Cornfield may have received an additional 160 deer days of use, bringing corn consumption down to 12.6 ears per deer per day. Analysis of The Cornfield data continues in an attempt to isolate the apparent error.

During the final survey of the remaining corn in The Cornfield, we sampled two transects across The Cornfield in order to see if deer favored the outer rows. While the results have not been tested statistically, it appears that four samples of the outer 120 stalks indicate that less corn remained in the outer rows than in the rest of The Cornfield, suggesting that deer prefer to feed on the external limits of cornfields.

The amount of corn left from the 839 stalks of corn purposely knocked down on March 6 surprised us. Even though the rest of The Cornfield still had eighty-nine percent of its corn remaining on April 21, only nine percent of the levelled corn remained. This situation indicates that deer prefer to feed on corn on the ground, probably because it's easier to get a grip on while feeding. In his *World of the White-tailed Deer,* Leonard Lee Rue III also notes that when strong winds knock cornstalks down, "deer are quick to find whatever corn is left and they will feed there each night until the corn is all devoured."

Deer Number 8, an adult doe, particularly interested us since The Cornfield existed in the center of her spring, summer, and fall home range. We had previously followed her for nearly four years. Each winter she moved 1.6 miles south to a separate winter home range. The presence of The Cornfield in December of 1984 made no difference. Toward the end of December, she moved south as usual. She remained in her winter home range until March 10, when we located her back in her summer home range. On March 19, we again observed her and three other deer using The Cornfield. These four deer continued to use The Cornfield regularly after this, although their use of corn lessened noticeably after the spring green-up.

The lack of adjacent woody cover apparently contributed to the low deer use that The Cornfield received. While a woodline existed ninety yards north of The Cornfield, the deer closest to the area wintered in a larger woods 400 yards to the east. Most of the deer in this part of BAAP fed on waste corn in a harvested cornfield 1070 yards southeast of The Cornfield, referred to as the "AP Cornfield."

Radio-telemetry indicated that deer from two areas used the AP Cornfield. One group of about twenty-five animals wintered in a mixed-wooded, old field 800 yards east of the AP Cornfield. These deer would have had to move more than a mile to reach The Cornfield. The other group of five deer wintered 260 to 530 yards north of the AP Cornfield. These deer would have had to move 400 yards to reach The Cornfield. Why they chose to move south to the AP Cornfield, rather than moving west to The Cornfield, remains open to speculation.

We suspect that, first of all, the deer found adequate food in the AP Cornfield and were not forced to look elsewhere. With abundant food available to their south, these deer may not have been aware of the standing corn to the west. Secondly, thick wooded cover surrounded the AP Cornfield, providing them with more substantial cover than the woodline near The Cornfield. Thirdly, tradition may have played a large role in the deer's selection. Four years of deer observations from a previous study indicated that deer used the AP Cornfield every winter from 1980 to 1984. The same study indicated that deer seldom used the area of The Cornfield during the winter. The presence of a new, abundant food source failed to entice them to change tradition. Perhaps if The Cornfield were allowed to stand for several years, deer would learn to use it. It appears that the deer made the right choice: They used a known, abundant food source rather than changing their habits for a food source that was not as reliable a choice over the long term.

The five-acre cornfield cost $1500 at market value. If deer eat five ears of corn per day, this five-acre field could have supported 200 deer for 100 days at a cost of $7.50 per deer for the season, or less than eight cents per deer per day. However, the value of the cornfield was not realized, since so few deer used it. In this area a cornfield of 0.25 acres in size would have sufficed.

In other parts of the plant, not even two acres of standing corn were enough. Deer cleaned out the three wildlife food patches by the first week of January. Their presence may have allowed deer to enter the winter in a healthy state, but accomplished little toward maintaining deer throughout the winter. The unfertilized food patches also offered little winter cover due to their sparse growth of cornstalks.

The food patches would have accomplished more if treated with the same fertilizer and herbicide that commercial cornfields receive. Economically, it makes little sense to plant poor quality food patches, since much of the cost of the food patches consists in the cost of the land being used and the labor required to plant it. With chemical treatment, the yields of the three food patches would have doubled, providing a better food source for deer. On the other hand, there would not have been such a fine stand of foxtail grass in Field 3, something that the quail favored.

We also made counts of songbirds sighted in the study fields. The majority of them fed on the ground. The quail, sparrows, and juncos frequently fed on weed seeds rather than on corn. The sparrows, cardinals, juncos, and quail also fed among the corn cobs discarded by the squirrels. Indeed, without the squirrels, it's questionable whether these birds would have such ready access to corn, since deer drop few kernels while feeding on standing corn. Bluejays fed on the corn by landing on the upright ears and tearing back the husk in order to get to the kernels. Downy woodpeckers, which we continually observed, searched for insects in the cornstalks.

One should also remember that standing corn does not represent the only way to provide food for wildlife. Modern mechanization of our farms, particularly in the harvesting of grain, provides deer and wildlife in general with a great deal of waste corn. Automatic corn pickers miss many ears of corn that would not happen if man husked them by hand. Wisconsin DNR researchers estimate waste corn left in the field after harvesting at five percent, or approximately five bushels per acre (280 lbs/acre). A reduction in fall plowing practices would clearly provide deer with a great deal of this corn and help to prevent soil erosion as well.

In a study conducted in central Illinois, Richard Warner of the Illinois Natural History Survey studied seventy-one cornfields. In 1981, he estimated waste corn in untilled, harvested fields at 384 lbs/acre compared with 40.5 lbs/acre in intermediately tilled fields (off-set discing), and 3.3 lbs/acre in plowed fields. Warner concluded that the amount of waste corn in untilled fields doubled since the early 1940s, despite modern technological advances in picker-sheller operations. Like many of us, he hopes that plowing and all forms of fall tillage decrease, thus leaving the residue to protect soils and to provide more food for the sustenance of white-tailed deer populations.

While studying the dynamics of waste corn and its nutritional quality on the Southern High Plains of Texas in southeastern Castro County (1979–1982), wildlife researchers from Texas Tech University observed a cornfield loss of 3.7 percent of a potential crop with a waste of 324.7 pounds per acre. First discing of harvested fields removed seventy-seven percent of initial waste, whereas deep plowing and hand salvage removed ninety-seven percent and fifty-eight percent, respectively. While changes in the nutritional quality of waste corn remain unknown, we do know that standing corn has a high vitamin A content and the grain of standing corn consists of 9.9 percent protein. Corn, however, as Aaron Moen of Cornell University observes, "is deficient in the amino acid lysine and as a result it is not a good single source of protein."

One field surveyed within our study area at BAAP contained thirty-nine ears of corn per acre after harvest; another had 228 ears of corn per acre. Other harvested fields surveyed in 1982 averaged 188 ears per acre. These results imply that about one percent of the corn in these fields remained unharvested. In this situation, a 100-acre cornfield, left unplowed, provides as much food to wildlife as one acre of standing corn. While it does not provide the amount of winter cover of standing corn, it does not cost as much either.

Corn obviously remains an important wildlife food during the winter months, especially for deer and squirrels. Deer often eat up to five ears of corn per day during the middle of winter. Yet, much of the damage that occurs to cornfields may be from squirrels, not deer. While deer readily utilize waste corn if found close to their winter cover, they will not immediately change their home range when presented with a new food source. It may take several years for them to learn to use new food plots.

Only one previous study exists that deals with corn consumed by deer in terms of pounds per day. In studying the food habits of white-tailed deer in southern Wisconsin in 1981, Wisconsin DNR researchers estimate that one deer consumes approximately two bushels of corn during the autumn months or 1.2 pounds per day. Their study, like ours, does not indicate that whitetails prefer waste corn to standing corn, but that whitetails do prefer to eat corn on the ground rather than corn attached to the stalk. The monthly use of corn by deer in the Wisconsin DNR study peaked in February and November. In converting our data into pounds of corn per deer per day, we found that the aver-

---

The energy and matter morphology of a corn plant.

Aerial Part Except Ears And Husks:

Ash	7.1%*
Protein	5.9%
Digestible Energy**	2,601 kcal kg^{-1}

Entire Aerial Part of Plant:

Ash	6.7%*
Protein	8.9%
Digestible Energy**	2,866 kcal kg^{-1}

Corn Cobs:

Ash	1.7%*
Protein	2.8%
Digestible Energy**	2,072 kcal kg^{-1}

Corn Husks:

Ash	3.0%
Protein	3.5%
Digestible Energy	3,219 kcal kg^{-1}

Corn Grain

Ash	1.4%*
Protein	9.9%
Digestible Energy**	4,012 kcal kg^{-1}

*Indicates percentages based on dry weight
**Indicates digestible energy

—Aaron N. Moen, *Wildlife Ecology*, 1973

Corn consumed by one white-tailed deer: September 23 - December 21					
	Sept.	Oct.	Nov.	Dec.	Total
Days (no.)	8	31	30	21	90
Food Eaten (Lb.)*	40	155	150	105	450
Volume In Corn (%)	14	15	37	20	24(Ave.)
Corn Eaten (Lb.)**	6	23	56	21	106
Standing Corn Eaten (%)	100	80	10	0	—
Standing Corn Eaten (Lb.)	6	18	6	0	30
Waste Corn (Lb.)	0	5	50	21	76

*Assuming 5 lb. of food eaten per day **56 lb./bu.

Charles M. Pils, et al., "Foods of Deer in Southern Wisconsin," 1981.

age cob from The Cornfield consisted of 0.38 pounds of shelled corn. We estimate that in consuming five ears of corn per day, a white-tailed deer eats approximately two pounds of corn per day.

Since 1900, whitetails in the Corn Belt drastically modified their feeding habits. Deer in these states today prefer cultivated crops such as corn to browse, the traditional white-tailed deer food of the past. Corn growing and harvesting practices also changed during this period of time from cultivation with horses and field-shocking to cultivation with tractors and mechanical pickers to herbicide applications and corn combining. The cornfields themselves changed as well, as Aaron Moen observes in his *Agriculture and Wildlife Management* (1983), "from field-shocks providing food and cover to cultivated but somewhat weedy fields to clean and efficiently harvested fields." Accompanying these changes, deer and hunters

alike found larger and larger increases in corn acreage providing the deer with a place to hide and the hunter with a place to stalk.

Stalking whitetails in cornfields on windy days with bow and arrow in hand, especially cornfields surrounded with stands of oak and tightly bordered with apple trees, provides me with endless hours of fascinating frustration and dramatic surprises. While stalking one buck in an upland cornfield of this kind, I suddenly looked behind me and discovered to my utter surprise an even bigger buck stalking me; his track indicated that he had followed me and the odor emanating from my scent vent for approximately sixty yards. Needless to say, I didn't get either one of them. But incidents like this one never cease to amaze me and keep me coming back to the cornfields for hunting and observation purposes.

Some cornfields frequently contain a single large oak tree within the field itself; this kind of a situation provides an ideal observation point to study deer movement in and around the field. While some hunters advocate using pit blinds and stepladders in the fields themselves, I prefer to locate my tree stand thirty to fifty yards into a woodlot adjacent to a secluded, upland cornfield, especially if it contains white oaks interspersed with crabapple trees. My most productive tree stand exists in a white oak overlooking a misshapen crabapple tree with a heavily used overhanging branch; the oak stands on the side of an east-west ridge with cornfields located on the upper side and alfalfa fields on the bottom. This situation provides me with a steady stream of antlered deer movement to and from the cornfields.

After feeding whitetails an average of

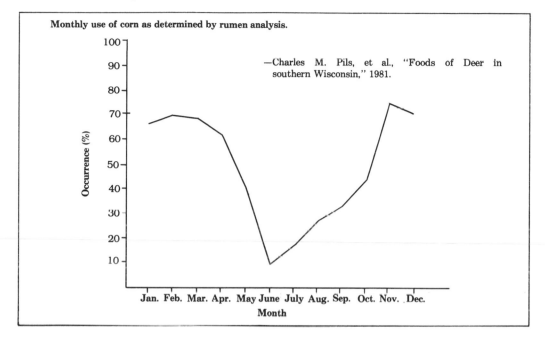

Monthly use of corn as determined by rumen analysis.

—Charles M. Pils, et al., "Foods of Deer in southern Wisconsin," 1981.

1300 pounds of shelled corn a month at a cost of $2.70 per day and observing their behavior at my corn feeders in front of my study window, I reached the conclusion that deer in the wild feed on corn, when available, at all times of the day; they voraciously eat shelled corn in an uninterrupted manner for as long as fifteen to twenty minutes, and they chew twenty-seven to thirty-four times per mouthful before bedding to digest these high protein kernels.

Even during the spring green-up, they follow their regular deer trails to the corn feeders. Scientists state that once a deer's stomach and intestinal tract become acclimated to corn they continue to ingest it until it disappears. Unlike the cornfields that fall prey to spring plowing, my feeders continue to provide corn year-round. Deer bed close to a known source of corn and, like Pavlov's dog, seem to react within minutes to the sound of corn pour-

ing into the feeders. Early in July the does introduce their fawns to the corn. Even though their first experiences include games of tag and hide and seek with the squirrels while at the feeders, they learn shortly to nibble on the shelled corn. The deer share my wildlife feeders with cottontails, gray squirrels, fox squirrels, raccoons, turkeys, grouse, chipmunks, woodchucks, blue jays, and sundry songbirds, but aggressively fight amongst themselves as to who will eat first.

When presented with shelled corn and corn on the cob, whitetails obviously choose the former; this is not, however, to suggest that whitetails will not carry a cob of corn with them as they leave the field. In fact, in separating items taken from the stomachs of whitetails, wildlife biologists from the Corn-Belt states frequently find large pieces of corn cobs; whitetails eat the stalks and silk as well. But when the white oak acorns drop in mid-August and

Stalking whitetails in cornfields on windy days with a bow and arrow provides the deer hunter with hours of fascinating frustration and dramatic surprises. *Photo credit William Vaznis*

the price of shelled corn drops dramatically, whitetails quickly abandon their voracious interest in corn.

The story of whitetails and cornfields reaches its ultimate conclusion in the Corn Belt, a region of fertile, well-drained soils comprising Iowa and parts of Illinois, Indiana, Ohio, Missouri, Kansas, Nebraska, South Dakota, and Minnesota. In this region, corn occupies approximately one-half of the cultivated land and produces about eighty percent of the nation's corn crop. This region also produces some of the nation's largest whitetails, both in antler dimensions and body weight. Minnesota claims the all-time record in body weight with Carl J. Lenander's buck shot in a cornfield in 1926,

weighing in at 402 pounds field-dressed, with a calculated live weight of 511 pounds. It's not surprising that one of the biggest nontypical whitetails of all time — the "Hole in the Horn Buck" measuring 342-3/8 points — comes from the fertile Corn Belt state of Ohio. Indeed, the "Paul Bunyans" among white-tailed deer come from the Corn Belt.

Hunters frequently take these large whitetails in the middle of cornfields. "Smart deer," as bow hunter Bob Chestnut of Illinois insists, "stay in standing corn where hunters can't get at 'em. The corn gives them cover and food and there's always water in bordering ditches." Some deer hunters even coordinate their hunting efforts with the farmer's schedule of corn picking in order to drive farmland bucks from the cornfields.

Studies show that deer stay in cornfields for several days at a time. In a study entitled "Deer Movements and Habitat Use of Irrigated Agricultural Lands in Central Wisconsin," University of Wisconsin researchers at the College of Natural Resources in Stevens Point observe that radio-collared deer frequently venture into unharvested cornfields and bed there throughout the day, thus using cornfields as refuge cover. Some of these deer actually stay in the cornfields for as long as three to four days at a time, bedding during the daytime and feeding in the evening. One yearling buck moved two and a half miles between September 28 and October 6, 1980, from his core area in a marsh to a 161-acre cornfield, where he remained for four days.

In analyzing the daily and annual harvests of white-tailed deer in Illinois over a seventeen-year period, deer researchers at the Illinois Natural History Survey found that the stage of the corn harvest had a dramatic and consistent effect on the daily and annual harvests of deer. Lower-than-anticipated kills took place when a substantial amount of unharvested corn remained at the beginning of the deer season. Researchers speculated that two factors contributed to the lower kills. First, whitetails use standing corn for cover and when standing corn prevails, deer simply scatter throughout the corn, making them less vulnerable to deer hunters. Secondly, farmers who would otherwise participate in the hunt may not do so in years when they fall behind in harvesting their crops.

Farmland deer feed on corn because it's there and available. I believe that habit and custom influence deer utilization of corn more so than any preference of palatability. However, deer are selective eaters; they will not eat that to which they are not conditioned. Leonard Lee Rue III, wildlife photographer and a resident of New Jersey, underscores this point:

"For years, hundreds of acres of corn were raised near my home. That corn helped to create a deer problem. When the farming was discontinued, the deer herd was much too large to be supported by the natural food available. We lost a great many deer to starvation because at that time we could not harvest does.

"When enough time had passed, our

If you are having trouble getting bucks such as this one, turn the shotgun over to the missus and have her hunt in and around the cornfield. *Photo credit Tom Huggler*

deer no longer knew what corn was. Each fall they came to feed on the dropped apples in an orchard near my home. One year the apple crop was exceedingly poor. Because I like to watch the deer, I put corn out for them. But no corn had been grown in the valley for about five years. The deer did not know what it was. They smelled it and were not afraid of any odors on the corn, but they would not eat it. None of the deer that came in had been alive when corn was a mainstay; the link was broken and the corn remained untouched."

Venison from corn-fed deer never remains untouched at my deer shack. It seems to take on a deeper and richer red color than venison from deer living exclusively on browse; it certainly tastes sweeter to me. Indeed, the sweet taste of venison tenderloins at the deer shack from corn-fed deer together with roasted sweet corn and Estate Bottled *Vin De Bordeaux*—1980, keeps me on the track of whitetails in the ripening, waving cornfields of Indian Summer.

Chapter 9

White Scars of the Deer Forest

In October my pines tell me, by their rubbed-off bark, when the bucks are beginning to "feel their oats." A jackpine about eight feet high, and standing alone, seems especially to incite in a buck the idea that the world needs prodding. Such a tree must perforce turn the other cheek also, and emerges much the worse for wear. The only element of justice in such combats is that the more the tree is punished, the more pitch the buck carries away on his not-so-shiny antlers.

—Aldo Leopold, *A Sand County Almanac*, 1949

Although the observant deer hunter begins to locate buck rubs in late August and early September in the North, it isn't until that glorious month of October (it occurs a bit earlier in the South) that these mind-riveting signposts proliferate, grab our attention, and haunt our imagination to the fullest. When we find one of these visual signposts, we measure the diameter of the tree, the length of the rub and its height, and we stand before it somewhat mesmerized, thinking of the kingly crown that made it and the buck's reasons for so doing.

Will the buck return to rub it again, we wonder? Is the repeated rubbing of a certain tree merely a chance occurrence? What environmental and behavioral and/ or physiological factors increase or decrease rub density? Can we distinguish the rubs of dominant bucks from those of the subordinate animals? Do deer prefer a particular species of shrubs or trees; that is, are certain trees given "preferred" treatment? Are certain areas within their home range preferred for rubbing? Can the observant hunter find centers of rubbing activity? Is rubbing a nocturnal activity? Why do so few buck rubs frequently occur in an area even when the resident buck population remains at a high level? How many rubs does a buck make? Are does attracted to them? When are the first and last dates of these rubbing episodes? What do buck rubs ultimately tell us about the buck population in any given area? What do they really indicate? Of what are they a sign? To what are they an obvious clue? In what way do they guide us to a successful hunt?

When we find a pronounced line of these large and dramatic signposts, these questions and others arise in our mind as our eyes rise upwards into the woodland canopy for the ideal placement of a tree stand. While deer hunters have philosophized and argued about buck rubs from time immemorial, here's what scientists and natural historians tell us about bucks and their rubbing episodes.

The earliest research in this regard occurred in the spring of 1943, when H. H. Chapman, one of America's most influential foresters and one of Yale University's most beloved professors of forestry, together with his students in the Yale School of Forestry, studied the relationship between a large white-tailed deer population and the mixed hardwoods in the Great Mountain Forest in Norfolk and Canaan, Connecticut. His survey indicated that bucks rubbed all species of forest trees with no evidence of distinct preferences, and that bucks frequently rubbed the same tree more than once.

Chapman dissected and measured more than fifty species of rubbed trees. The injured trees averaged twenty-two years of age, varying from eleven to sixty years. The average diameter reached about 1.5 inches, ranging from 0.5 to 4.7 inches. Most of the trees he examined were located in the understory, thus accounting for their relatively small size in relationship to age. In general, most buck rubs in his survey reached a height of about twenty inches above the soil, varying from ten to thirty-six inches. He did, however, find one basswood with a rub reaching fifty inches above the surface of the soil.

According to Chapman, "narrow wounds, covering only a small percentage of the stem circumference of rapidly growing trees, heal quickly (see Part A of accompanying photo page). Discoloration of the wood occurs in most cases and decay occasionally is evident. Large wounds heal more slowly and in most species decay is certain to enter (F,G,H,I). Trees having wood not resistant to attack by fungi suffer the most. Thus, wounded basswood stems are often reduced to mere shells owing to destruction of the heartwood by decay. Large wounds which are not healed quickly weaken the stems and render them liable to breakage by wind, snow, ice glaze, or other natural agents. The wood of injured spruces is rather resistant to decay and is commonly pitch-soaked (C)." After being rubbed, some trees die within a few years but many continue to live. If seriously injured and decay enters before complete healing takes place, the trunks provide man with little more than firewood.

In his study of a herd of mule deer on the Hastings Natural History Reservation in California, Jean Linsdale, a zoologist, and his co-workers at the University of California kept extensive field notes on buck rubs and rubbing episodes. Like Chapman, Linsdale observed that deer often rub the same tree year after year and, in the process, completely destroy the tree. But unlike earlier researchers, he made a clear distinction between two kinds of buck rubs. The rubs that appear in late July, August, and September he defined as a "beating and twisting" of small stems to assist the buck in removing velvet and polishing antlers. In this process, Linsdale reported in his field notes, "the antlers, at first a dull brown, acquire a vitreous finish and ivory-like tips."

But as the rut develops and the bucks

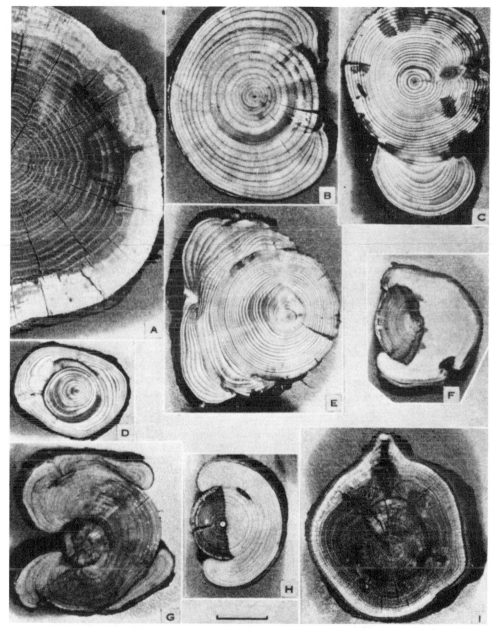

The Long-term Results of Buck Rubs:

Injuries to tree stems resulting from rubbing by deer antlers. (Scale at the bottom represents one inch.) A) Red oak wounded six years previously. B) White pine wounded six years ago. C) Red spruce wounded fifteen years ago. D) Hemlock wounded twice—eight and nine years ago. E) Red spruce wounded three times—thirteen, six, and four years ago. F) Red maple wounded four years ago. G) Striped maple wounded twice—fourteen and four years ago. H) White ash wounded eight years ago. I) Red oak wounded twice—thirteen and twelve years ago.

Reprinted from H. J. Lutz and H. H. Chapman. 1944. "Injuries to Young Tree Trunks from Antler Rubbing by Deer." Journal of Wildlife Management, *8(1):80.*

begin to feel their oats, they more vigorously thrash and chafe small tree trunks, leaving their signature on them as an expression of their sexual drive. Linsdale reported that rutting bucks repeatedly mauled arroyo willow clumps. In one thicket measuring twenty feet across, Linsdale found twenty-nine rubs. Unlike Chapman's conclusions, Linsdale observed that deer recognize peculiarities of certain shrubs and tree species and make their selection accordingly. The largest rub in Linsdale's study measured fifteen inches in length, 4.5 inches wide, and was scarred on a red willow eighteen inches above the ground with a 4.75-inch diameter. He found it unusual for bucks to work on such tough trees as live oaks.

The most interesting and significant finding of Linsdale's work revolved around his description and picture of a shrub that bucks virtually reduced to a cluster of mauled stubs by repeated use as a rubbing or whipping post during several seasons. Within several feet of this tattered and abused shrub stood another one of the same plant species, same size and equally accessible, but completely ignored by the bucks. In 1956, William Graf, a California deer biologist, followed up on this significant observation and put forth the interesting hypothesis that "the repeated use of the same signposts during a season (as well as year after year by individuals or by different bucks) . . . certainly indicates that there is more significance to these acts than the immediate fulfillment of the need for something upon which the buck can vent his surplus energy and spirits."

After studying the behavior of mule deer, blacktails, and elk, Graf concluded, unlike Linsdale, that antler rubbing for the sole purpose of removing velvet does not occur, although in some cases, velvet may be removed but only incidental to the rubbing of antlers for other more significant purposes. He observed mule deer bucks going for days and weeks with masses of stripped velvet hanging over their eyes without making any attempt to remove it even though it might have caused them a great deal of annoyance. He also noted that antler rubbing usually starts well after the disappearance of velvet.

Graf indicated that only dominant bucks make rubs and that most of these rubs are found in the bedding areas. He observed bucks "nosing" and sniffing the tree they chose to rub with great delicacy and the utmost precision, and recorded the entire series of actions lasting for a period of five to fifteen minutes. He interpreted the ultimate meaning and significance of these rubbing episodes as a manifestation of territorialism, a view generally opposed by other mammalogists of his time. He nevertheless defined buck rubs in a psychological sense as a form of "cold war," and argued that "what is perhaps more significant in regard to these signposts is not so much the recognition of the territory by the animal or animals making the signposts as the psychological effect that these signposts have on nonmembers of the territory by an intimidation of the stranger entering such an occupied territory."

Like the glowing spark of a campfire, this idea of buck rubs as psychological intimidators or cold war tactics—"combat practices intended to intimidate a rival"—burned hotly but died quickly. Or did it? One decade later, while studying whitetailed buck rubs on his farm in Puslinch Township, Ontario, Antoon de Vos, a zoologist at the University of Waterloo, reached conclusions comparable in many ways to those presented by Graf.

For two years during the rutting season, de Vos recorded the locations of rubbing by white-tailed deer in a 4.5-acre conifer plantation. The rubbings for the two different years could readily be separated since the color of the newest rubs were light in color instead of dark. He found that nine out of a total of thirty white spruce trees—or thirty percent of the spruce trees rubbed—had been rubbed by bucks in both years. He viewed this repeated rubbing of the same trees as more than a chance occurrence and speculated that the re-used trees may have served the function of territorial signposts as suggested by Graf. Like Graf, he too concluded that bucks gave preferred treatment to certain trees but gave no reasons for the preference beyond saying that "the vegetation selected has certain characteristics eliciting this reaction." In his study of the rubbing of conifers, de Vos, like many deer hunters, found centers of rubbing activity but gave no further explanation.

In the fall of 1971, research biologists from around the world gathered at the University of Calgary, Alberta, for an international symposium on the behavior of ungulates and its relation to management. Again the idea of buck rubs as signposts of territorialism surfaced—this time in the work of Larry Marchinton, an avid deer hunter and deer biologist from the University of Georgia, who reported in a very significant paper on the marking behavior of white-tailed deer that in some situations white-tailed bucks defend areas and use rubs or signpost markings to delineate these areas.

After an intensive study of fourteen bucks by radio tracking and analyzing 135 instances of antler rubbing, Marchinton

concluded that buck rubs express social dominance during the breeding season and tend to have clumped distributions. According to his observations, rubbing

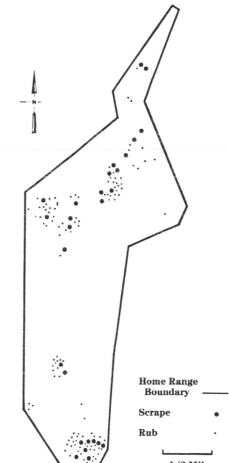

Home Range Boundary ———

Scrape •

Rub ·

├——┤ **1/2 Mile**

The spatial distribution of rubs and scrapes made by one Georgia white-tailed buck between October 14 and December 5. Note the clumped distribution or centers of rubs.

Reprinted from W.G. Moore and R.L. Marchinton. 1974. "Marking Behavior and its Social Function in White-tailed Deer." Page 452 in The Behavior of Ungulates and its Relation to Management. *IUCNN, Morges, Switzerland.*

behavior occurs primarily in the morning and evening, but only immediately prior to and during the rut.

"It was usually done by lone animals although the dominant individuals sometimes rubbed when confronted by another buck. The time spent making a rub averaged approximately fifteen seconds; however, there was considerable variation. It was common for an animal to pause for short periods while rubbing and to carefully sniff and lick the portion of the tree which was being rubbed. Eastern red cedar, winged sumac, sourwood, sassafras, shortleaf pine, and longleaf pine were most often rubbed. The plants selected for rubbing ranged from one-half inch to four inches in diameter, with the average being about one inch. A trained hound could detect deer scent on these trees and shrubs several days after they had been rubbed, and signs of rubbing remained visible for at least several months."

On several occasions Marchinton and his fellow researchers saw dominant bucks making rubs when encountering other male deer. Since snorts and intimidating postures accompanied these rubs, Marchinton viewed them as visual expressions of dominance with territorial implications, at least during the breeding season. His data suggested that rubs—which communicate a threat in the animal's absence—may play a major role in bucks maintaining their dominant position in a given area during the rut. He hastened to add that territorial behavior of bucks in this regard tends to break down at higher population levels, and, in any given area, the extent of the rubbing episodes may be related to the structure of the population and to the density of the population.

He concluded his landmark paper by telling deer biologists that "dominance areas involving sizable portions of the home range are marked by intensive rubbing early in the rutting season. There may be several such areas within the range of a mature buck. In these areas the buck

While establishing dominance, two bucks will occasionally take on the same tree at the same time. *Photo credit Richard P. Smith*

asserts his dominance by the ritualistic display of rubbing and by the visual and olfactory signposts (rubs) which result. It is our impression that physical combat is common during the period when dominance is being established. The buck, however, does not physically defend these dominance areas against males as long as the latter maintain subordinate postures. As a result, the presence of subordinate bucks within these areas is common. Observations suggested that an animal dominant in one area may act as a subordinate in the dominance areas marked by other bucks."

Buck rubbing can be especially devastating in orchards, deciduous hardwoods, and pine plantations. If we assume that most pre-rut rubbing is done by alpha bucks as an expression of dominance, then it would seem likely that the removal of the alpha buck during the velvet stage would minimize rub damage while maintaining a huntable buck population. However, H. G. Cumming, a research biologist with the Ontario Ministry of Natural Resources, told deer biologists at the international symposium in Calgary that his preliminary investigations in this regard indicated that removing territorial roe bucks in Scotland was ineffective in reducing rubbing because other territorial bucks immediately took their place and continued to rub while maintaining dominance. Cumming suggested that the destruction of the subordinate bucks, especially yearlings, proved more effective in reducing rub damage to tree plantations: "Since territorial bucks were always replaced in an area, but non-territorial bucks were seldom replaced, the best policy to reduce rubbing would seem to be to shoot the latter."

While the sight of peeled stems heightens the deer hunter's imagination and enthusiasm, it infuriates the orchardist or nurseryman. In dealing with this problem of rubbed trees and deer populations, Richard Prior, an English deer biologist, follows Cumming's advice and suggests that to reduce rubbing, deer managers should ensure a reasonably level sex ratio and cut the competition by eliminating the younger bucks. Like Cumming, Prior believes that well-established, territorial bucks have enough authority and presence to dominate subordinates by threat demonstrations and physical gestures rather than rubbing episodes, whereas young, nonterritorial bucks have to assert their vitality and aggression by constant demonstrations of rubbing. According to Prior, "a heavy harvest of surplus yearling bucks early in the season, preferably before they start to rub, will have a dramatic effect on the amount of rubbing damage. It is better to have a couple of resident bucks than many contentious youngsters. Removal of one territorial buck early in the season may lead to a group of yearlings taking his place." However, a good deal of experimentation needs to be done before we will have an informed harvest-management strategy for nurserymen dealing with the problem of buck rubs and before we know how that strategy would affect the sport of deer hunting.

While studying buck rubs, Cumming, like Marchinton, found that deer have a distinct preference for pines. Ninety-two percent of the 279 rubbed trees in his study were pines, although they composed only seventeen percent of the trees on the vulnerable area. In speculating as to why, Cumming remarked that "perhaps the relatively long section of stem without branches in pines facilitates fraying (rubbing) and the resilience of the stem may be suitable for mock fighting." While very few trees showed repeated rubbing in the same year, many of them were rubbed in successive years. Cumming estimated that each buck rubbed at least twenty-two trees per year and that about twenty-five percent of the trees rubbed eventually died. Other studies indicate that the average number of rubs per buck varies from sixty in the case of old bucks to 110 rubs for younger bucks. Larry Marchinton found that on the average a buck will make anywhere from sixty-nine to 538 rubs in one year, with an overall average of approximately 300 rubs per buck.

While not dealing with the number of rubs per buck, Al Brothers and Murphy Ray, two Texas deer biologists, report in their excellent book, *Producing Quality Whitetails* (1975), that buck rubs will usually be more numerous near the buck's bedding ground. I have found this to be true in my own deer hunting area, which has an unusually high ratio of bucks to does and exhibits a great deal of competition among bucks for breeding. The extent to which buck/doe ratios favoring females, population dynamics, and age structure affect these rubbing episodes — in terms of numbers of rubs and spatial placement — remains an unanswered question open to speculation. It would seem likely, however, that the closer the ratio approaches 1:1, the greater the competition and hence the greater the number of rubs.

During the 1970s Marchinton continued his detailed, scientific investigation of white-tailed buck rubs, especially their physical characteristics, seasonal changes, distribution patterns, and frequency as related to specific vegetation. After studying 193 buck rubs, he noted that the physical characteristics of rubs changed as the rut progressed. The early season rubs exhibited a lower visibility, but as bucks shed their velvet, "the proportion of highly visible rubs increased progressively until all rubbing ended." The average continuous length of exposed xylem (the water-conducting tissue of the stem) of the rubs increased from 6.4 inches in early September to 10.9 inches during the first two weeks of November.

While buck rubs generally occur in the same areas each year, Marchinton only discovered eight occasions of bucks rubbing the same tree. He found no evidence of bucks returning to the same tree in the same year to rub it again. The number of rubs increased from the beginning of September until the end of December with the most intense period of rubbing occurring just prior to the actual breeding season. However, he found a marked increase in the percentage of highly visible rubs during the breeding season and these rubs were generally associated with individual scrapes.

White-tailed bucks in the Georgia Piedmont preferred pines and black cherry for rubbing purposes, both being aromatic species. Indeed, Marchinton concluded that bucks are highly selective in their choice of tree species and that they prefer the physical characteristics of certain trees. They avoided trees with a rough bark texture and low-hanging branches, preferring smooth-barked trees with few low-branching limbs. Bucks seem to discriminate between trees based on subtle olfactory or taste factors, with pines remaining their favorite tree. Apparently, the aromatic quality of the pine enhances its utility as an olfactory signal and signpost.

Indeed, regardless of where you find the white-tailed buck, he chooses saplings

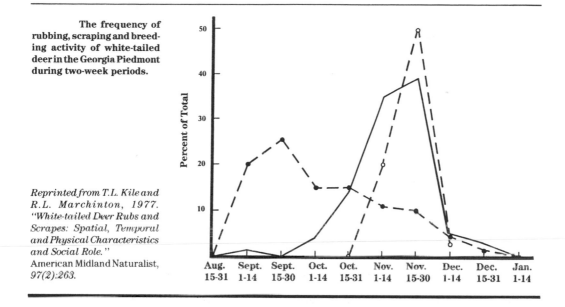

The frequency of rubbing, scraping and breeding activity of white-tailed deer in the Georgia Piedmont during two-week periods.

Reprinted from T.L. Kile and R.L. Marchinton, 1977. "White-tailed Deer Rubs and Scrapes: Spatial, Temporal and Physical Characteristics and Social Role." American Midland Naturalist, 97(2):263.

with a strong resinous sap above all other available kinds. On the east-Texas ranch of John Wootters, the Executive Editor of *Petersen's Hunting,* white-tailed bucks like the young pines so much that, according to Wootters, "They invariably kill every pine sapling before it reaches a trunk diameter of two inches. The parent trees themselves would not exist if they hadn't grown there before the re-stocked whitetail herd became large and old enough to have plenty of breeding bucks. Pines, hemlocks, cedars, and other conifers are favorite rubbing targets everywhere they may be available."

While studying the rubbing targets of bucks in a 900-acre nursery, deer researchers at the Ohio Agricultural Research and Development Center in Wooster report that, in a two-year period, bucks rubbed 1145 trees with a wholesale value of more than $30,000. These Ohio rubs also had a clumped distribution, with the rubs made during the rut being located near scrapes.

Only three percent of the trees were rubbed in both years and the percentage of the trees rubbed was inversely related to the tree diameter. Most pre-rut rubbing occurred at night.

According to David Nielsen, the principal investigator in this Ohio study, most, if not all, pre-rut rubbing was done by dominant bucks. Apparently, when the rut begins, dominant bucks rub less and concentrate their signpost marking to scrapes and overhanging branches. During their investigations, these Ohio researchers noted that rub density was exceptionally high for several years when a 4.5-year-old buck weighing 401 pounds on the hoof, with a Boone and Crockett typical score of 176-6/8, roamed the area as the dominant resident. The untimely death of this alpha male early in the rut, and in the absence of an immediate successor, resulted in a dramatic decrease in pre-rut rubs during the following year. Following his death only forty-eight trees

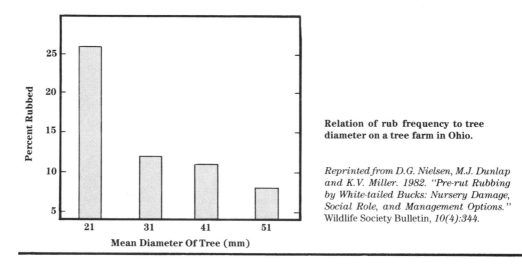

Relation of rub frequency to tree diameter on a tree farm in Ohio.

Reprinted from D.G. Nielsen, M.J. Dunlap and K.V. Miller. 1982. "Pre-rut Rubbing by White-tailed Bucks: Nursery Damage, Social Role, and Management Options." Wildlife Society Bulletin, *10(4):344.*

(4.6 percent) were rubbed in his area during the next pre-rut period, compared with 303 rubbed trees (twenty-three percent), when his kingly crown left the white scars of cold war dominance.

Although the function of buck rubs in the whitetails' social behavior is not fully understood, scientists generally agree that white-tailed bucks deliberately rub their glandular foreheads on the debarked trees, thus leaving a scent for other deer to identify the individual and the metabolic condition of the buck that made the rub. The scent left on the rub persists for several days, with the visible evidence lasting throughout the breeding period. Since does occasionally sniff, lick, and even mark buck rubs with their foreheads, we know that buck rubs ultimately function in the sexual communication between the sexes. However, as David Hirth and Larry Marchinton point out in the Wildlife Management Institute's *White-tailed Deer* (1984), "in populations with a high percentage of does and young age-structure among bucks (typical of many heavily hunted populations), the communicative

role of rubs and scrapes may be less significant." I believe this to be the case and herein lies the greatest lesson that we as deer hunters can learn from the scientists.

When locating buck rubs while scouting, the all-important clue to these centerpieces of breeding activity remains the diameter of the tree, for while large bucks frequently rub small stems and saplings, small bucks very seldom rub large trees. It seems that a definite correlation exists between the size of the buck and the size of the sapling or tree he attacks. Pay little attention to rubs on thumb-size tag alders or poplars; watch instead for rubs high above the ground on trees with a four-inch diameter or more, especially pines. When you find these kinds of rubs, you will find the wide, high, and very heavily beamed kingly crowns—the eights, tens, twelves or better. Spend your time scouting and searching for these kinds of rubs in an attempt to locate the main breeding area of a dominant buck, for his scrapes will generally be found within 100 to 200 yards of his massive breeding rubs.

Remember that these breeding rubs differ entirely in appearance from those made earlier in the fall; these savage rubs frequently have damaged or killed bushes, roots, and branches in and around the main rubbing target. One report in the literature even indicates that a buck actually rubbed so vigorously that he entangled his antlers in the branches above, and hung himself in the process. In making these breeding rubs, bucks often break low-hanging branches and limbs and toss them in the air while scarring all sides of the tree with their antler tines. The ground beneath these rubs frequently becomes torn, pawed, and gored with antler tines. These breeding rubs naturally appear much fresher during the hunting season than the pre-rut rubs located lower to the ground and on smaller saplings.

The largest breeding rub I have ever found was located on a high east-west oak ridge. The rub measured sixteen inches in length and was located sixty-two inches at its highest point above the surface of the soil; the rub was 3.5 inches wide, scarred on a white birch tree with a 4.5-inch diameter. Noel Feather, an antler rattler from Illinois, undoubtedly holds the record for finding the largest buck rub ever reported in the literature on deer and deer hunting to my knowledge. In his book entitled *Battling Bucks* (1985), he reports finding a buck rub on a cedar tree with a twelve-

Rubbing the forehead scent gland on the buck rub. *Photo credit Leonard Lee Rue III*

When locating buck rubs while scouting, the all-important clue for determining the size of the buck that made these centerpieces of breeding activity is the diameter of the tree. This buck rub occurred on a tree with a seven-inch diameter. *Photo credit Irene Vandermolen*

inch diameter, made by a Boone and Crockett, non-typical buck weighing 244 pounds dressed with a score of 220-1/8 that Feather shot very near the rub; the antlers and skull plate weighed eleven pounds alone.

If you haven't found a line of breeding rubs, keep looking, for being in an area of big rubs results in seeing big bucks. Watch particularly for areas that exhibit vigorous rubbing activity over a period of many years in the same small spots. Locating buck rubs in your area will provide you with a great deal of information about the resident buck population, the current stage of the rut, and the mental disposition of individual bucks; sometimes one can even guess the size of the antlers that

made the rub by closely observing the damage to secondary stems and brush behind the main rubbing target. If in doubt as to the freshness of the rub, take the back side of your knife and scrape away the bark next to the rub (if the tree belongs to you) and compare the color of the wood and the inner bark. Remember to take into consideration the humidity level and the rub's exposure to the sun.

Sometimes while scouting, the hunter will not only find buck rubs on saplings and trees but on fenceposts and power poles as well. While traveling through the deer forest one fall day, John Ozoga, a wildlife research biologist at the Cusino Wildlife Research Station in Upper Michigan, spotted a large-racked buck leisurely strolling across a powerline right-of-way. Instead of entering heavy cover as Ozoga expected, the buck "paused momentarily, then turned abruptly and retraced his steps to the nearest pole supporting overhead high voltage lines. Without hesitation, the buck lowered his head and raked the dry wood with his antlers. He nosed the pole briefly, seemingly satisfied with his effort, before continuing along an apparently predetermined course and out of my view. The entire episode lasted less than a minute."

Like many of us, Ozoga traditionally believed that buck rubs represented a place where bucks cleaned the velvet off their antlers and engaged in mock fights. But in this particular case, Ozoga knew that this large-racked buck had shed his velvet six weeks earlier, and the encounter with the power pole didn't look like any mock fight he had ever witnessed. Like other deer researchers, Ozoga learned from his own studies on white-tailed breeding behavior that few buck rubs exist as a direct result of rubbing off velvet or play-fighting with trees. We inherited this mistaken notion and myth from watching captive deer in pens. As John reminds us, "The antics of captive bucks confined to small pens and deprived of social contact are another matter entirely, as they'll battle just about any object within reach."

Actually, most buck rubs of the deer forest are made by a small number of "breeder-bucks" in order to advertise their high rank of dominance. While sub-dominants do make buck rubs, these rubs are relatively few in number when compared with those of the alpha male—the "number one" buck in the area. In his six-year study comparing the breeding behavior and performance of yearlings versus mature bucks, Ozoga found that yearling bucks did minimal rubbing prior to mid-October and made only about fifty percent as many total rubs per season as older

bucks. Scientists sometimes refer to these yearling bucks as "subdominant floaters," since they often float in and out of the social hierarchies, disrupting the population's social order in the process and frequently traveling from two to twenty miles from their natal range while so doing.

Like other researchers, Ozoga found that most buck rubs are made by alpha males and primarily serve as signposts to exhibit social dominance during the breeding period, whereas scrapes facilitate communication between the sexes. In his Michigan study, he observed that the frequency of antler rubbing decreased during the peak of the rut while scraping increased in intensity. When compared with mature males, yearling bucks demonstrated delayed rubbing and less overall rubbing in general.

While studying white-tailed breeding

A definite correlation exists between the size of the buck and the size of the tree he attacks. *Photo credit Richard P. Smith*

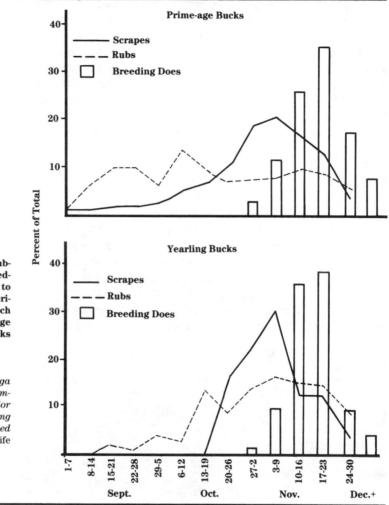

Frequency of rubbing, scraping, and breeding activity with respect to male age during weekly periods. Three years' data each are pooled for prime-age (1977-79) vs. yearling bucks (1980-82).

Reprinted from J.J. Ozoga and L.J. Verme. 1985. "Comparative Breeding Behavior and Performance of Yearling vs. Prime-age White-tailed Bucks." Journal of Wildlife Management, *49(2):368.*

patterns, Ozoga tested the response of whitetails to artificial rubs. He cut several aspen saplings with two-inch diameters from outside his study area and scraped them to resemble buck rubs; he then planted them within view of his blind. The first two bucks to approach the dummy rubs paid no attention to them. Ozoga was then surprised: "Nearly all of the dozen or so does and fawns that came near stopped to investigate. One doe

seemed particularly puzzled, making three repeat visits, each time carefully sniffing the dummy rub, apparently searching to identify the odor of the mysterious maker.

"When the area's number two buck came on the scene, he went directly to the fake rub, sniffed it briefly, then lowered his head and commenced converting the fake into an authentic rub. Unfortunately, I'd not 'planted' the stem deep enough, and after a few vigorous strokes of the buck's head, the sapling toppled to the ground. The buck stood over the fallen rub for a moment, then calmly walked away as though he'd previously experienced such disappointment."

In summarizing his findings, Ozoga reported that when excellent nutrition prolongs antler retention, you will frequently find buck rubs well into the winter and that most of them will be found in the area of the buck's preferred bedding site — an observation also verified by Al Brothers in Texas. After studying 378 buck rubs, Ozoga speculated that the experienced alpha buck's elaborate system of making them may be so sophisticated as to even permit does to solicit the particular attention from preferred males.

He ultimately reached the following conclusions of great significance for the deer hunter: "The intensity and seasonal pattern of buck rubbing activity reflects the age composition and degree of social stability among resident males. The occurrence of many rubs in September, for example, likely reveals the presence of an older, highly dominant buck, not necessarily many bucks. In contrast, delayed rubbing is more prevalent in heavily harvested herds comprised chiefly of young bucks, and is indicative of a lack of pre-rut social order."

At the 66th Annual Meeting of the American Society of Mammalogists in Madison, Wisconsin, in June 1986, I listened to Larry Marchinton present a fascinating paper entitled "Antler Rubbing by Bucks: Influences of Demography and Habitat," in which he again noted that rub aggregations represent dominance areas of a particular buck. While studying antler rub densities on five wildlife management areas in Georgia, he noticed that habitat type and food sources influenced the location and number of buck rubs: They were more common in oak and oak-pine types than in pine stands.

After months of tramping through rhododendron thickets, scaling mountains, wading rivers, and braving ice storms, Marchinton and his students located and measured 529 buck rubs. Rub densities on the five research areas ranged from approximately 500 to 1500 rubs per square mile, or one to three rubs per acre. Marchinton felt that during peak rubbing periods one buck may make from fifteen to twenty rubs per day. He established a direct relationship between buck rubs and acorns: Years of high acorn production coincided with an increase in the number of buck rubs. In years of poor acorn production, the intensity of the rut seemed reduced; apparently the buck's physical condition deteriorates more rapidly in the fall when acorns do not exist, and consequently they spend more time searching for food and less time fraying their antlers against oaks.

The most interesting theory with regard to bucks and their rubbing episodes came to me in the form of a letter to the editor of *Deer & Deer Hunting* magazine, from a deer hunter named Ed Tousignant:

"For the past couple of years we have been observing deer rubs with respect to the direction the rub is visible from. We hunt in an area where we have observed the rubs to be on the east-facing side of the tree in over ninety percent of the cases. Since 'East Rubs' are more visible from the morning sun, perhaps these rubs were made during the early morning hours and this area is frequented by bucks during these hours. Conversely, perhaps 'West Rubs' in another area would mean afternoon rubbings. The deer sightings in our area bear out our observations. Wouldn't it be nice to find a line of 'East Rubs' and know with a high degree of certainty that this is a good place for a morning stand?"

Indeed! But I cannot attest to the validity of this intriguing theory. All I know for sure is that these shiny white scars of the deer forest remain the most positive and only deer sign made exclusively by the antlered buck. As Sir Walter Scott once wrote, "We can show the marks he made, when against the oak his antlers frayed."

Chapter 10

Buck Movements and Hunting Pressure

A buck will come back to the same area where he grew his antlers the previous year; he may even fight the same brush, or shrub near it, where he rubbed off antler velvet last year. Undisturbed, a white-tailed buck will remain at any season within the confines of a few square miles, following the same routine day after day. Because he knows this place so well, a buck will remain there under heavy hunting pressure. He knows every trail, ridge, stream, thicket and grassy meadow in his domain many times better than you ever can know it within the limited time of a hunting season. And he will use that knowledge to outwit you.
— Arthur Carhart, *Hunting North American Deer,* 1946

When deer hunter, conservationist, and outdoor writer Art Carhart (1892–1978) penned these lines about white-tailed buck movements and heavy hunting pressure, he had little knowledge of the sophisticated, electronic and computerized techniques of present-day deer biologists for determining buck movements in response to hunter density. But nonetheless, much truth resides in Carhart's idea of a buck's fidelity to a small core area of his home range, especially when hunting pressure becomes intense.

Indeed, when deer hunters gather at the deer shack, regardless of the geographic area, one eternal question arises: How far do white-tailed bucks range from a certain locality during the hunting season? The typical dialogue sounds something like this: "Man, I shot three times at that buck on opening day and never touched him! My father-in-law killed him twenty miles away on the following Friday." This statement and many others like it cause lively discussions and arguments that circulate through deer hunting camps all across America. What is the likelihood of a buck traveling that far during the hunting season? Does intensive hunting pressure force bucks out of their normal areas of activity? Do harassed bucks concentrate in unhunted areas outside their normal home

In avoiding hunters, mature white-tailed bucks frequently run in a relatively straight line for considerable distances, quickly exiting their home range with high speed and great endurance; but unless shot, most return to their home ranges within a short time.
Photo credit Mark Wilson

range? How do individual bucks respond to heavy hunting pressure? Do they become more wary as hunting pressure continues? Are the oldest bucks shot later in the season?

Many deer hunters throughout America believe that the harassment of intense hunting causes mature white-tailed bucks to leave their home range and sojourn in remote, undisturbed areas during the hunting season. Deer biologists, however, who spy on white-tailed bucks with electronic surveillance, indicate that mature bucks in particular exhibit a strong affin-

ity for a known area, a restricted, core area that becomes almost unaltered by intense hunting pressure. While heavy hunting pressure may create the impression that bucks desert their home areas when heavily hunted, radio telemetry studies suggest that disturbances by deer hunters seldom force white-tailed bucks to permanently abandon their home ranges.

In their studies of deer movements, researchers generally distinguish between at least six different types of buck movements: (1) dispersal of yearlings; (2) migration between winter and summer ranges in the North; (3) occasional and seasonal shifting within, and temporary excursions or "wandering" outside of, their normal home range; (4) "homing" following translocation; (5) extended movement during the rut and; (6) erratic movement as a result of hunting pressure. A great variation in buck movements and home ranges exists depending upon such variables as method of measurement, age, predation, habitat type and change, weather (moisture, changes in humidity, temperature, wind, sunlight, lunar phases), food, water, salt, and finally the strongest and perhaps most interesting factor of all, hunting pressure.

As hunting pressure increases throughout the whitetail's domain, deer hunters, landowners, and lease-hunters voice one universal complaint: that "their" bucks are being killed miles away from "home." In responding to the case of the vanishing bucks, Jack Ward Thomas, a wildlife research biologist, trapped and tagged 241 deer on the Edwards Plateau in Texas, a very important deer range from the standpoint of hunting pressure, deer harvested, and economic return to landowners.

While studying the movements of these

deer, Thomas found that the average movement from trap site to death site for bucks approximated only 700 to 900 yards, thus lending support to the concept of a limited home range for bucks at least in that region. He concluded that bucks display a strong social affinity for a known area of less than 1.5 miles in radius and that knowledge and familiarity with that area apparently become the binding force that restricts greater movements during the hunting season. Indeed, although exceptions exist in the literature, most of the telemetry studies on deer movements indicate a small, restricted range for bucks, especially when put under heavy hunting pressure.

In Illinois, for example, Don Autry, a wildlife researcher, trapped and tagged 147 deer and set out to determine (1) if intensive hunting forces bucks to leave their normal areas of activity, (2) the relationship of their age to their movements, (3) whether they concentrate in unhunted areas, (4) the response of individual bucks to hunting and (5) whether they become more wary as hunting continues. He conducted his research during a controlled, public deer hunt on an 18,000-acre research area of the Crab Orchard National Wildlife Refuge at Carterville, Illinois. Researchers designed this hunt to reduce a high population of white-tailed deer with a pre-hunt estimate of one deer per eight acres. They judged the ten-day hunt as particularly harassing to deer, since 21,805 hunter-hours were expended over an area of approximately 14,000 acres, thus equalling about 9.5 minutes of hunting per acre per day. Thirty-two hundred hunters observed 13,595 deer, fired 5063 shots — killing 1450 deer during the hunt, which occurred on three consecutive weekends.

During the hunt, yearling bucks moved significantly greater distances than older bucks and thus the vulnerability to harvest varied by age with 1.5- and 2.5-year-old males being the most susceptible. Indeed, during the first three days of the hunt, especially opening day, hunters killed bucks in the 1.5- and 2.5-year-old class at a higher rate than any other sex and age class. Apparently, older bucks (3.5 years and older) learned from past experience; or maybe the transient nature of young males merely increased their chances of confronting a hunter, since in many cases yearlings on opening day occupy relatively unfamiliar territories as opposed to older bucks already well-established in permanent and familiar ranges.

Autry noted that after the hunt began, movements of bucks decreased from pre-hunt averages while movements of does increased. The mean distance between the last pre-hunt locations and the first post-hunt locations of bucks surviving the hunt

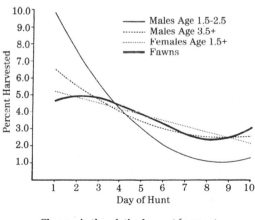

Changes in the relative harvest (percentage of available deer per 1,000 man-hours) of various sex-age classes with time.

Reprinted from J.L. Roseberry and W.D. Klimstra. 1974. "Differential Vulnerability During a Controlled Deer Harvest." Journal of Wildlife Management *38(3):499-507.*

averaged 0.57 miles. Interestingly enough, those bucks that remained more sedentary, tended to survive; intensive hunting seemed to restrict their mobility. On the other hand, the average distance between the pre-hunt centers of activity and the harvest-locations of non-surviving bucks approximated 1.92 miles. Those bucks that held tight and maintained their range fidelity tended to survive. Autry recalls how he walked through one section of the research area following the hunt and noticed a 5.5-year-old buck in his bed. The buck allowed him to walk past within a distance of twenty-three feet without taking flight. "Upon the return of two investigators about one hour and twenty minutes later, the buck remained in the same position but flushed when approached within twenty feet."

On the basis of 1200 observations of 147

marked deer before, during and after the hunt, Autry concluded that most of the deer remained in or very near their normal areas of activity and that they did not move into unhunted areas in any significant numbers. They responded to hunting pressure by hiding and decreasing daytime activity rather than utilizing unfamiliar areas; they became wary, inactive, and nocturnal. "The impression that harassed deer concentrate in remote, unhunted areas not a part of their normal home ranges was erroneous and efforts to transport hunters into such areas on that notion were unjustified." Hunters saw fewer deer each day of the hunt due to the interaction of daily harvest and wariness. Wariness increased about two to four times, remaining almost constant after the first day of the hunt. Autry ultimately concluded that the spatial distribution of deer

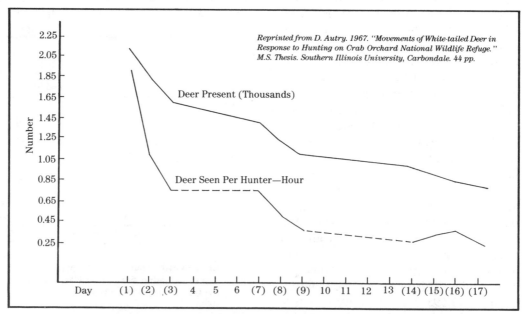

Reprinted from D. Autry. 1967. "Movements of White-tailed Deer in Response to Hunting on Crab Orchard National Wildlife Refuge." M.S. Thesis. Southern Illinois University, Carbondale. 44 pp.

The inactivity and wariness of deer during a ten-day controlled deer hunt on the Crab Orchard National Wildlife Refuge in southern Illinois. Numbers in parentheses indicate the days of the hunt. The gradual increase in deer seen during the closing days of the hunt occurred as a result of several supervised deer drives.

in general and bucks in particular apparently changes little during an intensive hunt.

Bucks that survive several hunting seasons become more elusive and warier than younger deer. While analyzing harvest data in New York, deer biologist Bill Severinghaus concluded that yearling males are initially less wary than older bucks, although the difference becomes negligible after opening day; apparently yearling bucks learn the characteristics of wariness quite rapidly. After studying the fall movements of deer in the Catskill and Adirondack regions, Severinghaus reports that older bucks are less vulnerable because of superior wariness. "Where hunting pressure is heavy, bucks are driven into the more inaccessible areas—either high mountain tops or regions of dense cover such as afforded by the extensive blowdown areas in the Adirondacks. Only those who have hunted such dense or inaccessible areas realize how difficult it is to move deer out of such a place. Not only bucks, but does and fawns too will let a hunter pass within a few feet in such cover."

In measuring the "flight behavior" of whitetails in response to humans (i.e., the distance to which deer may be approached before they flee) in two Adirondack forests—one hunted and one unhunted—researchers at the Huntington Wildlife Forest Station in northern New York observed that the flight distances of bucks were significantly longer on the hunted area: antlered deer on the hunted area maintained twice the flight distance as did bucks on the non-hunted area—fifty-eight yards versus thirty yards. Furthermore, bucks on the hunted area were more likely to run than walk when disturbed and more frequently snorted in response to the distur-

bance. Bucks on the unhunted area ran with their tails up more often than did their counterparts on the hunted area.

According to Don Behrend, the principal investigator of this study, "The less frequent tail-up flight behavior by antlered deer on the hunted area indicates wariness, for keeping their tail down proves valuable for hunted deer by rendering it more difficult to follow in flight." Like Severinghaus, Behrend found yearling bucks to be the least wary of all deer, and that during the hunting season mature bucks maintain very long flight distances and in many cases individuals with the longest flight distances, i.e., the wariest bucks, are never even seen by hunters. In many instances the beginning of the deer hunting season cuts into the rut like a catastrophic storm with mature bucks suddenly stepping up their flight distances. The harder you hunt them, the greater their flight distance; the more you subject them to hunting pressure, the more they run with their tails down.

In his study of the flight distances of whitetails, Behrend often approached deer more closely by vehicle than by foot. Other studies also show that deer become more frightened by the approach of the silent cross-country skier than by noisy snowmobiles. Other researchers indicate that they can more readily approach whitetails on horseback without causing much flight or disturbance, especially in areas where deer are not hunted on horseback. The results of Behrend's study support the hypothesis that the response of bucks to hunters is greatly modified by experience. According to the study, deer learn the objects of their fear anew from generation to generation.

White-tailed bucks are very good at learning; they adjust themselves on the basis of previous experience and remain highly sensitive to hunter disturbances of any kind. The older they get, the more they seem to restrict their movement to areas near escape terrain and heavy cover. They also specialize in detecting danger at great distances by means of their large ears and excellent nose and depart from their core area while you remain a great distance from them. On the other hand, the hunter frequently experiences great difficulties in moving them from their chosen core area or hidden sanctuary.

For example, with a hunter density of one hunter per 9.9 acres (sixty-five per square mile) on the Clark Hill Wildlife Management Area in the Piedmont section of Georgia, hunters failed to force white-tailed deer to leave their home ranges; the study area consisted of oak ridges interspersed with mature pine

stands that contained one deer per twelve acres. Using telemetric equipment, A. D. Marshall and R. W. Whittington, researchers with the Georgia Game and Fish Commission, found that radio-tagged deer remained within their telemetrically determined home range when subjected to heavy hunting pressure by archers and firearms hunters. In general, deer movement increased as hunting pressure increased but that movement occurred in a more restricted area. These researchers concluded that an absence of understory vegetation on the study area forced deer to move as hunting pressure increased; they indicated that a hunter density of five hunters per 100 acres (thirty-two per square mile) sufficed to move deer on areas containing sparse understory.

Marshall and Whittington focused in

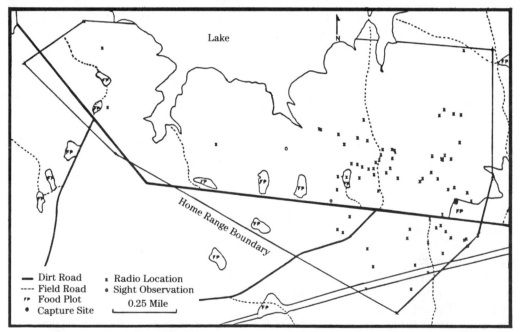

Lake

Home Range Boundary

— Dirt Road   x Radio Location
---- Field Road   • Sight Observation
🐾 Food Plot
• Capture Site   0.25 Mile

The 360-acre home range of Buck Number Three between October 12 and November 1 and between November 13 and November 18.

Reprinted from A.D. Marshall and R. W. Whittington. 1968. "A Telemetric Study of Deer Home Ranges and Behavior of Deer During Managed Hunts." Proceedings of the Southeastern Association of Game and Fish Commissioners *22:30-47.*

on a 1.5-year-old buck, Buck Number Three, and his response and behavior during periods of heavy hunting pressure. His home range approximated 360 acres. It was linear in shape and orientated in an east-west direction. In radio tracking him, researchers found that this yearling buck moved more than any other deer they studied. He usually traveled from one to 1.5 miles over a twenty-four hour period. Prior to the archery hunt he usually traveled in a circular manner during daytime hours, but traveled in a more linear pattern during the hunt. Heavy hunting pressure did not force this buck to leave its home range; he continually sought moderately dense understory and tended to become sedentary. Hunters eventually killed Buck Number Three on the fourth day of the hunt on the western boundary of his home range.

Other studies as well indicate that hunting disturbances seldom drive deer from their home range. While studying blacktails in the north coast ranges of California, Raymond Dasmann, a professor of zoology at the University of California, observed that the daily travels of bucks during the hunting season frequently become restricted to a small area not more than 100 yards across; they will remain for days in a small brush patch if need be. According to Dasmann, "Intensive hunting seems to restrict the mobility of deer. They find good cover and hide there. We attempted to drive deer from their home ranges using dogs, but were unable to do so . . . Each deer tends to escape by circling around and seeking patches of heavy cover within its home range. After the initial surprise, deer tend to adjust their feeding activities so that less time is spent in the open. Mature bucks, in particular, tend to stay close to dense cover, and resist

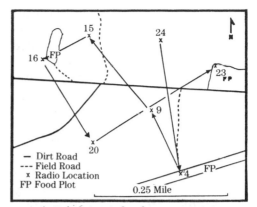

A typical twenty-four-hour movement pattern of Buck Number Three on 16 November 1967. He usually traveled between one and 1.5 miles in a twenty-four-hour period.

Reprinted from A.D. Marshall and R.W. Whittington. 1968. "A Telemetric Study of Deer Home Ranges and Behavior of Deer During Managed Hunts." Proceedings of the Southeastern Association of Game and Fish Commissioners 22:30-47.

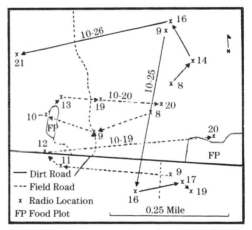

This map shows the normal daytime movement patterns of Buck Number Three on October 19 and 20 (broken line) and the daytime movement patterns during an archery hunt on October 25 and 26 (solid line). Numbers adjacent to radio locations are the hours (based on twenty-four-hour clock) during which the animal was located.

Reprinted from A.D. Marshall and R.W. Whittington. 1968. "A Telemetric Study of Deer Home Ranges and Behavior of Deer During Managed Hunts." Proceedings of the Southeastern Association of Game and Fish Commissioners 22:30-47.

the usual impulse to jump and run when a hunter or dog passes by. This may create the impression that the deer have deserted the area; but this has not been found to occur. Thus far, we have found no cases where disturbances by hunters or dogs have forced deer from their usual home range."

While studying the escape behavior of radio-tagged whitetails from hunting dogs in the mountainous habitat of North Carolina, deer hunter/biologist Larry Marchinton noted, unlike Dasmann's findings, that while deer could be forced out of their home ranges by intensive dogging, they usually returned in one day or less. In mountainous habitat they most frequently employed long-distance running. A typical chase, according to Marchinton, "consisted of a deer being jumped from its bed on a ridge and running a short distance uphill. After a few minutes, however, the animal usually turned and ran a relatively straight course downhill, crossing and paralleling streams. The chase often ended with the deer escaping in the relatively level terrain of stream valleys at lower elevations. Chases . . . revealed that certain escape routes were used repeatedly. These routes were most evident at points where they intersected roads and after a few chases it was possible to predict where the chase would cross. There was an apparent tendency for animals jumped anywhere within a watershed to use the same route when moving down into the valleys.

"An interesting aspect of escape behavior was that the deer often continued to travel for considerable distance in a direction away from the home range after the hounds lost the trail. The straight line distances moved from the point where the dogs lost the trail ranged from zero to 2.28

miles and averaged 0.71 miles in fifteen chases in which data were available."

Marchinton also monitored the responses of radio-tagged whitetails chased by hunting dogs in the south-eastern coastal plain environments of Alabama, Florida, and South Carolina. The chases averaged thirty-three minutes in duration and 2.4 miles in distance with maximums of 155 minutes and 13.4 miles. The deer responded to this type of hunting pressure by exhibiting five distinctive types of escape behavior: (1) Some held tight and remained bedded in dense cover, allowing the dogs to approach within ten feet; (2) Others, especially adult bucks, ran in a relatively straight line for a long distance, quickly exiting their home range with high speed and great endurance; (3) Others, especially does and fawns, took flight and ran in a complicated, zigzag, circuitous pattern, making brief stops at frequent intervals; (4) When grouped with other deer, some immediately separated from them, and; (5) Some deer sought water and repeatedly ran through streams, while others sought habitat escape in marshes and deepwater swamp areas.

While studying the movement patterns of deer and monitoring their escape behavior during an archery hunt in a 2322-acre enclosure at the Radford Army Ammunition Plant in Virginia, deer biologist Robert Downing reported that two-thirds of the deer studied moved out of their normal home ranges as a result of intensive hunting pressure. The harassment was intense: the habitat consisted of mostly rolling, open grassland, with scattered clumps of hardwood, cedar, and young pine plantations. During the hunt, bow hunters virtually occupied every clump of trees while hunters stalked the deer in the open as well. But again, all surviving deer returned to their normal home ranges after the hunt.

In a similar study of the movement patterns of white-tailed deer in eastern South Dakota along a fifteen-mile stretch of the Big Sioux River, Rollin Sparrowe and Paul Springer, wildlife researchers with the South Dakota Cooperative Wildlife Research Unit, concluded that hunting influenced deer movements and distribution more than any other factor. One yearling buck in their study, strongly influenced by hunter disturbances, ranged over a forty-seven-square-mile area. Archers in this study drove many deer out of marshes and wooded areas and broke up their breeding groups. Intensive hunting pressure caused one yearling buck to move seven miles from his summer range. Aerial surveys indicated that deer responded to the presence of archers by moving out of heavy cover into soil bank fields and cornfields during the day; spotlight surveys revealed that the deer returned to the marshes and river bottoms at night.

Rifle hunters also strongly affected deer distribution and movements. Driving marshes and river bottoms, gun hunters chased deer across open land for several miles. These deer, when pursued in this manner, according to Sparrowe and Springer, "stayed in the open fields where they could observe attempts to approach them. Aerial surveys showed that many areas occupied by numerous deer before the rifle season were devoid of deer after the first weekend." In monitoring the responses of individual deer to the hunters, these researchers observed that in one case hunters dispersed a herd of twenty-four deer; they located individuals from that herd ten miles away less than a month later.

But these situations of white-tailed deer roaming great distances in response to hunting pressure seem to be more the exception than the rule. This is not to suggest that white-tailed bucks will not travel great distances, especially when trapped and translocated to other areas. For example, Guy Colbath, a deer trapper for the Texas Game & Fish Commission, reports that a white-tailed buck released near Sheffield in Pecos County made its way back to the Aransas Wildlife Refuge in Aransas County, where Colbath trapped it a second time, thus traveling a distance of approximately 350 airline miles. But such record treks remain the exception.

In many situations deer simply remain unwilling to move, period. In his study of deer movements and hunting pressure on the Crab Orchard National Wildlife Refuge, mentioned earlier, Autry recalled what happened when he observed a deer for a two-hour period with a 30X spotting scope from a distance of 260 yards. "During the period of observation and at a distance of 300 yards, hunters were making considerable noise; they fired eleven shots within 250 yards of the deer. Despite all these disturbances, the deer remained bedded, faced away from the hunters except for once when it stood for about four minutes, obscured from the hunters by brush. It then pivoted 180 degrees, stared at the hunters for around two minutes, turned and bedded down, still facing away from the hunters; the animal seemed alert but undisturbed."

As a short-term adjustment to hunting pressure, white-tailed bucks, instead of shifting their home ranges, tend to become nocturnal and very wary, moving into cover earlier in the morning than does and leaving it later at dusk. Whereas does become more active when heavily hunted, bucks become less active. While does and fawns tend to circle back and use confusion-tactics after being jumped, bucks tend to remain rigid, silent and hide; they bolt, if need be, with a fast, flashy start-up, running longer distances than does before resuming a slow, sneaky, circular movement pattern, as frequently evidenced in detailed maps of wounded buck behavior. Their hiding strategy and explosive eruptions from concealment to galloping off low to the ground turn many pot-hunters into buck hunters, myself included.

Their escape is often triggered not by our appearance but by our disappearance: They will allow us to walk by and will sneak out behind us with great evasive maneuvers. Indeed, more and more telemetry studies suggest that mature white-tailed bucks remain especially prone to stay in their beds and allow the hunter to pass within a few feet without flushing. When badly frightened by hunters, however, instead of skulking they will bolt off at speeds of thirty to forty miles per hour and often run a relatively straight course; then stop once they gain distance and cover. In doing so, they reorient themselves to the hunter and in the process deprive the hunter of information of their whereabouts. In other instances, bucks will run a circuitous zigzag pattern, frequently crossing their own trails. Others will swim through water to avoid you, as well as submerge themselves in water under ditch banks with only their eyes and nose above the surface.

A classic example of these evasive tactics and Houdini-like disappearances occurred during a controlled deer hunt on the Holly Shelter Refuge in Pender County, North Carolina, when even the most tenacious efforts of well-trained deerhounds lost a hot buck trail. Fred Barkalow, a researcher at North Carolina State College of Agriculture and Engineering in Raleigh, recalls what happened and how white-tailed bucks will even exhibit skulking behavior while hiding in water:

"Three hounds started a young buck outside of the refuge and had been trailing it about thirty minutes before it entered the refuge and thick bay some two miles from our stand. The deer doubled back a number of times in the wet bay but was unable to escape. After almost an hour and a half of trailing, the dogs began to overtake the deer. Coming down-wind, it plunged into the water, swam the ditch and climbed out on the opposite bank. The young buck was obviously nearing exhaustion, but on sighting one of us only six feet away, it again crossed the ditch and backtracked rapidly for approximately two hundred yards. It veered sharply toward the ditch and was lost to sight. The hounds were less than five minutes behind it when they reached the initial crossing site. One of them quickly discovered the back-track and all tore off at full cry. On reaching the point where the trail again entered the ditch, they lost it instantly. After trying for several minutes to pick up the scent on both sides of the ditch, the dogs gave up.

"Some thirty minutes later, my hunting partner, Walt Keller, who had remained at his stand, noticed waves coming from beneath the overhanging bank. On investigating, he discovered the deer, completely submerged with the exception of its nostrils, forehead and eyes. Even the tips of the ears were laid back along the neck and submerged. Apparently, the deer made no effort to escape even though the dogs were

Some bucks will swim through water to avoid hunters, as well as submerge themselves in water under ditch banks with only their eyes and nose above the surface. *Photo credit Leonard Lee Rue III*

within a few feet of it. It also remained perfectly still while it was under observation. After some sticks were thrown in its direction, the deer came out on the bank, shook itself and trotted off . . . It preferred to skulk in the icy water under the bank rather than to continue attempting to escape by flight."

Indeed, white-tailed bucks with their hunter-avoidance strategies and tactics manage to successfully survive intensive hunting pressure as well as any big-game species on the North American continent and probably as well as any animal in the world. In addition to these evasive strategies and tactics, white-tailed bucks add a certain amount of unpredictability to their daily whereabouts, making it impossible

to predict accurately from day to day, or hour to hour, where a given individual buck will be, especially during the rut, when wandering bucks make many directional changes in their movement patterns. At this time, they seem easily distracted and oscillate between feeding, chasing does, and investigating breeding signs made by other bucks. During the rut, they will literally engage in random running while constantly shifting their locations so that no predictable pattern emerges; the unpredictable manner of the bucks now becomes their only constant characteristic.

While studying the movement patterns of live-trapped, radio-tagged, white-tailed does during the rut in Clarke County, Alabama, Keith Causey of Auburn University

White-tailed bucks with their hunter-avoidance strategies and tactics manage to successfully survive intensive hunting pressure as well as any big-game species on the North American continent. *Photo credit Leonard Lee Rue III*

observed an increase in activity but a decrease in movement. According to Causey, "The general pattern of movement during the rut changed from relatively long linear movements during pre-rut and post-rut to repeated crisscrossing movements of shorter magnitude within restricted areas." The average minimum home ranges of the does in Causey's study decreased progressively from 168 acres during the pre-rut period to 155 acres during the rut to 143 acres during the post-rut period. The does also significantly restricted their bedding areas as well from that of the pre-rut and post-rut period:

during the rut their minimum bedding areas averaged fifty-four acres. Pre-rut and post-rut minimum bedding areas were sixty-nine and sixty-four acres, respectively.

While the does increased their activity but with minimal and restricted movement, Causey's telemetry studies indicated that rutting, adult bucks frequently moved outside their previously established home ranges during the rut in search of receptive does. Their average home ranges during the rut approximated 425 acres; their pre-rut and post-rut minimum home ranges averaged 205 acres and 185 acres, respectively. Their average minimum total distance traveled during daylight hours increased more than one mile during the rut, and the area they used during the daytime hours more than doubled during the same period when compared to the pre-rut and post-rut period.

Causey explains this interesting phenomenon of does increasing their activity but within restricted areas while bucks expand their movement in the following way: "The *concentrated* movement and increased activity of does and the *expanded* movement of bucks provides optimum conditions for the location of receptive females by rutting males. If the female responded by increased mobility, scent deposition would be less concentrated. Since a singular female may attract males several days prior to and after she reaches her period of receptiveness, high deer numbers and unbalanced male/female ratios could result in a number of females reaching receptiveness in the absence of rutting males. Large numbers of does nearing estrus in a given area could result in multiple crossing scent trails which could tend to confuse males following scent trails. By restricting movement, scent trails of different receptive does are less likely to overlap, enabling the males to locate particular estrous does."

One universal complaint frequently heard throughout deer country revolves around the notion that deer travel great distances and expand their movement patterns to escape from hunters only to vanish into the protective cover of refuges. Reports often surface in and around deer camps of bucks moving great distances into refuges as a result of hunting pressure, but in most cases the scientific evidence suggests that these reported move-

ments are within the familiar home ranges of the deer involved. Deer researchers in various parts of the country (Minnesota, Wisconsin, Oklahoma, Georgia, and Iowa), set out to examine the relationship between hunting pressure and the use of refuges by white-tailed deer. Although their results sometimes conflict with one another, they are interesting nonetheless.

A low hunter success in conjunction with a high deer population prompted deer researchers at Oklahoma State University to conduct a two-year study to test the hypothesis that whitetails moved to an adjacent refuge during the hunting season. After radio tagging five bucks and fourteen does and studying their movements during the hunting season on the Fort Sill Military Reservation in southwestern Oklahoma, researchers concluded that although their daytime use areas increased dramatically — pre-season daytime use areas for bucks averaged 153 acres while hunting season daytime use areas approximated 468 acres — significant numbers of deer did not move to the adjacent Wichita Mountains National Wildlife Refuge during the hunting season. They attributed the discrepancy between a low hunter success and the high deer population to low vulnerability due to use of extensive blackjack-post oak cover type during the day.

Other research, however, reveals that whitetails will move to wildlife refuges during the hunting season. While studying the movements of deer in response to hunting pressure in the open farming country of Iowa, Michael Zagata, a wildlife biologist, observed deer moving up to one mile through croplands to reach the security of a refuge (Pilot Knob State Park) when harassed by hunters. He also observed wounded deer, in particular, moving toward the refuge. Bucks in his study exhibited the greatest variation in movement, with home ranges varying from forty-nine to 504 acres; their major axes varied from .62 to 1.9 miles with a minimum daily movement of .50 to 1.25 miles. Most bucks maintained a northwest-southeast home range orientation. According to Zagata, "Their escape movement varied with topographic and vegetative conditions. During the day, if deer were disturbed in timber patches, they usually fled into open cropland where they could more easily observe their surroundings. Although they demonstrated a reluctance to return to timber, they eventually did . . . It is difficult to determine what evokes a particular flight pattern as deer in similar situations react differently."

In studying the reactions of radio-monitored deer in relation to a refuge and a hunted area in northwestern Georgia, Kent Kammermeyer, a wildlife biologist with the Georgia Game and Fish Division, observed a seasonal, short-range migration of a large contingent of deer into a refuge with the opening of hunting season. He concluded that after substantial population expansions, some deer may develop a tradition of returning annually to a refuge to escape hunting harassment, and that inadequate harvests and overpopulations often result when whitetails move freely between contiguous refuges and hunted areas. According to Kammermeyer, "Variations in movement patterns indicate that habitat conditions, juxtaposition of refuge areas and the past history of hunting all play roles in the deer's response to heavy hunting pressure."

Marked changes, however, in the movement patterns and behavior of refuge bucks coincident with the beginning of the rut can actually work in the hunter's favor. While studying nineteen radio-tagged bucks in the Berry College Refuge in Floyd County near Rome, Georgia, Kammermeyer noticed how one buck, in particular, enlarged his range from 228 to 603 acres in a six-week period. This type of increased and unpredictable activity of bucks led to a thirty-two percent rate of buck dispersal from the refuge. These dispersal movements in Kammermeyer's study averaged 2.7 miles and ranged from 1.5 to 4.75 miles. These dispersals actually added a considerable number of bucks to the legal kill outside of the refuge.

With funding from the Pope and Young Club and the Minnesota State Archery Association, Dennis Simon, a wildlife researcher with the Minnesota Department of Natural Resources, set out to examine the effect of isolated refuges on deer behavior in heavily hunted regions. His radio-telemetry study entitled "Density, Migration and Mortality Patterns of White-tailed Deer using a Sanctuary in Southeastern Minnesota" (April 1986), supports the hypothesis that hunting pressure, harassment, and hunter selection can create migratory behavior among whitetailed deer.

In his study, most of the forty-eight radio-tagged does were in the refuge before the gun hunting season ever started, traveling an average distance of 6.8 miles to get there. But nearly all male progeny produced from this population dispersed from the refuge when 1.5 to two years old, and hunters harvested these bucks at high rates within the boundaries of public hunting areas.

"This pattern of buck dispersal and heavy mortality of yearling males," Simon believes, "indicates that refuges probably play little if any role in producing a higher than average number of older, trophy, white-tailed bucks for harvest."

To learn more about the activities and movements of adult white-tailed bucks during the deer hunting season in Mississippi, Harry Jacobson, a wildlife professor at Mississippi State and an avid bow hunter and blackpowder enthusiast, placed radio collars on twenty-eight white-tailed bucks. Hunting season home ranges for yearling bucks averaged 3737 acres compared to an average of 2618 acres for two-year-old bucks or older. Their home ranges tended to be elliptical in shape with the major and minor axis averaging 4.2 and 3.9 miles, respectively. The sizes of these home ranges greatly exceed those previously reported in the literature, due undoubtedly to the periodic flooding that occurred over large portions of their habitat.

The activity patterns of these bucks indicated a crepuscular activity cycle, with the greatest daytime activity during the hours of sunrise and sunset with a slight increase at midday. During each daytime observation of eleven bucks, Jacobson and his student, Kevin Herriman, recorded the number of hunters in the woods to determine the effect, if any, of hunter density on buck activity. They divided hunter density into three groups: (1) none; (2) one to ten hunters, and; (3) eleven to forty hunters. A cross-tabulation of deer activity with hunter density indicated an increase in the percentage of buck activity from 38 percent to 70 percent with one or more hunters in the woods.

Jacobson and his students quickly learned about the incredible ability of mature bucks to survive heavy hunting pressure. They radio tagged several bucks on a

private hunting club, a club that protects its deer by controlling hunting pressure. All of the bucks were killed during the next season. They then collared six bucks on a heavily hunted public area. All of them survived the next hunting season. In other words, whereas Jacobson and his students couldn't get one buck to survive the hunting season on a managed area with controls on hunting pressure, all six of their collared bucks survived in a heavily hunted public area without restrictions on hunting pressure. It's no surprise that some trophy hunters prefer to hunt on public land.

At the Ninth Annual Southeast Deer Study Group Meeting in Gatlinburg, Tennessee, in March of 1986, Steve Demarais of Texas Tech University, like Jacobson, also reported very large home ranges for white-tailed bucks between the ages of 3.5 and 7.5 years old. After radio tagging nine adult males in southern Texas, he estimated their average home ranges at 3363 acres, ranging from 790 to 9701 acres. The

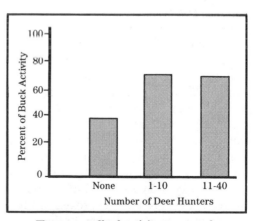

The percent of buck activity corresponding to the different levels of hunter density.

Reprinted from K. Herriman. 1983. "Hunting Season Movements of Male White-tailed Deer on Davis Island." M.S. Thesis. Mississippi State University, Mississippi State. 67 pp.

greatest movement occurred between 6:00 and 9:00 a.m. and between 6:00 and 9:00 p.m. While the age of these bucks may play an important role in these large movement patterns, the reasons for these extremely large home ranges still remain under investigation. Like Jacobson, Demarais found these home ranges to be elliptical in shape. Three of these bucks shifted their core area of activity within their home ranges throughout the year; six did not.

As a result of more and more radio telemetry studies nationwide focusing on buck movements and home ranges, deer researchers now know more about the internal anatomy of the buck's home range, especially his core area of activity. Deer researchers at Auburn University in Alabama, for example, report that in most cases instrumented bucks reveal smaller areas within their home ranges that contain most of the radio locations during a given time period. These core areas remain well defined and bucks seldom stay away from these activity centers for extended periods of time. These core areas, however, do shift from time to time in relationship to changing food supplies.

According to Art Hosey, a wildlife researcher from Auburn University who often lived with bucks for twenty-four straight hours at a time, bucks usually place these core areas at the end of their ranges or very near the end. While buck home ranges overlap, their core areas do not. Hosey found that one buck had two core areas, one at each end of his home range. These core areas approximated ten to fifteen acres of heavy brush; they usually contained a main entrance and exit, with optional runways for quick Houdini-like disappearances.

For the past decade (1975–1986), Professor James Kroll, an avid trophy hunter, and his students in the forestry department at Stephen F. Austin University have relentlessly tracked the movements of radio-tagged bucks on the North Boggy Slough Hunting and Fishing Club, located north of Houston, Texas, resulting in one of the nation's longest-running telemetry studies. Surrounded by an eight-foot fence, North Boggy Slough contains approximately 6000 acres of pure pine, mixed pine-hardwood, and bottomland hardwood stands with an average deer density of one deer per fifteen acres (forty-three per square mile, a 1979 estimate). While studying habitat selection and identifying core areas of whitetails, Kroll and his student, Randy Tucker, characterized core areas as frequently being part of younger stands of timber and often located near habitat edges. They found that core areas in spring occurred most frequently in upland sites with lower, overstory pines, while deer preferred core areas in the summertime near the banks of rivers, ponds, and small lakes.

During one season in this experimental area, Kroll allowed deer hunting for three days a week. As expected, the deer became less predictable and more erratic in their movements, but they stayed within their normal home ranges. The following year, the "deer doctor" prescribed hunting for every day of the season. Many deer responded by jumping the eight-foot fence to escape the relentless hunting pressure. Within six weeks after the close of the season, Kroll found the deer gradually drifting back into their home range. According to Kroll, "As soon as hunting begins, deer movements become very erratic. Deer become more secretive when they're hunted, staying closer to thick cover. They become more nocturnal. We've found that deer will tolerate a certain amount of hunting pressure, but once it reaches a critical point, they'll simply leave the area, even if it means abandoning their entire home range." Radio collars demonstrated that some of the bucks in Kroll's study traveled up to fourteen miles to avoid hunters, returning long after the season ended.

When hunting pressure becomes extremely intense, trophy bucks have two choices: (1) vacate the area, or (2) retreat to the heaviest and nastiest cover available in their home ranges. From his radio-tracking studies on hunted bucks, Kroll believes that many trophy deer completely abandon their home range until the season is over; returning only when the gunfire stops. Others, however, retreat to undisturbed sanctuaries in the thick cover (not to be confused with refuges), and move primarily along safe travel corridors between these hidden and inaccessible "buck sanctuaries." In Kroll's study area, trophy bucks preferred dense pockets of pine saplings for their sanctuaries. These dense thickets virtually excluded the hunters from entering them. Mature bucks only left them under the cover of darkness. The trick obviously becomes locating these hidden sanctuaries and hunting them successfully.

Human dimensions researchers report that the majority of deer hunters on public and private land place their deer stands less than 1500 feet from permanent roads and thus lessen their chances of seeing buck movements of any kind, for mature bucks quickly learn to avoid lines of newly erected tree stands. Kroll also found this to be the case in the Pineywoods of East Texas. "Deer are creatures of habits," Kroll explained in an interview with a reporter from the *Dallas Times Herald.* "They spend a lot of time exploring their home range, becoming very familiar with the terrain. They notice anything that's new or out of place. We've put up stands near existing game trails and had the deer create new trails to avoid the stands. Hunters think they can put up stands well before the season, and that deer will become accustomed to them. That ploy sometimes fails to work. I've seen deer look at a stand that had been in place for two years. They looked at it every time they came by, apparently checking to see if the stand was occupied."

Hunters who traditionally follow the crowd to these tree stands—hunting the same places in the same old ways—seldom see mature bucks. Buy and study aerial photos, topographic maps, and soil surveys and correlate every intricate detail of the terrain you hunt with the local hunting pressure; it will help you locate these buck sanctuaries. Avoid permanent tree stands and hunting near roads. When you do locate these sanctuaries, Kroll recommends that you never hunt them on consecutive days. Always wait several days between hunts and approach these thick areas via different routes; you need to be as devious as the bucks that use them.

Kroll also reports that "deer tend to be more active in the middle of the day. Many hunters go out before daylight and hunt until 9:30 a.m. or so. They piddle around camp in the middle of the day and then hunt again in late afternoon. A lot of deer movement occurs from 10:00 a.m. until noon. You'd be surprised how many good bucks are killed in the middle of the day, usually by pure accident."

In studying how individual bucks respond to heavy hunting pressure on the opening day of gun hunting in my area in southwestern Wisconsin, an area in which hunters kill sixty-five to eighty percent of

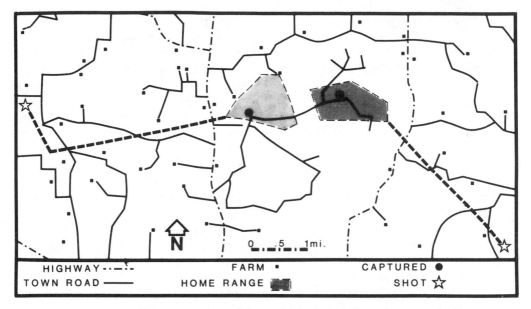

HIGHWAY ·—·—·—··   FARM ▪   CAPTURED ●
TOWN ROAD ——   HOME RANGE ▮▮▮   SHOT ☆

The gross movements of two adult bucks on opening day.

the entire season's legal buck harvest on the opening two days, my friend, Bill Ishmael, a game manager and frequent contributor to *Deer & Deer Hunting* magazine, clearly demonstrates from his radio-tagged bucks that those adult bucks that survive the opening weekend with hunter densities averaging one hunter per forty-nine acres (thirteen per square mile), do so by rarely straying from their home ranges, by holding tight to densely-wooded draws and ravines, and by running circular patterns within familiar dense cover, rather than running straight beelines into foreign territory; those that choose the latter option frequently decorate the meat pole.

Since the advent of radio telemetry in the early 1960s, thanks to the electronic wizardry of William Cochran of the Illinois Natural History Society, wildlife research biologists have amassed an incredible amount of data on deer movements

and home ranges. They have used all kinds of baits to entice bucks to trapping sites: everything from cattle range cubes to cabbage heads, from apples, alfalfa, and shelled corn to cottonseed cake and mistletoe. Yet, despite their refined tagging, trapping, and telemetry techniques, their use of Clover traps, rocket nets, Cap-Chur guns, and succinylcholine chloride, and their lengthy discussions of triangulation, range configuration, and convex polygons, escape routes, travel corridors, and buck sanctuaries, we still know very little about the movement patterns of bucks over the age of two and a half as they relate to hunting pressure and hunter density. Much of what we know comes from limited instances and small sample sizes.

We do know, however, that the posting of private land frequently creates small patches of different hunter densities and buck harvest rates within individual home ranges of deer, but little information on the movements of bucks in response to this variance exists. It is not known, for example, to what degree they use small areas of light hunting pressure or how long they might maintain altered movements resulting from high hunter densities. If altered movements occur, then harvest rates of deer in that area may be reduced. If mortality is reduced, then deer populations may increase. But we do not know whether deer will disperse from areas of this type into areas of higher harvest. Without an understanding of such movements and the resulting population dynamics, proper harvest strategies and management may not be attained.

It would be interesting to know if mature bucks return each rutting season to a constant and familiar breeding ground or whether they wander freely into unfamiliar breeding areas. It would also be valuable to know if bucks that leave the area in which they spent the first year or two of their lives regularly return to that same area when establishing social dominance. On neither of these points do we have adequate data.

Human dimensions researchers who spy on deer hunters and probe their minds and behavior report that as hunter density and pressure increase, personal satisfaction in the deer hunt generally increases as well, especially if more bucks are sighted, shot,

and bagged. While it's difficult to compare the overall satisfaction levels across different studies and geographic areas, it appears that increased levels of seeing, shooting, and bagging bucks override the negative effects of high hunter density (i.e., crowding, interpersonal conflict and poor sportsmanship), at least for most urbanite deer hunters surveyed in such states as Michigan, Maryland, and Wisconsin.

"High levels of satisfaction," as human dimensions researcher Ed Langenau of the Michigan Department of Natural Resources observes, "are attained even under extreme conditions of crowding, as long as the buck kill remains at a high level."

While compiling the data and information on what we know about buck movements and hunting pressure at the Conservation Library Center in Denver, Colorado, Art Carhart summarizes the buck hunter's dilemma: "There never will be a complete exposition of how to get your white-tailed buck. Too much depends on the buck and your own woodsmanship. One may lay a foundation for good deer hunting, but beyond that, there are individuals in bucks, individuals among men, and the results of the hunt lie in pitting wits against wits, and the will of the Red Gods of the outdoors."

Chapter 11

Buck Movements During the Rut

I have seen some very silly stuff in print about the ease with which any blockhead can kill a deer in "running time."
— T. S. Van Dyke, *The Still Hunter*, 1882

This cryptic warning remains as true today as when Van Dyke issued it more than 100 years ago, especially in light of what the chemical industry would have us believe. Today, the popular literature seems saturated and cluttered with nonsense about the ease with which bucks can be killed during the rut, or the "running time" as our forefathers called it. Apparently, all we need to do is to pick up another bottle of chemical juice No. 7C-4 and start shooting. But what do we really know about rutting bucks in the wild? What do we know about the changes in their movement patterns, home range sizes, and activity patterns? Deer researchers have asked these questions since the early 1930s. While the results of their research on buck movements during the rut, pre-rut, and post-rut periods are still incon-clusive and tentative, they nonetheless remain interesting and fascinating for the die-hard buck hunter.

Considerable interest exists among deer hunters throughout America with regard to the movement patterns of white-tailed deer, especially the movement patterns of bucks during the rut. As deer hunters, we never seem to have enough information about the sizes and shapes of the home ranges of white-tailed bucks during the rut, as well as their normal movement and activity patterns during a twenty-four-hour period. With the advent of radio telemetry in the early 1960s and the subsequent interdisciplinary cooperation in the fields of biology and electronics, deer researchers began to document very detailed information concerning buck movements during the rut.

While studying the influence of the reproductive cycle on the rutting behavior of bucks in the Southeast, Larry Marchinton, professor at the University of Georgia, detected a great deal of variation in the twenty-four-hour movement patterns of bucks during the rut. He found, for example, that one yearling buck, Eglin No. 8, increased his movement at the onset of rutting behavior and bedded less frequently and only for brief periods of time. This buck moved from one extreme end of his home range to another but did not leave his telemetrically established home range of 147 acres during the rut. In other words, Eglin No. 8 did not expand his home range but merely bedded less and moved more within his established home range. Yet, Marchinton points out in his "Telemetric Study of White-Tailed Deer Movement-Ecology and Ethology in the Southeast" (1968), that other "more physically capable bucks may very well expand their home ranges during the breeding season."

While tracking Eglin 8 for a twenty-four-hour period, Marchinton found a direct cause and effect relationship between rainy weather and reduced buck activity: during a twenty-four-hour period of light rain with relative humidity near 100 percent, Eglin 8 greatly reduced his activity.

After five intensive years of tracking whitetails with radio equipment, Marchinton reached the following conclusions

Some bucks do not expand their home range during the rut but merely bed less and move more within their established home ranges. *Photo credit Leonard Lee Rue III*

with regard to the bedding activities of whitetails: (1) You will find deer beds widely distributed over the deer's entire home range; (2) Although a great deal of variation exists, most whitetails, both bucks and does, show a marked tendency for placing daytime beds at one extreme end of their home ranges and nighttime beds at the other; (3) Some whitetails bed repeatedly in the same spot, while others rarely do so, and; (4) Practically all whitetails bed regularly in certain localities.

One late December evening, while maintaining his tracking vigil, Marchinton encountered the following display of mating behavior in an alfalfa field: "About 10:20 p.m. I was prompted by a sudden change in the radio signal to shine a spotlight into the field. The light showed three does running across the field followed by a six-pointer. In a few seconds a larger, ten-pointer appeared on the edge of the field and apparently offered a challenge to the first buck. A fight followed, but after several clashes, the smaller buck disengaged and walked off in another direction. The larger animal then started toward the group of does, which had remained calmly watching the spectacle from a distance of about 100 yards. He singled out and pursued Auburn No. 1 (a semi-wild doe Marchinton released in his study area), causing her to run wildly, dodging and jumping fences. The buck, on the contrary, seldom broke out of a trot while following. This continued for several hours with most activity centered around the alfalfa field and with a relatively small total area being encompassed. Although the doe appeared to be in frantic flight, the area covered was less than fifty acres. This agrees with the observation by Edwin D. Michael, a wildlife biologist, that does when pursued by bucks usually move in wide circles and seem reluctant to leave their regular feeding areas."

While studying the movement patterns of does pursued by bucks in the Coastal Bend area of Texas, Michael compiled rare, in-depth, numerical data on this subject, especially with regard to the meteorological factors affecting it. With the aid of forty-foot observation towers and 20X spotting scopes, he observed more than 150 marked and unmarked deer over several hundred acres. He found that the arrival of cold fronts greatly increased the frequency of pursuit. He also concluded that in most cases more than one buck pursued a doe. On one occasion, he observed eleven bucks chasing one doe; the chase consisted of large circles within the doe's regular feeding area.

"Most bucks," according to Michael, "exhibited characteristic behavioral patterns prior to chasing a doe. They stretched their necks forward, raised their noses in the air, curled back the upper lip, and gave the appearance of sniffing the air . . . After curling back their lips, bucks usually ran quickly toward the doe and gave chase . . . Bucks also gave out low bleats, pants or moans prior to or during the pursuit."

While observing the pursuit of does by bucks, Michael concluded that the hour of day was not significantly correlated with the number of bucks pursuing does. He also found no correlation between the phases of the moon and bucks chasing does. However, he did find a slight increase in the number of chases during the first and last quarters but hastened to add this only indicated "that moderate amounts of moonlight, as compared to very dark or very bright conditions, may be associated with an increase in rutting activity. This pattern, however, was not prominent and I feel that moonlight does not play an important part in mating behavior."

Michael's observations indicated that more chases occurred during periods of much-below-average temperature. He applied statistical tests to determine what effect, if any, the arrival of cold fronts had on bucks chasing does. He concluded that more chases occurred on dates that were at least six days after the arrival of a 15°F drop in temperature. Few chases occurred on dates that were seven or more days after the arrival of such a cold front. In his study, seventy-two percent of all chases occurred on dates that were six days or less after the arrival of a 15°F cold front. He also conducted statistical tests of 20°F cold fronts. He expected that more chases would be observed during the days immediately after 20°F fronts than after 15°F fronts, but this did not happen. Whereas seventy-two percent of the chases were seen within six days after a 15°F front, only thirty-two percent were seen during the same period after a 20°F front. In other words, significantly more chases occurred during the six-day period after the arrival of 15°F cold fronts.

Michael noticed that extreme drops in temperature (20°F or greater) coupled with precipitation caused a dramatic reduction in bucks chasing does. When correlating cloud cover with the number of bucks pursuing does, he reported that the greatest activity occurred with a cloud cover of from eighty to 100 percent. Increased wind speeds also increased the chasing of does. The greatest number of chases took place with wind speeds of 14 m.p.h. or more.

While Michael observed the pursuit of does by white-tailed bucks in Texas, and Marchinton studied the movement patterns of whitetails in Florida, Alabama, and Georgia, Robert Downing and other researchers conducted a six-year study (1967–71) of the seasonal changes in the movements of white-tailed deer in a 2322-acre enclosure at the Radford Army Ammunition Plant in Dublin, Virginia. Downing and his associates marked more than 100 bucks with streamers of plastic tape affixed to aluminum ear tags and studied their movement patterns during the breeding season.

Like Michael and Marchinton, Downing noted striking changes in buck movements during the rut. Almost forty percent of the yearling bucks moved outside their normal home ranges during the rut, but none moved as far as three-quarters of a mile from their established center of activity. Sixty percent of the 2.5-year-old bucks moved outside of their normal ranges, with thirty percent of them moving more than three-quarters of a mile. Does in this Virginia study did not move outside their home ranges during the rut. No permanent changes in home ranges resulted from the rutting movements of either sex. However, Downing observed one 3.5-year-old buck three times during a two-week period during the rut more than one mile from his normal core area. Downing's findings, based on direct observations of free-ranging, individually marked bucks, seem to suggest that greater buck movement occurs with increased age. But whether older and more mature bucks travel greater distances than yearling bucks during the rut or vice versa remains a greatly debated, but unanswered question.

Long-distance movements of bucks during the rut were impossible in the Radford enclosure, which measured only 1.9

The percentage of white-tailed bucks moving one-half to one mile or more from their center of activity for each month of their lives.
Reprinted from Robert Downing, B.S. McGinnes, R.L. Petcher and J.L. Sandt. 1969. "Seasonal Changes in Movements of White-tailed Deer." Proceedings of the Symposium on White-tailed Deer in the Southern Forest Habitat, U.S. Forest Experiment Station, Nacogdoches, Texas. pp. 19-24.

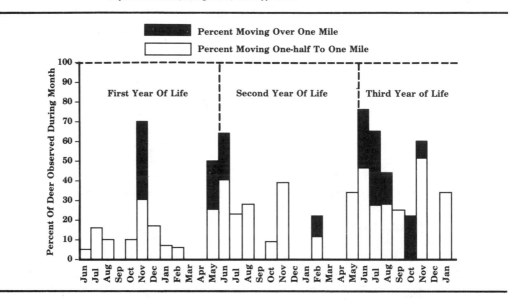

by 2.7 miles. Other researchers across the country, however, report greater distances for buck-roamings during the rut. March-inton, for example, observed one buck near Athens, Georgia, move three miles outside his normal home range during the rut. John Ellisor, a deer researcher with the Texas Parks and Wildlife Department, reported that a buck moved 2.6 miles between observations during the breeding season in the brush habitat of southern Texas. David Urbston, while working as a researcher at the Savannah River Project in South Carolina, also noted that hunters killed a buck, tagged as a fawn in May of 1967, 14.5 miles distant in November of 1968.

In 1976 Kent Kammermeyer and Larry Marchinton described extensive dispersals of competitive, breeding-age white-tailed bucks. They defined dispersals as "long-range movements without return to previously established home ranges of breeding-age bucks." While radio tracking white-tailed bucks in northwestern Georgia, they observed major increases in buck movements at the onset of the rut in early November. Buck No. 11B, for example, enlarged his range from 228 to 603 acres in a six-week period during the rut. The home range of this buck overlapped the home ranges of four other radio-tagged bucks. According to Kammermeyer, "several other bucks, including a large dominant male, also resided in this area. The amount of range overlap suggested a potential for intense breeding competition with three of the radio-monitored bucks and probably a fourth dispersing during the early part of the rut . . . Most long-range movements were made during the rutting season by 1.5- and 2.5-year-old bucks that were of breeding age but apparently participated little in breeding because of their subordinate social status. Therefore, sexual competition among bucks occupying the same habitat was probably the main stimulus for dispersal."

Of the nineteen bucks Kammermeyer and Marchinton tagged or radio collared, at least six (thirty-two percent) dispersed from their home ranges. Their movements averaged 2.7 miles and ranged from 1.5 miles to 4.75 miles. If we consider only the 1.5- and 2.5-year-olds in their study, five of ten (fifty percent) made long-range movements during the rut.

While studying the movements of eight unhunted white-tailed bucks with telemetric devices in southwest Alabama, Keith Guyse, a deer researcher at Auburn University, found that the home ranges averaged 679.5 acres for five bucks during the pre-rut, 469.5 acres for six bucks during the rut, and 432.4 acres for five bucks during the post-rut. In other words, for unhunted bucks on the Stimpson Sanctuary in Clarke County, the actual sizes of their home ranges *decreased* during the rut. The minimum distances moved during a twenty-four hour period averaged 2.9 miles for five bucks during the pre-rut, 3.0 miles for six bucks during the rut, and 2.4 miles for four bucks during the post-rut.

In his study, Guyse reported that the home ranges of most of these bucks contained smaller activity centers but that no well-defined pattern existed for their bedding sites during the rut. These bucks spent little time seeking preferred bedding sites. Guyse noted, however, that their activity pattern increased from fifty-eight percent during the pre-rut, to sixty-eight percent during the rut, and to seventy per-

cent for the post-rut, but that these increases were not significant. He defined his study period in the following way: pre-rut (September 24 to December 31), rut (January 1 to March 1), and post-rut (March 2 to May 10).

During the later part of November and early December, a heavy acorn drop occurred in one part of Guyse's research area. An examination of his telemetry data revealed that none of the five instrumented bucks near that area had been there before the acorn drop. But four of the five bucks near the acorns immediately increased their home range to include that area. Not only does acorn production affect buck movements during the rut but it also seems to have a direct bearing on the number of buck rubs we find: The greater the acorn production, the greater the number of rubs per acre.

Overall, Guyse concluded that the eight bucks he followed with radio transmitters did not significantly increase their home range size, activity, or distance moved in a day's time during the rut. This unusual conclusion, which conflicts with much of the literature, may be explained by the fact that these bucks were not being subjected to hunting pressure. The high population density in his study may have been another factor, for the average size of a buck's home range appears to decrease as the population increases. Density-related social behavior may also have affected Guyse's conclusion, for as the size of the home range increases the number of individuals a buck competes with for his position in the dominance order also increases. The bucks Guyse followed may have limited their movements to an area whose size facilitated an acceptable level of social pressure.

On several occasions, Guyse encoun-

A twenty-four hour movement pattern for white-tailed buck
number eight as determined by radio telemetry locations taken
on October 16 and 17 on the Fred T. Stimpson Sanctuary in Clarke
County, Alabama. The time for each location is indicated. The buck
travelled a total minimum distance of 2.5 miles.

*Reprinted from K. Guyse. 1978. "Activity and Behavior of Unhunted White-tailed
Deer Bucks During the Rut in Southwest Alabama." M.S. Thesis. Auburn University, Auburn, Alabama. 134pp.*

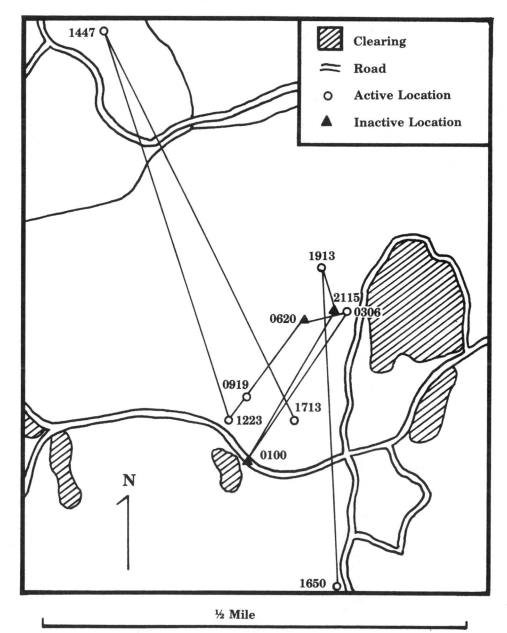

The aggressive sidling approach of an angry white-tailed buck. *Photo credit Leonard Lee Rue III*

tered bucks behaving in a manner he termed "highly active." For example: "At 3:10 p.m. on January 21, the investigator was watching a twenty-five-acre field with about forty deer in view. A large, seven-point buck entered the field alone and threatened an eight-point buck with a sidle. The eight-pointer turned away and continued to feed. The seven-pointer began moving about the field, chasing all does and threatening all bucks. During the next hour, he covered the field two or three times and encountered almost all of the deer at least once and many of them two or three times. All other deer retreated at his advance including three large, eight-pointers. At one point, he stopped and urinated over his tarsal glands while rubbing them together. Later,

he rubbed his antlers on a small shrub at the edge of the field, smelled an overhanging limb, bit part of it off and pawed the ground beneath it. At the end of an hour, he slowed down and started feeding but he still made occasional advances at does until the investigator left forty-five minutes later.

"At 3:50 p.m. on January 29, I watched the same field with about fifty deer in view. The same seven-pointer was present and had been feeding quietly for an hour and fifteen minutes. He suddenly began trotting around while smelling the air and ground; he chased all does and threatened all bucks. He would stop occasionally and look around. If he saw another buck chasing a doe, he would run to that area, even if it was completely across the field. All deer retreated from his advance including four eight-pointers. When he passed nearby, I could hear grunting noises. Once he stopped nearby and the investigator could see that he was breathing deeply; saliva dripped from his mouth. After thirty minutes, he singled out a doe and chased her continuously for about five minutes after which the doe stood for the buck to mount. He stayed with the doe for approximately forty-five minutes and then lost her while trying to keep other deer chased away . . .

"At 4:20 p.m. he again singled out the doe and chased her continuously. They ran in wide circles with the buck running fifteen to twenty yards behind her, making grunting noises while running. The buck ran behind her, head low, ears back and rear end crouched. After about five minutes, the doe slowed and the buck trotted along two yards behind her. The doe

The extreme aggressive posture of a white-tailed buck. *Photo credit Leonard Lee Rue III*

stopped and the buck licked her vulva for twenty seconds. The buck then nudged the doe's rear with his chest; she crouched down and he mounted. There was a four-second pause with no detectable movement; the buck dismounted without any movement from the doe.

"The buck then stood still, displaying a head-high threat for twenty seconds. He then moved up and nudged the doe's rear with his chest. She crouched down and he mounted. A twenty-second pause ensued. Then the buck thrust hard, raising his head up and straightening his body. This pushed the doe forward about two yards. The buck walked away, licked his penis and began feeding. The doe walked about five yards in the opposite direction, urinated and began feeding. After five minutes the doe started walking away slowly. The buck followed ten yards behind her. When she stopped to feed, he would resume feeding. When she moved again, he would move along with her. After ten minutes of following the doe, the buck moved toward her in courtship-pursuit display. She ran away into a group of deer sixty yards away. The buck followed and chased the other deer away from her.

"Two eight-point bucks were feeding thirty yards away. The seven-pointer moved toward them, displaying a sidle; they both retreated. When he returned the doe had moved into another group of deer. The seven-pointer charged at the group in courtship-pursuit display and they scattered. The buck walked around for two to three minutes, smelling the ground and air, but he did not contact the doe. He then started moving about all over the field, chasing all does and fawns and threatening all of the bucks. That continued for thirty minutes; then it became too dark to see."

These continuous chases of does by bucks before mounting generally last about five minutes. While running in wide circles, the buck follows fifteen to twenty yards behind the doe.

In a follow-up study to Guyse's, Arthur Hosey, another wildlife researcher at Auburn University, attempted to determine the movement patterns of unhunted white-tailed bucks before, during, and after the rutting season. Hosey live-trapped and radio-marked eleven bucks on the Strimpson Sanctuary; he monitored their movement patterns for a five-month period and reached somewhat different conclusions. During the pre-rut period, the minimum total distance moved (MTD), i.e., the sum of the linear distances between sequential locations of an individual deer during a particular twenty-four-hour period, was 2.7 miles; it increased to 3.9 miles during the rut and again decreased to 2.7 miles for the post-rut period.

Their home range sizes approximated 205 acres for the pre-rut period and 425 and 185 acres for the rut and post-rut, respectively. Like the findings of Robert Downing, Hosey noted that the home ranges of the younger bucks tended to be smaller and increased less dramatically during the rut than those of the older and more dominant bucks. The sizes of these ranges tended to be long and narrow in shape during the pre-rut period and more elliptical during the rut and post-rut period.

Their time periods for being active also increased from fifty-two percent to sixty-four percent and seventy-four percent for the pre-rut, rut, and post-rut periods. Hosey attributed the increase in activity during the post-rut period to a decrease in the availability of food. Unlike Guyse,

Hosey concluded that the increases in home range, MTD, and percentages of activity were all significantly different and resulted from breeding activity. Indeed, his research suggests that the mean distance moved by his radio-tagged bucks increased dramatically during twenty-four-hour periods during the rut. These bucks became much more active during the daytime than at night; but these bucks, we must remember, were not being subjected to hunting pressure.

In his notes on behavior, Hosey reported that during the "sidle display" (i.e., when bucks of nearly equal position in the hierarchy stand with broadsides toward each other, with heads in the high threat posture, and move slowly together), bucks circle for at least 120 degrees and generally in a counterclockwise direction. According to Hosey, whitetails "may have a handedness, dominant side or eye. The coriolis effect (i.e., the force created by the earth's rotation), may also influence this directional tendency."

In another follow-up study on this same wildlife sanctuary in Clark County, Alabama, Tim Ivey, a wildlife researcher with the Department of Zoology/Entomology at Auburn University, radio tagged and monitored ten female white-tailed deer during the rut. He discovered that their minimum home range did not differ statistically among the pre-rut, rut, or post-rut study periods. He also observed that during the rut the doe's total distance moved during twenty-four-hour periods significantly decreased. The distance between their extreme twenty-four-hour locations, the actual area covered, and the portion of their home range utilized, all decreased during the rut.

The general pattern of their movement, according to Ivey, "changed from rela-

Mean distance moved in meters by hour during each period for fifty-eight diel (twenty-four hour) studies on seven white-tailed deer bucks conducted from 7 November 1975 through 26 March 1976 on the Fred T. Stimpson Sanctuary in Clarke County, Alabama.

Reprinted from A. Hosey. 1980. "Activity Patterns and Notes on the Behavior of Male White-tailed Deer During the Rut." M.S. Thesis. Auburn University, Auburn, Alabama. 66pp.

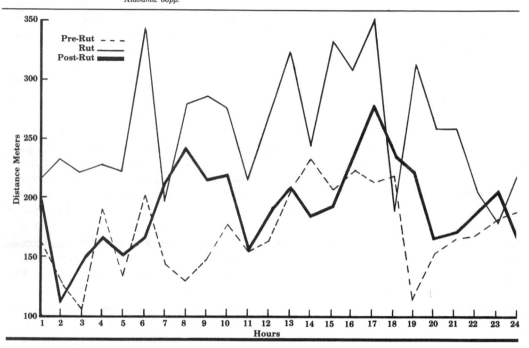

tively long linear movements during the pre-rut and post-rut periods to repeated crisscrossing movements of shorter magnitude within restricted areas during the rut." He associated this *increased activity* and *decreased movement* for does during the rut with the breeding activity and movements of bucks, for this increased activity with minimal movement greatly enables males while expanding their movement patterns to locate particular estrous does.

Deer researchers in other parts of the country also examined the influence of rutting behavior upon the home range sizes and movements of yearlings and adult bucks. David Mech, for example, while radio tracking white-tailed bucks in the Superior National Forest in northeastern Minnesota, observed that adult males moved extensively from three to five miles in, and/or adjacent to the areas they used in the summertime. Like Downing, Mech found that yearling bucks moved much less during the rut than older, adult males.

In another study in the central Adirondack Mountains of New York, Don Behrend and his colleagues at the State University of New York—Newcomb, radio-tracked fifty-two bucks in the Huntington Forest. In their eight-year study, adult bucks showed a dramatic shift in their center of activity during the autumn

Photo credit Leonard Lee Rue III

The ultimate in buck movements during the rut.

Photo credit Charlie Heidecker

months. They attributed this shift in the center of activity to the increased possibility of coming in contact with does in estrus on the periphery of their home range; they observed dispersal movements up to seventeen miles for 1.5- and 2.5-year-old males.

Despite all this, there exists very little systematic research dealing with the question of how far white-tailed bucks will roam during the rut. These studies deal with very small sample sizes and in several cases deal with bucks on non-hunted areas. When we turn our attention to the other members of the deer family, we do not get much beyond general observations. For example, while studying the movements of red deer during the rut in Scotland, a species closely related to the American wapiti, F. F. Darling, an animal behaviorist, noted in his classic of naturalistic prose, *A Herd of Red Deer* (1937), that stags cover considerable distances in short periods of time. In his study, some stags traveled ten to twenty miles at a stretch. He followed one rutting stag for an hour and a half; during that period it traveled seven miles.

In his classic study on the life history of mule deer in California, Joseph Dixon, a field naturalist and pioneer deer biologist, states that mule deer bucks during the rut travel as much as ten miles overnight. Other researchers in western Washington, while observing the movement patterns of rutting mule deer bucks, found that 2.5-year-old bucks, based on hunter tag returns, ranged from zero to sixteen miles. In another study, Raymond Dasmann, a wildlife biologist, reported that during the rut black-tailed bucks in Lake County, California, became much more active throughout the day and spent a great deal of time in riparian woodlands. According to Dasmann, "all bucks during the rut became more conspicuous, occupying commanding heights from which they can search the surrounding area and traveling widely from one group to another."

A great deal of unexplainable behavior still exists with regard to buck movements during the rut, regardless of the species. While studying the movement patterns of one white-tailed buck in South Carolina one night, Marchinton recorded that "around midnight the buck began trotting in a relatively straight line, and by sunrise he was more than seven miles from his original range. He remained for six days within a 200-acre area at the new location. For the next fifteen days, he wandered back and forth along the travel route, entering his original range twice and the temporary range once, but remaining only one day in each. Eventually the buck established a new home range about halfway between his movement extremes."

These unusual and unexplainable movement patterns of bucks keep hunters in the deer forest and the deer biologists on the endless trail of future theories and hypotheses; they add flair to the sport of American deer hunting and the study of white-tailed deer.

Chapter 12

Deer Trails

There are many kinds of deer trails, and some of them appear mighty appealing to the hunter, even though they have long been abandoned by the animals.

—George Mattis, *Whitetail*, 1969

These words of wisdom by deer hunter and trail watcher George Mattis epitomize the irresistible mystery of deer trails. Even after deer abandon them, deer trails call out to be followed, suggesting to us that if we follow them they will yield their secrets and lead us to even more amazing deer signs. They fascinate us; they stretch before us like mysteries to be solved. We track down these highways of the wilderness like hunters possessed, hoping to find tracks, scats, rubs, scrapes, licking branches, shed antlers, you name it.

Historically, deer trails have fascinated the imagination of the deer hunter for time immemorial. Some deer trails date from prehistoric times. Indeed, when man first explored this continent, he used deer trails as main avenues of travel. Like human roads, they never run straight even when the terrain sufficiently opens and

allows them to do so. Their tactical value, structural quality, and ideal placement defy the imagination. At first glance, it's hard to believe that individual deer produce them in an attempt to follow the path of least resistance, thereafter using them by memory, and that they are not preconceived works of the human mind.

It always delights this deer hunter to observe how unerringly deer trails cross through heavy and inaccessible terrain at the most convenient places. Ask any mountain man and he will tell you that deer trails provide you with an infallible guide for traveling through heavy cover via the path of least resistance. Some of the deer trails I travel along on hillsides almost seem to be engineered: the passage of countless hooves along these steep hillsides pushes the soil and stones slightly downhill, creating a firm, narrow terrace

Even after deer abandon them, deer trails call out to be followed, suggesting to us that if we follow them they will yield their secrets and lead us to even more amazing deer sign. *Photo credit Leonard Lee Rue III*

that accommodates hunter and quarry alike in moving through the deer forest.

In one way or another I have been traveling deer trails all my life, whether it be following them through my deer hunting turf, threading them, fiddling around with automatic game counters, reading stories such as *The Trail of the Sandhill Stag,* or studying about them in the naturalistic lore and the scientific literature. Here's what I learned about these important objects in the social life of the white-tailed deer, these telltale signs of the whitetail's whereabouts that enliven so many deer camp discussions.

Deer make trails during all seasons of the year, and some biologists in various states use them as population indexes and as a means for evaluating fall deer habitats. Actually, counts of white-tailed deer

trails in your hunting area can give you a fair estimate of deer abundance per square mile of deer range. Deer biologists generally define deer trails as distinct and pronounced paths or runways in the low-lying vegetation of the forest floor caused by repeated use. Deer hunters, however, often use the words "runways" and "crossings" interchangeably, but they are not quite the same thing, as Larry Koller points out in his *Shots At Whitetails* (1948): "A runway is a well-defined path followed by deer, whereas a crossing is a limited area where deer are likely to pass through." Whereas the hunter readily encounters deer trails, deer crossings remain less evident. When searching for deer crossings, study aerial photos of your hunting terrain and watch for narrow strips of timber between open fields and meadows, between heavy swamps and dense thickets. While hunting in the Catskills and Adirondacks, Koller frequently found deer crossings in saddle-shaped depressions in the ridges of hills.

Deer trails, unlike crossings, typically move into the wind so deer can scent trouble ahead. While some trails seem to meander, they generally allow the deer to approach feeding or bedding areas into the prevailing wind. Indeed, wind changes and prevailing air currents shape deer trails. If the wind shifts, whitetails simply choose a different trail. The more trails you study and map, the clearer deer movement patterns in your hunting area become.

Sometimes deer trails result from years of travel; but at times these routes change suddenly and dramatically. Never take it for granted that last year's main trail will again be the focus of attention this year without detailed examination. Just because deer used a certain trail in August is no assurance that they will favor it in any other month of the year. With changes in the seasons, weather, food supplies, water, and wind, or some combination of these elements, deer abandon old trails temporarily or permanently and establish new ones.

Deer trails vary greatly in length. One deer camp discussion led to the somewhat tenuous conclusion that one of the camp's hunters could walk from the East Coast to the West Coast while continuously staying on deer trails. Longer deer trails, however, often wind around lakes and feeding grounds, and they frequently parallel rivers. Side trails branch off from these longer trails and eventually finger out into individual tracks. Shorter deer trails, on the other hand, tend to avoid crossing the path of obstacles such as swamps, steep rocky ledges, windfalls, snowdrifts, and thick tangles of vegetation.

While studying and mapping deer trails in the Adirondack Mountains, deer biologist Bill Severinghaus observed that "deer trails connecting areas intensively used by deer often take an easy grade to the lowest saddle or gap in a ridge, run along the side of a hill from one good observation point to another, skirt the end of a ridge, hill or encampment, or wend around hills in such a manner that each saddle can be crossed. They follow the natural lay-of-the-land and are usually the easiest routes of travel, although in brushy country in the western mountains they might be quite steep. Deer trails are interlaced so that escape routes may be found quickly."

In his study of trails and runways, Severinghaus observes that deer trails used in the "Plains" area along the South Branch of the Moose River in New York during the 1890s were still heavily used during the winter of 1951. Heavily used winter trails in the Adirondacks provided Severinghaus with an index for malnutrition: He used trail counts versus tracks in winter for determining the foraging ability of deer. According to Severinghaus, "When individual deer tracks outnumber deer trails and group tracks, deer are foraging enough to maintain their physical condition. Conversely, when deer trails and group tracks equal or outnumber individual deer tracks, their foraging range has become so restricted that they are unable to secure adequate nourishment."

While studying deer trails in Maine, Chester Banasiak reported that within forty-eight hours after a snowstorm whitetails usually open up their deer trails but as travel becomes more difficult, they keep fewer trails open. He found that the distances deer travel on trails in deer yards varies considerably. He noted that deer in the northern yards do not generally venture more than a quarter of a mile from bedding areas to feeding areas. Yet, in his *Deer In Maine* (1961), Banasiak reported that he observed deer trails up to a mile long between bedding sites and logging operations. He also found continuous trails running from two to three miles in length that connected areas of activity of several groups of deer. Whether individual deer traveled the entire length of such trails he failed to determine. "Most likely," according to Banasiak, "several groups of deer maintained common feeding grounds and traveled to them in an overlapped manner."

During the 1970s, deer researchers in Wisconsin began to count deer trails as a secondary index to estimate deer populations. Assuming deer trails in an area to be reasonably proportional to the deer population using them, researchers designed a systematic method for counting

With the exception of the rut, mature white-tailed bucks tend to use their own trail network. *Photo credit Tom Edwards*

deer trails that employed a one-quarter mile transect. After tallying deer trails at four-chain intervals (every 264 feet) in spring and fall, they used the mean number of trails per transect for comparing deer use among areas and forest types, and for estimating fall populations and subsequent buck harvests. Using research-run trail counts and adjusted sex-age-kill estimates, they found that deer density per square mile could be estimated by multiplying the mean number of trails per transect by five. Their counts of deer trails in northern hardwood timber averaged 5.74 deer trails per one-quarter-mile transect. Deer trail counts in agricultural areas averaged 13.3 trails per transect.

According to Keith McCaffery, a Wisconsin DNR researcher, neither the habitat type nor the soil type directly affected the observability of deer trails in Wisconsin's annual deer trail surveys (1969–1981). He observed, however, that deer trails became more readily noticeable "in the dead and dormant vegetation following a severe frost." Like many observant deer hunters, he reported that several factors affect the visibility of deer trails: (1) cessation of herbaceous growth; (2) presence of deer; (3) rutting activity; (4) changes in food habits from summer to fall, and; (5) some time-lapse following leaf drop.

In his study of deer trails, McCaffery found that deer added few trails after late autumn. "Systematic recounts on marked permanent transects," he reported in the *Journal Of Wildlife Management,* "indicated that most trails were made by deer during late summer and fall. Of 161 trails counted on permanent transects in spring, only thirty-five percent were visible and recounted in July despite continuous presence of deer. New and re-opened trails began to appear in August when vegetation growth slowed, with the greatest addition of trails occurring after frosts and leaf-fall in mid-October. By November, 157 actively used trails were counted, including eighty-one that originally had been counted in spring. Little change in trail abundance was evident from fall to the subsequent spring on the permanent transects."

While studying deer trails, McCaffery learned that many trails recur in approximately the same place year after year as a result of habitat configuration and topography, but that few deer trails persist annually without regular use. He found the greatest abundance of deer trails in areas dominated by such sun-loving trees as aspen, jackpine, pin oak as well as upland brush and grass, and the lowest average number of deer trails in forest types containing a significant number of sugar maple trees.

While mapping deer trails in the Pilot Knob area of Iowa, deer biologist Michael Zagata clearly illustrated the detailed and complex network of trails whitetails establish. He found that major deer trails in his study area ran in an east-west direction. Deer trails running in a north-south direction connected feeding areas with bedding sites. The most heavily traveled trails bordered fields of corn and soybeans. He also observed that trails follow the path of least resistance, and that deer quickly re-establish them after fresh snowfalls.

After studying the patterns of deer trails in the Smoky Mountains in east Tennessee, my friend Kent Horner, a biologist and field editor for *Deer & Deer Hunting* magazine, concludes that does teach their trail patterns to each succeeding generation of fawns. Although whitetails alter some of their trail patterns, Horner argues, "according to the seasons, food supplies, water, herd density, social dominance, air temperatures, weather, terrain alterations, and hunting pressure, deer seldom leave their home range for any extended length of time; consequently, after the fawns once learn their home range trail patterns from the doe, they tend to continue using at least a major portion of the main runways and escape routes." Horner found that whitetails in the South seldom travel on all of their trails every day but more often walk certain trails every other day, or every third or fourth day, and then on a most variable schedule.

While observing the speed of travel on deer trails at the University of California's Hastings Reservation, deer researchers report that even badly frightened deer rarely

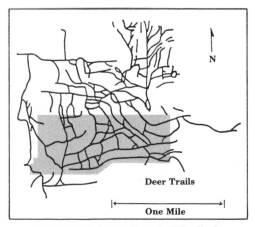

Heavily used deer trails at the Pilot Knob study area in Iowa.

Reprinted from Michael Zagata. 1972. "Range and Movement of Iowa Deer in Relation to Pilot Knob State Park, Iowa." Ph.D. Dissertation. Iowa State University, Ames. 249pp.

trot or gallop steadily for more than one-eighth of a mile. In following well-worn deer trails, they note that few of them continue for more than a mile before intersecting divergent and convergent trails and ending in cover or at some foraging place. Although deer trails widen with heavier use, they found that most vary in width from five to eight inches. In their great compendium of deer facts, *A Herd Of Mule Deer* (1953), Linsdale and Tomich tell us that despite the intricate and complex nature of deer trails, overlapping activity or use on the same trail seldom occurs in any given twenty-four-hour period.

A person on foot in rough country, these deer researchers maintain, can generally depend upon deer trails to lead him most easily and directly over the terrain. Other animals benefit from deer trails as well. Deer trails leading to waterholes provide game trails that other animals such as gray foxes, coyotes, badgers, skunks, squirrels, turkeys, and cottontails use regularly. Annuals also tend to grow in deer trails, but the trampling of hooves eventually affect their growth.

Linsdale and Tomich perhaps best summarize the utmost importance of deer trails when they write that, "The development, use and maintenance of trails are of great importance to the deer. Getting over the ground on a route free from obstructing vegetation improves the efficiency of deer in their living. Transversing individual trails becomes habit, and this learning aids in finding the way from one point to another. Deer in orderly retreat will go off on a well-known trail, if one leading in a general direction away from danger is available. Since retreat leads to no den or burrow, the deer are bound by no instinct to retreat directly from a danger source;

they can retreat to any quarter. If suddenly startled, a deer will rush off, not on a trail, but on some escape route suited to momentary needs."

We must also underscore the great significance of deer trails to man in helping him to interpret the activities of these animals. Yet, in so many situations runways seem to start nowhere and end nowhere — vanishing as mysteriously as they begin. This phenomenon and the frequent, random wandering of deer in general are perhaps what lead Aldo Leopold to write in that great nature essay, "The Gila" (1929), that "a deer never follows anything." Perhaps this random wandering also prompted T. S. Van Dyke to seriously question the entire validity of runways from the deer hunter's point of view in his book *The Still Hunter* (1882): "The habits of deer in forming and traveling in runways or paths are peculiar and vary with localities in a way difficult to reduce to rule . . . They also change their trails so often that when you find one you cannot feel certain that it will be traveled again at all. And they often have so many that you cannot decide whether the next travel upon any one will be today or next week. The best thing to do with runways is to let them entirely alone."

Most of us, however, would probably disagree with both of these statements even though they come from master woodsmen who developed woodsmanship to the highest of arts. They certainly do caution us against putting too much faith in deer trails and in doting on them when planning our next deer hunt. This is not to suggest that trails are valueless for watching the movements of deer. Just make certain that the trail you watch has a specific use by deer for the specific season in which you hunt. As Townsend and Smith emphasize in their study entitled *The White-tailed Deer In The Adirondacks* (1933), "with the change of seasons and the development of other food plants in a new locality new paths will be worn, and the old ones abandoned for the season, to be used again, perhaps, the following year."

In the vast configuration of deer trails, deer maintain morning trails and evening trails. The threading of runways and the use of automatic game counters can help us distinguish between these two types of trails. With the exception of the rut, most major deer trails contain the movement pattern of does, fawns, and yearling bucks. Adult bucks avoid these major trails for the most part, except during the rut. Their trails often parallel the distinct, major deer trails twenty to thirty yards away. These less pronounced trails become more noticeable to the hunters who look for lines of buck rubs in heavy cover.

When you find a well-worn deer trail winding through deer country, map the trail and study it until you find the relationship between the trail and the nearest bedding locations and food sources. A common mistake many of us make revolves around setting up tree stands too close to the food source; the closer we approach the bedding area for stand placement, the better.

In the spring of 1977, The Stump Sitters Whitetail Study Group, a national organization of deer hunters devoted to studying the white-tailed deer, put into operation electronic equipment designed to monitor deer trails on a twenty-four-hour basis. We also designed "Deer Trail Survey Sheets" for our national membership to help us compile data on deer trails. After thousands of hours of trail watching, many interesting details emerged. (1) We learned that deer almost always travel in the same direction on some trails while on other trails they employ two-way traffic. (2) Deer use major trails throughout the year while using minor trails at varying times of the year depending on the availability of food. (3) Deer commonly use one trail when traveling to a feeding area and a second trail when leaving that feeding area. (4) Deer generally use certain trails only at specific times of the day. (5) Few deer trails are used at the same time of day throughout the entire year. (6) We learned the hard way that a deer trail getting heavy use a few weeks before the opening of bow season may not be used at all shortly after the opening of bow hunting. It should be noted, however, that this change in trail usage relates to changing food sources and not hunting pressure associated with the opening of bow season. (7) Don't waste time hunting in the evenings on a morning trail. (8) Always ask yourself four basic questions. Where are the trails? Why are they used? When are they used? And how often are they used? (9) Four types of trails generally exist in all hunting terrain: highway trails, feeding trails, bedding trails, and escape trails. (10) The deer trail always remains a primary consideration whether you still-hunt, drive a section of timber, or stand hunt.

In 1981, Dean Herschede, an Ohio deer hunter, conducted an intensive one-year study of deer trails in the farm country of Ohio. The general movement pattern of the deer he studied consisted of deer moving north through hardwoods of red oak, white oak, hickory, ash, and maple. The deer eventually ended up in field crops approximately one-half mile from their bedding site. He found that does, fawns, and

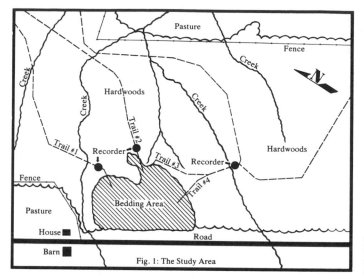

Fig. 1: The Study Area

In conjuction with scouting activities, the deer hunter greatly benefits by drawing detailed maps of the deer trails in his hunting area like this one of Dean Herschede's deer-trail study in Ohio.

Reprinted from Dean Herschede. 1981. "A Study In Deer Movement on the Farm." *Deer & Deer Hunting* 4(5):5.

small bucks used these trails. With electronic equipment, he recorded the movement patterns according to the number of deer, date, time of day, sunrise, sunset, temperature, humidity, wind, barometric pressure, and moon phase.

Herschede learned one obvious fact from his study: Deer are not "creatures of habit." While they feed and bed in the same general area, they do not enter or leave their bedding areas via the same trail or at the same time each day. They used an individual trail on two consecutive days *only* twenty-four percent of the time. On average, they only used each of the four trails Herschede studied twenty-four percent of the days in the one-year study; they used all four trails only forty-seven percent of the time.

Herschede learned, to his great disappointment, that Saturday rated last with only eight percent of daily trail usage. Monday, Tuesday and Wednesday constituted the days of greatest trail activity with each of the remaining days of the week showing below-average deer-trail activity. In his trail study, ninety-eight per-

cent of the deer movement on trails occurred with a wind velocity of 15 m.p.h. or less. Herschede found no correlation between moon phases and deer trail activity. Sixty-two percent of the deer-trail travel took place on sunny days, twenty-nine percent on rainy days, and nine percent on cloudy days.

Herschede found that, on the average, whitetails in his study returned to their beds twenty-nine minutes after sunrise and left their beds fourteen minutes before sunset on overcast, cloudy days. This situation varied little on rainy days, with deer returning to their beds twenty-nine minutes after sunrise and leaving their beds eight minutes before sunset. On sunny days, however, deer returned to their beds, on the average, seven minutes after sunrise and left their beds two minutes before sunset. Translating these interesting results into hunting strategy, Herschede reached the following conclusions from his study:

"If we apply this information to hunting, we can see that on all days (sunny, cloudy, and rainy), we would have shooting light at the time of deer movement if we hunted near the bedding area. First light arrives approximately thirty minutes before sunrise on a sunny day and darkness arrives approximately thirty minutes after sunset. These times would change somewhat on cloudy days, but deer movement also changes.

"If you choose to hunt near the feeding area in the evening, your chances of having more deer pass by your stand would apparently increase because the trails funnel together by the time they reach the nighttime feeding area. But, assuming the deer take approximately thirty to forty minutes to move and browse between the bedding and feeding areas, you probably would not see very many deer in the evening because they would arrive just after dark. For instance, on an average sunny day, the deer leave their bedding area only two minutes before sunset and if it takes thirty to forty minutes to travel and browse that one-half mile, they would arrive two to twelve minutes after dark (darkness arriving thirty minutes after sunset). On rainy or cloudy, overcast days, the timing would be worse; with darkness setting in much earlier, the deer again arrive after dark.

"There would be a better chance of seeing deer in the morning near the feeding area than at night. They apparently leave the feeding area on sunny days just as first light is arriving. On rainy or cloudy, overcast days, deer leave just about at sunrise or a little earlier, which again is about at first light.

"On the one hand, you have a low percentage of deer sightings at the bedding area but good shooting light, while on the other hand, you have a higher chance of seeing deer, but little or no shooting light.

Possibly the place to put yourself for general deer hunting is somewhere between the bedding area and the feeding area where you can benefit from the advantages of both areas."

Following, studying, and mapping deer trails becomes a yearlong activity. In the northern terrain, the deer-trail melt-down in spring provides the deer hunter with the unique situation of being able to distinctly see for a very short time the white, ice-packed trails in sharp contrast against the rest of the mud-covered forest floor. If tracking wounded deer during the fall, always make a map of the deer's trail. These maps will usually illustrate an intricate maze of deer trails formerly unknown to the hunter. I have always learned a great deal about the deer-trail network in my hunting area from these kinds of maps, although some wounded deer will blaze new trails.

It might seem farfetched to say that when everything else fails, make your own deer trails. But is it? On several occasions I have cut a swath through the woods in order to approach my tree stand in a silent manner in the predawn darkness, only to

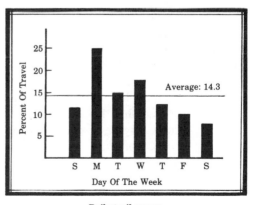

Daily trail usage.

Reprinted from Dean Herschede. 1981. "A Study in Deer Movement on the Farm." *Deer & Deer Hunting* 4(5):8.

return several days later and find that the deer incorporated my blazed swath into their network of trails. In the fall of 1981, Dan Watkins, a reader of *Deer & Deer Hunting,* wrote me a letter summarizing his similar experience in Iowa.

"I hunt from a tree stand, and there are a lot of weeds between the cornfield I must cross and my stand. Every year in July I go to the woods and cut the weeds from where I enter the woods to my stand. I cut a path about four or five feet wide, so when the season opens I have a clean trail to walk on as I approach my stand.

"There are several main deer trails that have been used every year since I started hunting and these trails intersect fifteen yards from my tree. I have noticed that the deer start using the path I cut almost as soon as I clear it. I change the path every year, but it seems no matter where I put the path, the deer follow it to my tree, bucks and does alike. I checked my path for this year yesterday. After clearing sticks and branches from it, I found that my path is full of tracks going in both directions. The tracks indicate that various-sized deer have been using my path again throughout the early fall."

For many years that master woodsman, Aldo Leopold, while sitting under an elm, watched white-tailed deer pass along a trail a quarter of a mile east of his shack. At one point along the trail, the deer became briefly visible from the shack. He always positioned his chair toward the best spot for watching the deer trail. One hot afternoon in August, he decided to cut a swath so that more deer could be seen

from the shack as they passed along the trail. He always pointed the "deer swath" out to his weekend guests for the purpose of watching their reactions to it. Some forgot about it almost immediately, while others watched it as chance allowed. After many years of observing his weekend guests' reactions to the deer swath, he categorized four distinct types of outdoorsmen: deer hunters, duck hunters, bird hunters, and non-hunters. "These categories," Leopold wrote in that splendid nature essay entitled "The Deer Swath," "have nothing to do with sex or age, or accouterments; they represent four diverse habits of the human eye. The deer hunter habitually watches the next bend; the duck hunter watches the skyline; the bird hunter watches the dog; the non-hunter does not watch."

I killed most of my bucks in some thirty years of deer hunting while trail watching, and it comes as no surprise that a survey of the readership of *Deer & Deer Hunting* magazine indicates that trail watching remains the most popular deer hunting technique. The most thrilling aspect of trail watching for me revolves around the mysterious and magnificent way white-tailed deer suddenly materialize from nowhere without warning and disappear in a similar manner like a flash of lightning. I cannot disagree with George Mattis, that lone, solitary trail watcher, when he tells us that "a deer hunt is hardly complete without a day or two reserved for serious trail watching. It is a change in pace that can round out the experience and pleasure for every hunter."

Chapter 13

Deer Licks

Salt, of course, is a great delicacy to the deer, as it is to all animals. The largest salt lick I have seen was probably an acre in extent, put out by hunters. No deer were ever shot there as far as I know, but after each season's hunt the salt left over from the camp was thrown on the old stumps a quarter of a mile from camp. Deer trails led to it from all directions. The stumps were torn to pieces and cut away down into the solid wood inside, which also showed the marks of much chewing. The earth was torn up a foot deep around these stumps and it looked as if the deer that came there had become frantic in their desire to get the last grain of salt.
— William Monypeny Newsom, 1926

Some states already outlawed the use of salt for deer hunting purposes by the time William Monypeny Newsom penned those lines. The impetus for that legislation came from sportsmen such as Newsom, who argued that no self-respecting sportsman would ever kill deer over a salt lick. Nevertheless, during the early days of this republic, the pioneer deerslayers killed many of their deer at licks. Historical evidence indicates that hunters killed as many as 10,000 deer at the famous deer licks near the north fork of the Trinity River near Helena, California, before it became a national game refuge in 1911.

While the term "lick" derives from European origins, hunters in colonial America used the term most frequently when describing their deer hunting exploits. Natural deer licks became so conspicuous to the pioneer deerslayers that even to this day the names of a few places in Pennsylvania still honor the long-vanished deer licks and deer hunting shoot outs of yesteryear: Slate Lick, Lick Island, and Deer Lick. In Pendleton County, West Virginia, near the Shenandoah River, we find such names as Buck Lick Run, Beech Lick Run, and Clover Lick Knob. Indeed, geographical references that refer to deer licks occur widely throughout America.

In reading the diaries and journals of early American hunters, we learn that they understood the whitetail's craving for salt, but Ernest Thompson Seton, that great student of deer, best described that craving in his *Lives of the Hunted* (1901): "Oh, it was the most delicious thing they had ever tasted! It seemed they could not get enough; and as they licked and licked, the dryness left their throats, the hotness went from eye and ear, the headache quit their brains, their fevered itching skins grew cool and their stomachs sweetened, their listlessness was gone, and all their nature toned. It was like a most delicious drink of life-giving cordial, but it was only *common salt*."

Common salt and hand augers to bore holes into hollow oak logs became standard equipment in the 19th century deer hunter's backpack. After observing deer chewing on old stumps and logs for minerals, many of the old-time deerslayers such as Philip Tome in the Allegheny Mountains of Pennsylvania, Oliver H. Perry in the deer forests of Michigan, Meshach Browning in the mountains of western Maryland, and David W. Cartwright in the hardwoods of northwestern Wisconsin placed salt in strategic places and built scaffolds nearby in order to shoot from elevated positions. Their hunting maps indicated the precise locations and names for these deer licks, whether man-made or natural. Their deer hunting excursions often revolved around traveling from one lick to another. In their scouting activities, they searched endlessly for deer licks. Indeed, the deer lick became the focal point for early American deer shooting. The deer, as Philip Tome wrote in his *Pioneer Life; or, Thirty Years A Hunter* (1854), "would keep near the salt licks in large droves, sometimes as many as forty could be seen together near a lick."

Shooting deer over salt, although never considered sportsmanlike, frequently occurred in the South. In Lieut. Col. P. Hawker's *Instructions to Young Sports-* *men* (1846), an Arkansas deerslayer named T. B. Thorpe, Esq., developed the shooting of deer over salt to a fine art. Not only did Thorpe shoot from scaffolds over deer licks, but he added the novel idea of constructing a fire light of pine knots above the scaffold. He then built a seat beneath the scaffold. With the scaffold casting a shadow immediately below the fire, the deer could not see the hunter. The fire light, Thorpe tells us, "glared brightly like a spark in the surrounding gloom. The brightness of the fire dazzled their eyes to such an extent as to entirely shroud any object under the scaffold to total obscurity." In five nights of fire hunting over deer licks in this manner, Thorpe killed twenty-two deer.

Since salting for deer has always been a traditional trick of the poacher, the whole subject matter remains shrouded in controversy. My friend Lennie Lee Rue tells us that on two occasions he saw hunters putting out salt blocks that they intended to hunt over. According to Rue, "One even had a bag of potato peelings mixed with salt. They evidently thought that deer were all starved for salt and would smell salt and come running."

Deer do eat salt but whether they locate salt by odor or accidently and then remember its location I cannot say. Most whitetails have easy access to salt put out for cattle and horses in my area in southwestern Wisconsin. Not only do they lick the blocks but they eat the salt-saturated soil beneath the blocks as well, resulting in large holes in the forest floor measuring up to a foot or more in depth. After injesting the salt-saturated soil from such locations, bucks have been observed withdrawing their heads with black soil hanging from their faces and noses.

The first time I saw a buck with black soil hanging from his face and nose was at an artificial lick near Black Earth, Wisconsin, before hunting season. I returned to my study with more questions than answers. How far will bucks travel to get salt? How much salt do they need? How does salt affect their body weights and antler development? What role do licks play in the life cycle of the white-tailed deer? What fundamental relationship exists, if any, between the chemistry of rock types, soils, plants, and deer populations? What is a natural deer lick and where do we find them? How do deer behave at deer licks? What do the deer doctors tell us about "lick biology?"

Among nature's special places, mineral licks (commonly known as salt licks or deer licks) attract deer and excite the curiosity of naturalists and sportsmen with the same intensity as do licking branches with their modern-day hype and chemical mystique. Deer biologists and hunters alike know that well-worn deer trails lead to salt licks like spokes in a wheel. In 1912, George Shiras III, the father of modern deer photography, pointed out in an article in *National Geographic* that few deer ranges in America exist without earth licks. But what are these so-called earth licks, deer licks, or mineral licks—words used so interchangeably?

In the minds of most deer biologists and hunters interested in the natural history of deer, deer licks represent places in the landscape, some man-made and some natural, where deer concentrate at certain times to satisfy their need for sodium and magnesium. In their natural setting, they frequently consist of moist areas or pools with an apparently higher concentration of minerals than usual. They show signs of being walked in, stirred up, ingested, and eroded into deep holes in the forest floor. The deer's use of them fluctuates seasonally, with the heaviest use occurring in spring and summer due to antler growth and lactation; the craving tapers off in fall and drops to a low ebb from November through March.

During the month of March, motorists frequently kill deer on the highways in the North because the animals come to the roads in search of the salt residue from the road-salting operations of the winter months. In his *Game Management* (1933), Aldo Leopold noted that the nighttime killing of deer by motorists on highways salted to reduce dust during the late 1920s often became quite serious. "In 1929, sixty deer were thus killed on twenty-five miles of highway in Michigan—over two deer per mile per year. In 1930, block salt of the kind used for cattle was put out by the Conservation Department to decoy the deer away from the road salt. The losses promptly fell to eight deer, or one-third deer per mile per year."

During the late 1940s, Irven Buss, one of Leopold's students, set out to examine the activity patterns of deer at salt licks in relation to lunar phases. After watching a heavily used salt lick area for thirty-four days during the months of July to September in the Blue Mountains of southeastern Washington, Buss reported that fully developed mule deer bucks usually reached the lick area well after most does and yearling bucks arrived and that these older bucks seemed to maintain definite groups while feeding on salt. All deer approached the lick area from the same direction each day. Buss observed that three distinct groups of large bucks consistently used the same trails leading to the lick area. During rainy periods, deer tended to stay away from the lick area.

While at the salt lick area, does in particular exhibited a definite pecking order: Individual does maintained a definite priority on choice licking sites, and all does contested and defended their choice places against mature bucks that they drove away in most cases. Fierce fighting, however, occurred only infrequently. But skirmishes between yearling bucks and does occurred frequently, with the does driving them from the area by rearing up and striking out with their front hooves. Mature bucks exhibited a more pronounced wariness and distrust of the lick area than did all other deer.

After studying the activity patterns of 689 deer at the salt lick area during the thirty-four-day period, Buss found a striking correlation between the period of

bright moonlight and the occurrence of deer at the licks. With a full moon, Buss counted twenty-nine deer at the lick area; as the moon waned, the frequency of deer activity at the deer lick declined as well, leading Buss to conclude "that deer change the time of their feeding activities which are correlated with changes in the moon." While "moon magic" continues to entice the imagination of deer hunters, modern-day research does not seem to substantiate Buss's conclusion with regard to deer licks and lunar phases, a conclusion based on a rather small sample size, but interesting nonetheless.

While coping with the seasonal changes

Phases of the Moon and Occurrences of Deer at a Salt Lick.

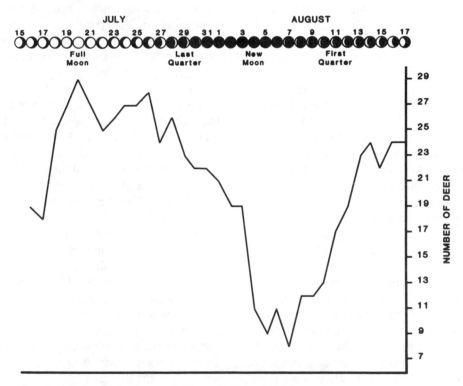

Reprinted from *Journal of Mammalogy.* 1950.
31(4): 426-429

in the catchability of whitetails for research purposes, deer researchers sometimes resort to salt as a bait for trapping and immobilizing whitetails with the Cap-Chur Gun. Deer researchers in the Huntington Wildlife Forest in Newcomb, New York, for example, emphasize the effectiveness of trapping deer with rock salt mixed with moistened soil during the months of May through July. They also underscore its effectiveness wherever salt is seasonally attractive and not available naturally.

In 1979, deer researchers in Texas studied the effectiveness of deer hunting while shooting in the proximity of salt blocks, a widespread legal practice throughout the major white-tailed deer range of that state. They assigned one-half of the deer hunters on the Engeling Wildlife Management Area to salt-baited deer stands with thirty-three-pound "deer blocks" placed within forty yards of the stand during ten hunting periods in 1979 and 1980; they assigned the other half of the hunters to unbaited deer stands. A maximum of seventy deer hunters participated in each of the ten hunting periods; researchers held a drawing prior to the commencement of each hunt to randomize the placement of hunters on the salt-baited or unbaited deer stands.

Deer hunters on the salt-baited stands exhibited a higher success rate (32.9 percent) than hunters on the unbaited stands (26.7 percent). Deer hunters on the salt-baited stands, according to David Synatzske, the principal investigator of the study, "experienced greater harvest opportunity while observing more deer, shooting at more deer, and firing more shots than hunters on the unbaited stands. Less time was required to harvest deer from the salt-baited stands and kill distances were less. Deer hunters more readily observed and harvested bucks from the salt-baited stands. A higher percentage of yearling bucks and fawns was also noted in the harvest from the salt-baited stands. Trend data indicated that while the observability of deer and hunter success was initially higher for baited stands, it declined more rapidly than unbaited stands as the deer hunting season progressed."

Synatzske concluded his study, entitled "Effects of Baiting on White-tailed Deer Hunting Success" by noting that shooting deer over "deer blocks" represents an effective tool for increasing the harvest of deer in areas where higher harvest rates are needed, and that the practice would benefit most management programs in Texas. According to the Wildlife Management Institute's *White-tailed Deer: Ecology and Management* (1984), thirty states or provinces allow deer hunters to use salt blocks as a hunting aid; twenty-six states or provinces do not.

Interestingly enough, the difference between the success rates for deer hunters using salt and for those hunting on unbaited stands remains quite small: 6.2 percentage points. White-tailed deer undoubtedly learn very quickly to avoid salted bait stations, as most deer researchers will tell you. Fred Goodwin, that legendary buck hunter from Maine, warns us against placing too much faith in the effectiveness of salt for deer hunting purposes:

"Do not put too much stock in the tales of salt licks and the big herds of deer that congregate around them. Those stories are of little value except to pass away an evening when better yarns are scarce. True enough, deer do come to salt licks, but in late fall when most hunting seasons are open, deer have less desire for salt than at

The Legal Use of Salt Blocks for Deer Hunting

State or province	Legal use of mineral blocks	State or province	Legal Use of mineral blocks
Alabama	No	Nevada	Yes
Alberta	No	New Brunswick	Yes
Arizona	Yes	New Hampshire	No
Arkansas	Yes	New Jersey	Yes
British Columbia	Yes	New Mexico	No
California	No	New York	No
Colorado	No	North Carolina*	Yes
Connecticut	No	North Dakota	Yes
Delaware	No	Nova Scotia	Yes
Florida	No	Ohio	Yes
Georgia	No	Oklahoma	Yes
Idaho	Yes	Ontario	Yes
Illinois	No	Oregon	Yes
Indiana	No	Pennsylvania	No
Iowa	No	Quebec	Yes
Kansas	Yes	Rhode Island	No
Kentucky	Yes	Saskatchewan	Yes
Louisiana	Yes	South Carolina	Yes
Maine	No	South Dakota	No
Manitoba	Yes	Tennessee	Yes
Maryland	Yes	Texas	Yes
Massachusetts	No	Utah	Yes
Michigan	No	Vermont	No
Minnesota	Yes	Virginia	No
Mississippi	No	Washington	Yes
Missouri	Yes	West Virginia	Yes
Montana	No	Wisconsin	No
Nebraska	Yes	Wyoming	No

any other season. If deer have the habit of coming to salt licks during the spring and summer, it is more likely that they will use the same route in the fall and winter through force of habit rather than a craving for salt. Trophy bucks heed the call of other cravings in late fall far more than salt licks."

The importance of sodium, calcium, and magnesium to phenotypic development in deer, especially the development of antlers, has been the subject of intense speculation since the late 19th century. More recently, during the early 1970s, Harmon Weeks, a deer researcher at Purdue University, studied natural and artificial deer licks in south-central Indiana and the behavior of whitetails while using these licks. Weeks identified sodium (Na) as the key element sought by deer. Maximum use of deer licks occurred in early spring and moderated during the summer and early fall; no winter use occurred. According to Weeks, adult males were clearly dominant at the licks and displayed a great deal of aggressive behavior. Unlike Buss, Weeks found no evidence of deer using the licks as a focal point for the formation of a dominance hierarchy as is

Aggressive interactions frequently occur among whitetails using the same deer lick; antlerless deer often strike out with a foreleg. *Photo credit Leonard Lee Rue III*

typically the case with the licking branch. Indeed, aggressive-submissive interactions commonly occur among whitetails simultaneously using the same deer lick. The hard stare usually becomes the most frequently employed threat posture by lick users, although antlerless deer frequently strike out with a foreleg.

While observing deer behavior at deer licks from elevated blinds, Weeks noted that deer of all ages and sexes used licks with the exception of young fawns (zero to four months of age); young deer licked with as much intensity as the older animals. Few diurnal visits occurred. Deer approached the licks slowly and cautiously, but directly. Most of their visits lasted approximately thirty minutes.

Weeks reported that deer ingested the lick material in various ways. They did not lick the soil; instead, they picked up the

Natural deer licks are often found in non-wooded bottomland situations and in soils classified as Stendal silt loam, a poorly drained soil type found in the lowest parts of bottomlands. *Photo credit Judd Cooney*

loose soil with their lips; others gnawed it loose with their incisors. They invariably chewed the soil prior to swallowing. An analysis of fecal samples collected in the spring in the vicinity of the licks that Weeks studied contained an average of 29.4 percent of inorganic matter, with values as high as 87.5 percent. This activity lead to the characteristic, telltale hole in the forest floor—the ultimate sign of the whitetail's love of salt.

Weeks closely examined eighteen active, natural deer licks—i.e., deer licks not originating as a direct result of human activity. He located all of these deer licks in non-wooded bottomland situations and in soils classified as Stendal silt loam, a poorly drained soil type found in the lowest parts of bottomlands. Virtually impermeable, Stendal soils contain a subsoil with a high clay content. Natural deer licks form in the following manner: runoff water collects in these low areas over Stendal silt loam and, being unable to move downward, it stands until dissipated by evaporation, leaving behind its dissolved minerals.

During the 1980s, Gary Wiles, one of Weeks's students, continued to study the movement and use patterns of white-tailed deer using natural licks in south-central Indiana. Nearly all of the forty-eight free-ranging whitetails that Wiles marked with ear tags and radio transmitters used natural licks. Most of the deer used licks within their home ranges, but others left their home ranges to find and use natural licks. One deer traveled 1.98 miles to use a lick outside of its home range, but most trips were less than 0.93 miles. Other movements outside of their home ranges Wiles attributed to exploratory trips, temporary flight from human disturbances, and permanent yearling dispersals.

Individual deer used an average of 1.9

licks and visited them once every 3.16 days during their peak use period. Most of their visits to licks occurred one to two hours after sunset, but Wiles also noted a second peak occurring three to four hours after sunset. Although both sexes craved sodium, lactating does seemed to have a greater need for it than bucks; the age ratio of lick users was skewed toward adults and yearlings.

Wiles located and studied ninety-six mineral licks, both natural and artificial, and reached the conclusion that deer establish patterns of lick use when fawns begin to follow their dams to licks in late summer and early fall. In this manner, they learn the location of and travel routes to deer licks. When the lick use resumes in early spring, the pattern becomes firmly imprinted. Thus, deer establish an affinity for certain licks through tradition during the first twelve to fourteen months of their lives. Smell may aid deer in finding mineral licks, but once found, sodium-deficient deer quickly learn their location. Yet, it may take more than one year for deer to establish an affinity for a new lick site.

In terms of management implications, Wiles concluded that providing artificial deer licks would probably not greatly alter either deer distribution or habitat use. Salting, however, does benefit deer in several ways: (1) it improves their body condition; (2) it reduces physical exertion caused by long-distance travel to natural licks; (3) it might aid in reducing deer-auto accidents; and (4) it may reduce disease and parasite infection from dung deposited at natural mineral lick sites.

While social historians attribute a strategic part to salt in many of the great military engagements of the last four centuries, wildlife biologists report intense, aggressive interactions among deer at mineral licks. According to Wiles, "agonistic behavior among visitors to lick sites occurred in competition for preferred feeding sites inside licks . . . Dominant animals forced submissive individuals to feed in the less preferred, outer portions of licks; to leave after having fed briefly or not at all; or to wait outside until dominant animals had left." Wiles noted that "the hard look-ear drop" occurred most frequently, followed by the head high threat and chases and strikes.

When providing salt for deer, Wiles recommends spacing salt blocks approximately one mile apart in order to be readily accessible to deer, but not closer than eighty yards from roadsides to avoid deer-auto accidents and to allow deer to remain undisturbed while ingesting the soil. Placing salt blocks in bottomland habitats on clayey soils increases the life of the lick by avoiding the leaching of deposited sodium. Wiles also suggests placing artificial licks in thick vegetation to make deer feel more secure as well as to reduce poaching opportunities in states that prohibit deer hunters from shooting deer over salt blocks.

Deer will go to great lengths to satisfy their mineral requirements; they will even chew weathered, shed antlers for their mineral content. In their study, *A Herd of Mule Deer* (1953), Linsdale and Tomich observed mule deer in the wild chewing on fallen and disintegrating antlers. From their photographs we can see that when deer chew antlers, they rasp the opposite surfaces of tines toward flatness. Shed antlers that I have found indicate to me that bucks beat me out on two scores: Not only do I fail to hang their antlers on the mantel, but I also fail to find their shed antlers intact without partial deterioration. Yes, deer seem to eat everything from birds to porcupines, from dead frogs to newly burnt ground, from fish to deer bones. During a two-year study in Big Bend National Park in Brewster County, Texas, deer researchers observed an adult mule deer buck chewing the dried pelvic bone of a fawn. They speculated that a phosphorus deficiency may have been the reason F. F. Darling even records in his book, *A Herd of Red Deer* (1937), how he observed a hind chewing a stag's antlers while they were still on his head.

In his book, *Our Wildlife Legacy* (1954), Durwood Allen, the distinguished wildlife researcher, wrote that "like the crops we cultivate, all living things reflect in number and vigor the quality of the earth that bears them." Indeed, large-bodied whitetails with massive antler development and high rates of productivity come from fertile soils. In 1985, two scientists from Illinois, Robert Jones and Harold Hanson, looked closely at the habitats of large-antlered white-tailed deer from the Midwest, and clearly related the trophy antler development of 122 deer that placed among the first 153 positions of the Boone and Crockett system to what they called "alkaline earth-rich habitats" with adequate levels of calcium and magnesium.

According to Jones and Hanson, "calcareous rocks, limestones, dolomites and shales and the more recent, thick deposits of loess—which tend to be base-rich in the upper Mississippi Valley—are the ranges of large whitetails of high reproductive capacity . . . Forage growing on soils developed from all these rocks is highly nutritious. The contents of bases are higher and the nutritional needs for amino acids and energy are met at what appear to be optimal levels." Does this description characterize your deer hunting area? If not, study soil survey maps and move.

How much salt do deer consume in the wild? A difficult question to answer, but an Arizona investigator reports that while the nature of the forage, air temperature, and exercise all affect salt consumption, deer under penned conditions consume about 0.1 pounds per month.

For time immemorial, whitetails have visited deer licks where they eat and lick the earth to satisfy subtle but specific needs in their diets. Such deer licks may be muddy places around springs, certain rocky outcroppings, or brackish pools where whitetails eat mud. Artificial licks may be salt blocks in the back forty or rock salt deposits from salt spread on the highways to melt ice. Deer hunters may simply refer to deer licks and let it go at that.

But as mentioned earlier, the whole subject of deer and salt seems somewhat shrouded in controversy. For many of us, shooting deer over salt strikes us as similar to stalking and shooting heifers at the lick behind the barn. I suspect that even though thirty states and provinces allow hunters to legally shoot deer over salt, many hunters, myself included, believe that the most legitimate and best use of salt in the deer forest revolves around flavoring the venison and preserving the hide. I find it ironic that while thirty states and provinces legally allow hunters to shoot deer over salt, virtually no commentary on this somewhat controversial and often-called unsportsmanlike practice exists in the more than 600 volumes on the subject of deer and deer hunting in my library. My research on the lure of salt and the practice of shooting deer over salt turned up only three comments on the subject: one from a self-confessed deer poacher from Colorado, where the practice is not legal; a second interpretation from a buckslayer in the deer forests of Louisiana, where the practice is legal; and a third commentary on the practice from a professional trapper . . .

First, Ragnar Benson speaks his piece on gunning 'em down over salt blocks in that infamous tour de force, *Survival Poaching* (1980):

"Recently a farmer in our area discovered a mineral block that I put out for deer. In many cases it is a foolish waste of time and money to pack salt in for deer, since they can get all they want from blocks set out for cattle. But in this case a nice little woods with an abandoned apple orchard lay especially far from anything else, so I thought it was worth the effort.

"The farmer called the warden, who went out to examine the situation. After a close scrutiny, our intrepid warden decided that the salt was indeed set out for deer and that he had better stake out the location. It was the middle of September. Our warden waited patiently five days for someone to show up, his truck parked right out in the open on the road. We all laughed about the possum sheriff's stupidity, but at least he wasn't snooping around someplace else during that time.

"In case the reader does not know this, deer won't generally come to salt in the fall. They may stay in the area, or come by the lick every week or so, but salt is not the magnet for them in fall that it is in the spring. This holds true for elk, moose, and bear as well.

"Should the poacher decide to put salt out, I recommend a location that is high and dry, yet near to water. The ground should be clay, if possible, and the location sheltered by trees or heavy brush. It is best to find a spot that is used by deer at present, or plan to wait at least three years before activity builds around a new lick.

"If detection is a problem, use rock salt rather than blocks. The deer will eat the ground after the salt is melted, and is therefore not as easy to spot."

Next, we read these lines of advice from Ronnie "Big Buck" Glover, taken from his *More Than Luck: A Guide for Hunting the Trophy Buck* (1980):

"One of the means of attracting deer and contributing to the growth of their racks is the use of salt licks. We had to do a lot of experimenting in Louisiana before we came up with a kind of salt lick that the deer in our area really go for. We tried all of the more obvious things first. We placed the large salt blocks out in the woods; we tried placing salt in sacks and hanging them from trees so that the salt would drip on the ground when rained on, and we stashed it on old rotting stumps. None of these approaches was as successful as the technique we finally came up with through our conversation with an old hunter. Using pure salt plus dairy minerals mixed fifty-fifty, we dig a broad shallow hole about three feet wide and throw in the salt, mix it up with the dirt, pat it all back into place, and cover it up with leaves so that it appears natural. This has worked beautifully. After a few weeks, we checked out these salt licks and found that deer had been by and literally torn that ground up getting to that salt. Deer really need salt, especially during certain seasons of the year, and this has been the most effective way we have found to attract them to a salt source."

Thirdly, we find this interpretation in *Successful Hints on Hunting Deer* (1976), written by Hollis Callender, a one-time professional trapper for the Louisiana Wildlife and Fisheries Commission, who documents how he created deer licks throughout his deer hunting lease by placing table salt in dirt and re-salting every six months. Hollis reports that he has "been putting salt (the chemical NaCl), in holes creating salt licks for years. Some of these licks are large enough to put a car in, they have been used so much." But Hollis hastens to add, "We don't kill deer around these licks, however, because that would defeat our purpose of promoting deer growth and development." He then curiously adds that "some of our friends have used mineral salts with success on deer licks." No doubt.

If the non-hunting public, not to suggest the antihunting public, were aware of the common practice of shooting deer over salt, we would probably all be headed for the state capital tomorrow, regardless of which state we live in, with our briefcases packed with exquisite, euphemistic double-talk.

Given the fact that the practice of shooting deer over salt legally exists in thirty states, I'm surprised that the chemical stands at the "deer classics" throughout America have not yet added salt blocks to their lineup of products. At least I haven't seen salt blocks displayed on highly varnished and polished rotting-oak stumps via plastic fantastic at the classics I've attended.

Actually, "stump chewing" emerges as the most interesting aspect of the entire story of the deer's salt-drive phenomenon. Yes, I said stump chewing, not stump-sitting or stump "setting," as it is so often pronounced. While we know that deer frequently chew at old stumps, it sometimes remains hard to distinguish their work in this regard from bears chewing stumps for ants. But unlike the bear, which usually tears the stump into large pieces, deer tend to merely chew at the exposed corners, creating a fine shredding of wood fibers. But the answer to why a deer chews at a stump of rotten wood still remains elusive and open to speculation and deer shack debate. William Monypeny Newsom, that great popularizer of information about white-tailed deer, believed that deer acquire a certain amount of mineral matter in the process; he also mentioned in this regard that deer go into burnt-over areas shortly after a fire, apparently being attracted to the ashes in a similar manner.

Yes, deer will go to great extremes to satisfy their sodium deficiency and man, the hunter, *homo tyrannicus,* will likewise encourage this salt drive phenomenon as an aid to his deer hunting strategy. Historically he has done so, and he continues to do so in the present.

PART III

THE DEER HUNTING MYSTIQUE

Chapter 14

Blue-Chip Deer Books: The Nineteenth Century

There have been fewer books written by Americans about life in the American wilderness and the chase of American big game than one would suppose—or at least fewer books which are worth reading and preserving; for there does not exist a more dismal species of literature than the ordinary cheap sporting volume.

—Theodore Roosevelt, 1893

When not scouting or hunting for deer, the deer hunting aficionado searches for deer books that reflect his interests and dedication to the sport. For the past twenty years, I have combed the antique and second-hand book stores of this country and scoured the out-of-print sporting book catalogs in search of blue-chip deer books. Indeed, ever since the age of sixteen, I have been an avid deer book fan, constantly checking the local bookstores for the newest releases. Invariably, I devour these books in one or two sessions, tucking away in my memory small snippets of information on deer and deer hunting and the literature of the sport.

Like most novice book collectors, my first volumes were primarily of a how-to nature written by dilettante outdoor writers and self-proclaimed experts. But in time and after a serious drain on the exchequer, I gradually acquired top-shelf deer books written by the nation's leading deer biologists and serious books on deer hunting of a where-to and wherefore nature written by first-rate authors. Today, part of my library contains a deer book collection of more than 600 volumes dealing exclusively with deer and deer hunting, with the earliest volume being William Scrope's *The Art of Deer-Stalking* (1838), and the latest vintage volume being the Wildlife Management Institute's *White-*

tailed Deer: Ecology and Management (1984). For an annotated list of these deer books and how to obtain them, since most of them and especially the great ones are unfortunately out of print, see the appendix entitled "The Deer Hunter's 400," in the author's *Deer & Deer Hunting,* Book 1 (Stackpole Books, 1984).

Many of these books were written by deer hunting guides, amateur naturalists, professional journalists, scientists, famous book authors, explorers, as well as self-proclaimed experts, outdoor writers of various persuasions, and backwoods pioneers without any formal training. But all of these men shared a common love for white-tailed deer and the hunting of them. Whether we read the polished prose of T. S. Van Dyke's *The Still Hunter* (1882) or the brilliant, briar-patch philosophizing of William Long's *Following the Deer* (1901), these vintage volumes from the past provide us with an entertaining and engaging record of the American deer hunting experience.

While I was writing *Deer & Deer Hunting,* Book 1, my study of the literature of the American deer hunting experience became particularly extensive. During the preparation of that book, it became impossible to avoid comparing the different eras in which these deer books appeared. I reached the conclusion that the second half of the nineteenth century produced this country's greatest literature on deer hunting as well as the first scientific treatise on deer: John Caton's *The Antelope and Deer of America* (1877). In this chapter, I briefly examine the great deer books of the last half of the nineteenth century.

The first great, vintage volume appeared in 1841. In this novel, entitled *The Deerslayer,* James Fenimore Cooper

(1789–1851) depicted the early American deer hunter in intimate harmony with nature. His moral character and worth, Cooper argued, depended upon his degree of reverence and respect for deer, his direct relationship to nature, and the manner in which the hunter perceived his natural environment.

Natty Bumppo, the hero of this romantic tale, killed deer only out of necessity, and then lovingly, and not for plunder. "They call me Deerslayer. I'll own; and perhaps I deserve the name, in the way of understanding the creature's habits, as well as for the certainty in the aim; but they can't accuse me of killing an animal when there is no occasion for the meat or the skin. I may be a slayer, it's true, but I'm no slaughterer . . . I never yet pulled a trigger on buck or doe, unless when food or clothes was wanting." The Deerslayer's chief virtue resided in the fact that he did *not* view the presence of a live deer as an insult to his powers. He hunted deer both for food and for the spiritual satisfaction of participating in the ennobling rite of the kill.

The Deerslayer's deep connection with the teachings of nature and his mastery of the intricate details of the deer forest create a rich and intensely exciting story— filled with romance and theatricality. A story to be cherished by all deer hunters; in it Cooper invested the deer kill with an ennobling purpose. But by the time of his death in 1851, Cooper's conception of the deer hunter's life as an untrammeled existence of necessary hunting was quickly evaporating—giving way to the arrival of a new social and industrial order.

Before that new social and industrial order took command, another romantic tale of the deer stalker appeared on the scene: Frank Forester's *The Deer Stalkers*

(1843). In this short, fancy sketch of early American deer hunting in the southwestern counties of New York, Henry William Herbert (1807–1858), writing under the pen name of "Frank Forester," constructed a brilliant portrait of the chase based on the ethical proposition, as he so aptly proclaimed, "that there is not only much practical, but much moral utility in the Gentle Science of Woodcraft." In this work as well as in all of his writings, Forester preached the need for adapting English sporting ethics to the American scene, taking a bitter and unrelenting stand against all deer poachers and pot-hunters. In the sporting journals of his time, he politicked for game laws and a sporting ethic.

Herbert's annual deer hunting trips to the woodlands of Orange County and the lakes of the Adirondacks, especially an area known as "Old John Brown's Tract," provide the background for this classic tale unequaled in the annals of the literature on American deer hunting. The following poem sets the stage for Forester's portrait of the early American deer hunt:

Mark! How they file adown the rocky pass, —
Bright creatures, fleet, and beautiful, and
    free, —
With winged bounds that spurn the unshaken
    grass,
And Swan-like necks sublime, — their eloquent
    eyes
Instinct with liberty, — their antlered crests,
In clear relief against the glowing sky,
Haught and majestic!

Like most deer hunting stories, Forester's tale begins with the first flush of autumn as Frank's boys cross the woodland hills in a horse-drawn carriage en route to the Dutchman's Tavern. Through the fast-fading twilight they rattle along —

HENRY WILLIAM HERBERT, Esq.
(1807–1858)
"Frank Forester"

"Frank Forester," the author of that great tale entitled *The Deer Stalkers.*

singing, laughing, and jesting all the way, making the deer forest ring with sonorous music. Just as the young moon climbs into the sky, they arrive at the little, old, stone Tavern nestled so closely into the wooded terrain that its existence remains unsuspected.

Dutch Jake, the owner, opens the door as Frank's boys enter the bar, a large room dimly lit by home-made tallow candles and blazing and snapping hickory logs in the large, open fireplace. Forester describes the shelves of this holy sanctum for us: "They were garnished with sundry kegs of liquor, painted bright green, and labelled with the names of the contents in black characters on gilded scrolls. These, with two or three dull-looking decanters of snakeroot whiskey and other kinds of 'bitters'; a dozen heavy-bottomed tumblers, resembling in shape the half of an hour-glass, set up on the small end; and a considerable array of tobacco-pipes, constituted all the furniture of Jake's bar, and promised but little for the drinkableness of the Dutchman's drinkables."

Despite the questionable nature of Jake's snakeroot whiskey for the more refined tastes of Frank's sporting companions, they nonetheless made their way to the bar with the vociferous Fat Tom, a fictional character based on the mammoth and eccentric Tom Ward of the village tavern, a well-known man to the sportsmen of New York in those days, hollering, "Jake, you darned old cuss, look alive, carn't you? and make a gallon of hot Dutch rum torights!" With a burst of laughter the deerstalkers begin to steep their souls in old Dutch Jake's strange compound of Santa Cruz rum, screeching hot water, allspice, brown sugar, and peppercorns. After several doses of this antique concoction, one of the boys howls, "I knowed it, jest as I 'spected, adzactly. Them's prime sperrits!" Following a brace of larded grouse and brazed ham, brought forth with odoriferous steam and numerous quart pewter mugs of champagne, imported to the Dutchman's Tavern from New York for the occasion, Frank's boys indulge in yarn spinning until late into the evening. Shortly after midnight they remove their tomahawks from their sashes, hang up their stout buckskin leggins, and retire for the evening to dream of shining, antlered bucks silhouetted against the eastern sky.

When the kitchen clock strikes four, the deerstalkers are afoot. After a hearty breakfast of ham and eggs, "not least, two mighty tankards smoking with a judicious mixture of Guinness's double stout, brown sugar, spice, and toast — for to no womanish delicacies of tea and coffee did

the stout huntsmen seriously incline," Frank's boys shoulder their rifles and strike forth while the stars still shine in the sky.

The first flash of dawn in the eastern horizon finds several of Frank's boys, Harry Archer and Dolph Pierson in the company of Smoker, their noble, Scottish, wirehaired deer-greyhound, hunting deer from a canoe while floating down the numerous, narrow streams of the Adirondack country. After miles of floating in an unbroken silence, they suddenly encountered two bucks. Forester recalls the scene for us:

"Under the shade of a birch stood two beautiful and graceful deer, one sipping the clear water, and the other gazing down the brook in the direction opposite to that from which the hunters were coming upon them.

"No breath of air was stirring in those deep, sylvan haunts, so that no taint, telling of man's appalling presence, was borne to the timid nostrils of the wild animals, which were already cut off from the nearer shore before they perceived the approach of their mortal foes.

"The quick eye of Archer caught them upon the instant, and almost simultaneously the hunter had checked the way of the canoe, and laid aside his paddle.

"Pierson was already stretching out his hand to grasp the ready rifle, when Archer's piece rose to his shoulder with a steady slow motion; the trigger was drawn, and ere the close report had time to reach its ears, the nearer of the two bucks had fallen, with its heart cleft asunder by the unerring bullet, into the glassy ripple out of which it had been drinking, tinging the calm pool far and wide with its life-blood.

"Quick as light, as the red flash

gleamed over the umbrageous spot, long before it had caught the rifle's crack, the second, with a mighty bound, had cleared the intervening channel, and lighted upon the gray granite rock. Not one second's space did it pause there, however, but gathering its agile limbs again, sprang shoreward.

"A second more it had been safe in the coppice. But in that very second, the nimble finger of the sportsman had cocked the second barrel; and while the gallant beast was suspended in mid air, the second ball was sped on its errand.

"A dull, dead splash, heard by the hunters before the crack, announced that the ball had taken sure effect, and, arrested in its leap, the noble quarry fell.

"For one moment's space it struggled in the narrow rapid, then, by a mighty effort rising again, it dashed forward, feebly fleet, keeping the middle of the channel.

"Meanwhile the boat, unguided by the paddle and swept in by the driving current, had touched upon the gravel shoal and was motionless.

"Feeling this as it were instinctively, Harry unsheathed his long knife, and with a wild shrill cheer to Smoker, sprang first ashore, and then plunged recklessly into the knee-deep current; but ere he had made three strides, the fleet dog passed him, with his white tushes glancing from his black lips, and his eyes glaring like coals of fire, as he sped mute and rapid as the wind after the wounded game.

"The vista of the wood through which the brook ran straight was not at the most above fifty paces in length, and of these the wounded buck had gained at least ten clear start.

"Ere it had gone twenty more, however, the fleet dog had it by the throat. There was a stern, short strife, and both went down together into the flashing waters.

Then, ere the buck could relieve itself, or harm the noble dog, the keen knife of Archer was in its throat—one sob, and all was over."

No you will not, unfortunately, find a copy of Frank Forester's *The Deer Stalkers* in Waldenbooks. No outdoor publisher has re-issued it; you will have to locate it in a used bookstore or in an out-of-print sporting book catalog. Since its publication, the book went through various editions with the last edition being published by the Derrydale Press in 1930. The 1985 issue of Angler's & Shooter's Bookshelf catalog lists a faded copy of the book for $50; I purchased my fine copy for $60 several years ago from Larry Barnes of Gunnerman Books. Good luck in your hunt for this jewel! It is worth every dollar spent for this short, fancy sketch of early American deer hunting.

Although this stirring sketch—written in eloquent prose with a spirited and graphic tone—provides us with a colorful portrait of the chase, in reading his great essay entitled "Deer Hunting" published in 1849, we learn that Frank Forester took a dim view of the general quality of the deer hunt during this time. "Deer hunting proper and scientific, I may say there is none." Too many hunters, in his opinion, were waging promiscuous havoc on the deer herd—not respecting the seasons, age, or sex of the animals.

Of the two most popular modes of deer hunting during the 1840s, driving and still-hunting, Forester favored the latter. "It is by far," he writes, "the most legitimate and exciting, as it demands both skill in woodcraft, and endurance, on the part of the hunter; whereas driving requires only the patience of Job, added to enough skill with the gun to knock over a great beast, as big as a Jackass, and as timid as a sheep, with a heavy charge of buck-shot."

Forester delivered a tremendous charge of buckshot against the idea of fire hunting as a mode of deer hunting. His critique of this form of deer poaching resounded throughout the deer forest like the sudden crack of a rifle on a quiet, crisp November day: "There is nothing of fair play about it. It is a dirty advantage taken of the stupidity of the animals; and, apart from its manifest danger, ought to be discountenanced. It is utterly unsportsmanlike, and butcherly. The great drawback to this species of sport, apart from the not slight odor of pot-hunting which attaches to it, is that other animals than deer often approach the treacherous blaze; and instances are not uncommon of hunters shooting their own horses and cattle, —nay, every now and then, their own companions, sisters, and sweethearts."

Forester's conception of a deer hunting group never exceeded four hunters, for Frank took a mighty dim view of large deer hunting parties often numbering twenty or thirty guns, presenting a situation in which as he exclaims, "the odds are, perhaps, a hundred to one against so much as even hearing the distant bay of a hound." Whether or not we agree with these odds, I am sure that many of us can relate to his final assessment of the sport of deer hunting:

"Here there is no work for the feather-bred city hunter, the curled darling of soft dames. Here the true foot, the stout arm, the keen eye, and the instinctive prescience of the forester and mountaineer, are needed; here it will be seen who is, and who is not the woodsman, by the surest test of all—the only sure test—of true sportsmanship and lore in venerie, who can best set a-foot the wild Deer of the hills, who bring him to bay or to soil most speedily, who ring aloud his death halloo, and bear the spoils in triumph to his shanty, to feast on the rich loin, while weakly and unskillful rivals slink supperless to bed."

While Frank Forester and his boys tramped the picturesque passes of the Adirondack highlands in pursuit of deer, Philip Tome (1782–1855), probably the greatest Pennsylvania deer hunter of his time, wrote his memoirs of early nineteenth century deer hunting in the hills and river valleys of the Keystone state. Since I discussed his book of stirring tales in Chapter Four, I will merely say that his book of hair-raising adventures contains everything from fire hunting deer to capturing grown elk alive on the waters of the Susquehanna. All lovers of the hunt will enjoy reading about his exciting deer hunting episodes in the hills of Warren County, Pennsylvania.

Tome's thrilling adventures can only be matched by those of one of his contemporaries, Meshach Browning (1781–1859), a very successful Maryland deerslayer who hunted the Allegheny Mountain section of western Maryland. Reportedly, Meschach Browning killed somewhere between 1800 and 2000 deer during the first four decades of the nineteenth century.

One January evening while staring at my bookshelves as the dying embers of my woodburning Morso shot their shadowy ghosts upon the antique book bindings, my eyes gradually focused on his soiled, tattered, gold-colored volume entitled *Forty-Four Years of the Life of a Hunter* (1859). I had retrieved this quaint and curious volume from Paul's Used Bookstore on State Street in Madison, Wisconsin, during the Christmas holidays; shelved and forgotten about until that wintery night in January, its rare and entertaining deer hunting lore had escaped my attention.

Born in Frederick County, Maryland in March of 1781, this pioneer Marylander carved a living for himself and his family of twelve out of the Maryland wilderness much like Philip Tome had done in the hills of Pennsylvania. Whitetails provided him not only with meat and hides but with a source of income as well. At that time venison sold for twelve and a half cents a pound. What he could not use for his family, he sold. The money raised eventually enabled him to buy a small farm. Like Philip Tome, deer hunting represented not only Meshach's favorite pastime, but his basic source of livelihood as well.

He understood the whitetail's habitat; he knew their mating seasons, gestation periods, and browse preferences. He used candles in bark reflectors to spotlight them at night while floating down streams in his canoe. On the subject of deer hunting he wrote: "If a man undertakes a dangerous enterprise with a determination to succeed or lose his life, he will do many things with ease and unharmed which a smaller degree of energy would never accomplish."

Even though his livelihood depended upon venison, he claimed to live by a certain ethical code toward wildlife suggesting, in much the same way as did Cooper and Forester before him, that the chase was more important than the kill. Ultimately, he insisted that self-reliance was vital to anyone who would hunt deer in the wild. Since the rifles of his day were so inaccurate and the powder so poor that even at thirty yards they lacked killing

power, Meshach frequently confronted his quarry with knife in hand. While reading his autobiography, I encountered with great delight one hair-raising incident of deer hunting lore that I shall never forget: Meshach's fight with a wounded buck in the Yough River.

After Meshach badly wounded a ten-pointer with a heavy charge of buckshot, his half-breed greyhound took to the heels of the animal and drove him into the river where the dog and the buck engaged themselves in a desperate battle. Due to the river's deepness, neither hound nor deer could get a foothold. In his chilling memoirs, Meshach tells us what happened:

"I concluded to leave my gun on shore, wade in, and kill him with my knife. I set my gun against a tree, and waded in—the water in some places being up to my belt, and in other places about half-thigh deep. On I went until I came within reach of the buck, which I seized by one of his horns; but as soon as I took hold, the dog let go, and struck out for the shore, when the buck made a main lunge at me. I then caught him by the other horn, though he very nearly threw me backwards into the river; but I held on to him, as I was afraid of our both being carried into the deep hole by the swift current. I dared not let him go; for if I did, I knew he would dart at me with his horns. I must kill him, or he would in all probability kill me; but whenever I let go with one hand, for the purpose of using my knife, he was ready to pitch at me. I called and called the dog, but he sat on the shore looking on, without attempting to move.

"After awhile, it occurred to me to throw him under the water, and drown him; whereupon I braced my right leg against his left side, and with my arms jerked him suddenly, when down he came with his feet toward me. Then it was that my whole front paid for it, as his feet flew like drum-sticks, scraping my body and barking my shins, till ambition had to give way to necessity, and I was not only compelled to let him up, but even glad to help him to his feet again, though I still held on to his rough horns. From the long scuffle, my hands beginning to smart, and my arms to become weak, I took another plan.

"I threw him again, and as he fell I twisted him around by his horns, so as to place his back toward me and his feet from me. Then came a desperate trial, for as this was the only hope I had of overcoming him, I laid all my strength and weight on him, to keep him from getting upon his feet again. This I found I could do, for the water was so deep that he had no chance of helping himself, for want of a foothold. There we had it round and round, and in the struggle my left foot was accidently placed on his lowermost horn, which was deep down in the water.

"As soon as I felt my foot touch his horn, I threw my whole weight on it, and put his head under the water, deeper than I could reach with my arm. I thought that was the very thing I wanted; but then came the hardest part of the fight, for the buck exerted all his strength and activity against me, while I was in a situation from which I dare not attempt to retreat.

"I was determined to keep his head under, although sometimes even my head and face were beneath the water; and if I had not been supported by his horns, which kept me from sinking down, and enabled me to stand firmer than if I had no support, that stream might have been called, with great truth, 'the troubled water'; for I know that if it was not troubled, I was, for often I wished myself out of it. I know that the buck would have had no objection to my being out; though he probably thought that, as I had come in to help that savage dog, he would give me a punch or two with his sharp points, to remember him by. Indeed, that was what I most dreaded; and it was my full purpose to keep clear of them, if possible.

"In about two minutes after I got my foot on his horn, and sank his head under water, things began to look a little more favorable; for I felt his strength failing, which gave me hopes of getting through the worst fight I had ever been engaged in during all my hunting expeditions.

"When his strength was but little, I held fast to his upper horn with my left hand, and keeping my foot firmly on his lower horn, I pressed it to the bottom of three feet of water and, taking out my knife, when his kicking was nearly over, I let his head come up high enough to be within reach, when at a single cut I laid open the one side of his neck, severing both blood-vessels. This relieved me from one of the most difficult positions in which, during all my life, I had been placed for the same length of time."

I cannot imagine a better volume to read on a wintery night, especially if one is a connoisseur of great deer hunting tales and continually scouting for deer hunting anecdotes and lore. His backwoods style and strange, peculiar phraseology hold great appeal. Unfortunately, Browning's book has been out of print for the past forty years; it remains scarce even though it went through ten editions between 1859 and 1942. When found, a first edition of this book (1859) in fine condition will probably cost $65. For the addict of deer books, it serves as a rich compendium of American deer hunting lore of the first half of the nineteenth century. If you are interested in the heroic, picturesque adventures of fighting with wounded bucks and catching deer barehanded in the snow, you will want to read this exciting, rustic volume.

While Meshach Browning prowled the deer forests of Maryland subduing wild, white-tailed bucks with knife in hand, Judge John Dean Caton (1812–1895), that ardent deer hunter and prominent judge from Illinois, studied the natural history of whitetails under penned conditions in Ottawa, Illinois, with pen in hand. In 1877, he published America's first great treatise on deer: *The Antelope and Deer of America*. Although an amateur naturalist, his book is still regarded by scientists as a standard reference volume on the subject. The work was published by Hurd and Houghton. *The Antelope and Deer of America* quickly went out of print after going through a second edition.

This thorough and extraordinarily fine volume, as mentioned in chapter one, includes a very impressive chapter on the chase, in which the author discusses the true virtues of deer hunting and reminds us that "to the cultivated mind capable of understanding and appreciating the works of the Divine hand, the pleasures of the pursuit are immeasurably enhanced by a capacity to understand the object taken." You will indeed understand "the object taken," if you read this remarkable volume of personal observations on all facets of deer anatomy and behavior.

Following in the tradition of James Fenimore Cooper, Caton placed deer hunting in the context of natural history, formulated a classic hunting ethic, and even argued that deer biologists have much to learn from deer hunters. "The pleasure of the sportsman in the chase," Caton insisted, "is measured by the intelligence of the game and its capacity to elude pursuit, and in the labor and even the danger involved in the capture . . . No matter how abundant the game, none but a brute would ever kill it for the mere pleasure of killing. The feeling of utility must be associated with its capture. If it cannot be utilized, a pang of regret must take the place of gratification."

The glorious chapter entitled "The Chase" is worth the price of the book itself regardless of whether you buy the first edition (1877), the second edition (1882), or the inexpensive 1974 reprint. In that chapter we find this eloquent description of the deer kill:

"The trusty rifle is quickly brought to the cheek, and the next instant, with a lofty bound, the magnificent but graceful form of the stately stag bursts forth from the border of the covert, his face in a horizontal line, his antlers thrown back upon his shoulders, so that every branch and vine must easily glance from the backward-pointing tines, his scut erect, and his bright eyes glistening in the excitement of the moment, when instantly and while he is yet in mid-air, a sharp report is heard, when, to use a hunter's expression, 'he lets go all holds,' his hind feet, propelled by the great momentum, are thrown high in the air as if his very hoofs would be snapped off, and he falls *all in a heap* or turns a complete somersault, and then rolls upon the ground pierced through the heart, or with both fore shoulders smashed; or if the deer was descending in his leap, perhaps the shot was higher than was intended, and a stitch is dropped in the spinal column. In either case, the monarch of the forest is laid low, never to rise again. It is a glorious moment, and unsurpassed by human experience."

While the honorable Judge Caton studied, observed, and stalked whitetails on the wild prairies of Illinois, T. S. Van Dyke (1842–1923), that prince of the sporting writers, still-hunted them in the primeval forest of northwestern Wisconsin. If Caton's book is the first great scientific treatise on deer, Van Dyke's *The Still-Hunter* (1882) is without doubt the first and greatest treatise on the art of still-hunting deer—the likes of which we have never seen since. Since I have dealt with this famous American deer hunter and his classic treatise on the art of deer stalking in my book, *Deer & Deer Hunting,* Book 1 I will merely say that if you have not read *The Still-Hunter,* you have thus far missed the greatest, most intense happiness that could conceivably be crammed into a couple of hours in front of your fireplace. The deer hunter who reads this book will vividly relive his own days afield. The book's spirited and lifelike descriptions will make every deer hunter who has ever found enjoyment in still-hunting whitetails tingle with the delight of pleasant recollections. An unsurpassed classic! Fine copies of the later editions sell for approximately $35 to $50.

Oliver Hazard Perry (1817–1864), that rugged and robust deerslayer from Cleveland, Ohio, and author of that marvelous book of deer hunting reminiscenses entitled *The Hunting Expeditions of Oliver Hazard Perry*, published in 1899. From his reminiscenses we learn that his annual deer hunts lasted for two to three months at a time in the vast, unbroken wilderness of the North, where Perry and his boys chased many an "Old Hemlock Ranger" and consumed large quantities of hickory nuts washed down with a judicious amount of "Old Jamaica Rum." From an oil painting. *Photo credit The Library of Congress*

In 1899, the nineteenth century ended for the American deer hunter with a dramatic blast, when friends of Oliver Hazard Perry (1817–1864) posthumously published his extraordinary deer hunting journals in a volume entitled *Hunting Expeditions of Oliver Hazard Perry* (1899). Unfortunately for us, they only published one hundred copies—making the book extremely rare and expensive. Nonetheless, this greatly-sought-after book provides the reader with the finest account we have of the daily adventures of a mid-nineteenth century deerslayer in the deer forests of northern Michigan. His journal is replete with vivid descriptions of chasing the "Old Hemlock Rangers" through Michigan's boundless and trackless forests. After reading this account, I can still hear Perry's primitive rifle belching out its thunderous notes as he tramped through cedar swamp after cedar swamp—eventually arriving at the Buck Horn Tavern, a solitary log cabin, to dine on venison, potatoes, and snakeroot whiskey. His tales of how the deer "unfurled their white flags to the breeze" have to be read to be believed. His backwoods jargon carries the reader along with great intensity. He didn't shoot deer; he "put their lights out!" After a stiff drink of "Old Bald Eye" at the Buck Horn, he spent the evening playing Eucre with the boys. First-rate whiskey, pie, and cheese capped the night. Before the night ended, Perry's boys talked about "flocks of deer."

"The Sandhill Stag," by Ernest Thompson Seton.

In 1899, Ernest Thompson Seton (1860–1946), that brilliant naturalist who waxed so eloquently on deer and deer hunting, put the final touches to the blue-chip deer books of the 19th century by adding to the list *The Trail of the Sandhill Stag* (1899), one of the most thought-provoking, sensitive, moving tales ever written on the long, endless pursuit of a black-tailed stag. I highly recommend it for boys of twenty and for boys of sixty and over! In this deer hunting tale, Seton challenges and examines the basic philosophy of the chase.

Unlike most tales of early American deer hunting, when Yan, the main protagonist of his tale, finally encounters the Sandhill Stag in his rifle sights, after several years of intensive study and elusive chase, he refrains from shooting. As he stands in front of the magnificent monarch of the woods with his nerves and senses at their tightest tone, he says to himself, "shoot, shoot, shoot now! This is what you have toiled for!" But shoot he does not. Instead, he says to himself while staring into the soul of the stag:

"We have long stood as foes, hunter and hunted, but now that is changed and we stand face to face, fellow-creatures looking into each other's eyes, not knowing each other's speech—but knowing motives and feelings. Now I understand you as I never did before; surely you at least in part understand me. For your life is at last in my power, yet you have no fear. I knew a deer once, that, run down by the hounds, sought safety with the hunter, and he saved it—and you also I have run down and you boldly seek safety with me. Yes! you are as wise as you are beautiful, for I will never harm a hair of you. We are brothers, oh, bounding Blacktail! only I am the elder and stronger, and if only my strength could always be at hand to save you, you would never come to harm. Go now, without fear, to range the piney hills; never more shall I follow your trail with the wild wolf rampant in my heart. Less and less as I grow do I see in your race mere flying marks, or butcher-meat."

Although the original edition of this book is out of print—only 250 copies were published—it went through numerous editions, and copies of these later editions can be readily found in used bookstores and at a reasonable price. This little volume of less than 100 pages will arouse the spirit of any deer hunter. It is a fascinating record of long searches that usually end in an unsuccessful manner; it captures the spell of the woods and the joy of the hunter. A story to read and reread! In the fall of 1899, the *New York Times* instantly recognized it as a classic. "It is in every way thoroughly pleasing, both through the beauty of the story—one which once read, we think, can never be forgotten—and in its illustrations and general make-up, all the details of which are worthy of the charm of Mr. Seton's style."

Several weeks of deer hunting experiences out of fifty-two do not thoroughly or reasonably satisfy the deer enthusiast. Consequently, we turn to good books to stretch out the season. If you're like me, you probably enjoy reading blue-chip deer books in front of the fireplace. The books discussed in this chapter represent some of the all-time greats. In reading them, you will quickly discover that we have not learned a great deal about hunting the white-tailed deer that our forefathers did not already know. These books not only enhance the image of the American deer hunter, but the experiences found within their pages frequently parallel our own in many ways; although their deer hunting exploits often make our modern hunting trips look like genteel tea parties. These classics not only add a universal flavor to the deer hunting tradition, but they warm our memory and provide pleasant evenings next to the fireplace.

Chapter 15

Deer Camps in the Land of Hiawatha

Go, my son, into the forest,
Where the red deer herd together,
Kill for us a famous roebuck,
Kill for us a deer with antlers!
— The Song Of Hiawatha, 1855

Ever since time immemorial, Michigan deer hunters have heeded the call of Hiawatha. Indeed, ever since 1855, they have gone to the tall, mature forestland of the North to kill a deer with antlers and to seek relief from civilization in those magical places—the deer camps of yesteryear. This chapter narrates the story of some of those Michigan deer camps of yesteryear and underscores the adventurous spirit of those early deerslayers on their long, arduous excursions into wild deer country. As one modern-day deer hunter from Michigan exclaims: "Our grandfathers and great-grandfathers *hunted* in those days, and there was little stump-sitting so commonly seen in these times . . . It was a way of life for the old-time deer hunters, and should they rise from their graves and gaze upon orange-clad hunters today, I'm sure they would be thankful for the deer hunting days they spent on this earth."

The earliest record we have of those deer hunting days of the 1850s we find recorded in a marvelous book of deer hunting reminiscences entitled *The Hunting Expeditions of Oliver Hazard Perry,* published in 1899—a greatly-sought-after and highly cherished blue-chip deer book. In that delightful volume of deer hunting adventures, we learn that Perry (1817–1864), a rugged and robust deerslayer from Cleveland, Ohio, and son of the famous naval officer with the same name, hunted deer primarily in the state of Michigan, especially near the Cass River in Tuscola County.

Perry enjoyed nothing more than a

The hanging of deer during 1850s. Taken from a painting by Courtier. From left to right: Hiram T. Merrill, Johnstown, Burry County, Michigan, and John Nichols of Battle Creek. *Michigan Historical Collections*

"protracted encampment" with his deer hunting partners in the depths of Michigan's boundless and trackless deer forests during the mid-1850s, when no restrictions of any kind existed on the harvesting of whitetails. His deer camps became the center and rendezvous for extensive deer hunts in all directions. Deer camp camaraderie, however, was by no means indispensable for Perry. As one of his deer hunting companions remarked: "It was not an uncommon occurrence for him to start out solitary and alone upon one of his great hunts, occupying several months, relying for society — where none intrudes — only upon nature as she always appeared to him in her multitudinous charms."

While on his hunting expeditions, Perry camped in tents for the most part, although he frequently slept in large, hollow logs lined with straw, using large coon skin robes as bed clothing. En route to his favorite haunts, he traveled via steamship, train, horse and buggy as well as cutters during heavy snowfalls. When inclement weather curtailed his tramps afield, his group passed the time away very merrily, as he recalls, "with a good stock of tobacco, cigars, hard bread, rum, brandy, sugar and codfish."

He situated his deer camps so far back into the wilderness that he could hear no noise from any settlements; a dead silence reigned supreme around his deer camp, broken only by the infernal din of the hunting pow-wow music of Saginaw Indians or the occasional "nasal twang" of his hunting partners. After traveling for days on end over corduroy roads, roots of trees, and black, deep mud, these early deer stalkers spent days just in the preparation of their camps; not surprising when we realize that their annual deer hunts lasted for two or three months at a time in the vast, unbroken wilderness of the North.

After a two-year absence from one of his favorite deer camp locations, Perry reflected in his journal on the ultimate meaning of deer camp life: "Sad and gloomy thoughts came into my mind when I viewed the well-known trees and other objects and witnessed the wild desolation, that deep and solemn silence. Here two years before a happy party of us, in the springtide of our existence, spent a portion of the most pleasant period of our lives. All was life and animation. The noise of singing, laughing, talking and hooting made the woods resound. But now how different! The great changer Time had intervened, and a part of that merry Company were scattered to all portions of the earth, while two of them were then gazing in melancholy silence on the ruins of their old deserted Camp before them."

In the evenings, Perry and his partners consumed large quantities of hickory nuts. With the aid of a gallon of "Old Jamaica Rum," interesting incidents of earlier deer camps translated themselves into legend. Having no clock, these deer-slayers of yesteryear frequently depended on an old, veteran rooster from a local farmhouse. "This crowing of the old Game-Cock of the wilderness was the morning revelry for all hands to muster forth for duty." Breakfast consisted of fried venison and a cup of Spice-bush tea. Indeed, venison was the main staple of these deer hunters. As they roamed the hemlock forests, they continually hung venison in the trees. In the fall of 1854, Perry writes in his journal that he "found some Venizon hanging in a tree, took one Ham and left stuck in a crotched stick a quarter of a dollar for it."

At the first ray of light, they "bent their course" through the fields and thickets. Perry vividly describes how one of his partners, D. W. Cross, a zealous disciple of Nimrod, headed for the deer forest: "Cross put a good quantity of his favorite 'bald eye' in his stomach, a few bullets in his pocket, shouldered his rifle, and turning over with ecstatic delight an old 'chaw' of Tobacco in his mouth, started into the woods, the sound of his footsteps reverberating back the exhilarated state of his mind and body."

These early deer hunters, with tomahawks and knives belted to their sides, hunted like tireless hounds; with red faces sweating and begrimed with dust, they pursued their quarry with the deadly determination of Hiawatha. Yet, despite their determination, these old time Nimrods did not completely escape the effects of that dreaded, eternal disease — buck fever. Perry encountered the disease while shooting twice at a noble buck with large and magnificent antlers. After missing it, he exclaimed: "The buck fever seized me in a moment. I was all shakes and made two foolish shots at the Old Patriarch, who hearing a noise and smelling gunpowder, threw up his head, hoisted his flag, gave a snort and bounded away forever from my sight, leaving me to suffer from chagrin and mortification at the results of my two shots." After experiences of this nature, Perry frequently imbibed enough stimulating fluid to lighten his heart and content himself with the world.

In addition to buck fever, Perry fought an eternal battle with deer mice. On October 1, 1854, he wrote: "I am so overrun with deer mice that I can hardly live in the woods. They eat the Strings of my Tent, my Shoes, Pork, Hard bread, Gloves, leather strings, Bags, etc. and commenced last night working in my hair, and planting their cold noses on the scalp of my head. I have tried one experiment in trapping them, but it did not succeed. I must devise some way of killing them, or leave the woods."

While in the deer woods, violent storms added to his problems and frequently forced him to leave. In his hunting journal, he records how the dreadful winds and the roaring, awful sounds of screeching treetops, breaking limbs, and falling trees would drive him out of his tent onto the shallow riffles of the Cass River in order to avoid crashing hemlock trees, branches, and brush. He would remain in the middle of the river for hours on end waiting to return to his endangered tent site.

Perry experienced other problems as well. Because of the dire need for venison to survive and the primitiveness of his weapons, many deer were hit but never recovered. His journal is replete with vivid descriptions of endless tracking procedures that lasted for days on end with many "old Hemlock Rangers" dying in water-filled swamps and remaining unretrieved. Too frequently the crude rifles belched out their thunderous notes but to no avail, for the distance was too great or the shocking power too light. In one instance, Perry recalls that when he raised his rifle to shoot a deer he could not see his sight because of darkness; consequently he fired at the deer "by looking along the barrel." This kind of helter-skelter blazing away, putting lead on their tracks but not bringing them to bay, characterized much of the 1850s' style of deer hunting.

While it is hard to distinguish the killing of deer for sustenance or simply for sport, by the early 1870s a larger number of Americans followed Perry and went afield primarily for recreation. Rapid industrialization brought wealth and leisure to greater numbers of people and thus resulted in the opportunity to hunt deer for sport. Deer hunting, however, did not become the hobby of the butcher, the baker, and the candlestick maker overnight. That event had to wait for a generation or more, but for those Nimrods who could afford it, deer hunting became a popular pastime during the 1870s.

Michigan deer hunters of the 1870s, unfortunately, did not diligently chronicle their deer camp experiences for posterity. In reconstructing the early deer camp experience, we are forced to rely upon an occasional sketch or reminiscence found in a more general book on hunting and fishing. One such account, "A Sketch of the Nichols Deer Hunting Camps," appeared in William B. Mershon's *Recollections of My Fifty Years of Hunting and Fishing* (1923); it was written by Edwin C. Nichols, a prominent manufacturer of threshing machinery in Battle Creek, Michigan.

From his account, we learn that although some deer hunters insisted on camping in hollow logs, most deer camps during the 1870s took the shape of primitive tents with black, protruding stovepipes belching smoke into the pines, not to mention "the goodly number of deer in the hangings," as Nichols so aptly described it in an unpublished letter to conservationist Mershon. Nichols's fascinating sketch of his deer hunting camps in the 1870s and 1880s needs to be reproduced in part to capture the very essence of an early American deer camp in the land of Hiawatha.

"Our camp in the early days was an unpretentious affair compared with its somewhat luxurious development in later days. The usual procedure then was to hitch a pair of horses to a big lumber wagon in which was placed a heavy canvas tent, some suitable blankets, a supply of tin table china, very primitive cooking utensils including of course the coffee and tea pots, plenty of salt pork and a bag of those home-made doughnuts, a small supply of groceries, to all of which was to be added the choicest selection of deer meat, game birds and excellent fish. The latter were to be obtained at will on short notice at the very threshold of the camp. There was never lack of grand food and plenty of it.

"Under this shelter and amid these attractive surroundings would come the little band of happy hunters, each armed with a muzzle-loading rifle, down which the powder and ball were pushed with a long ramrod, and carefully primed with a percussion cap. For this was the day before the invention of the murderous repeating rifle with its magazine of cartridges, enabling the shooter to pour a volley on the poor deer without much regard to skill or marksmanship. The olden hunter had his single barrelled muzzle-loading rifle, giving him but one shot and one chance at the deer, and thus requiring on his part steady nerve, accurate eye and

delicate trigger finger to make this one chance a killing one. It was indeed a good sporting accomplishment to place this one little rifle ball in a vital part of a running deer, of which the modern hunter with his magazine rifle knows nothing. The imaginative lover of these goodly scenes who has enjoyed, as some of us have, these wonderful surroundings would not willingly lose the memory of those happy and thrilling events.

"The party usually carried one and sometimes two deer hounds mainly for tracking wounded deer, but occasionally to make a drive in the early morning to stir them up a little. Any true sportsman who has on a keen, frosty early morning listened to the music of one or two loud baying hounds following the wily buck in full swing will not soon forget the electric thrill that the chase brings to every hunter within hearing; each hoping the deer is headed for his stand and with every sense acute, every muscle tense, he listens to the echoes and re-echoes of the baying dogs as they follow on the track of the flying deer.

"Thus it was, that year by year the Nichols Deer Hunting Camps were located for several weeks each season in various parts of the Lower Peninsula of Michigan. The outfit gradually increased in its hospitable features until there was a large cooking and dining tent with a good wooden floor, capacious table with its white tablecloth and napkins, a fine show of modern chinaware and table silver, comfortable chairs, a large cooking stove with hot water reservoir, and an especially large pancake griddle, capacious sleeping tents with comfortable bedding, a commissary tent for the storage of provisions with auxiliary tents for extra guests or other purposes, so that it was not uncommon to have a hunting party of twenty persons, all invited guests, and the hunt frequently lasted thirty to forty days. The importance of these annual hunts and the hospitality of its founder became quite well heralded throughout the country.

"One of the most interesting of the Nichols Deer Hunting Camps was on the Au Sable River in the fall of 1876, when the party were taken by rail to Roscommon and then down the South Branch of the river. This party of hunters, with its extensive equipment and all needful provisions for a six weeks sojourn in this beautiful wilderness, together with ten thoroughbred deer hounds, was loaded into five big scow boats which were prepared and transported there for the purpose, and they went gaily sailing down that beautiful stream on a bright October day. The South Branch at that time was densely wooded with overhanging trees along the margin, and grand strips of Norway and white pine bordering it. It was a fine rushing torrent down which the boats sped with little effort except to dodge the overhanging sweepers and clear the treacherous whirlpools.

"A temporary camp was made before reaching the junction of the main stream of the Au Sable. On the following day the permanent camp was located a few miles below the junction near what was then known as Ball's Bridge. This camp had every attraction of location and surroundings and with abundance of game and fish and the fine companionship of the goodly family gathered on its shores, it will always remain a most cherished memory.

"Our favorite hunting camp site and one which we occupied for several successive years was on the north bank of the river a few miles below where the North Branch joins its rushing waters with the majestic main stream of the Au Sable. It was a beautiful hillside crowned with a grove of stately Norway pines, sloping gently down to the water's edge, forming a delightful frontage looking up stream. When our Tented City was in full regalia on this beautiful hillside, it presented a very interesting and charming picture as one rounded the river bend above and came into full view."

The annual Nichols deer hunts continued for many years, mostly on the famous Au Sable River and its tributaries. The accompanying photos of these deer camps vividly describe the features of their forest homes and suggest to the sympathetic and experienced deer hunter the many pleasures and comforts to be found in deer camp. When Michigan outlawed the use of hounds for deer hunting in 1887, the E. C. Nichols deer hunting camps formally suspended operations. These diehard muzzleloaders could not accept the outlawing of hunting hounds nor the development of the repeating rifle. In the words of E. C. Nichols, "the party saw no real pleasure or true sport in the mere potting or killing of deer by the hunter who sits shivering on the runway and waits for the poor deer to show himself within range of the murderous repeater, which gives the deer but little chance, while it contributes considerable danger to the surrounding neighborhood." They hung up their rifles and stored their equipment; but the memory of their romantic camps and their happy days afield remains gratefully and lovingly cherished in the annals of American deer hunting.

Michigan's deer camps of yesteryear have become living legends and models for the American deer hunter. Deer Camp Erwin on the banks of the Au Sable,

The E. C. Nichols deer hunting camp located on the bank of the Sturgeon River in Dickinson County, 1886. When this "Tented City" was in full regalia on this beautiful hillside, it presented a very interesting and charming picture as one rounded the river bend above and came into full view. *Michigan Historical Collections*

where John Erwin's boys consumed vast quantities of venison and bedewed the deer shack floor with strong infusions of Virginia plug, comes to mind. One also thinks of Deer Camp Hiawatha along the banks of the beautiful Tah-qua-me-non, where A. D. Shaffmaster and his crew raised the art of still-hunting to an all-time high. Since I discussed these two vintage deer camps in another context, I merely mention them here. For a detailed discussion of them, see the author's *Deer & Deer Hunting*, Book 1 (Stackpole Books, 1984), pp. 182–195.

Undoubtedly, the best-known and most cherished deer camp to emerge from the land of Hiawatha remains the Whitefish Lake deer camp of George Shiras III, the father of wildlife photography whose world-famous deer photos of the 1890s remain unsurpassed in quality, clarity, and composition.

In 1886, this leading sportsman/naturalist replaced his earlier, primitive shacks by constructing a substantial log cabin with two bedrooms, a living room, and a dining room as seen in one of the accompanying photos. At this Whitefish Lake log cabin, Shiras started a deer camp log wherein his visitors recorded their impressions of the daily events and unusual happenings of deer camp life. These narratives indicate the mood induced by the wilderness when deer hunters cast aside all cares and genuinely relax in good fellowship.

In Shiras's camp log for 1894, a fellow sportsman visiting Whitefish Lake uniquely constructed the following intimate portrait of a different camp, a portrait of the congenial gathering of the Galster deer camp, a camp he had visited in the previous year. His detailed description of the Galster deer camp characterizes the fellowship and camaraderie not only of that well-organized camp in Ontonagon County, but of the Shiras deer camp as well. It bears quoting since it epitomizes

the very essence of an early American deer camp; his enthusiastic rhetoric stimulates the modern-day deer hunter as well.

"The Galster party camps at the old, abandoned Nonesuch mine location, one of the early-day copper properties located near the Porcupine Mountains about twenty miles from Ontonagon. The hunter's main camp is a large building used in the old days as a warehouse by the mining company. It is a long log building, substantially built and warm. One-half of it is used as a living room and the other half for sleeping quarters. Two sections of bunks, built in three tiers, each section

A. O. Jopling, a hunting partner of Shiras's, poses with his trophy buck of extraordinary size. The photograph was taken in the early 1890s and pictures the backside of one of Shiras's more finely constructed deer shacks. **George Shiras III.** © *National Geographic Society*

Michigan's famous Deerfoot Lodge, owned and operated by that well-known sportsman, editor-author, traveler, the Hon. Chase S. Osborn. From left to right: Barney, the deer camp cook, Governor Osborn, and two unidentified slayers of prime venison, 1897. *Michigan Historical Collections*

accommodating twenty-four men, make up the 'boudoir', or 'Nellie's room' as it is labeled by a sign on the door.

"A lean-to built along one side of the building gives ample space for dining room and kitchen, and meals are served at a long table at which forty guests may be fed without crowding. And at dinner in the evening the table is none too large, because Captain John Galster and his boys dote on good fellowship and there is seldom a dinner without a few guests.

"The writer was privileged, recently, to be one of a group of five guests at dinner with the Galsters and their happy family of 'kids' grown up, and the experience brought a few hours of unforgettable pleasure.

"First of all, the dinner, prepared by an expert colored chef and served by his staff of four young men aides, was so good that there are no words to describe it. Imagine a meagre menu of soup, fried fish, roast beef, venison steak, mashed potatoes, peas, pudding, cherry sauce, angel food cake, coffee, tea, cigars.

"And as cigars were being consumed, Captain Galster arose from his seat at the head of the table and gave a brief talk which bubbled over with good-fellowship, formally welcomed the guests and reported the day's best yarns, taken from the hunting experiences of his pals.

"That day one of the boys had shot a fine buck. The hunter had walked up to the prone deer and was preparing to dress it when he noticed that the buck's tail wagged every few seconds. Concluding that the animal was not dead, he decided to shoot it in the head, but as he lifted his gun, Mr. Buck leaped off the ground and darted away, five shots following it.

"Certain that the animal was mortally wounded, the hunter pursued. But there was no snow, and the trail was hard to follow. After three hours the buck was found, lying a quarter of a mile from where the hunter had first dropped him.

"Captain Galster concluded his address with a serious, heart-to-heart message to his party. He said: 'Boys, another day has passed. We have all hunted and we are all here, safe and sound. Remember, tomorrow is another day and I want every one of you to be careful. There must be no accidents. Don't shoot until you are certain it is a buck. Wait till you see antlers.'

"There never has been an accidental shooting in the Galster party and there is not likely to be. One might suppose that a party of twenty-five or thirty deer hunters would be something of an unorganized mob. Not so with the Galster group. It is well organized, in and out of camp. It has rigid rules of conduct, and they are obeyed. In camp each man has a place to put his rifle, a place for his clothing, a place for all of his belongings and everything must be in its place.

"Near the main camp building the Galster party has constructed a Finnish bath house, and one of the camp rules is that each man must take a bath each day. No trouble, though, enforcing this rule.

"The twenty-three men in the Galster gang this season represent almost that many different vocations. There are young men and old men. One is about twenty, and one seventy-nine. There are merchants, bankers, a circuit judge, doctors, newspaper publishers, farmers, a police officer, and manufacturers. All are banded together for a good time and, above all, man-to-man comradeship. Of course, they hunt deer and try hard to fill their licenses, but if they fail — what of it? Who cares?

"After dinner in the Galster camp the boys waddle in from the dining room, let out their belts several notches and sink down into the many easy chairs to smoke, swap stories of the day's experiences, plan tomorrow's hunting and 'chin' in general. There is radio music, of course, and just to top off the dinner the chef sends in a basket of apples and two dish pans filled with buttered popcorn.

"To quote one of the men: 'Yes, we have plenty of fun and our gang has been together a long time. And our fun doesn't end November 30. From then until the end of next summer we talk about what we did this season, and there is no end of material to talk about. And when fall begins, we start planning for and talking about the next trip. Great stuff. Keeps us young and teaches us to love our fellow men. Keeps the blood red and makes us live longer.'"

All of these deer camps in the land of Hiawatha — whether it be Perry's, Nichols's, Shiras's, or Galster's — make one idea crystal clear. The American deer camp experience consists of three elements: anticipation, realization, and reminiscence. Like Hiawatha, we all dream of that lucky and radiant opening day when amidst our traditional deer camp surroundings the early-rising eastern sun casts its shining glint of light upon the branching antlers of a mighty whitetail as he browses his way into our rifle sights.

Chapter 16

An Album of Reflections
on Deer Hunting
Through the Decades

RAAB & CAREY GOOSEBERY CROSING
LAKE CO. MINN. NOV. 18 - 1918

In A Dusty, Rustic Old Cabin

We are in a dusty, rustic old cabin
Up in the brush,
We have porcupines gnawing at the door,
And a den of skunks under the floor.

Some of the boys are cussing about the heat,
Others are complaining of cold feet,
Some of the boys sleep in pajamas,
Others in their drawers.
All these things don't make any difference
Everybody goes to bed and everybody snores.

Some of the boys are killing deer that's been
Dead for twenty years or more,
Others are still fighting the first World War.

Some of the boys are sitting at the table,
Hollering fifteen two and fifteen four,
With part of the cards on the floor.
A few more rounds of Roses Four,
They would still be hollering
Fifteen two and fifteen four if
All the cards were on the floor.

There is the good cook standing
By the door, he says, "Boys you have
Time for just one hand more, then
Clear the table and put on the
Plates and get ready for your
T-Bone steaks, some of you like
Them rare, some like them well,
You will eat them the way I
Cook them or go plum to Helena."

Such is life in a dusty, rustic
Old cabin up in the brush.

— Author Unknown

Photo credit Minnesota Historical Society

Whitetails aren't often hunted in real wilderness. They are often hunted in the tamest of farmlands. But even in a horseweed patch at the edge of a cornfield, a deer lends special wildness to the land so that wherever the deer is found it is a truly wild place. Deer carry wilderness entangled in their antlers; their hoofprints put the stamp of wildness on tame country.
—John Madson
  "The Secret Life of the Cottontail Deer,"
  Deer & Deer Hunting 5(3):15

Photo credit Mark Haggerty

461 Pounds on the Hoof

This white-tailed buck, shot in 1955 by Horace Hinkley, had a dressed weight of 355 pounds, which puts him at an estimated 461 pounds on the hoof. According to the records of the Biggest Buck in Maine Club, Hinkley's buck still remains the largest buck ever shot in that state. Indeed, it is one of the largest whitetails, in terms of weight, ever shot anywhere.

It was shot on a rainy day in November; the year was 1955. Lennie Rue recalls the tale:

"Horace Hinkley and his wife, Olive, were hunting on the Kennebec River near Bingham, Maine. It was a good hunting day because a hunter could move through the woods silently and there was only a light breeze to move scent around. Mr. and Mrs. Hinkley took stands on opposite sides of a ridge. At about 9:20 that morning, Hinkley fired at a buck but missed. A few minutes later, Olive Hinkley's rifle cracked, and after a few minutes she shouted that she had downed a big buck. Hinkley, certain that there were more deer in a thicket of scrub beech where he had missed the first one, remained where he was and did not respond. Suddenly a huge buck came crashing out of the brush toward him. Hinkley dropped the animal with one shot. It was so heavy that the Hinkleys had to get help to haul it out.

"The buck was not officially weighed until three days later. The weighing was performed by Forrest Brown, an official state sealer of weights and measures, and there were two witnesses. Hog-dressed, and after three days of drying out, it still scaled 355 pounds (160.8 kg.). Bob Elliot, of Maine's Department of Game, originally calculated the live weight to be at least 450 pounds (203.8 kg.) and more probably 480 pounds (217 kg.). Records of the Biggest Bucks in Maine Club officially established the weight at 461½ pounds. The buck's rack was excellent, but not in keeping with its body size. There were 8 points on each side, with a spread of twenty-one inches (53 cm.) and a beam length of 24.5 inches (63 cm.)."

Several bucks have come close to this record. One thinks of Dean Coffman, who shot a 440-pound Iowa buck in 1962. Or Robert Hogue, who reportedly shot a buck in Sawyer County, Wisconsin, in 1924 that had a dressed scale weight of 386 pounds (174.8 kg.) and an estimated live weight of 491 pounds (222.4 kg.). Unfortunately, Hogue's buck was not officially witnessed. One also thinks of the huge southern whitetail taken in Worth County, Georgia, in 1972 by Boyd Jones. Hog-dressed, it weighed 355 pounds (160.8 kg.) with an estimated live weight of 443 pounds (200.6 kg.).

Minnesota, however, claims the all-time record with Carl J. Lenander's buck shot in 1926. Field-dressed, it scaled 402 pounds (182.1 kg.). The Conservation Department calculated its live weight to be 511 pounds (231.4 kg.), making it the largest whitetail ever officially recorded in North America.

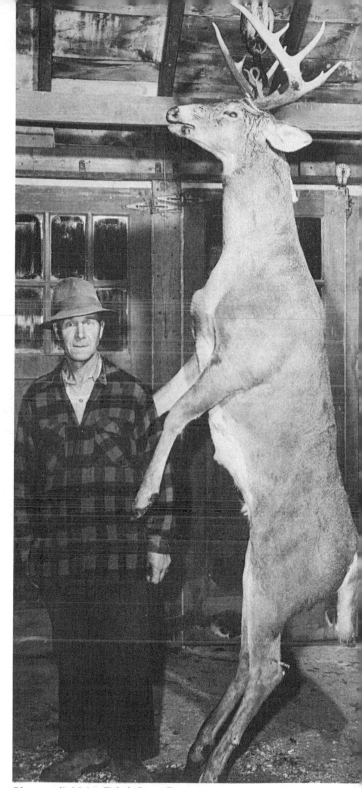

Photo credit Maine Fish & Game Department

Upstate New York, *circa* **1857** — "A loud and repeated hurrah! burst from us all as our oars struck the water and sent our little boats bounding over the rippled surface of the beautiful Saranac.

"This is indeed a beautiful sheet of water. The shores were lined with a dense and unbroken forest, stretching back to the mountains which surround it. The old wood stood then in all its primeval grandeur, just as it grew. The axe had not harmed it, nor had fire marred its beauty. The islands were covered with a lofty growth of living timber clothed in the deepest green. . . .

"Four or five miles down the lake is a beauti-

ful bay, stretching for near half a mile around a high promontory, almost reaching another bay winding around a like promontory beyond, leaving a peninsula of five hundred acres joined to the main land by a narrow neck of some forty rods in width. Our first sport among the deer was to be the 'driving' of this peninsula. We stationed ourselves on the narrow isthmus within a few rods of each other, while a boatman went round to the opposite side to lay on the dogs. We had been at our posts perhaps half an hour, when we heard the measured bounds of a deer as he came crashing through the forest. We could see his white flag waving above the undergrowth, as he came

Photo credit Adirondack Museum, Blue Mountain Lake, New York

bounding towards us. Neither Smith nor Spalding had ever seen a deer in his native woods, and they were, by a previous arrangement, to have the first shot, if circumstances should permit it. The noble animal came dashing proudly on his way, as if in contempt of the danger he was leaving behind him. Of the greater danger into which he was rushing, he was entirely unconscious, until the crack of Smith's rifle broke upon his astonished ear. He was unharmed, however, and quick as thought he wheeled and plunged back in the direction from which he came; Spalding's rifle, as it echoed through the forest, with the whistling of the ball in close proximity to his head,

added energy to his flight.

"The rifles were scarcely reloaded when the deep baying of the hounds was heard, and two more deer came crashing across the isthmus where we were stationed. The foremost one went down before the doctor's unerring rifle and cool aim, while the other ran the gauntlet of the three other rifles, horribly frightened, but unharmed, away. The hounds were called off, and with our game in one of the boats, we rowed back around the promontory and passed on towards the Saranac River."

—S. H. Hammond
Wild Northern Scenes, 1857

Photo credit Leonard Lee Rue III

Then the Buck Was There

Then the buck was there. He did not come into sight; he was just there, looking not like a ghost but as if all of the light were condensed in him and he were the source of it, not only moving in it but disseminating it, already running, seen first as you always see the deer, in that split second after he has already seen you, already slanting away in that first soaring bound, the antlers even in that dim light looking like a small rocking-chair balanced on his head.

— William Faulkner

The solo hunter learns to become self-reliant for he knows his success and enjoyment afield are strictly of his own making. He becomes sort of a lay naturalist because in his unhurried step and loitering at vantage points, he has ample time to observe all animal behavior. In short, he becomes a part of his hunting grounds and not an intruder of them.

And the lone hunter feels a sense of elation by bagging his game through his own efforts and knowledge of woods lore. Regardless of his success venison-wise, he enjoys the hunt because he loves the intimate contact it gives him with the outdoors.

—George Mattis,
"The Preserving Solo Hunter,"
Deer & Deer Hunting 5(4):25

Photo credit Michigan Department of State Archives

Deer of Tremendous Proportions

There are still deer of tremendous proportions—wise three-, four- and five-year-old bucks, typical and atypical, with thick necks and spreading rocking-chair horns that get tangled in the brush and make clacking noises as they move through the trees. Bucks that lie down on their belly when they hear a hunter and do not run but lie still and hide and wait until he is gone before silently sneaking off and away from that area for good, forever. Bucks that feed only at night, and sleep in the day, and have no friends, no other deer they travel with, for fear one of the other deer will do something stupid that will affect all of them—step on a twig, twitch a tail, snort a blow, step into a pasture at the wrong time. Instead, they drift through the woods alone, browsing acorns, growing fat, getting older, raising their heads and staring down the creek bottoms whenever they hear any sound at all, even a natural one.

—Rick Bass
The Deer Pasture, 1985

Photo credit Michigan Department of State Archives

The deer camp cook samples the venison stew. *Photo credit Michigan Department of State Archives*

A rustic North Woods cabin affords the deer hunters safe haven from the winter's chill. *Photo credit Minnesota Historical Society*

Schlitz beer comes to the American deer camp. *Photo credit Michigan Department of State Archives*

Northern Wisconsin, 1893. The refined taste in dress surely outweighs the crudeness of this deer shack. With the chores completed and the socks drying in the rafters, the alarm is set and the weary hunters turn in. *Photo credit State Historical Society of Wisconsin*

Opposite above: **The deer camp intellectuals catch up on what transpires in the "civilized" world.** *Photo credit Michigan Department of State Archives*

Opposite below: **The eternal card game — a deer camp recreation interrupted only by deer stalking.** *Photo credit Michigan Department of State Archives*

Things Permanent & Priceless

We cannot live in close touch with beautiful scenes and stimulating environments without being enriched by them. Is it unlikely that we will forget the way the wilderness appeared on a certain autumn morning when every brilliantly hued leaf was encased in glittering snow-crystals and kindled into prismatic fires by the beams of the rising sun? Do we cease to remember the advent of the Hunter's Moon—a blood-red and fabulous lantern as it peered at us across the lonely mazes of a black spruce swamp? Do we fail to recollect the spellbound mystery of a secluded lake, girdled by virgin timber, and sleeping like a liquid tourmaline in the shadowland of twilight? These are things permanent and priceless—poems of loveliness and beauty impressed upon the mind by nature in her wild state. These are things that time cannot take from us as long as memory lasts. The deerskin on our study floor, the buck's head over the fireplace, what are these after all but the keys which have unlocked enchanted doors, and granted us not only health and vigor, but a fresh and fairer vision of existence?

—Paul Brandreth
Trails of Enchantment, 1930

These Michigan women were obviously at home in that male bastion, deer camp. Their pump shotguns, repeating rifles, pistols, knives, and well-stocked ammunition belts indicate their preparedness for hunting in the deer forest. The trophies displayed on the meat pole are indeed an impressive collection. A half-century later, hunting women are still in the minority, constituting about 3 percent of the deer hunting population. *Photo credit Michigan Technological University Archives*

These hardy, rugged 1923 Minnesota deer hunters arranged their trophies—white-tailed bucks, does, and snow-shoe hares—on a birch bark meat pole. *Photo credit Minnesota Historical Society*

Photo credit Leonard Lee Rue III

Something Important Is About to Happen

In the long hours (of waiting for deer), I occupied a separate world of introspection where reverie could mature into reality. The stimulus was Nature in its impartial offerings of song and fruit, death and birth, and a sense of imminence: Something important is about to happen. It did not matter that I was surrounded by oaks and maples, ash and hemlock; the trees might well have been ghostly gums of the Australian Murrumbidgee, or kahikatea in New Zealand, or the dwarf palms and bamboos of Indian sal forests.

The aloneness of the deer hunter, and his thoughts of his hunting past, are the very genesis of primitive energy. He is always a young man, and making his most daring journeys. He will not think of middle age, and even the responsibility of his family will be dim as he pauses, every sense alert for the sound of what he plans to kill. This is really the only time that he is fully alive. All the rest is the dreaming time.

—Franklin Russell
The Hunting Animal, 1983

Al Herman and Carl Bing collected these fine specimens while deer hunting at Ash Lake, Minnesota, in 1925. *Photo credit Minnesota Historical Society*

These "city slickers" returned to civilization to display their quarry, which demonstrated for their womenfolk and families the results of their annual trip to deer camp. The memories of the hunt will survive long after the last package of venison is consumed. *Photo credit Minnesota Historical Society*

These dignified gents obviously desired a photographic record of their deer hunting trophies. (1908–1909). *Photo credit State Historical Society of Wisconsin*

The results of the 1919 deer hunt are displayed by these Minnesota deer hunters. *Photo credit Minnesota Historical Society*

The young deer hunter who shot this spike buck will turn this early success into a life-long November habit of stalking the white-tailed deer. *Photo credit Michigan Department of State Archives*

Adirondack deer hunters pose for a solemn photograph of the mighty buck atop the woodlot hearse. *Photo credit Adirondack Museum, Blue Mountain Lake, New York*

I Go Deerstalking . . .
"Just Because"

I go deerstalking because I like to. I love the usually beautiful mountains and bush where deer are found. In comparison the weekday surroundings of the working world are monotonous and ugly.

I go deerstalking sometimes just to escape the urban world and its crowds of people; to escape the artificial world of television and social life; to escape the things most of us tolerate but don't love.

Getting out in the hills is a way of returning to reality where things are logical, fresh, pure and clean; where there are no interruptions from telephones, television or other trivialities.

I go deerstalking because it exercises my patience, relaxes my mind and sheds my daily cares and worries. There is a special quietness and humility among good sportsmen in the hills. I go because I can find sweet solitude yet never be lonely; because a stew in camp always tastes better than one back home; because a cup of tea or coffee becomes the nectar of the gods after a hard slog with a pack; because one day I may find a big, big stag and will decide whether to kill or to show mercy. Going deerstalking is so important. Like all good outdoor sports once you get out there, the worries and cares of the city are somehow put into perspective and seem less important.

I go deerstalking just to enjoy myself, perhaps for a morning, an evening, a weekend or occasionally longer. I am a "very average hunter," but like so many who go deerstalking I go "just because."

—Tony Orman
Reflections of a Deerstalker, 1979

Photo credit Tom Huggler

Youthful success stories are the beginnings of long-time, dedicated hunters. In 1955, Dad was their hunter-safety instructor.
Photo credit Minnesota Historical Society

Photo credit Michigan Department of State Archives

The Cabin on the Bay

The huntin' season's comin' on,
I feel the old pulse stir,
I see the leaves a-flutterin' down,
I hear the partridge whirr:
I see the buck's track in the snow,
An' straight my fancies stray
To where the hills looks down upon
A cabin on a bay.

Oh, it's huntin' up the Mink Run Road,
An' peerin' all around,
An seein' everything that moves,
An' hearin' every sound:
An' trailin' where Mount Ida's top
Salutes the comin' day,
An trudgin' back at nightfall to
The cabin on the bay.

The crooked runway's windin' line
Invites my willin' feet
'Twas made by those who never knew
The trammels of a street:

By woods an' hills an' lakes an' rills
It leads its steadfast way,
An' those who foot it know full well
The cabin on the bay.

Oh! it's huntin' up the Cliff Lake trail,
An' seein' every track,
An' throwin' up your rifle quick,
An' hearin' it go crack;
An' cuttin' poles to hang him up,
The only proper way—
An' tellin' all about it
In the cabin on the bay.

What though the city's noisy streets
Confine our steps today,
'Tis not for long, an' soon we'll see
The cabin on the bay.

—Horace Kent Tenney, 1924

Chapter 17

Buck Fever

Any sportsman who can kill his deer without the tingling spine, the quick clutch at his heart, the delicious trembling of nerve fibers when the game is finally down, has no place in the deer woods.

—Larry Koller, 1948

I have always known how dangerous the sport of hunting for white-tailed bucks can be and know personally some of its casualties. However, I speak not of its physical dangers—although many American deer hunters become the victims of heart attacks, perhaps brought on by the excitement of confronting the biggest buck of their lives. But these cases of heart stoppage as a result of buck fever remain comparatively few nationwide; the danger I refer to is more widespread and insidious, for it is mental and emotional. Indeed, that eternal desire to hunt up a buck has wrecked men's marriages and ruined many a career.

I know of one buck hunter from Alabama called "Crazy Eddie" who goes through one wife and one job each buck season. The Dean of Students at the University of Wisconsin once called my mother to retrieve me from the deer forest for final exams. Chasing bucks, if begun early enough in life, can prevent people from ever getting around to either marriage or a career; it can turn people into lifelong celibates and ne'er-do-wells. One buck hunter I know had the Nietzschean strength of will to cure himself of chronic alcoholism but failed to control his obsessive addiction for white-tailed buck hunting. Some backwoods deerslayers quit their jobs at an early age, sponge off their relatives, remain lifelong bachelors, and do whatever the call of the wild dictates to keep them on the track of white-tailed bucks. A good number of deer hunters even view this kind of behavior as an exemplary form of life. While the healthy, well-balanced mind usually withdraws in distaste and fright from all excess, when it comes to the sport of white-tailed buck hunting many of us become excessive in everything we do. The zeal for the activity has no bounds or limitations; we make a passion out of our pastime and in the process often fail to understand or even recognize the word "moderation."

That "delicious trembling of nerve fibers," as Larry Koller, that great Catskill deer hunting guide, suggests, represents an essential ingredient of buck fever. But what is buck fever overall, and how does it affect man, the hunter? When we consult the *Oxford English Dictionary,* we find no such concept. We don't find it listed under the subject headings in the card catalog of the public library either. But deer hunters all across this land confront it and pour their souls into understanding and coming to terms with this malady. Although absent as a concept in standard bibliographic references, the literature on the subject of American deer hunting contains countless examples of how buck fever affects man and how man, the hunter, describes that fever and searches for a cure.

I get buck fever when I merely take Eldridge Reeves Johnson's classic book, *Buck Fever,* in hand. Sneaking this $300, rare blue-chip deer book bound in a fully dark, green pigskin and illustrated with nostalgic deer hunting pictures past my wife Maren Lea, the Chancellor of the Exchequer, is what I call buck fever! Paying that kind of money to Ken Callahan of Callahan and Company Booksellers of New Hampshire, at a time when I'm living on $50 a week and all the road kills I can eat, gradually undermines the cement of the marriage contract — even though my wife is a deer hunter.

The musty, ancient smell of *Buck Fever,* the black-and-white plates with printed

"Oh, a good buck track just sets me to quivering!" — **Larry Benoit.** *Photo credit Leonard Lee Rue III*

overlays — especially the one entitled "The deer turns and goes slowly on. Bang! Bang! and good-bye." — and the watered silk endpapers paralyze my emotions, and if read in the deer forest will render the deer hunter, regardless of his mental constitution, foolishly harmless upon the sighting of any buck. Published in 1911, this privately printed jewel seriously questions the universal notion that buck fever only affects amateurs and disappears as the deer hunter gains experience. Johnson, the one-time president of the Victor Talking Machine Company, remained convinced, as does this author, that buck fever is far more reaching in scope and certainly more tenacious than the popular conception would indicate.

Like many hunters, Johnson directly confessed to being hopelessly susceptible to buck fever or to what he called that "expensive, intermittent, business-disturbing mania." He rightly compared this intermittent mania to malaria in that you can depend on it to return at certain times of the year and argued that "in some cases it can be subdued only by the rigid enforcement of the game laws." Actually, that fine line between chronic buck fever and deer poaching has never been fully explored. As most buck hunters learn sooner or later, the chief end of a trophy, white-tailed buck focuses on one basic instinct: keeping his head on his own shoulders and not on your mantelpiece or as a statistic in the record book next to your name.

In striving to add their name to the record book, some overzealous buck hunters try to turn the odds in their favor by committing what they euphemistically call "minor infractions" of the game laws. Yes, buck fever has been the undoing of some trophy hunters in their obsessive desire to collect trophy antlers. While trophy hunting and antler display, sometimes called "trophyism," has come under attack, no adequate explanation has ever been given for this form of human behavior and its intimate connection with buck fever. But the connection obviously exists.

In his explanation of buck fever, Johnson observed that this interesting disease does not limit itself to the single matter of marksmanship but runs deep into the blood of the human condition. "Buck fever," Johnson writes, "is a blood affection; it is contagious and hereditary. A well-developed case will impart the disease to many innocent persons in a comparatively short time, if opportunity can but secure them as audience. Buck Fever, in truth, is nothing less than a tormenting desire to go and rough it a bit, —a continuous longing to get back close to Mother Nature, who is always calling to her truants."

Like many deer hunters before him, Johnson believed that a mild dose of buck fever does little harm but actually adds a little spice to the deer hunt where spice is needed. We all miss bucks sometimes, and Johnson acknowledged that it takes a good deal of experience and a tremendous amount of self-control to gracefully acknowledge missing a close, easy shot. Most deer hunters like to fall back on those weird tales of buck fever to explain their misses, but these tales often constitute little more than what Johnson calls "disappointed, disgusted Mr. Missed-the-Buck's explanation of why it happened." Whatever buck fever may be, Johnson thought it had a lot more to do with hunting than the mere incidence of missing a very close and easy shot. He experienced buck fever as a long-standing, irritating, restless attack of one age-old thing: a haunting desire to hunt and hang on the meat pole a trophy, white-tailed buck.

That haunting desire drove Johnson to the deer forest each fall to pursue a buck. He called his deer camp "Harvey's Inn," named after one of his guides. He prepared a sign for his camp for use in the event of the guide's absence. It read: "HARVEY'S INN—But Harvey's Out." While deer hunting out of Harvey's Inn, Johnson experienced buck fever in various degrees of intensity. One day shortly before returning to Harvey's Inn, he spotted a buck reaching a small clearing at an easy trot. He recalls the incident in *Buck Fever:*

"I suspended breathing and threw every nerve and muscle into the aim; I never aimed quite so hard before. Bang! Now I will see a deer do some running, flashes through my mind. But no, the deer stops short and looks in my direction. No amount of reasoning can forecast what a deer is going to do at such a time, but I am astonished. Didn't even scare him, is my thought. Bang! again. The deer turns and goes slowly on. Bang! Bang! and good-bye. Well, I couldn't expect to make a long shot like that, I say to myself by way of comfort, but it is no comfort. When the shooting is over, I am all out of breath from the strain.

"Missed, just missed! What an awful thing it is to miss. Three thousand miles and two days' waiting for a shot—and missed! Missed! I can never become reconciled to that experience.

"Over the hill I trudge with heavy heart, to see that our second best case of Buck Fever has killed the first buck he ever shot at. He limps about in that fullness of soaring spirits and joyful pride that comes to all who have the real sporting blood in their veins—the real blue blood. His is that mysterious unreasonable joy of the first kill. He limps, because after he tumbled the deer fifty feet down the hill, he tumbled down after it in excitement and twisted his ankle. He never knew it until he returned to camp—Buck Fever! How many things it has to answer for!"

Buck fever also plagued T. S. Van Dyke, that great American still-hunter, who often saw "venison vanish down the vale with bounding hoof and flaunting tail" after missing one of those so-called perfect, ideal shots. In doing so, Van Dyke would merely smile and view that flaunting flag as a chilling, mocking farewell to hope. Van Dyke considered the disappointment and humiliation as a result of buck fever to be his best teachers, for he studied why he missed the deer and always turned the situation into a learning experience.

Buck fever is certainly not a unique American phenomenon. Augustus Grimble, the famous English deerstalker, experienced the problem as well. In his classic manual on *Deer Stalking* (1888), he warns us that, "The disease must run its course. Advice will not cure it, neither will whiskey."

The disease affects hunters in the deer forest all across America. In checking the *Bucks Camp Log* (1974), a Wisconsin deer camp diary, we find the following entry dated November 25, 1917:

The bunch drove the vicinity of Poise stump this afternoon. Mr. E. W. Hill, Sr. was feeling well enough to join the bunch. A lead mine could be started with bullets we left down there. We had five deer surrounded. The bombardment sounded like an English barrage. Deer were running everywhere. They were so thick around Mr. Hill, Sr. that he had to push them away beyond the end of his gun so he could shoot them. He got buck fever so bad that he was shooting in a circle. Mr. True said the air was so thick around Mr. Hill, Sr. that he could not shoot through it.

This kind of buck fever has no scientific name nor does the medical profession recognize it. As one medical doctor exclaimed while deer hunting in the Adirondacks with William Monypeny Newsom: "Why should any healthy man dissolve into nervous hysteria in one form or another merely at the sight of a deer? As far as I've seen in my own practice, I don't believe it is possible." The doctor made this statement while on his first deer hunt with Newsom. Shortly after pronouncing those words of wisdom on the subject, he shifted his rifle from his shoulder to the hollow of his left arm and walked down a trail for an afternoon stand.

Several hours had passed when Newsom suddenly heard a shot from the ridge the doctor had headed for. "Evidently the doctor had gone into action," Newsom thought to himself. Newsom arose from his stump to listen. He heard one shot only, which could have meant anything or nothing. Newsom listened for ten minutes. Then down the trail came the bewildered doctor in great haste. Newsom noticed that the doctor's face took on a pale, peculiar yellow tint. He trembled to such a degree that he could hardly hold onto his rifle. He started to speak to Newsom, but stuttered, hesitated, and stopped before trying again.

"A b-b-b-buck!" he finally blurted out as if he made some world-shaking discovery. "I d-d—don't b-b-believe I e'er t-t-touched 'em," he continued.

Newsom took the frenzied doctor up the ridge again to investigate and discovered that a buck had stepped out from behind a windfall and stood broadside less than twenty-five yards from the doctor's stand. Fifteen feet to the right of where the buck stood, Newsom found a birch sapling with the top broken off. The fresh cut made the mark of the bullet plainly visible. The doctor had missed the buck by fifteen feet. Newsom looked for the empty cartridge but could not find it.

"Why didn't you shoot again?" Newsom asked. The doctor told him somewhat sheepishly that he couldn't remember how to work the action. "When I finally threw a new cartridge into the chamber—it was too late," the doctor claimed.

Newsom glanced at the bolt of the doctor's rifle; the safety lug was in a position to shoot—not in the safety position. Newsom took the rifle, opened it, and an empty cartridge case came out. Newsom handed the empty cartridge to the doctor, who looked quite amazed.

Newsom became so fascinated with the whole question of buck fever that when he returned to New York City, he sought out an eminent psychiatrist who pronounced these words of wisdom on the subject of buck fever and its victims:

"Of course buck fever is a violent form of nerves, but there's a good reason for it. You will notice it is more apt to hit a man who goes from the city to the deer country. Before he goes he says he 'needs a rest' or he 'ought to get away.' In other words he's saying he is out of adjustment with his city environment. Perhaps he doesn't realize it, but he's antagonistic to and fighting against his city life and the hurry of it all. Quite unconsciously he's pulling against the stream instead of pulling with it, though he doesn't see the current. Naturally, when he hits the deer woods, he's out of adjustment with *that* environment too. He goes from one bad adjustment to another bad adjustment. Then instead of taking it easy mentally, he fusses and frets over little things like a late start in the morning. He is mentally pushing himself along harder than he should. Besides which he usually overworks physically the first few days or so—walking too far, getting over-tired, and perhaps not sleeping well the first few nights. But always *striving* mentally toward the deer. The natural result is, without his knowing it, the nervous system is overtaxed and breaks under the strain when the climax comes and the object of the trip is sighted. And that is particularly true of short deer hunts because there is much jammed into a short space of time and there's a constant rush to get it done. There is little chance to become adjusted under such circumstances."

Some deer hunters refer to these circumstances of buck fever as "the shakes," and a strange sort of craziness. In the South, hunters sometimes call it "buck ague." One deer hunter from Louisiana defined it this way: "When a person endures rain, wind, cold, heat, mosquitoes, thirst, and hunger—and even forgoes tobacco, coffee, and almost anything to be out in the woods deer hunting, he has what is known as Buck Fever. It is a contagious disease and each year in Louisiana it becomes increasingly more difficult to contain."

Others think that this mysterious, humorous malady afflicts only greenhorns. For many it is a real barrier to good shooting, and sometimes to any shooting. It sometimes throws the hunter's aim so far off that the deer couldn't be safer. The initial symptoms remain familiar to most deer hunters: Your heart speeds up, your temples pound, and your arms and legs weaken. One deer hunter in Ohio referred to it as an unpredictable and unconscious thing forcing the hunter to choke up and freeze. Ben East, the long-time field editor for *Outdoor Life,* called it "a very queer affliction and I have yet to hear a really good explanation of it. It can result from excitement, fear, a trance-like concentration on getting game, even from fascination, or from a combination of all of them."

One thing remains certain: The deer camps of America never run short of buck fever stories. The last volume of deer hunting tales to cross my desk was even written by an author named Buck Fever. The real author obviously heard of the American author Sherwood Anderson and his famous *Buck Fever Papers*.

In trying to explain buck fever, deer hunters talk about palpitations, jammed cartridges, incoherent mumbling, and quick jolts of adrenaline. Russell Thornberry, a trophy white-tailed deer hunter from Alberta, best explains it as a product of fear. He argues that the "number one fear is that the buck will get away due to the hunter's inadequacies in delivering a fatal shot." I find this explanation particularly relevant to the bow hunter. While buck fever never plagues me during the gun season, it haunts me during the bow season when the odds greatly favor the buck. The only partial cure I have found for buck fever revolves around spending more time in my tree stands throughout the entire year and learning to live with live deer so close that you can hear them chew acorns and break wind. But as Thornberry warns us, we will probably never find a 100 percent cure for buck fever, nor should we:

"It is only fitting that there should be no 100 percent cure for buck fever in a sport that offers no guarantees anyway. When the biggest buck you ever have seen walks out in front of you and you feel no surge of adrenaline, check your pulse to be sure you still are alive. If you find you still are among the living, go home and hang up your gun or bow. It would be a crime for a hunter with no thrill left in his veins to bag such a magnificent creature. It is not that we desire to eliminate buck fever, because that is part of the thrill of the hunt. We only want to learn to function with control through it. The thrill of the opportunity combined with the sweet taste of success is the combination we seek."

Other deer hunters such as John Madson, the poetic outdoorsman from the prairie land of Illinois, compares buck fever to "a form of shell-shock" that so overwhelms the mind and paralyzes the nervous system that some deer hunters, as Madson tells us, "perform amazing maneuvers that have absolutely no logical connection to the job at hand, such as jacking a magazineful of hulls through the rifle without firing a shot and maybe even yelling 'bang!' each time they throw the bolt." Madson, like Larry Koller, mourns for the guy who's never experienced a glowing flush of buck fever and rightly doubts whether he has ever really been hunting. After all, Madson asks, who really has the most fun? The cold, detached, clinical deer hunter? Or the shook-up buck hunter who bites through his pipe stem when a white-tailed buck jumps into sight?

Buck fever is perhaps as common as wet feet. A classic example of an A-number-one attack of buck fever occurred when Emil Winter, the one-time president of the Pittsburgh Steel Company, went deer hunting at the Woodmont Rod and Gun Club in Hancock, Maryland, with Henry Bridges, the secretary and game master of the club. Winter wanted to kill a buck for a stag party he planned to give in his Pittsburgh home. After a good deal of effort moving deer around on the Woodmont acreage, one of this country's finest hunting clubs, Bridges finally got Winter within 500 yards of a magnificent white-tailed buck coming along an oak ridge.

When Winter, a big-game hunter with many years of experience, finally saw the sun glinting off the buck's massive rack, he bolted upright from the stump he had been sitting on. He seemed startled; sweat beads popped out on his forehead. The buck seemed to float through the oaks in a ghostlike manner as it approached the hunters. Bridges saw Winter's hands begin to tremble; the foreign-made, custom-built rifle in his hands wobbled and shook. Winter's glassy eyes stared straight ahead; his mouth hung wide open.

The buck approached the two hunters and soon stood broadside between two white oaks, less than fifty yards away. "Shoot!" Bridges whispered to his agitated colleague. "Shoot him!"

Winter looked at Bridges dumbfoundedly and gasped for air. "I can't shoot him, Henry. I can't even see him!"

"There he is, Emil! Right in front of you," Henry whispered again. "Shoot!"

"Henry, I can't see any buck! I tell you I can't see him," Winter insisted somewhat in a state of delirium. "Henry, you shoot him!"

"No!" Henry whispered. "He's your deer. You shoot him!"

While trembling and shaking and as the fever intensified, Winter sat back on his stump. He mumbled inaudible sounds and looked blindly about himself. "I can't see him, I can't see him," he kept muttering in muffled tones.

Henry slowly raised his rifle and aimed it at the buck. Incredibly enough, the buck still stood there, patiently offering a perfect broadside shot. "Look down my rifle. It's aimed at the buck. Now, pull the trigger, Emil," Henry whispered.

Winter leaned forward and squinted down Henry's rifle barrel. He trembled with such excitement that he could hardly keep his head above the barrel. "I don't see any buck," he finally blurted out loud. The buck tensed up, ready to spring forward.

"Shoot!" Henry said. "He's heard us—he's ready to bolt!"

But Winter just sat there and trembled as the buck bounded off. So Henry shouldered his rifle and shot twice. The buck staggered but managed to keep going. Henry's two shots seemed to break Winter's fever, for he now jumped to his feet and shot just as the deer stumbled and went down. After walking over to the fallen buck, the somewhat dazed Winter asked: "Henry, did I—did I get him?"

Trying to keep the humor off his face, Henry replied, "Yes, you hit him and I missed."

Winter stood there shaking his head and breathing hard, as if coming out of a delirious dream. A moment of silence occurred, followed by this one-liner: "Henry, my boy," Emil proudly pronounced, "I want you to come to my stag party, and if we find two bullets in this buck, I'll give you credit for one of them!"

Indeed, buck fever affects veteran and novice alike, and appears in about as many different guises as there are individuals who succumb to this frenzied derangement of deer hunting behavior. Whether it be loss of judgment or helpless confusion or utter loss of composure, it differs only in its effect on the hunter and the intensity of the feverish attack. The proximity of the deer often plays a considerable part in stirring the hunter's emotions. A buck standing off at a great distance does not seem to excite the fever as much as when that same buck comes close enough for the deer hunter to see the intricate details of its anatomy and the distinct structure of its rack. The booming of the

deer rifle and the sight of a mortally wounded buck struggling to regain the spark of life also play a strong psychological role in that complex affair we call buck fever.

Regardless of the variables or the different ways it's experienced, the end result remains pretty much the same: The buck escapes. That might strike some of us as an excellent state of affairs, at least from a selfish point of view. If buck fever did not exist, few white-tailed bucks would be left in the woods for the rest of us.

I doubt whether any wildlife ecology student in America has yet received a Ph.D. degree for a doctoral dissertation on the subject of buck fever, but the problem has received attention in the technical literature. While trying to explain this confused state of mind and body we call buck fever, Harry Ruhl, the one-time chief of the Michigan Game Division, offers us this technical interpretation:

"What happens? Under great emotional stress, a temporary block momentarily occurs between the straining mind and the willing but uncontrolled muscular system. The effects are different in individuals. Some persons are simply paralyzed. Others are victims of muscular incoordination so pronounced that the simple act of pointing a gun becomes impossible. Others may perform complicated muscular maneuvers, but their actions may have no logical relation to their immediate objective. Hunters have been known to rack their guns until every cartridge in the magazine lay unexploded on the ground. One of the most regrettable reactions may be the peculiar visual aberration whereby a man, cow, or other animal appears to the victim as a deer. In such a case, the old story of shooting a man for a deer may be reenacted.

"Buck fever is a peculiar variation of the situation referred to by medical men as nervous shock. Mind and body do not function as a unit. Each responds intensely to the sharp stimulus of the sight of big game. All of those fine adjustments built up through the years suddenly break down. The heart speeds up. Blood pressure rises. Hormones are spilled into the blood with reckless abandon. Blood sugar rises, then drops. The whole voluntary and autonomic nervous system goes awry. The more the victim struggles, the worse his condition becomes. The last flick of a white tail disappearing in the distance is likely to break the spell. The hapless victim revives with electric suddenness. The self-condemnation and maledictions sent in the direction of the vanished deer are scarcely less violent than the inward struggles occurring at the height of the 'fever.'"

However we define it, many different things cause buck fever to stir in my blood regardless of the season. Finding a fresh scrape with a pool of urine in it does the trick, as does seeing a massive eight-pointer at my corn feeders the day after the gun season closes. Encountering a rutting buck trotting down a major runway with its tail standing straight out and with its nose tight to the ground in hot pursuit of a white-tailed doe in estrus fires the fever. Observing a buck licking an overhanging branch in the middle of July, or watching a fashion show of fourteen different bucks in an alfalfa field with the sun in the sky in early autumn, intensifies and sustains the fever throughout the year. Finding shed antlers in the deer forest in spring, seeing newly-shed velvet hanging from bloodied antlers in late summer, and locating the devastating buck rubs of the "Birch Bark Buck" all inflame the heat of the fever. Reading Seton's *The Trail of the Sandhill Stag* or Horace Kent Tenney's poem entitled "The Cabin on the Bay" stirs the pulse of the fever in my veins, as does viewing Michael Sieve's "Evening Stand" or the deer paintings, prints, and illustrations of A. F. Tait, Sir Edwin Landseer, and Ned Smith, or the deer photos of George Shiras III and Leonard Lee Rue III.

Hearing the low, guttural grunts of a rutting buck in November agitates the fever, while smelling the distinct aroma of buckskin ignites it as well and forces me to drive out of my way to visit the show-

If you've ever been victimized by buck fever, you know what a big buck can do to your mental constitution. *Photo credit Leonard Lee Rue III.*

Photo credit Missouri Department of Conservation

Photo credit Dr. Charles T. Arnold

While many of us dream of shooting Boone and Crockett bucks such as the Jordan head and that monster from Missouri, most of us shoot does, yearlings, and bucks with mediocre racks.

rooms of Mid-Western Sport Togs, Custom Coat Company, and the W. B. Place Company, America's leading manufacturers of deerskin products. Going to the Southeast Deer Study Group Meeting each year in February with my friend Kent Horner and listening to the distinguished deer doctors expound upon their theories of buck behavior during the rut heightens the degree of all the symptoms and leads me to dream of the Jimmy Jordan record typical head and that monster Boone and Crockett non-typical buck found dead along a fence line in Missouri with a Boone and Crockett score of 333⅞, when in reality I shoot does, spikes, forkhorns, and the scraggliest bucks Iowa County, Wisconsin, can produce. Finding buck tracks cut deeply into Deer Foot Road as I tramp to the mailbox hoping to receive a

new issue of *The Journal of Wildlife Management* in Box 98A keeps the heat of the fever warm. But finding in Box 98A a letter from a subscriber of *Deer & Deer Hunting* magazine written with a fountain pen in very distinct penmanship on the very subject of buck fever and written on the back of a NRA target renews the fever.

Dear Dr. Wegner,

I write to you with some hope inside of me, for a cure for my "ailment." I don't know what else it could be called. There are many fine people in the deer hunting world, but I need to feel I'm writing to someone whom I feel is of a sensitive nature.

I'd like to sit here on my couch, thinking that I can write some sort of a smooth sounding piece, but the fact is I'm a house builder, not a writer. I'm thirty-seven, father of two healthy children. My wife Barb is a nurse and a very good wife, as well as understanding.

My ailment is a severe case of post-season depression. (I must admit I don't know what your degree is in and I'm not really looking for a health cure. I don't think so anyways!) My life revolves around two things: my family and deer hunting, in that order. Sometimes one gets ahead of the other, though.

Every year that goes by it gets harder for me to accept the reality that deer hunting is over for nine or ten months. I don't know what it's like for a drug addict to go cold turkey, but I think I can imagine. I have done and read more than the average hunter experiences after the season, but it just doesn't cut it anymore. I hunt in five states with rifle, bow and arrow, and muzzleloader. Right now I still feel I need to do more. I'm not really rich and I have to work, but as long as I know there is a deer hunting season on, I keep wanting to be there. That can put a strain on family life, and I can see my wife's point of view after I've hunted for the entire month of November and some of October and December.

Killing a deer means nothing to me as far as pleasure goes. It's everything that happens before and after.

I've hunted in Saskatchewan this year for the first time. Met some wonderful people and I had a great trip. I even got a nice eight-pointer. The whole trip was beautiful. After returning only two weeks ago, I'm wanting to be out again. I even tried to ease myself down by hunting a couple of days in the southern zone of New York. I'm supposed to work tomorrow but thoughts of the muzzleloader season in southern New York are just dancing all through my little pea brain. It's gotten so that once in a while I'm on the border of skirting some of my responsibilities. I guess that's where the problem is now that I see myself writing this letter.

I do have one consolation, however. I have gotten to know Dr. Charles Arnold quite well in the past three to four years. He lives in my home town of Nashua, New Hampshire. I have a picture of my son holding the James Jordan buck. I look at it and it gives me comfort and solace. Oh, the Lord was such a creator and still is. I guess knowing he will create another Jordan head someday is cause to be jubilant.

Well, what do ya think Doc? Is there salvation? Do you know of any good cures? It's frustrating. Why I couldn't even find a piece of lined paper in my house, so I had to write this letter on a target. Ironic!

I was starting to come down a bit and then I got the February issue of Deer & Deer Hunting. Seeing that cover just shot me to the stars. I would like to thank the editors and Mr. & Mrs. Brakefield.

I'm looking forward to any help you can give me.

Ron Boucher
Wallingford, Vermont
December 13, 1984

That letter drew this response:

Dear Ron,

Yes . . . there is salvation! There are several cures you might try. But before I discuss the cures let me just say this with regard to your "ailment."

Aldo Leopold, the father of wildlife management, usually referred to the symptoms you describe as "congenital hunting fever." I have had this chronic, infectious fever ever since the age of ten when I saw my first eight-point buck in the hills of southeastern Wisconsin. The sight of that buck, as I tramped behind my father carrying a stick as a substitute for a gun, so enamored me with the white-tailed deer that I have been pursuing deer in one way or another ever since. I think about deer. Read about deer. Observe deer. Write articles and books about deer. Feed deer. Hunt deer. Butcher deer. Eat deer. Wear deerskin clothing. And dream about deer. You know the obsession is peaking when you dream about them. Indeed, when I cannot do these things, I too suffer from what I call deer depression.

But Ron, you and I are not alone. A research report from the North Carolina Division of Wildlife that just crossed my desk indicates that 203,000 people from that state alone are afflicted with this disease each fall. The report goes on to suggest that "the disorder passes in time causing little damage but much domestic discord." Much domestic discord . . . yes! But I doubt whether that disorder ever passes in time!

Here are some of the cures that I have employed to ease the pain, if "pain" be the right word, for I tend to like this psychotic disorder.

First of all, I built a personal library on the subject so that I could enjoy the experiences of others, but that only brought a great deal of domestic discord and financial ruin. Secondly, I got a job as a writer dealing with the subject of deer, but $50 a week is not a great deal of salvation as my wife, the Chancellor of the Exchequer, will be the first to tell you; you will make more money building houses. Thirdly, I built a deer shack in heavily populated deer country where I now reside. This step brought great relief, for I now have deer wandering around the house at all hours of the day. Now and then they drop off their fawns on my front porch. Fourthly, the greatest comfort and solace came when I read Ortega's Meditations on Hunting (1942), a book that ultimately defines deer hunting as the purest form of human happiness and portrays human nature as inseparable from the hunting instinct. Ever since reading this classic, deer hunting for me has become a form of personal evolution. The fifth and final cure to the whole dilemma came when my wife joined the ranks of the American deer hunters, thus ending, once and for all, all traces of domestic discord.

Dr. Rob Wegner, Editor

When I was a young Nimrod of twelve, the convoys of covered trucks heading north toward deer country on the highways and backroads brought forth the first traces of buck fever. Today, the mere examination of a new issue of *Deer & Deer Hunting* as it comes "hot" off the press, even though I have already seen every inch of it while editing it, induces a good jolt of buck fever. But the fever peaks for me when I watch the sunrise in the east while the moon slowly sets in the west next to Doc's Rock during the closing days of the bow season, and as I stare at a large, gray, antlered image moving through the young birch stand in front of Doc's Rock, for I then think of the deer hunter's eternal paradox: Why do I kill the object I love best?

While thinking about this eternal paradox, these lines from Ortega y Gasset's *Meditations on Hunting* (1942) always come to mind: "Every good hunter is uneasy in the depths of his conscience when faced with the death he is about to inflict on the enchanting animal. He does not have the final and firm conviction that his conduct is correct. But neither, it should be understood, is he certain of the opposite." Because of this eternal paradox, buck fever will always afflict man, the hunter, and it will always be associated with the most controversial issues of modern-day deer hunting: accidental deaths, crippling losses, poaching, and the numerous illegalities involved in the current American antler craze.

PART IV

THE DEER HUNTER

Chapter 18

Stalking the Deer Poacher

Poaching may be considered more like "stealing bases" than stealing a public resource.

—Robert Giles, *Wildlife Management,* 1978

In 1739, the state of Massachusetts initiated the job of deer wardens to protect this country's white-tailed deer population. To defy, trick, and circumvent these first deer wardens (later to become more popularly known as game wardens or conservation officers), deer poachers appeared on the scene. The conflict between deer wardens and deer poachers, the reverse sides of the same coin, goes back to the legend and tradition of Robin Hood and farther back into the golden age of medieval hunting in England and Europe. I say the reverse sides of the same coin, because I wonder whether poachers and wardens have not at one time or another played both sides of the coin? The *Oxford English Dictionary* states the paradox more sharply: "The warden is only a poacher turned outside in and a poacher a warden turned inside out." We even read in W. M. Smith's *The Romance of Poaching in the Highlands* (1919), that "poaching is the best possible training for gamekeeper."

Actually, deer poaching may well be considered "the second oldest profession." Some consider it a skilled and ancient craft, for the poacher is both hunter and hunted, trying to evade the wardens as his quarry, the white-tailed deer, tries to evade him. Indeed, deer poachers remain elusive characters with Ph.D.'s in evasion. As warden J. A. McQuerry of the Arkansas Game and Fish Commission states, "The harder you press him, the more educated he becomes. A good many of ours have B.A. degrees, I am sure; if you ever chased one on a dusty, gravel road at night, you'd know he is not too easy to catch even after you have located him." Indeed, most deer poachers school themselves in the entrance, exit, and evasion theme. According to one self-confessed deer poacher with more than forty years of experience, "The ability to move in and out of a chosen piece of posted country is to a great extent an art. Truly successful poachers are like smoke. They move silently and invisibly wherever and whenever they please."

We know very little about deer poachers and their social backgrounds. Any portrait of them must be built on many different sources, for deer poachers obviously do not write a great deal about their activities and the current state of their nefarious art. We need to consult the hunter education, law enforcement and human dimensions literature, diaries, and journals of game wardens, court records, newspaper clippings, and the esoteric journals of the social scientists. But above all, we need to consult the literary work of Edmund Ware Smith (1900–1967), that superb spinner of deer poaching tales based on fact, who gave us a consummate portrait of the all-American deer poacher in the infamous character of Thomas Jefferson Coongate, one of the most ingratiating rascals in American literature. In studying these various sources, a fascinating story of deer poachers and poaching emerges riddled with humor, inconsistencies, entrenched social prejudices, bigtime commercial profits, the daredevil aspects of small-scale operations, prehistoric savagery, and murder.

Let us then meet some of the legendary deer poachers — both past, present, and in our imagination.

When Thomas Jefferson Coongate was out of jail and sober, his chief occupation revolved around poaching deer, outwitting the game warden, and playing Robin Hood by peddling venison loin to his neighbors in the woods of Maine. Smith based the character of Jeff Coongate — "the greatest deer poacher this country ever heard tell of" — on the pathological poacher who persists in the "cops and robbers" syndrome, who gets as much satisfaction from outwitting the warden as from his criminal gain and who delights himself in the thrill of the chase, the getaway, and the cool-off. He introduced the Coongate character to the American outdoorsman in his *Tall Tales and Short,* published by Derrydale Press in 1938:

"Old Jeff Coongate was composed solely of vices. He was a chewer of tobacco, a drinker of bottled goods in any alcoholic form and a kind of marathon blasphemer. He was a sworn breaker of game laws and an enemy of the State. He was a jacklighter of deer, a gillnetter of salmon, a dynamiter of trout and above all else, a plotter against the lives of game wardens. In fact, he was currently in the clink for shooting the stern off a game warden's canoe with an automatic shotgun. Happily the warden was a good swimmer."

Jeff Coongate, as Smith tells us, never shot a legal deer except once — by mistake. Through the skillful pen of Smith, Coongate becomes a deer poacher of gigantic proportions, awesome prowess, and mental agility. Like many of the boys who feast on illegal venison, he violates the game laws as an act of human dignity. For Jeff Coongate, the violation of the deer laws merely represents an act of self-affirmation; he violates them as an instinctive response to the challenge of nature. In so doing, he thinks that he asserts his human dignity.

A double hunt takes place in Smith's classic tales of the One-Eyed Poacher of Privilege: the poacher pursues his venison loin while warden Tom Corn pursues his victim. Smith found this antagonistic relationship between poacher and warden peculiarly interesting and observed that solid friendships frequently spring up between poacher and warden; friendships cemented together by a continuous cat-and-mouse routine.

Smith places his deer poacher-game warden feud on a sporting basis within the fixed penalties of the law; it becomes purely a battle of wits without much blood being spilled other than that of the deer. But when this classic feud erupts in reality, as in the 1981 case of Claude Dallas and wardens Bill Pogue and Conley Elms in Idaho, blood spilling reaches tragic proportions.

In his deer poaching tales, wardens and poachers frequently play both sides of the coin as Smith found the case to be in reality. "I knew the cream of the two opposing crops," he writes, "one representing the law, the other holding out for a high protein diet, low meat bills, if any, and the mythical and nefarious 'summer hunting license.'" As a result, Smith admired and befriended poachers and wardens alike in his attempt to understand the mind of the poacher. In an autobiographical essay entitled "My Game Warden Friends and Outlaw Companions," Smith gives us an example of the exchange of roles:

"I knew an old-time warden, and a good one—call him Ike Spencer. Ike had just about reached the age of retirement, and had trained a younger warden—Dick Royce—to carry on in his snowshoe beat.

"'Ike,' said the young warden, 'what're you going to do when you retire?'

"Old Ike considered briefly, and said: 'Well, I'll tell you: I'm goin' to take me out a summer license, an' poach a deer or two, now an' then. Venison is never better than in early September.'

"'You do, Ike,' said Dick, 'an' I'll catch you, sure as hell. I'll throw the book at you, too.'

"'I think you would, at that,' said old Ike.

"And Dick did!"

Like a goodly number of American deer poachers, old Jeff Coongate remained faithful to the keg and interpreted most of the game laws via "the vast, dim understanding of whiskey." When constantly hounded by wardens, the precious rum with the infamous trademark of Hernando's Fiery Dagger (hundred an' ten proof), cheered him through many a storm, giving him strength and purpose. When out of reach of his beloved Hernando's Fiery Dagger, Jeff Coongate "dreamed of the first, cool feeling of rum in his mouth, then the shock and fire in his throat, then the strangling sensation, and at last the huge glow in his belly and the roaring in his brain."

There wasn't a whisker of truth in the old boy. When not scheming against the wardens, or droolin' for a hunk of venison loin, or carrying on with his poaching forays against the deer herd, he spun woodsmoke tales of great intrigue in Zack Bourne's deer shack on the shore of Mopang Lake, interrupted only by an occasional jet stream of Strong Jaw tobacco juice splashed through the bottom draft of Zack's woodstove. Old Jeff Coongate loved to hear the illegal rifle shot break the stillness of the closed season. Dreary, foggy nights amplified with buck snorts and lightened with a single ray from his jacklight heightened his sense of consciousness. He represented a breed of men who believed that the fish of the waters and the deer of the forests were theirs for the killing and that was that—a tradition carried on in this country by Earl Durand and Claude Dallas. Yet, many folks living in Mopang County, Maine, still insisted that "he's a good feller, jest the same."

Coongate justified his belief in the woodsman's "inalienable right" to shoot deer in any season on the grounds that "it ain't anyways sinful; moose and deer ain't even once mentioned in the Ten Commandments." One wonders whether he believed in a life hereafter? Apparently not. "Ain't aimin' to go to heaven—too much harp-playing' and I ain't musical. I expect to go to hell where it's more home-like."

To this day, the people of Mopang, Maine, insist that Coongate was born clutching a jacklight in one hand and a quart of Hernando's in the other. If you look hard enough when the hunter's moon prevails in the November sky, you will see the tall, slender figure of Coongate, the One-Eyed Poacher of Privilege, with the pale, piercing, blue eye, clutching his weather-beaten Winchester 45-70, as he stalks unsuspecting deer after hours. If in doubt, ask the game wardens around Mopang.

On March 16, 1939, in Cody, Wyoming, a young, bearded, tangle-haired deer poacher named Earl Durand came forth from the pages of reality like a fictional cousin of Jeff Coongate's. On that day, Undersheriff Noah Riley jailed Durand for poaching deer. That evening, when Undersheriff Riley brought Durand's supper to his cell, Durand clubbed him with a milk bottle and snatched his revolver, thus beginning an astonishing saga. In *American History Illustrated,* author George Morrill describes the event as "the prolonged flight from an armed posse by a latter-day Daniel Boone. For nine tense days, twenty-six-year-old Durand zigzagged through snowy wilderness. He backtracked down lonely trails, trading shots with his pursuers. News of the western drama kept millions of Americans tuned to their radios. By the time the manhunt ended, the posse had called in bloodhounds, trench mortars, a 37-millimeter howitzer, and an airplane, and six men had been killed." Something about that shaggy fugitive's doomed defiance of twentieth century game laws still haunts us to this very day.

Instead of going to high school, this young, modern-day mountain man tramped the Tetons, stalking deer and learning the ways of nature. As a superb hunter, Durand could toss a baseball into the air and drive four bullets through it before it returned to the ground. "I'm too good with a rifle," he admitted. "It's no fun shooting because I always hit where I shoot." Becoming bored with the rifle, he took up the bow and arrow. For weeks at a time, he would vanish into the Bear Tooth Mountains east of Yellowstone National Park, carrying only his bow, arrows, and a knife. Like Jeff Coongate, he would periodically appear at neighboring ranches with gifts of venison loin and then leave silently. He weighed 250 pounds and stood six-feet-two-inches. Living in a dilapidated tent in the deer forest, his Daniel Boone lifestyle earned him the nickname "Tarzan of the Tetons." He slept in caves and hidden shelters as well, which he called his "forts." His hair grew to his shoulders, his beard to his bulging chest. Living off the land in a free-roaming manner, killing deer as needed and pitching his tent wherever and whenever his spirit dictated, the Wyoming bandit soon became something of a hero and something of a joke in the towering Teton Range. In his "Ballad of Earl Durand," folk singer Charlie Brown characterized his lifestyle as:

Boundin' lightly crag to crag, Earl Durand
would hunt the stag;
Elk and moose meat, too, he brought just to
fill his hungry bag.
Skinned 'em out and used the hides to keep
warm his young insides
With the buckskin clothes he wore on his
lonely mountain rides.

After subduing Undersheriff Riley, Durand forced Riley to take him to the Durand family ranch in Powell Flats, twenty-five miles from Cody. While Durand argued with his bewildered parents, Undersheriff D. M. Baker and Marshall Charles Lewis advanced on the ranch house in an attempt to make an arrest. Durand killed both of them with two quick shots and vanished into the thick willows along Bitter Creek with rifle, knapsack, and ammunition. Outraged citizens immediately assembled a posse, fanned out through the wooded countryside, and in a blinding snowstorm traced the poacher's trail with bloodhounds and horses into the craggy Bear Tooth Mountains. For five days, while living on a diet of raw fresh venison, the barrel-chested poacher evaded the posse by wading through mountain stream after stream.

It's not surprising to learn that deer poacher Durand once sat through two showings of the movie *Jesse James*. The posse would never take him back to jail: at least, not alive. This was his bailiwick — the Bear Tooth Mountains. Here this brush savage could survive indefinitely with only his rifle and knife, eating venison raw by preference and sleeping in caves.

On the sixth day of his rampage, he kidnapped rancher Art Thornburg and forced Thornburg to drive him to Clarks Fork Canyon, near the Shoshone National Forest. Now wanted for deer poaching, breaking jail, kidnapping, and a double murder, he wrote Sheriff Frank Blackburn, leader of the posse, a caustic letter warning the game wardens who initially arrested him to always carry weapons.

". . . Tell King and Kennedy (the game wardens who arrested him) to always carry a pistol. If I ever meet them I will give them a chance for an even draw — something I won't give you . . .

"Of course I know I am done for and when you kill me I suggest you have my head mounted and hang it up in the courthouse for the sake of law and order. Your beloved enemy, Earl Durand."

For a return address he grimly wrote, "Undertaker's Office, Powell, Wyoming." As Charlie Brown points out in his ballad, "the folks back in town didn't dig this scene very much."

On the seventh day, the posse, now swollen to one hundred guns, forced Durand into a stony fortress 400 feet up the side of a steep ridge. Two deputies, Arthur Argento and Orville Linaberry, stormed Durand's fort. The poacher shot twice and two more lawmen crumpled dead in their tracks. Durand's incredible marksmanship held the posse at bay, not even allowing them to retrieve the deputies' bodies. In anger, Sheriff Blackburn ordered up a Montana National Guard howitzer detachment to blast the deer poacher from the mountainside.

"That's right, folks," Charlie Brown sings in his ballad, "howitzers and mortars and the National Guard, after one lone man sittin' up there on a ridge." As darkness fell on March 22, 1939, the besieged raw-meat-eating fugitive remained entrenched in his citadel of mountain rock.

On March 23, the *New York Times* reported that Bill Monday of Cody flew over the area and tried to drop dynamite bombs and tear gas on the poacher's citadel but failed to locate either the hideout or the fugitive from the sky. With a thirty-seven-millimeter howitzer and a three-inch trench mortar en route to the scene, the poacher managed to escape from his canyon stronghold. Under darkness he approached the corpses of the downed lawmen and took the rubber-soled boots from one and the bootlaces from the other. After smashing their rifles, he disappeared into the mountains like the wild cats he tracked. The mountains fell silent. Day eight died.

On March 24, at about 1:30 p.m., the twenty-six-year-old fugitive deer poacher strolled into the First National Bank at Powell with his 30-30 in hand. Dressed in a mountain man's jacket and denim levis, six-shooters hung from his hips; his pockets jingled with cartridges. *Time* magazine records what happened:

"Bank President Bob Nelson, his three employees and five customers, reached for the ceiling. Durand grabbed $3000 in cash, then started shooting crazily through the bank's windows and walls. 'They'll plug me anyway,' he told his frightened captives. When he had fired forty or fifty shots, he bound Nelson, Cashier Maurice Knutson, and Teller John Gawthrop together by the wrists with rawhide. 'Come on, boys,' he said, 'we're going out.'

"Pushing the three in front of him, he stepped into the street. No one was on the sidewalks but bullets from angry townspeople began whanging at him from all around, shattering the bank's front windows, splintering the woodwork. Durand began shooting at random. Gawthrop slumped to the pavement, mortally hit.

"Across the street in a filling station, Otis Gillette, the proprietor, loaded his rifle and thrust it into the hands of Tipton Cox, a high-school boy who had scuttled in for shelter. Cox, like all the boys in town, knew and admired Earl. Unlike Earl he had never shot a big rifle, but he lay on the floor and took aim. As Durand spied him and raised a smoking rifle, Cox fired. Earl Durand crumpled with a grunt, hit in the chest. He crawled back into the bank, put his revolver to his own temple, and pulled the trigger. Bank President Nelson pumped one more bullet into the shaggy, dead head just to make sure." The final score: five murders, two kidnappings, and self-destruction.

While Durand was shooting up his hometown bank in Powell at the end of this bloody nine-day flight from the law, the furious, baffled posse continued its hunt for Durand in the mountains, even though bloodhounds failed in their attempt to pick up Durand's trail. Meanwhile, Captain C. W. (Buck) Wheat and his boys of the Montana National Guard had established their trench mortars and howitzer in readiness for their ultimate bombardment.

One wonders why this mountain man, the son of a respected rancher, preferred to die rather than to comply with the game laws. Why the comparatively minor offense of shooting a deer out-of-season led to Durand's killing rampage. What nudged him into crazed rebellion: the stringent enforcement of game laws or some innate villainy? His sister tried to explain: "My brother didn't belong in this modern world. There was no place for him here."

His father speculated on this question as well: "I think when he was sent to jail he went crazy thinking about having to give up his outdoor life." One thing is certain: Like Jeff Coongate, he believed that the deer of the forest were there to be shot and that was that. One hundred years earlier, his crime of deer poaching would have been a way of life. But in 1939, his act of deer poaching did not go unpunished. In 1967, folk singer Charlie Brown popularized Durand's plight:

Earl just wanted to live free, just the same as
  you and me.
But the game laws said, 'Oh no!' So this
  free soul had to go.
And his flight was called a crime, although in
  an earlier time,
He'd have been a mountain man instead of
  shot down in his prime.

Forty-two years later another mountain man, deer poacher, and backwoods desperado became one of this country's most wanted men. After gunning down two Idaho game wardens on January 5, 1981, who had come to Claude Dallas's deer camp to investigate complaints against him for poaching deer, Dallas, like Durand, fled into the vast, vacant stretches of the bush. But unlike Earl Durand who died in a bloody, Jesse James shoot-out, Dallas lived to tell his story of giving the wardens "a chance for an even draw" to an Idaho jury, a jury that exercised backwoods justice in the Jeff Coongate tradition by "looking the other way," convicting Dallas not of first-degree murder, but of voluntary manslaughter, in a Wild West trial that has been called incredible, in-

comprehensible, and most bizarre. His friends say he's just a good old boy born 150 years too late.

Like Durand, Dallas, the son of an Ohio dairy farmer, fled from civilization and settled into the rugged mountains of Idaho, Nevada, and Oregon at the early age of eighteen. He became an expert rifleman, deer hunter, trapper, and a master at wilderness survival. Like Durand, he preferred to live in the past and off the land—poaching deer as needed, regardless of society's laws. "Nobody else lives like I do," he proudly boasted. "A man's got to eat. You've got two things to eat: You either eat venison or you eat beef. And I've never killed another man's beef."

Like Jeff Coongate, Claude Dallas viewed the game wardens as intruding on him, not him intruding on society. In Dallas's mind, the game wardens were trespassing in his domain. He lived according to the seasons, not the legal hunting season. He knew he was violating the letter of the law when killing deer out of season, but for him, as Jeff Long argues in *Outlaw: The True Story of Claude Dallas* (1985), "it was the spirit of the law that was paramount. That the deer season was closed did not mean he couldn't kill a deer, because the 'season' was for other men . . . When it came from a lawman's mouth, 'season' was a limiting term, and Dallas was beyond limits. His relationship was to nature, not the law, to the seasons, not the 'season.' Over the years, to various people, he had evoked the ambiguous, informal subsistence law which holds that a man should be able to take an animal when he is hungry."

Dallas had previously been arrested for draft evasion and for game law violations in Nevada. He told law officers that he would never again be taken into custody.

He was raised by a father who maintained a great distaste for the law. According to Long, "standard procedure offended Claude Dallas' sensibilities." A 357 Magnum hung from his hip at all times, a bullet in the chamber. Indeed, he trained well for a fast-draw gun battle. In his camp, officers found three books: *Firearm Silencers, Kill or Be Killed,* and *No Second Place Winner,* a book about fast draws which suggests that you "be first or be dead—there is no second-place winner in a gun fight."

Game warden Bill Pogue, fifty years old, was an excellent and fierce protector of the game laws, a naturalist and a loner. He was not well-known for compromising. His fellow officers viewed him as the lawman's lawman. With more than twenty years of wildlife law enforcement work behind him, he stood diametrically opposed to the poaching ways and free-roaming lifestyle of Claude Dallas. The clash seemed inevitable.

On January 5, 1981, Pogue entered Dallas's camp accompanied by fellow warden, Conley Elms, to check out complaints against Dallas for poaching deer and bobcats. Illegal venison hung from the meat pole and illegal bobcat pelts hung on the back wall of the tent. Pogue left the camp in the back of Dallas's truck with two bullets in his chest and one in his head. Officers found Elm's body floating in the Owyhee River. Dallas insisted that in the ensuing gun battle Pogue reached first for his gun, and that he, Claude Dallas, merely acted in self-defense. The jury eventually believed the story. According to one jurist, if Dallas hadn't also fired one additional bullet into each man's head, trapper style, they would have acquitted him.

But before the jury had an opportunity to exercise backwoods justice, Dallas van-

ished into a heavy fog. Unlike Durand's nine-day flight from the law, it took law enforcement officials fourteen months to capture Claude Dallas. But when the law finally caught up with deer poacher Dallas in the northern Nevada desert in April of 1982, the final chase was no less than spectacular.

When a Huey helicopter swooped down on a weather-beaten trailer where Dallas was holed up—in an area the local people called Poverty Flats—the deer poacher burst through a glass window and screen. Within seconds he plowed his old Ford pickup through a barbed-wire fence and roared off into the prairie with the old flatbed bouncing four to five feet in the air. While the helicopter dogged him from the air with a submachine gun, he eventually encountered SWAT teams from the FBI, county sheriff officers from Idaho and Nevada, and several federal agents—about two dozen lawmen in all. They were armed with M-16s, 45 caliber submachine guns, shotguns, and rocket launchers. They sprayed the old Ford pickup with bullets, wounding Dallas in the left heel. After dragging himself and his lever-action rifle into the sagebrush, he suddenly surrendered quietly. After one of the most extensive and frustrating manhunts in modern times, many of his pursuers couldn't believe it ended so quickly.

But then it didn't end so quickly. Claude Dallas was sentenced to thirty years in prison in January 1983, but on Easter Sunday, March 30, 1986, he cut his way through two fences at the Idaho State Correctional Institution near Boise and vanished once again into the deer woods. "Claude Dallas knows every damn gopher hole in the Northwest," said one of his friends. How long would the poacher escape FBI agents this time?

Dallas roamed from Oregon to Mexico

for nearly a year. He was the subject of two books, one 45-rpm record, and a CBS-TV flick. FBI agents finally arrested Claude Dallas, unarmed, on Sunday, March 10, 1987, as he left a convenience store in Riverside, California. Thus, the trail of the outlaw poacher ended once again.

After airing a story on the dangerous profession of game wardens entitled "The Real Law of the Jungle," on ABC's "20/20," host Hugh Downs asked the recurring question: "Why would a guy like Claude Dallas, facing just a small fine for poaching deer, kill two game wardens?"

The answer to this question and the truth about who drew first in the gun battle will undoubtedly remain, as Russell Martin, author of *Cowboys,* observes, "as elusive as water on the desert wastelands." One thing seems certain: Wardens Pogue and Elms tried to convince Dallas that time had passed him by, that he must bend to the views of society, to the established rules of wildlife management — a message Claude Dallas did not want to hear. Generations of what was once right and "traditional" can often be difficult to declare wrong, especially when the rules are imposed by bureaucrats living beyond the bush.

The Earl Durand and Claude Dallas stories are not just isolated incidents or occasional enactments of old Jeff Coongate shooting the stern off game warden Tom Corn's canoe with an automatic shotgun. But they represent part of an ever-growing problem: the increased assault rates on conservation officers nationwide. After studying the statistics of this problem for the past sixteen years, William B. Morse, the western representative of the Wildlife Management Institute, notes that in 1983, poachers and viola-

tors assaulted 150 conservation officers throughout the country. "The overall national assault rate," according to Morse, "was 2.72 per 100 officers during 1980–1984. At that rate almost 82 percent of them would be assaulted during a thirty-year career."

Indeed, today's 7180 conservation officers face the most dangerous law enforcement job of its kind. In his memoirs of thirty dangerous years of combating wildlife violators, warden Dave Swendsen underscores the point in his *Badge in the Wilderness* (1985): "I have been shot at, sworn at and swung at. I have been lied to and hidden from; I've received pay-off offers and life threatening phone calls, and have had deer shiners try to run over me with their car. I've worked nighttime deer shiners from the air as an observer, when we had to use a car's headlights at one end of the runway and another car's taillights at the far end for us to land."

On November 10, 1984, thirty-six-year-old Terry Hoffer, a wildlife agent with the Washington Department of Game, was shot and killed in his car on a logging trail near his home in Buckley. He waved down two elk hunters to make a routine license check. One of the hunters had a loaded rifle in the vehicle. While he attempted to quickly unload it, the weapon discharged and killed agent Hoffer. The hunters fled the scene but were later arrested.

On December 13, 1984, twenty-six-year-old Peggy Park, a wildlife officer with the Florida Game and Fish Commission, was shot and killed while on a routine patrol in rural northeastern Pinellas County; she died next to her patrol car with its blue lights still flashing. Two Pasco County men were arrested on December 25 and charged with first-degree murder.

Ask John Savage, a wildlife law enforcement officer with thirty years of ex-

State Law Enforcement Data—1984

West	No. Arrests	No. Acquitted or Dismissed	Fines Levied	Cases Appealed	Written Warnings	Times C.O. Assaulted
Alaska	3,049	—	920,000	—	2,634	3
Arizona	5,457	432	197,177	—	0	0
California	29,317	2,325	1,685,486	—	—	8
Colorado	5,847	—	367,742	—	—	2
Hawaii	610	101	13,551	—	7,256	1
Idaho	4,079	422	115,007	—	1,196	4
Montana	3,342	60	—	—	466	—
Nevada	2,167	56	102,475	—	17	2
New Mexico	3,101	307	246,402	—	447	4
Oregon	10,832	—	—	—	11,727	0
Utah	4,446	132	101,979	—	286	2
Washington (Game)	8,500	600	—	—	—	0
Washington (Fish)	2,754	78	—	—	0	0
Wyoming	3,059	150	278,447	—	0	1
Total	86,555	4,662	—	—	24,012	27

Midwest	No. Arrests	No. Acquitted or Dismissed	Fines Levied	Cases Appealed	Written Warnings	Times C.O. Assaulted
Illinois	9,005	—	265,729	—	2,376	0
Indiana	10,975	—	—	—	3,591	6
Iowa	6,997	262	—	—	—	0
Kansas	4,256	46	191,485	—	—	3
Michigan	24,061	1,388	—	—	—	5
Minnesota	10,604	249	450,624	—	—	0
Missouri	7,362	189	328,086	—	—	8
Nebraska	5,343	180	178,668	—	—	0
North Dakota	955	40	64,750	—	—	0
Ohio	9,897	161	472,495	—	—	1
South Dakota	1,721	100	107,537	—	—	3
Wisconsin	18,820	1,042	601,958	—	—	4
Total	109,996	3,657	—	—	5,967	30

perience with the North Carolina Wildlife Commission, if he thinks that a warden's career can be dangerous:

"On November 1, 1984, barely two months short of retirement, I checked a report of fire lighting for deer in a field adjacent to Merchants Mill Pond State Park near Gatesville. As I approached the field, a vehicle left and headed toward the Virginia line about twelve miles away.

"I followed and turned on my blue lights and siren. As I came up behind the truck and began copying down its license numbers, a man on the passenger side of the vehicle leaned out the window. Then, I heard rifle shots. At the same time, two men in the back of the truck began shining a spotlight in my eyes, and threw out heavy objects to make me swerve off the road. One of the things they threw at me was a portable circular saw. One of the

Northeast	No. Arrests	No. Acquitted or Dismissed	Fines Levied	Cases Appealed	Written Warnings	Times C.O. Assaulted
Connecticut	3,585	—	—	—	2,475	5
Delaware	902	—	—	—	1,063	0
Maine	4,497	224	263,815	—	2,308	14
Massachusetts	—	—	—	—	—	1
New Hampshire	1,180	22	47,005	7	—	0
New Jersey	2,905	124	166,000	30	1,056	2
New York	14,449	1,190	904,948	—	2,098	2
Pennsylvania (Game)	12,087	324	667,628	144	—	4
Pennsylvania (Fish)	12,767	102	536,342	—	29,079	6
Rhode Island	1,048	(2)	61,309	—	308	4
Vermont	1,435	172	74,361	—	—	—
West Virginia	9,350	—	498,210	—	1,179	9
Total	64,205	2,158	—	181	39,566	47[1]

[1] 1 hospital, 8 outpatient (one loss of hearing) over 93 days lost

Southeast	No. Arrests	No. Acquitted or Dismissed	Fines Levied	Cases Appealed	Written Warnings	Times C.O. Assaulted
Alabama	13,000	600	448,207	—	0	0
Arkansas	5,533	171	382,918	—	589	0
Florida	23,281	1,483(est)	—	—	7,279	16
Georgia	14,621	—	663,797	—	9,462	3
Kentucky	7,540	2,536	—	—	—	0
Louisiana	27,000	—	—	—	0	7
Maryland	8,468	15-20%(est)	415,512	—	2,723	7
Mississippi	12,559	2,488	606,301	15	0	15
North Carolina	13,134	958	185,452	—	—	2
Oklahoma	6,460	—	—	—	—	—
South Carolina	11,727	561	396,379	—	—	1
Tennessee	5,596	—	87,157	—	—	2
Texas	49,522	2,476	2,254,148	—	0	3
Virginia	17,741	3,422	680,987	—	—	0
Total	216,182	14,695	—	15	20,053	46[1]

[1] Includes 8 hospital, 6 outpatient, 63 days lost

—William B. Morse, *Wildlife Law Enforcement*, 1984.

shots they fired also hit an occupied home.

"I radioed Virginia authorities and pursued the truck across the state line. I had the window rolled down and heard three or four more shots. Then, I smelled smoke and the car began to slow down. Both front tires were shot out and there was a hole in the radiator the size of a fifty-cent piece. All of the water and anti-freeze drained out of the radiator. Suffolk police soon arrived where I was waiting with the disabled car."

As a result of the publicity surrounding these deaths and the ever-increasing number of assaults by poachers on conservation officers throughout the country and the ever-growing difficulty of managing deer populations due to the unknown fac-

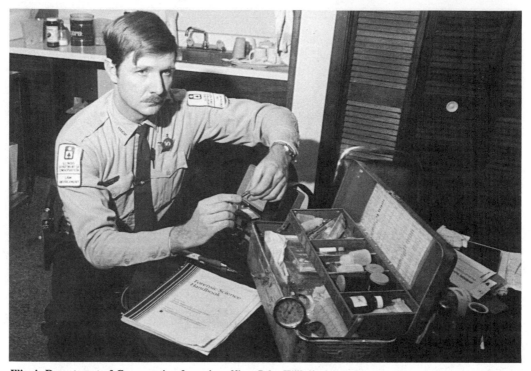

Illinois Department of Conservation forensics officer John Will displays a forensic kit that contains equipment and chemistry enabling conservation officers to make time-of-death and wound analysis determinations in the field. *Photo credit Illinois Department of Conservation*

tor of deer poaching, wildlife researchers began to stalk the deer poacher as early as the late 1960s all across this country.

The long stalk began in Idaho in 1968, well before Idaho's game-warden tragedy, when James Vilkitis, a researcher in wildlife management at the University of Idaho, interviewed thirty-two big-game violators and twenty-nine deer hunters, surveyed 1750 selected hunters—half known to be violators of deer laws—and studied arrest reports and violation simulation acts, Vilkitis concluded that big-game violators possess certain characteristics that distinguish them from hunters and that they poach more deer than the public generally realizes. According to Vilkitis, the stereotypes are generally industrial workers in their twenties with

three children; they own a car and rent a home; they are less conscious of class structure, spend more time on public land than the average deer hunter, and prefer just to hunt. Vilkitis reached the following conclusions:

(1) Both violators and hunters definitely refuse to report a friend for violating. Violators, however, are more likely than hunters not to turn in a violation by a stranger. (2) The violator is less likely than the hunter to possess a telephone. (3) Violators enjoy more forms of outdoor recreation than hunters. (4) Violators, contrary to hunters, perceive hunters' crippling losses as higher than official estimates. (5) Closed-season violators, more than open-season violators, tend to be in the twenty to twenty-nine-year age group and

be single or divorced and remarried. (6) Between January 1 and June 30, 1967, Idaho deer poachers killed an estimated 8000 big game animals during the closed season. (7) Further research should delve into the extent of big-game violations by outfitters and guides. (8) The hunting public, although being opposed to big-game violations, will condone them. "He's a good feller, jest the same," as the folks around Mopang, Maine, characterize Jeff Coongate and associates. This public indifference remains one of wildlife law enforcement's basic problems.

Continuing this line of research, Paul Amidon, a researcher in the College of Forestry at Syracuse University, compared violators and nonviolators of New York's deer hunting laws in the Adirondacks and the Catskills. He surveyed 1140 New York deer hunters in 1968, who were known to have violated deer hunting laws as well as deer hunters who were not known to have done so. Like Vilkitis, Amidon found several differences and similarities between deer poachers and deer hunters. As with a great deal of the human dimensions literature, Amidon found that poachers and hunters alike express strong dissatisfaction with regulations based mainly on laws that regulate hunter distribution and hunter behavior rather than with laws that directly affect the number of deer harvested.

When asked why they thought deer were killed illegally, both hunters and poachers alike agreed on three major reasons: (1) Tangible benefits such as food and/or profit — fifty-four percent. (2) Psychological reasons such as challenge and excitement — twenty-six percent. (3) Unintentional reasons such as mistaking an antlerless deer for a buck — twenty percent.

Amidon found that violators legally killed significantly more deer per year of hunting experience than nonviolators. This conclusion underscores the research of Wisconsin's Professor Robert Jackson, who also argues that the most successful deer hunters often show a marked tendency for violating. Thus, the question arises whether increased deer kill success precipitates a strong probability of being a deer law violator. We know that as deer populations rise, hunters become conditioned to a high probability of success. When game managers add laws and restrictions to lower the probability of deer kill, the number of violators increases. A corollary question arises as to whether wildlife management thus conditions some hunters to a high level of deer kill success and then, by reducing this high level of expectation, inadvertently encourages violations of deer laws.

How determined does the average hunter or the trophy hunter become when fulfilling his preconditioned expectations of success? Does he simply see certain regulations as unnecessary restrictions and subconsciously and/or intentionally ignore them? After studying New York deer hunters, Amidon came to the conclusion that more than half of all deer hunters believe that hunting regulations place too much emphasis on what they view as the less important aspects of hunting such as the proper tagging of harvested deer, use of licenses, and other legal technicalities. Several deer hunters, via letters, suggested to the editors of *Deer & Deer Hunting* magazine that we should view violations of the tagging law as "minor infractions and frivolous technicalities." I suggest that when deer hunters belittle the legal tagging of deer, they are approaching the beginning of the end.

Deer tagging regulations, as conservation officer Dave Swendson rightly argues in his *Badge in the Wilderness* (1985), are "not to be twisted or bent to suit the occasion . . . Without tough tagging and record-keeping regulations, all (illegal deer hunting activity) becomes untainted, untraceable—clean and legal."

Amidon concluded his study of violators and nonviolators of New York's deer hunting laws with several interesting hypotheses: (1) The greatest illegal deer kill occurs in heavily wooded areas with low human population densities. (2) The probability of being a deer law violator increases with a hunter's deer kill success but not with the amount of time he spends pursuing the animal: the more successful hunters may be more likely to violate deer laws. (3) Deer hunters exaggerate their reported legal deer kill by as much as 300 percent when questioned about the subject in a mail survey. (4) Violators seem to encounter conservation officers in the field twice as often as nonviolators. (5) Both violators and deer hunters alike believe that conservation officers spend too much time regulating behavior after a deer has been killed rather than regulating behavior prior to shooting a deer.

In a similar study comparing the attitudes and characteristics of violators and nonviolators of Michigan's deer laws in the Upper and Lower Peninsulas in 1974, James Kesel, a wildlife researcher at Michigan State University, observed that sportsmen held more professional and management positions than violators, and that conversely, violators held more jobs in labor and transportation than sportsmen. When asked in Kesel's survey to estimate the number of deer lost as cripples by jacklighters, both Michigan violators and sportsmen felt that for every 100 deer hit an average of twenty-nine were lost as cripples.

While studying jacklighters in Virginia,

Michael Kaminsky, a wildlife researcher at the Virginia Polytechnic Institute, noted that the number of jacklighting violations increases during the month of October, peaks in November, and decreases in January. Virginia wardens make the largest percentage of arrests on Saturday evenings—the average time being 11:37 p.m. Deer poachers favor clear weather conditions and hunt private cornfields surrounded by a mixture of oaks and pines. Poachers who have killed a deer are more apt to elude the warden when approached than the deer poacher who fails in his efforts.

The most common reasons given for spotlighting deer included the following: (1) Hunting for excitement; (2) Hunting meat for home consumption; (3) Market hunting; (4) Frustration in not obtaining a deer legally; (5) Could not resist the opportunity; and (6) "Getting back" at the warden. According to Kaminsky, "violators dressed in everyday, street-type clothes in 61.4 percent of the cases, in hunting clothes in 35.7 percent, and in camouflaged outfits in 1.4 percent of the cases. The large percentage in everyday clothes may indicate that the violators were not seriously engaged in hunting for meat, but would support the idea that they were looking for excitement or spotlighting for kicks."

Like Jeff Coongate, Virginia's deer jackers remained faithful to the keg. According to Kaminsky, violators were drinking or under the influence of alcohol in 32.9 percent of the cases. When compared with other studies, this figure remains very conservative. Most research in this regard indicates that alcohol plays a very prominent role in the complex group behavior of deer poaching. Willie Parker, a special agent of the United States Fish and Wildlife Service and one of this country's toughest game wardens, reports that "most jacklighters I've caught over the years were drinking and many were drunk." How drunk? In his *Badge in the Wilderness,* officer Swendsen observes that "I arrested a deer poacher so intoxicated that when I had him in my car on his way to jail, he said suddenly, 'There's a deer.' He tried to get at his confiscated rifle in the back seat to shoot a big buck that was standing alongside the road." Indeed, deer poaching and drinking seem to go hand-in-hand, as the Englishmen constantly remind us in their vast genre of literature on deer poachers and poaching. R. J. Machie, for example, author of *A Keeper's Book* (1911), likens the poacher to a drunken, slinking scoundrel—"a cast-off from honest trades, a grain in the sediment of society, whom drink has, as a rule, in its grip."

After a thorough analysis of deer poaching as a complex sociological phenomenon, Kaminsky concluded that numerous influences besides alcohol enter into the decision to spotlight deer. They include such desired benefits as food for the family, money from the sale of venison and trophy antlers, a chance for excitement, or a chance to outwit the game wardens. The risks include the likelihood of being arrested, the probability of high fines and penalties if ultimately convicted, and the social stigma attached to such events. Other influences include the current level of the deer herd in the area, knowledge of the game warden's patrol activities, and the association with other individuals involved in spotlighting activities. The cultural, educational, and economic status of the individual influence the weight assigned to the risks and benefits prior to the violation.

In New Jersey, Gary Sawhill and Robert Winkel, wildlife researchers at Stockton State College, continued this line of research by interviewing 148 admitted violators of deer laws ranging in age from fourteen to sixty-six in an attempt to determine the behavioral aspects and methodology of their deer-jacking activities. Sawhill and Winkel placed deer poachers into three categories: the accidental, the opportunist, and the premeditated or criminal. They focused on the third category: the locally known deer jackers.

Their findings indicate that deer jackers in New Jersey commit their violations in a group of two to three men who have a better than fifty percent chance of either being drunk or in the process of drinking. Ninety percent of them hunt in the same group during the legal deer season. The majority of them jack deer on lands or bordering lands that they hunt during the legal season. Forty-seven percent of them use four-wheel-drive vehicles. Of those poachers that wardens apprehended or pursued, all still jack deer. Seventy-one percent of them come from families whose relatives also poach deer. According to Sawhill, "the most alarming reason given for jacking deer was for 'the hell of it.' Eight percent admitted shooting deer just to see if they could hit them; they had no interest in picking up the animal for any purpose."

In 1977, the New Mexico Department of Game and Fish released some shocking statistics on deer poaching when they estimated that poachers killed 34,000 deer while legal hunters killed only 20,000. They estimated the animal losses at $4 million and noted that wardens discover less than one percent of the violations. Worse, after simulating a great number of deer poaching incidents by an undercover agent, law enforcement officials reached the conclusion that residents of New Mexico viewed deer poaching as a socially accepted activity. One wonders why people let poachers get away with it. Undoubtedly, the myth that the deer poacher is just a poor guy trying to feed his family while not really doing any harm plays a prominent part in people's perception of a poacher.

But the deer poacher is not just a poor guy trying to feed his family. "The fact is," says enforcement research specialist Dan Pursley of New Mexico's Department of Game and Fish, "very few poachers are in any serious need. The great majority of adults cited for game-law violations were employed, driving expensive vehicles, and owned reasonably good firearms. The poacher is a cheat who takes every advantage of the animal and the ethical hunter that he can. He is a glutton who takes all he can get. He is a danger to himself and to others, shooting off into the dark, often drunk and in a hurry. He cripples more game than he retrieves, because of his haste and ineptness, and he does not give a damn whether he is disrupting a breeding season, blasting a pregnant animal, or leaving an orphan." Pursley, like many wildlife researchers, does not believe that the poacher makes much of an attempt to recover cripples, since his most immediate concern is not getting caught. Thus, the cripples that make it to the brush and escape the range of his spotlight normally remain behind as wasted animals. Even after taking inordinate measures to recover any animal he crippled, the undercover agent, whose marksmanship was excellent, lost twenty-five percent of all deer he attempted to take while simulating poaching incidents for research purposes. We can only guess what percentage the real deer poacher leaves behind in his haste.

The only bright spot in this story seems to be the following UPI item entitled "Deer Poacher's Dog Turns Informant":

Austin, Texas — Illegal deer hunters often are reported to lawmen by other people, but one East Texas poacher recently was turned in by his own dog.

"Texas Parks and Wildlife Department Game Warden Jesse May of Mount Pleasant was checking on a report that a man living near there had killed a deer out of season and had taken it to his residence.

"After obtaining a search warrant, May and three other wardens searched the man's house for signs of the deer but found none. As the officers were leaving, the man's bird dog trotted up to their car clutching a deer's leg bone in his jaws.

"May took the bone from the dog, which turned and trotted toward a barn. The officers followed, and a renewed search behind the barn turned up parts of two deer, plus several raw furbearer pelts. Two persons arrested after the incident were found guilty of possession of deer and furbearer pelts out of season and fined more than $400.

"The dog's owner ruefully commented to the game wardens that 'the blankety-blank dog never retrieved anything for me.'"

While stalking deer poachers in Alberta, Canada, a province well-known for its trophy white-tailed deer, wildlife researcher Michael Melnyk found several significant differences between violators and nonviolators. Violators were significantly younger than nonviolators, with respective averages being 29.9 and 35.4

years. The majority of both groups were married but violators were proportionately more prone than nonviolators to either be single or divorced. Whereas hunters as a whole lived in urban areas, violators resided in rural areas. Violators received less education than nonviolators, and like the violators in Michigan and Idaho, worked primarily in blue collar occupations; nonviolators were more heavily concentrated in white collar occupations. Ironically, violators had more formal training in hunting than nonviolators.

Like many states with high deer populations, Michigan, like Canada, experiences a great deal of difficulty with deer poachers violating the deer game laws both during the hunting season and the closed season. In fact, Michigan conservation officials report that one third of their 1984 elk hunters had game law violations on their records. They estimate that poaching costs Michigan taxpayers $28.5 million a year with deer poachers taking 120,000 whitetails annually. Indeed, poached venison provides easy money for idle people. "This is big business," as one self-confessed deer poacher acknowledges in the *Detroit News*. "Some guys are making in excess of $50,000 each year while drawing unemployment, and a few are downright dangerous. There's some poachers that wouldn't think twice about wasting an officer or anyone else that gets suspicious of their activities or how they make their money." This type of activity obviously goes well beyond the moonshining rampages and home brew episodes of Robert Traver's Danny McGinnis and his boys in Hungry Hollow on the rugged Upper Peninsula of Michigan.

It doesn't take a Ph.D. in social criminology to realize that deer poachers move a lot of artillery around the countryside to waste whitetails: Look at the road signs or what's left of them. According to one Michigan conservation officer, "The subjects in fifty percent or better of the cases have been drinking, are drunk, or high on dope. A large percentage of these people, because of their intoxication, do not or cannot behave in a rational manner. Many of them have appeared before judges for crimes such as arson, assault, breaking and entering, muggings, murder, negligent homicide, rape, and other drug-related activities."

Yet, the public in general, according to a DNR report entitled "Michigan Deer Hunters' Perceptions and Attitudes Towards Law Enforcement," still follows the old tradition of "looking the other way." In surveying more than 4500 Michigan deer hunters in 1978, wildlife researchers observe that while deer hunters express a serious concern toward illegally harvested deer, a profound gap exists between that concern and action in reporting violations and illegal deer hunting activities. Michigan deer hunters, like the Idaho hunters, apparently rely exclusively on conservation officers to provide efficient big-game law enforcement with minimal active public support.

In this survey, only one out of every five deer hunters expresses a serious concern for deer tagging violations. One out of every three deer hunters reports seeing at least one illegally killed deer. The survey indicates that a "significant relationship exists between days hunted and the proportion reporting seeing an illegally taken deer. The reporting of illegally killed deer increases from twenty-five percent for hunters out one to five days to over fifty percent for hunters spending more than fifteen days afield."

Concern . . . yes. After surveying 3322

How Michigan deer hunters view the seriousness of the effect of common natural resource law violations on deer populations and their deer hunting enjoyment.

Hunting Violation	Effect On	Seriousness of Effect					
		Extremely Serious	Quite Serious	Moderately Serious	Slightly Serious	Not Serious	Total
Trespass	Deer Population	12.7%	13.0%	19.4%	20.6%	34.3%	100.0%
	Hunting Enjoyment	23.2	16.2	18.8	14.8	27.0	100.0
Shining	Deer Population	34.8	19.4	16.1	12.3	17.3	100.0
	Hunting Enjoyment	31.3	16.0	13.1	11.4	28.1	100.0
No Hunting	Deer Population	25.1	12.4	14.2	15.6	32.7	100.0
License	Hunting Enjoyment	28.0	12.4	11.3	12.0	36.3	100.0
Non-Season	Deer Population	46.2	18.9	15.9	9.7	9.3	100.0
Deer Kill	Hunting Enjoyment	46.0	17.5	12.7	7.9	15.8	100.0
Loaded Guns	Deer Population	34.0	16.5	17.3	14.1	18.1	100.0
in Cars	Hunting Enjoyment	38.1	13.4	12.8	10.7	25.0	100.0
Kill Doe in	Deer Population	50.4	18.9	13.6	8.6	8.5	100.0
Non-Doe Area	Hunting Enjoyment	49.9	17.2	11.6	8.3	13.0	100.0
Fail to Post Camp	Deer Population	4.8	5.2	12.6	17.4	60.0	100.0
Registration Card	Hunting Enjoyment	5.4	5.4	10.7	16.5	62.0	100.0
Not Tagging	Deer Population	20.8	17.1	18.3	17.0	26.8	100.0
Your Deer	Hunting Enjoyment	21.4	15.0	16.0	15.0	32.5	100.0
Not Wearing a	Deer Population	12.1	9.0	13.7	16.7	48.5	100.0
Back Tag	Hunting Enjoyment	15.0	9.7	13.1	15.8	46.5	100.0

—Harry Hill, *et al.*, "Michigan Deer Hunters' Perceptions and Attitudes Towards Law Enforcement," *Proc. West. Assoc. Fish Wildl. Agencies*, 1978.

Missouri deer hunters in 1980, Wayne Porath, a wildlife biologist, notes that 3200 of those surveyed perceive poaching as the greatest and most severe threat to the sport of deer hunting. Indeed, deer poaching probably does more to promote antihunting sentiments and a bad public image of the American deer hunter in general than any other practice. But why the universal condonation? Why the tradition of "looking the other way"?

In his book entitled *The Game Warden and the Poachers,* Lewis Reimann, a raconteur of backwoods deer poaching tales, points his finger at the attitude of the courts, which in many cases are more sympathetic toward the deer poacher than toward the protection of the natural resource. "Many violators, when arrested and brought before a justice court, will ask for a jury trial. Juries selected in a few towns are made up of violators or the beneficiaries of violators themselves, so it sometimes is impossible to secure a verdict of guilty. Frequently, the justice or the jury is convinced that the prisoner is guilty but, because of the financial condition of his family, will find him innocent. For many families living in the woods or in small settlements where work is seasonal, securing an adequate income is a real problem. Nothing seems more logical to them than for the head of the family to turn to nature and her bountiful supply of game and fish." Is deer poaching then socially acceptable at the local level?

Wildlife biologists and conservation law enforcement officials have asked that question for more than four decades in the peripheral Adirondacks of northern New York and attribute the illegal deer kill in that famous deer hunting mecca primarily to the attitudes of the local residents who apparently view deer poaching as a socially acceptable activity. Biologists believe that such attitudes are rooted in tradition and reinforced by a lack of respect for conservation laws in general. Indeed, the entire American tradition of deer jacking began in the Adirondacks.

In the early 1980s, human dimensions researchers at Cornell University undertook several research projects to assess New York public opinion on various aspects of deer poaching. In summary, their research showed an inclination on the part of the public to tolerate the accidental killing of illegal deer during the open season as well as poaching deer for meat. According to Daniel Decker, a research biologist, "Critical and as yet unidentified subgroups of the general population are tolerant of illegal deer hunting, and although many residents of the Adirondacks indicate that the practice is not

acceptable to them in principle, they may do little to abate it."

Despite prevailing public opinion against deer poaching, it occurs at a level sufficient to prevent an increase in the deer population of the peripheral Adirondacks, which biologists estimate at only one third its potential size. Deer poaching not only suppresses deer populations, but strains relationships between sportsmen and landowners and limits the recreational experiences for law-abiding hunters.

When does most deer poaching occur? In trying to answer this question, Ron Glover, a Research Specialist with the Missouri Department of Conservation, examined 660 confirmed deer poaching incidents during a two-year period, 1979–1981. He discovered that while deer poaching occurs year-round, more than eighty percent of the violations took place between September and February. Fifty-four percent of the violations occurred on Fridays (18.9 percent), Saturdays (20.1 percent), and Sundays (14.6 percent). Five p.m. to midnight (62.8 percent) represented the peak hours for poaching, which occurred primarily along gravel roads.

When we ask the self-confessed deer poacher this question, his answer readily agrees with these scientific observations.

Comparison of the number of days spent afield by hunters and the proportion that reported seeing an illegally-killed deer.

Saw an Illegally-Killed Deer	Days Spent Hunting			
	1-5	6-10	11-15	>15
Yes	25.2%	34.3%	43.5%	56.5%
No	74.8	65.7	56.5	43.5
Total	100.0	100.0	100.0	100.0

—Harry Hill, *et al.*, "Michigan Deer Hunters' Perceptions and Attitudes Towards Law Enforcement," *Proc. West. Assoc. Fish Wildl. Agencies*, 1978.

Ragnar Benson, for example, tells us in his *Survival Poaching* (1980), the most outrageous book ever written on the subject, that "it is very important that the deer poacher get out and make his harvest early while the critters can still be taken easily. 'Early' varies from one section of the country to the other, but is usually from September first through the end of October. The deer are much more relaxed, there are few people in the woods, and the days are longer. When the days are long and hot the deer will get hungry and thirsty before dark. If they have no reason to be suspicious, the poacher can be sitting there waiting for them at dusk, and have his pick of good shots. As an added bonus, early hunting will eventually alarm the deer. They will be shy during the regular season, protecting the resource for the poacher who can easily collect all he needs after hunting season ends."

In age, deer poachers range from fifteen to sixty-five years old, but average twenty-eight years of age. Three-quarters of them complete high school and most of them (81.3 percent) work in blue collar jobs, primarily construction, sawmill operation and logging, truck driving, and farm labor. Most of them earn less than $14,000 a year and thirty percent of them are unemployed when arrested. Surprisingly, unemployed deer poachers frequently admit that they poach deer as much for fun as for the venison. It seems that unemployment leads to poaching but more so to combat boredom than to secure tablefare. Forty percent of the poachers support only themselves. Many of them remain lifetime residents of the county in which they poach deer. The sex ratio of deer poached in Missouri remains nearly even.

According to Glover, forty-seven percent of deer poachers have been arrested for traffic violations and almost twenty percent commit felony violations including murder, attempted murder, felonious assault, manslaughter, armed robbery, rape, and various drug violations. Missouri deer poaching, as in other states, is typically done by a group of people and tends to be a socioeconomic, class-oriented activity. Many poachers see the activity as a means to gain excitement in a

Social and economic characteristics of closed-season deer poachers convicted in Missouri, July 1, 1979, to June 30, 1981.

Characteristic	Number	Percentage of Total
Sex		
Male	392	98.7
Female	5	1.3
Age		
15-20	80	20.1
21-25	129	32.5
26-30	58	14.6
31-35	44	11.1
36-40	32	8.1
>40	54	13.6
Education		
Elementary school only	16	4.7
Some high school	68	19.9
High school graduate	252	73.9
College graduate	5	1.5
Estimated income		
$ 6,999 or less	121	35.4
7,000- 13,999	161	47.1
14,000- 20,999	52	15.2
21,000 or more	8	2.3
Work status		
Employed	278	70.0
Unemployed	119	30.0
Occupation		
Blue collar	318	81.3
Farmer	28	7.2
Student	19	4.8
White collar	11	2.8
Retired	6	1.5
Disabled	5	1.3
Military	3	0.8
Housewife	1	0.3

—Glover/Baskett, "Socioeconomic Profiles of Missouri Deer Poachers," *Journal of Wildlife Management*, 1984.

Frequency of prior misdemeanor and felony arrests* for 385 convicted deer poachers in Missouri by age group.

Age	Number	Wildlife arrest		Traffic arrest		Felony arrest	
		n	%	n	%	n	%
15-20	107	3	2.8	46	43.0	7	6.5
21-25	162	14	8.6	92	56.7	29	17.9
31-40	70	11	15.7	28	40.0	21	30.0
Over 40	46	11	23.9	16	34.7	9	19.6
All ages	385	39	10.1	182	47.2	66	17.1

*Records showed only arrests in Missouri.

relatively humdrum life; it not only includes drinking but frequently becomes the main social event of the day. In this subculture, the desirability of violating deer laws apparently exceeds the undesirability of doing so. Only sportsmen's magazines communicate the undesirable impact of deer poaching, but most poachers do not read these types of magazines.

The principal reasons given by Missouri poachers for committing deer violations revolve around acquiring meat (50.6 percent) and recreation-vandalism (34 percent). "About one-half of the poachers stated that they poached for meat. A possible reason for this high percentage might be that poachers were attempting to make their arrests seem less culpable to local citizens and to elicit sympathy for acts of poaching. If this assumption is correct, recreational poaching may be even more of a reason for poaching than our study indicated."

Another reason for deer poaching and its associated criminal activity revolves around the astonishing craze for antlers, as epitomized in the following UPI story:

"*Three Indicted in Antler Scam.* Three men have been indicted on charges that they implanted stolen antlers from Canada onto the carcass of a deer and then claimed they had killed a record whitetail in Mexico.

"William Mark Day, fifty-three, an Austin, Texas, investor, was indicted by a federal grand jury for allegedly paying a Canadian hunting guide $20,000 for the antlers.

"The indictment charged that Day gave the guide, Lloyd McMahon, thirty-five, from Edmonton, Alberta, two $10,000 checks for the antlers, which were allegedly transported to the Mexican ranch owned in part by the third suspect, George Vogt, forty-eight, of Houston, in January 1984.

"Day was photographed with the allegedly altered deer carcass and then returned to Texas with the stolen antlers and claimed he had killed a Mexican whitetail that scored an extremely high 212 points.

"Day, McMahon, and Vogt are charged with conspiring to transport and receive stolen goods, giving false statements to U.S. border agents, and violating the Lacey Act, which regulates the sale and international transportation of wildlife.

"The break in the case came when a taxidermist, Alex Muirhead of Edmonton, saw a photograph of Day with the carcass.

"'I saw the picture in *Petersen's Hunting Magazine* and recognized the antlers as being the same antlers stolen from my taxidermy studio December 4, 1983,'

Reasons for closed-season deer poaching given by 379 poachers convicted in Missouri, July 1, 1979, to June 30, 1981		
Reasons	Number	Percentage of Total
Meat	192	50.6
Recreation—vandalism	129	34.0
Commercial	9	2.4
Failure to kill deer in open season	30	8.0
Other reasons	19	5.0

—Glover/Baskett, "Socioeconomic Profiles of Missouri Deer Poachers," *Journal of Wildlife Management*, 1984.

Muirhead said. 'The deer had actually been killed about 1973.'"

While stalking the deer poacher and trying to eliminate the myth of him as a "backwoods good ol' boy," Mike Bessey, a deer hunter and wildlife researcher at the University of Manitoba, interviewed ninety-five self-admitted deer poachers who were never prosecuted by law. In openly discussing their deviant deer hunting activities, a majority of them told Bessey that they prefer to poach in daylight hours. Indeed, a significant amount of daylight deer poaching goes undetected. Nine percent of them reported that they do not hunt deer during the legal deer season because "it is too dangerous." These non-prosecuted deer poachers indicated that they increase their poaching activities on Thursdays and Fridays. Like the Virginia deer poachers, they reported killing more deer on cool, clear nights without moonlight than on cloudy nights.

They gave Bessey five primary motivations for poaching deer: (1) Because venison was an inexpensive supply of meat; (2) Because it was a social activity related to alcohol; (3) Because the opportunity presented itself and the risk of apprehension was low; (4) Because rural people have a "natural right" to deer living off their crops; and (5) Because legal deer hunting seasons are too restrictive and dangerous.

Bessey estimates that more than 5000 whitetails—twenty to thirty percent of the annual legal harvest—fall prey to the poacher in the province of Manitoba. "It's the pioneer mentality we seem to have . . . it's the key stumbling block to all of our problems. We're losing out to the poachers. We've failed somewhere in our education . . . In terms of its sociocultural significance, deer poaching, in conjunction with the continuing destruction of white-tailed deer habitat, constitutes the most serious challenge or threat to the future of the deer resource." After posing as a deer poacher for two years while conducting his research, Bessey even encountered police officers poaching deer.

How many wardens and poachers play both sides of the coin at one time or another? A 1985 Pittman-Robertson report from Louisiana on the illegal spotlighting of deer teases us with a possible answer. While measuring the incidence, frequency, and timing of deer poaching at night from public roads, the Louisiana Department of Wildlife and Fisheries constructed life-like silhouettes of deer made of cardboard with reflective eyes. Researchers placed these deer decoys along roads in known hotspots for deer poaching. A study team of deer biologists kept them under surveillance for twelve continuous hours each day beginning one hour after sunset and extending to one hour before sunrise. The study periods occurred within five days before or after the fifteenth of the months of November, December, January, and February 1981–82 and 1982–83. According to J. W. Farrar, the deer study leader,

North Carolina was one of the pioneers in using aircraft to combat deer poaching at night as well as during the day. They started using planes in the early 1950s and other states followed suit. Today, state departments of conservation own 157 aircraft and lease nineteen more. Twenty-five states report 25,328 hours of flying time used for law enforcement. *Photo credit Rex Gary Schmidt, North Carolina Resources Commission*

"persons in law enforcement vehicles from sheriff's offices, town and city police departments, etc., showed nine responses to the fake deer and took three shots for a thirty-three percent violation record."

Deer poaching remains a problem in every area where man and deer exist; it is a nationwide problem and an unknown variable in determining deer populations. As early as the late 1960s, social scientists and wildlife researchers began to stalk the deer poacher in an attempt to understand the social demographics of deer poachers and the extent of their activity. All of these studies seem to suggest that the serious deer poacher, wherever he be found— in Idaho, New York, Michigan, Virginia, New Jersey, New Mexico, Alberta, Missouri, or Manitoba—tends to belong to a subculture from which he acquires his own distinctive norms and values. In this subculture, unemployment, alcoholism, and other extensive crimes often influence and direct his behavior. Within this Jeff Coongate subculture, deer poaching becomes a socially acceptable activity often categorized as a sport; it becomes a recreational function without any social stigma attached; it becomes a measure of the member's manliness. It is entirely possible, Ron Glover argues, that this type of behavior could influence people outside the subculture:

"Young adults who are seeking a means to raise their social status might observe the positive recognition given to deer violators by members of the subculture. These youngsters may select poaching as an immediate solution to their social shortcomings and subsequently become members of the subculture. If this happens, the net result will be persistence and perhaps growth of the subculture, ensuring that deer poaching will remain a major wildlife management problem."

Like the descendants of old Jeff Coongate, these so-called "deer hunters" of the subculture maintain a mad passion for hunting deer, legal and otherwise. Mostly otherwise! They tend to see hunting restrictions as interference from bureaucrats and environmentalists. As one reformed deer poacher acknowledged in an interview with the editors of *Outdoor Life,* "A man who poaches deer year-round is just as wild as the game he hunts. He wants no part of time clocks, regular schedules, and the rules and regulations of society."

Deer poachers shoot from vehicles, kill does illegally, fail to tag the deer they kill, kill over the limit, hunt during the closed season and after legal hours, and hunt off posted private property. "Land hunted by their fathers and grandfathers," as freelance writer Jeff Wheelwright points out in his classic essay entitled "Deer Week" published in the 1976 November issue of *Country Journal,* "does not suddenly become off limits because someone who made money in the city comes along and buys it." Deer poachers of the subculture shoot at whatever moves in the woods and flagrantly violate every legal and moral code on record. They think of themselves as masters of the deer around them, ignoring rules and regulations like spoiled children.

Curbing the illegal killing of deer by poachers remains one of the most important thrusts of current wildlife law enforcement work. Although citizen sympathy and tolerance appear to be wearing thin, and forty states now have some sort of a public-pinch-the-poacher program based on the principles of New Mexico's Operation Game Thief, too many deer still fall prey to the poacher. Despite the increasingly successful "sting" operations of the United States Fish and Wildlife Service and the emphasis on better forensics, sensors, computers, night vision devices, and lead deposit kits, too many deer are being wasted. Whether it be outdoor outlaws poaching elk antlers in Yellowstone National Park for their aphrodisiac value in the Orient or backwoods pot growers slaughtering deer in the mountains of California to protect their marijuana patches, or the lone Wisconsin farmer in the backwoods forty adding to the larder, or television's "Six Million Dollar Man" poaching deer in northwestern Oklahoma, or the massive deer poaching rings dealing in tons of illegally poached venison in Green County, Kentucky, or the new breed of Texas head-hunters poaching white-tailed bucks with massive antlers to sell as trophies for the record books netting themselves $15,000 to $20,000 per head, deer poaching remains a major wildlife management problem.

In editing *Deer & Deer Hunting* throughout the years, it has come to my attention on many occasions via news releases and letters to the editor that deer hunters are fascinated with poacher-warden confrontations, with the deer poacher's eternal battle with authority. After a great deal of intensive research on this highly romanticized subject with strong class overtones, I conclude that so long as deer roam the forest, wardens will be trying to preserve them and poachers trying to kill them. When asphalt and concrete completely cover America, when we shut the last whitetails into safari parks, deer poachers will be at work within the wire fences, for the roots of this nefarious art are deep: they go back to Robin Hood and even the young William Shakespeare.

In his *Poacher's Handbook* (1952), Ian Niall, a chronicler of the vagabonds, shiftless characters, and moonshining rascals of the deer forest, writes that "poaching is said to be a dying art, but I do not believe this. No great art dies. Congenital poachers will father poachers. It is an old thing. Hunting is in the blood. So long as there is a warren to shelter a rabbit, a holly bush in which a bird roosts and a hollow or a hill for a hare, there will be a man or a boy who will put his natural cunning to stalking the deer, hunting the wild thing and outwitting both the quarry and the representative of authority."

Chapter 19

Crippling Losses Revisited, 1985

The total elimination of crippling loss is an unrealistic goal, however efforts should be made to reduce it to a minimum level. Unfortunately, little can be done to reduce losses until the component factors contributing to crippling losses are measured. Until these determinations are made the myths and misunderstandings of crippling losses shall persist.

—Michael Lohfeld, 1978

In the October 1981 issue of *Deer & Deer Hunting,* the editors published an editorial essay entitled "Crippling Losses and the Future of American Deer Hunting." The article suggested that, on the average, the equivalent of thirty percent of the reported legal deer harvest remains in the woods: wounded deer that hunters fail to recover for whatever reason. That article was based on the findings of fifty-two scientific studies conducted throughout America between 1916 and 1979. That article, with its controversial subject matter, generated more mail than any other article published in the history of the magazine, with the possible exception of an article dealing with maned deer.

Since the publication of that article, five new scientific studies have addressed the problem of crippling losses by white-tailed deer hunters. In the interest of bringing deer hunters up to date on this subject and *facing facts as they are,* this chapter briefly summarizes these new studies and their findings. Three *additional* studies also came to my attention since the publication of the original article; they are summarized here as well. While only two of the studies discussed in the earlier article dealt with archers, all of the studies in this chapter deal with deer hunting with the bow and arrow. Unfortunately, all of them reach similar conclusions with regard to the number of wounded deer, as a percent of the legal harvest, unrecovered by deer hunters. (See the accompanying table, which is a continuation of the original table of the fifty-two crippling loss studies published in the October 1981 issue of *Deer & Deer Hunting*.)

In the first of these studies, Robert Croft of the Georgia Game and Fish Commission surveyed 578 Georgia bow hunters in 1963. The results of his mailed questionnaire indicated a bow hunting success rate of 24.5 percent, or approximately one deer for every four bow hunters. His data showed an estimated kill of 141 deer and an estimate of 111 wounded deer, or 78.7 percent of the harvest. The number of deer wounded but not recovered per bow hunter varied from

one to four deer. "The number of deer wounded," Croft argued by way of a disclaimer, "should not be taken as crippling losses, because some sportsmen indicated that the deer were only superficially wounded, yet others were sure that the deer would die."

In a similar study of bow hunters done under the auspices of the Vermont Fish and Game Department in 1968, Lawrence E. Garland surveyed 673 bow hunters from the state of Vermont, a state well recognized for its vociferous reactions to controversial deer management practices. His mailed questionnaire indicated that most deer were killed from tree stands of mixed growth and in orchards. Most suc-

A COMPREHENSIVE REVIEW OF CRIPPLING LOSSES—CONTINUED				
WILDLIFE RESEARCHER (Or Organization)	**YEAR**	**TYPE OF SEASON**	**PLACE & TYPE OF INVESTIGATION** (S) Field Search (Q) Questionnaire	**CALCULATED CRIPPLING LOSS** (% of legal harvest left in woods
Robert L. Croft Georgia Game and Fish Commission	1962-1963	Either Sex Archery	Georgia (Q)	78.7%
Lawrence E. Garland Vermont Fish and Game Department	1968	Either Sex Archery	Vermont (Q)	35%
Michael Lohfeld New Jersey Division of Fish and Game	1975-1976	Either Sex (Archery) Bucks-Only (Shotgun)	New Jersey (Q & S) Allamuchy State Park	10% (% of total hunting-related losses)
H. Lee Gladfelter, *et al.* Iowa Conservation Commission	1976-1979	Bucks-Only (80% of hunters) Either Sex (20% of hunters) Archery	Iowa (Q)	1976: 47.1% 1977: 58.5% 1978: 52.4% 1979: 60.4%
Sheriff, Haroldson, Giessman Missouri Department of Conservation	1980	Either Sex Archery	Missouri (Q)	100%
Kelly B. McPhillips South Dakota State University	1981	Either Sex Archery	South Dakota (Q)	48-56%
Thomas J. Landwehr Minnesota Department of Natural Resources	1982-1983	Either Sex Archery	Minnesota (Q)	116.7%
John S. Herron University of Wisconsin-Madison	1981-1983	Either Sex Archery	Wisconsin (S & Q)	S/Q 1981: 18/64% 1982: 19/59% 1983: 8/45%

Accurate information regarding the number of deer lost through hunter crippling is frequently inadequate, lacking, or greatly distorted with biases — the inherent evil of interviews and questionnaires. Worse, complete field studies are both expensive and difficult to carry out. *Photo credit Leonard Lee Rue III*

cessful archers shot their deer at distances of less than thirty yards. Successful bow hunters in this study reported locating mortally wounded deer within an average distance of 138 yards. Although Garland's figures showed a crippling rate of thirty-five percent of the legal harvest, he offered us this caveat: "There is no sure proof that these deer were mortally wounded since deer are occasionally examined during gunning seasons that have arrow wounds."

What deer hunters report on surveys, however, and what actually transpires in the deer forest frequently represent two different things. In the interest of comparing deer hunter surveys with field estimates (counting and examining dead carcasses), Michael Lohfeld, a research associate with the New Jersey Division of Fish, Game and Wildlife, studied the extent and importance of crippling losses of white-tailed deer by bow and shotgun hunters on a limited hunter-access area in northwestern New Jersey during the fall deer seasons of 1975 and 1976.

Lohfeld reached the conclusion that deer hunter reports prove to be a poor indicator of crippling losses for a variety of reasons: (1) This method *assumes* all wounded animals die; (2) It is difficult to determine if several hunters are referring to the same carcass; (3) Surveys do not consider salvaging, i.e., one hunter recovering another's kill; and (4) Survey estimates of this nature may be negatively influenced by the hunters' failure to report cripples because of fear of penalty.

Lohfeld's study indicated a crippling loss of ten percent of the total hunting-related losses (not a percentage of the legal harvest). When expressed in this manner, the percentages are substantially lower. In doing so, he carefully tried to distinguish which deer died of illegal kill, unrecovered kill, crippling, abandonment, and accidental kill. In comparison to other studies, his percentages remain quite low due, perhaps, to the controlled nature of the hunt: whether hunting under heavy restrictions, high warden visibility, and fenced conditions reflect deer hunting conditions in general remains an unanswered question. Furthermore, tree stands were prohibited. And since the area had only recently been opened to deer hunting, lack of familiarity prevented hunters from killing deer much less wounding them. In addition, the mature hardwoods with a small amount of understory more than likely facilitated the recovery of wounded deer; the high hunter density levels (one hunter per fifteen acres) undoubtedly encouraged salvaging. These special conditions and his small sample size may well have affected Lohfeld's conclusions.

Lohfeld's study also noted that once a deer frees itself of the arrow, blood trails frequently end and end abruptly.

One must exercise a great deal of caution when comparing the results of these different studies, since differences in terrain, habitat, type of weapon used, type of season, and the sociological character-istics of the hunters themselves affect the rates of loss. The most important aspect of this study, however, demonstrates the great disparity between hunter surveys and field estimates for crippling losses. Yet, surveys remain the most commonly used method for loss estimation.

In a survey of more than 12,000 Iowa bow hunters conducted by the Iowa Conservation Commission, H. Lee Gladfelter found a bow hunting success rate of twenty-six percent — almost equaling that of Iowa's gun hunters. His 1981 survey results indicated a crippling rate of from 47.1 percent to 60.4 percent of the legal harvest for compound bow users between 1976–1979. According to Gladfelter, "Reported crippling rates (percent of hunters hitting but not retrieving a deer) for compound bow hunters were slightly higher than for other bow types for most years, but these differences were not significant. The higher compound bow hunter crippling rate may be a factor of chance or due to differences in the use or performance of the compound bow. Compound bow hunters may attempt longer shots because they are more confident in the capability of their bow. Also, compound bow users hunted more days, which may have increased their opportunity to make a crippling shot.

"Survey data indicated that the odds of crippling a deer were 1.4 times greater for unsuccessful hunters than successful hunters. One reason for this may be that unsuccessful hunters spent more time in the field. Chances of crippling increased with number of days hunted regardless of bow type. Logically, more days in the field leads to greater opportunity for shots which may result in crippling.

"The crippling rate remained fairly constant for both compound and other bow types regardless of number of years of hunting experience. It was expected that increasing hunter experience might lead to less crippling, but no such case could be demonstrated from this data. One conclusion that could be made is that crippling is not correctable by increased training or field experience and is therefore a by-product of the sport. Another conclusion could be that inexperienced hunters may be more reluctant to report crippling than experienced hunters."

Gladfelter's data pose several difficult questions: (1) Does the improved efficiency of compound bows pose a threat to the primitive status of bow hunting? (2) What effects will future technological advances in compound bows and related shooting devices have on deer utilization and allocation?

While dealing with these difficult questions, wildlife researchers from the Missouri Department of Conservation surveyed 5000 archery deer hunters in Missouri in 1980. They found that eleven percent of the bow hunters harvested a deer and that eleven percent wounded but did not recover a deer, thus giving us a crippling rate of 100 percent of the legal harvest. Like the Iowa survey, the Missouri results indicated that "respondents who wounded and lost a deer tended to have more bow hunting experience than those respondents who did not wound and lose a deer."

The Missouri survey of bow hunters reached the following conclusions: (1) Forty-two percent of the bow hunters who killed a deer shot a deer at a range of between eleven and twenty yards; (2) Bow hunters who used longbows wounded proportionately fewer deer than recurve and compound bow users; (3) Crippling rates were not substantially influenced by the draw weights of the bows; and (4) Users of tree stands more frequently wounded deer than users of other kinds of stands.

In surveying South Dakota's archery deer hunters in 1981, Kelly Brian McPhillips, a wildlife research biologist at South Dakota State University, found that twenty-nine percent of 840 bow hunters were successful in harvesting a deer during the 1981 archery deer season. According to McPhillips, 1.84 deer were harvested per 100 hunter-days. Eight hundred and forty bow hunters took an average of four shots at deer during the season; they harvested one deer per 13.8 shots. Twenty-three percent of the successful hunters indicated that they crippled at least one deer, while fifteen percent of the unsuccessful hunters crippled at least one deer. The crippling rate of deer by South Dakota bow hunters approximated one unretrieved deer per one harvested deer. One bow hunter reported hitting five deer and failing to retrieve all five. This survey showed that bow hunters crippled 1.7 deer per 100 hunter-days; they crippled 0.92 deer per every deer harvested. According

Number of Missouri bow hunters that wounded but lost deer, by draw weight of bow.

| Draw Weight (Lbs.) | Deer Crippled | | No Deer Crippled | |
	Number	Percent	Number	Percent
36-45	29	10.36	251	89.64
46-55	124	10.06	1,109	89.94
56-65	113	12.43	796	87.57
66-75	18	12.59	125	87.41

Reprinted from: S. Sheriff, K. Haroldson and N. Giessman, "Survey of Archery Hunters of Deer and Turkey in Missouri, 1980," 1983

Number of Missouri bow hunters that wounded but lost deer, by type of stand used.

Stand	Deer Crippled		No Deer Crippled	
	Number	Percent	Number	Percent
Tree	233	12.32	1,659	87.68
Other	47	7.23	603	92.77

Reprinted from: S. Sheriff, K. Haroldson and N. Giessman, "Survey of Archery Hunters of Deer and Turkey in Missouri, 1980," 1983

to McPhillips, South Dakota bow hunters crippled one deer for each fifteen shots taken.

While wildlife managers perceive crippling rates and failure to retrieve deer as a problem of concern, some deer hunters apparently do not. When posed with the question, "Do you feel that wounding by other archery deer hunters is a problem in South Dakota?" 671 bow hunters, or seventy-eight percent of the total, responded in the negative. Yet, Professor Robert Jackson in a 1982 study of Wisconsin bow hunters found that sixty-six percent of the bow hunters he interviewed felt that wounding deer was a serious problem for bow hunting. George Reiger, the conservation editor for *Field & Stream*, summarized the public's concern when he stated, "Recent public surveys indicate that people (non-hunters) are not so much bothered by the killing of wildlife as by the thought that poorly trained shooters are crippling game."

Unlike the survey done in Iowa, this study concluded that successful deer hunters cripple significantly more deer than unsuccessful hunters. McPhillips

also noticed that almost thirty percent of the bow hunters in his survey had no archery instruction, thus creating the potential need for a broader-based hunter education system, at least in South Dakota. A broader educational program for bow hunters, he argued, should treat the areas of ethics, equipment, and deer anatomy.

No major deer hunting state seems to escape the careful scrutiny of deer hunters by scientific investigation. Minnesota is no exception in this regard. The archery deer hunter survey conducted by Thomas J. Landwehr, of the Minnesota Department of Natural Resources, noted in 1982 that neither the type of bow nor the method of hunting appeared to affect wounding or success rates; but rather success and wounding appeared to be related to such variables as experience and type of area hunted, e.g., forest versus farmland.

Landwehr's random sample of more than 55,000 Minnesota archery license buyers indicated that "in addition to the respondents' harvest of 419 deer, 489 deer were reported hit and not retrieved (116.7 percent of the retrieved harvest). If this wounding rate is expanded to a statewide

Frequency of crippling and success reported by 840 South Dakota bow hunters, 1981.

Number of Deer Crippled Per Hunter	Unsuccessful Hunters		Successful Hunters	
	Number	% of Total	Number	% of Total
0	499	83%	166	70%
1	89	15%	56	23%
2	7	1%	13	5%
3	3	< 1%	3	1%
4	2	< 1%	1	< 1%
5	0	0%	1	< 1%

Reprinted from: Kelly Brian McPhillips, "Characteristics and Success of South Dakota Archery Deer Hunters," 1983 estimate, almost 6500 deer were hit with an arrow and unrecovered in 1982. The following breakdown shows the hunting methods used when deer were wounded: deer drives (4.1 percent of total deer wounded), ground stands (19.0 percent), still-hunting (19.4 percent), tree stands (57.5 percent)." The high percentage of wounding from tree stands merely reflects the greater number of hunters using this method.

While analyzing the factors affecting wounding and success rates in Minnesota, Landwehr reached the following conclusions: (1) The most significant factors determining success revolved around previous experience and type of area hunted (higher in farmland than forest); (2) Type of bow used and method of hunting did not appear to be important; (3) The wounding rate increased with increased days of hunting, increased number of hours spent drive-hunting, and increased years of hunting experience with the compound bow; and (4) Bow hunters in the farmland zones tended to wound deer more often than the hunters in the forested areas. This situation might be explained at least in part by the fact that more bow hunters hunted the farmland zones in his study than the forested areas. Landwehr did not elaborate on this unique conclusion.

Another study analyzing deer harvests and wounding losses associated with bow hunting white-tailed deer occurred in Wisconsin in 1984. In this study, John Herron of the Department of Wildlife Ecology at the University of Wisconsin-Madison, surveyed and interviewed more than 700 bow hunters at the Badger Army Ammunition Plant in south central Wisconsin. He also conducted field searches after the bow hunts from 1981–1983. Based on his questionnaire, Herron estimated the crippling rate at between forty-five and sixty-four percent of the legal harvest. His field searches for unrecovered dead deer indicated a loss of from eight to nineteen percent of the legal harvest. (See table at start of this chapter.) The 1983 bow hunt took place with snow on the ground and with a very high hunter density, thus allowing hunters to more readily retrieve wounded deer.

Bow hunters in this study averaged 9.4 shots for each deer harvested. In interviewing hunters as they left the Plant, Herron noted that they reported missing seventy-one to eighty-two percent of their shots. "Such high percentages of reported misses," Herron observed, "may indicate that bow hunters are wounding deer without realizing it."

His analysis indicated that the unretrieved kill at the Badger Plant equaled 28.6 percent, 32.4 percent, and 16.7 percent of the number of deer reported wounded in 1981, 1982, and 1983 respectively. Herron concluded that on the average twenty-six percent of injured deer died of their wounds. He estimated that thirteen percent of the January deer population after the hunt were recovering from arrow wounds.

He also observed that some wounding loss occurs after the bow hunting season. "In February 1982, we captured, marked, and released an adult buck as part of another study. An arrowhead and part of an arrow shaft were found embedded in his left front shoulder. We made an unsuccessful attempt to remove the arrowhead before releasing him. During the next month, this buck was seen several times moving between a wooded area and a cornfield where he fed. He died in mid-March 1982, presumably from the arrow wound. The arrow was still imbedded in his shoulder when he died. Other deer may also take months to die of an arrow wound and may be difficult to distinguish from other forms of mortality."

Herron reached the following conclusions with regard to the aspects of bow hunting that can be manipulated in order to reduce the wounding loss: "Bow hunters can be encouraged to hunt in parties or to at least use a buddy system in order to retrieve more wounded deer. Managing areas to increase bow hunter density may also reduce wounding loss. Restricting or extending the season to periods of snowfall should also enable bow hunters to retrieve more wounded deer. Managers should encourage hunters to become familiar with their hunting area and assist them whenever possible by providing maps and information. Not all managers or bow hunters will find these approaches acceptable, but they are at least starting points that should be considered as possible steps towards reducing wounding loss."

In analyzing the factors associated with hunter retrieval of wounded deer hit by arrows and shotgun slugs, Edward E. Langenau, a wildlife research biologist at the Rose Lake Wildlife Research Center in East Lansing, Michigan, surveyed all deer hunters receiving permits to hunt on the Shiawassee National Refuge, located on the Saginaw Bay in the east-central part of Southern Lower Michigan during November 1–20, 1983. A total of 457 bow hunters (ninety-three percent of the permittees) responded to his mailed questionnaire; 143 shotgun hunters (ninety-five percent of the firearm permittees) responded as well.

Langenau reached the following conclusions: (1) Both archers and shotgun hunters missed a lot of deer. Bow hunters reported that eighty-one percent of the deer they shot at they missed; shotgun hunters missed sixty-six percent of the deer they shot at; (2) Twelve percent of the deer hit with arrows traveled zero yards after being hit; the remaining deer traveled an average of 262 yards before being retrieved. Fifteen percent of the deer retrieved by bow hunters showed evidence of former wounding; (3) Thirty-two percent of the deer hit by shotgun slugs traveled zero yards after being hit; the remaining deer traveled an average of eighty-five yards before being retrieved. Eleven percent of the deer retrieved by shotgun hunters showed evidence of former wounding; (4) The ratio of deer hit and not retrieved for each deer tagged Langenau estimated to be 1.4 for bow hunting and 0.3 for shotgun hunting; and (5) Archers retrieved twenty-nine (forty-three percent) of the sixty-eight different deer hit by arrows. Shotgun hunters retrieved forty-two (eighty-one percent) of the fifty-two different deer hit.

Langenau observed that three variables were independently related with regard to hunter retrieval of deer hit with arrows. Retrieval occurred most frequently when the archer hit the deer at close range, when the archer hit the deer either quartering-away or quartering-on, and when the archer had tagged several deer on previous bow hunts. The range of the archer's shot demonstrated a direct linear relationship with the wounding rate. Archers failed to retrieve any deer hit with arrows at distances of more than thirty yards away. No deer were retrieved that were hit in the head-on position.

Langenau also found that three variables were independently related with regard to hunter retrieval of deer hit with shotgun slugs. Retrieval occurred most

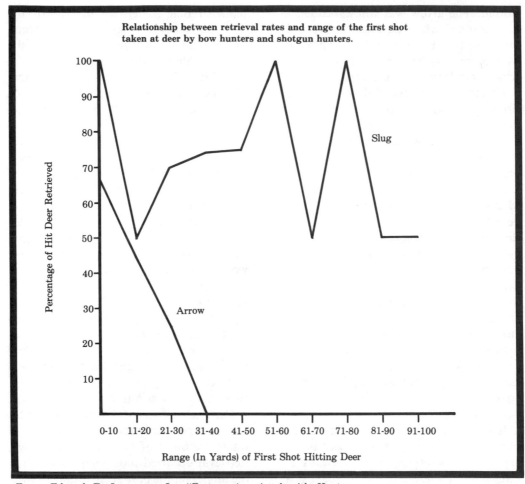

Relationship between retrieval rates and range of the first shot taken at deer by bow hunters and shotgun hunters.

From: Edward E. Langenau, Jr., "Factors Associated with Hunter Retrieval of Deer Hit by Arrows and Shotgun Slugs," 1985

frequently when the shotgun hunter hit the deer while it was standing or walking, when the shotgun hunter had previous bow hunting experience, and when the shotgun hunter had tagged few deer during prior firearm hunts. No difference in retrieval existed for deer hit with slugs while broadside, quartering, or in the head-on position.

These retrieval rates are almost identical to those reported by Stormer *et al.* for deer hunters using the Crane Ammunition

Depot in Indiana in 1979. Langenau's study confirms prior research indicating that hunters wound large numbers of deer. Although some of the deer hit and not retrieved might recover from their wounds, the rate of wounding reported in his study may be unacceptable to some groups of hunters and non-hunters as well.

What is surely unacceptable is that hitting and not retrieving a deer did not reduce hunting satisfaction: Ninety-seven percent of the bow hunters and ninety-one percent of the shotgun hunters who wounded deer but did not retrieve them reported that they had a "good" or a "very good" hunt. Langenau's study showed "that wounding was a positive event that created a better hunt than not getting a shot."

Contrary to the findings of Stormer in Indiana and Gladfelter in Iowa, Langenau's study showed that the inexperienced bow hunters wounded more deer than did the experienced bow hunters. His study indicated, however, that the reverse relationship held for shotgun hunters: experienced shotgun hunters wounded more deer than did the inexperienced hunters.

The position of the deer when hit emerged as a very important variable related to rates of retrieval. "Deer hit with arrows in broadside positions were retrieved at a lower rate than deer hit quartering-on or quartering-away. Although further research is needed here, it appears that arrows hitting broadside deer may not penetrate the scapula. Arrows striking the chest at quartering-on or quartering-away positions probably were able to strike vital organs because the arrow was behind or in front of the scapula. Also, a surprising number of deer in this study were taken by hunters who hit deer in the hindquarters, thereby severing the femoral artery. Nearly all hunter education material recommends chest shots at broadside deer. The results of this study suggest that these training manuals and targets be re-evaluated if chest shots at deer in quartering-away or quartering-on positions are more efficient in penetrating or bypassing the scapula."

Shotgun hunters, Langenau argues, need to be educated in the difficulties involved in estimating the range of shots taken at running deer. Too many hunters fail to lead deer enough and consequently hit them in the stomach or hindquarters rather than in the chest.

Several methods, according to Langenau, might be used by game managers to reduce the amount of wounding associated with deer hunting. "Certain types of equipment might be encouraged or prohibited. Hunters could be better instructed in shooting and tracking and some minimal level of proficiency in marksmanship could be required for purchasing a hunting license. Habitat management and trail design could be modified to encourage environmental conditions that favor retrieval. Hunting times and dates could be better adjusted to consider tracking conditions and social behavior of deer. Legal and ethical aspects of party hunting and the salvage of deer killed by another could be more clearly defined."

Whether we like it or not, the topic of crippling losses and wounding rates continues to rear its ugly head at scientific conferences and deer hunting seminars alike. The percentages in the table at the start of this chapter, we must remember, are coming from the deer hunters. We ourselves are supplying the scientists with this information.

When discussing this problem at various meetings, we frequently exhaust ourselves in the ambiguities of "crippling" semantics; debate on the subject usually exhibits more heat than light. Worse, we often wind up discussing two even more difficult and controversial subjects: the role of succinylcholine chloride (SCC) and the use of specially trained dogs for tracking wounded deer.

While attending the 10th Annual Meeting of the Southeast Deer Study Group in Gulf Shores, Alabama in February 1987, I listened to Horace Gore, Whitetail Program Director for the Texas Parks and Wildlife Department, present a paper entitled "Archery Wounding Loss in Texas." His data indicated a bow hunting wounding rate of about fifty percent (calculated as the percentage of animals hit but not retrieved.) In other words, for every deer bagged, one is hit and not retrieved. His data for public archery deer hunts on Texas Parks and Wildlife management areas indicated "1 deer killed and 1 deer reported wounded per 21 shots fired."

Gore pointed out that even this high rate of wounding by bow hunters does not present a problem from a biological and management perspective. But the ethical issue potentially does. He summarized the real problem:

"The real problem comes from the ethical-moral-humane perspective as viewed by the nonhunting public. Bow hunting and trapping have historically been the 'Achilles Heel' of hunting. This has been demonstrated over the years with both coming under attack by anti-hunting and humane organizations. These groups theorize that if they can win the small battles with two relatively small hunting factions, the legal foundation and precedent will help them take on hunting in general. Archery wounding loss and the lack of data open the door for legal action from these anti-hunting organizations."

Gore stressed the critical need for conclusive data on both gun and archery wounding rates and proposed three research parameters: (1) the proficiency of the hunter in hitting the vital area; (2) the efficiency of the broadhead; and (3) the proficiency of the hunter in finding a hit animal.

He also proposed the following research procedures: "(1) Radio collar a statistically valid sample of deer from any of several research facilities; (2) Use state of the art archery equipment—60-pound compound bows, aluminum arrows, and multi-bladed, pre-sharpened broadheads; (3) Utilize bow hunters with varying degrees of experience and expertise; (4) Shoot deer as encountered in typical hunting situations; (5) Simulate standard tracking procedures; (6) Monitor deer through various means until death or recovery from wounds; and (7) Collect data on the following: distance of shot, angle of shot, location of hit, penetration, initial distance traveled, total distance traveled, total time till death or recovery, deer found/not found by tracker, necropsy dead animals to determine cause of death, follow-up monitoring of wounded animals not found, calculate recovery rate, wounding rate/loss and, survival rates of wounded animals not found."

Gore concluded his discussion by noting that in all probability, the use of drug-tipped arrows would significantly increase archery recovery rates, thus reducing wounding losses. But before advocating or condoning the drug-tipped arrow, research on broadhead efficiency should be conducted to determine the magnitude of the problem.

Regardless of one's personal opinions in these matters, no simple method of solving the problem of crippling losses exists. As Albert Hochbaum, that distinguished professor of wildlife ecology, solemnly remarked, "It will always remain a personal issue with the individual hunter."

Indeed, the problem of crippling losses not only remains a personal issue with each of us, but still remains without doubt the most serious and the most controversial problem plaguing the American deer hunter and deer biologist. Accurate information regarding the number of deer lost through hunter crippling is frequently inadequate, lacking, or greatly distorted with biases—the inherent evil of interviews and questionnaires. Worse, complete field studies are both expensive and difficult to carry out; due to the problem of semantics, comparative studies currently do not exist.

Yet, accurate crippling loss figures must be had as a basis for sound deer management. As Aldo Leopold, the father of game management, observed, "The more I think about it the more I am convinced that crippling loss figures must be had as a basis for intelligent game management of any kind. While I certainly concede that the sentimentalists will use and probably misuse figures of this sort and thus do some possible harm to sport hunting, I do think such harm would be a drop in the bucket compared with the harm which would result from a policy of unwillingness to face facts as they are."

In the final analysis, whether we consider these percentages in the table at the start of this chapter as great or small remains a subjective question. Indeed, it is difficult to ascertain whether these losses constitute too big a price to pay for all the man-days of recreation derived by deer hunters across this land. If the prime consideration is conservation of the natural resource, these losses, high though they may be, do not seem to constitute a major threat to the deer herd. Yet, these losses remain a personal issue with many American deer hunters; they tarnish the image of this recreation and they create tension between firearm and archery deer hunters.

A. H. Rohlfing, the executive director of the National Shooting Sports Foundation, summarizes the overall importance of this problem in his research on hunter conduct and public attitudes toward hunting when he reminds us that when surveyed, Americans list wounding twice among the four most frequently given reasons for opposition to hunting: (1) hunters kill other hunters accidentally; (2) wounded animals die a slow death; (3) wounded animals die a painful death; and (4) hunters don't have to know anything to buy a rifle.

Chapter 20

Wounded Deer Behavior: The Myth of the Waiting Game

Because of the considerable amount of information that can be gained from a careful examination of a wounded deer's trail, this phase of wood-craft has been attended by a certain amount of myth.
— Francis E. Sell, 1964

A review of the literature on the subject of American deer hunting indicates that more ink has been spilled on the subject of wounded deer behavior and the tracking of wounded animals than on any other subject in the history of this sport, with the possible exception of the Almighty Rut. Indeed, readers of *Deer & Deer Hunting* magazine tell this editor via reader surveys that wounded deer behavior remains a topic of highest interest. No surprise, for the topic remains engulfed in such controversies as determining rates of crippling loss, using dogs to retrieve wounded deer, shooting drug-tipped arrows, as well as implementing proficiency testing as a requirement for the deer hunting license.

Undoubtedly, the most controversial aspect of this topic revolves around the question of whether to pursue the wounded animal immediately or to wait for a predetermined amount of time. Throughout the annals of American deer hunting, we have been told, *"Thou Shalt Not Pursue a Wounded Deer Immediately After a Hit!"* This eternal mandate seems like the eleventh commandment — delivered from the mountain by Moses. This chapter reviews the literature on the subject, summarizes the current state of knowledge, and ultimately questions the validity of this holy dictum.

This sweetly delusive formula was first issued in America in 1882 by none other than T. S. Van Dyke himself: "Excited by the sight of blood and signs of stumbling, burning with anxiety to retrieve the game, and impatient of any delay one is almost certain at first to rush ahead after a crippled deer. But you must remember that all means of pursuit, the trail, the blood, etc., if any, will generally be just as available in four or six hours, perhaps even the next day, as they are right after shooting. *By waiting you generally lose nothing. By not waiting you may lose all.*

"If the deer goes off," Van Dyke argued, "let him go and for several hours do nothing to disturb him. If it is near night you had better let him go until next morning. If he is badly hurt he will probably never rise after lying down a while, and at all events is likely to get so *sick and stiff* as to be quite easy of approach. But if followed up at once he will be watching, and unless very much hurt will be too keen and too lively for you."

The waiting-game philosophy probably worked during the years when Van Dyke tramped the deer forest, since hunter density remained marginal, thus allowing the hunter to track his deer without fear of someone else taking possession of it. Hunter density surely never led him to question the waiting-game idea, but snowfall did. When snow begins to fall, he insisted, pursue the animal immediately. While Van Dyke never recommended starting out in hot pursuit under any conditions like a rocket at the report of the gun, he eventually came around to seriously questioning the validity of the waiting game, interestingly enough, even though he initiated the idea.

In his treatise on still-hunting, he wrote: "It is common to hear people talk as if it were only necessary to let a wounded deer alone and it will lie down and either die or get sick. This is true enough if it be badly wounded and time enough be allowed it. But *when* will it be so sick that it will cease to watch upon its back track and either run away before you get within shot at all or go plunging through brush at your ap-

proach and give you a poor running shot? Of course *it is only a question of time,* but you will find that sweetly delusive formula very poor consolation when night closes in upon you and you wish to go somewhere else in the morning, when falling snow covers the bloody trail, when it leads into heavy windfalls or brush, and on bare ground when the blood ceases to flow and the cripple settles to a walk on ground where tracking is hard."

Yes, Van Dyke not only first proposed the theory of the waiting game but questioned it as well—thus leaving it for us to argue about. And deer hunters have argued about it for the past 100 years.

His twelve general observations on wounded deer behavior as a result of being shot with a gun, however, have received little or no argumentation; they remain virtually unchallenged:

(1) A deer shot in either the head or the spinal column will drop immediately.

(2) A deer shot through the kidneys or in the rectum will nearly always do the same.

(3) A deer shot anywhere in a six-inch circle behind the front shoulder will frequently drop at once, but is quite capable of traveling up to 200 yards or more.

(4) A deer shot from the fifth rib to the hip-joint—nearly half the body of the animal—may be regarded as a paunch shot—the worst shot of all.

(5) Deer are amazingly tough and sometimes get away when mortally wounded.

(6) You cannot be certain about the movement of a wounded deer except that it will generally run to the roughest and most brushy cover within reach.

(7) The number of deer lost on bare ground by the best of trackers is almost incredible.

(8) The deer's action when wounded de-

After being hit with an arrow, deer usually move away at break-neck speed. A deer shot through the heart does not necessarily drop immediately. After the first jump, which is often hardly perceptible and no doubt over-looked by the average deer hunter, it generally makes off at top speed, running in a mad, belly-to-the-ground dash. Bow hunters should not expect animals to pile up on the spot. *Photo credit Leonard Lee Rue III*

pends largely upon where you hit the deer, but mainly upon whether he sees you or not.

(9) If jumped and shot on the run, deer will probably run much farther than if shot while standing and not suspecting danger.

(10) Wounded deer, if not too badly hurt, will continually watch their back track.

(11) Individual deer differ with regard to their vitality in escaping: large bucks will drop in their tracks with the same bullet hole in the same place that another deer will carry for great distances before falling.

(12) Van Dyke observed that sighting the hunter often revives wounded deer in an amazing manner.

Not until 1909 did anyone add substantially to Van Dyke's original observations. In that year Joseph Brunner, a deer hunter and lay naturalist from Germany, systematically recorded the variation in deer tracks depending upon the nature of the wound. He recorded eight different sets of tracks for eight different types of wounds.

In addition to recording these variations in tracks, he suggested that deer tend their wounds. "During snowless times if a deer has been wounded and gets away, hunting a day or two after, along streams in the district will often bring to bay the wounded animal. If it has the strength, it will hunt up water to cool the wound, and then crawl into the densest cover that is near. I have found many deer in this way, dead and alive—and still more skeletons to which the tracks of varmints led me in the later season." Whether deer necessarily head for water when wounded remains a debatable point: some do and some do not.

Evidence suggests, however, that deer do in fact tend their wounds. Case in point: Leon Lyons, a Michigan deer hunter, reports that while skinning the shoulder area of a doe, he found a wound apparently received early in the fall. "The bullet had entered in front of the right shoulder, passed between the leg bone and her ribs, clipped about one inch out of a rib behind the shoulder and exited. The hole was closed on both ends. There was a

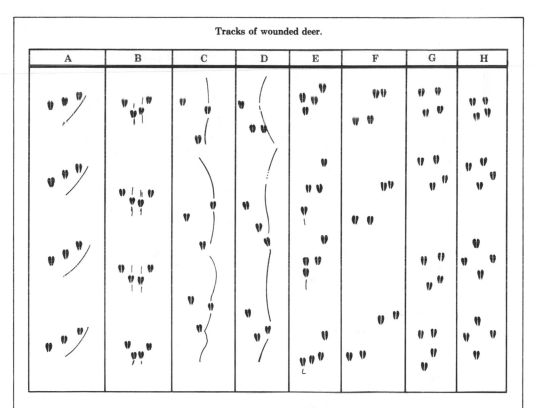

Tracks of wounded deer.

(A) Trail of a deer shot through brisket with leg broken low in shoulder. (B) Trail of a deer shot high through the shoulders. (C) Trail of a deer with a broken foreleg—the lower the leg is broken, the more pronounced the drag mark. (D) Trail of a deer with a broken hind leg—the lower the leg is broken, the more pronounced the drag mark. (E) Trail of a deer shot through the ham. (F) This trail usually means that the animal was shot through the intestines, liver or lungs; the animal will not go much over a mile, even if not given time to get sick; death results in less than two hours. (G) Same as F but did not penetrate to the lungs. The animal dies slowly, and after a couple of hours is usually shot in its bed. (H) The cross jump results from a bullet through the intestines or liver with the animal standing broadside to the hunter—usually the slowest killing shot.
—Joseph Brunner
Tracks And Tracking

wad of vegetation in the wound consisting of ferns, ripe choke cherries, grass, and leaves. The wad of vegetation approximated the size of a baseball." Lyons marveled that the deer could have so much foreign matter in that area. Perhaps Brunner was right: Deer do tend their wounds.

After many years of following the tracks and trails of wounded deer and systematically recording his findings, Brunner reached the following conclusions with regard to wounded deer behavior:

(1) The most important sign to observe is the action of the deer when it receives the bullet or the arrow.

(2) If struck somewhere in the front half, it usually jumps into the air.

(3) If struck in the hind half, it will kick out with its hind legs.

(4) When shot through the heart, deer generally make off at top speed running very hard and close to the ground—the hunter can follow at once.

(5) A deer shot through the lungs generally goes off, after the initial jump, as if nothing happened. This trail may be followed immediately.

(6) A deer shot through the liver will kick and at other times hump itself up, but it always exits with great speed, leaving a trail like a lung shot deer with a cross jump here and there. Brunner smoked a pipeful of tobacco before taking up this trail.

(7) A shot through the intestines causes the deer to kick violently, hump its back and go off in a slow manner. Deer shot in this way should not be followed for at least two hours.

(8) A hard, sharp sound conveys to the hunter that he hit a bone while a dull "thud" indicates he hit a soft part of the body.

(9) Deer hair cut off by the bullet frequently assists the hunter in determining the location of the wound; torn-up needles or leaves on the ground often show if the animal jumped or kicked.

Like T. S. Van Dyke and others, Brunner marveled at the whitetail's incredible ability to recover from hunter-inflicted wounds. Some of his deer hunting anecdotes, however, tend to stretch his credibility. For example: "I once killed an elk three days after we had fried parts of its liver which had dropped out through the hole made by a projectile from a heavy-caliber English rifle, used previously for hunting elephants. At another time I killed a deer one year after having shot it through the liver. When killed, this deer was apparently as well and fat as could be, though in place of the soft liver we found a hard mass." WHEW! Mr. Brunner certainly had a vivid imagination.

Brunner had mixed feelings with regard to the waiting game. He pursued immediately heart-shot deer. He also followed immediately lung-shot deer, deer shot high in the shoulders, and deer with a broken leg. Before pursuing liver-shot deer, he smoked a pipeful of tobacco. He waited for two hours before chasing deer shot in the intestines. But the rhyme and rhythm for these various durations of waiting remained unstated. He did give us these words of caution: "Remember that the successful deer hunter is never in a hurry, and minutes spent in close observation will often save hours of exhausting chase."

The next great contribution to the problem of wounded deer came in 1926, when William Monypeny Newsom (1887–1942), an Ohio-born deer hunter and naturalist, conducted surveys with American deer hunters primarily in the Northeast, as mentioned in chapter two, to determine their knowledge of white-tailed deer anatomy. He tested all types of deer hunters:

experts from training and experience who were capable of instructing others, good hunters with average experience, as well as the novice who depended upon the instructor. Newsom discovered that hunters did not know their anatomy and when presented with a broadside sketch of a deer could not pick out the precise location of the heart. Out of 139 replies from a selected list of well-known guides, eighty-nine (sixty-four percent of them) missed the heart location altogether. From his field observations, he concluded that hunters, for the most part, were shooting too far back of the fore-shoulder and too high to hit the heart area.

Believing that deer hunters must know the deer's anatomy, Newsom set out to do something about the problem. Working with the staff of the American Museum of Natural History in New York, he secured a deer, dissected it, and photographed its internal anatomy with the lungs inflated and deflated. His remarkable photographs of the internal anatomy of the deer's organs soon appeared in sportsmen's magazines all across America. The precise nature of the photos so enamored this deer hunter that I asked wildlife photographer Leonard Lee Rue III to recreate Newsom's work in color. (See color section, which precedes this book's title page.)

With his usual, unfailing energy, Newsom also designed illustrations of deer skeletons indicating the heart area in relationship to the bone and rib structure from various positions. Next, he published articles on his findings together with his photos and illustrations in the leading outdoor magazines of his time. *"One Shot — no cripples"* became his popularly recognized slogan; it should be emblazoned on every deer hunting license issued. Dr. F. A. Lucas, the director of the American Museum of Natural History,

rightly concluded in a letter that Newsom's photos of the internal anatomy of deer "diminished the number of lingering deaths due to ignorance of where to aim and actually increased the hunter's bag." One hopes that Leonard Lee Rue III's updated version of Newsom's work will do the same.

With regard to wounded deer behavior, Newsom denied the idea that deer always clamp their tail down after being hit. Some do, some don't, he argued. He reminded us that when we find a big, wide trail of ordinary red blood of no distinguishing feature, we should not jump to the conclusion that the amount of blood indicates a sure kill in a few hundred yards — it doesn't. On the contrary, a mere flesh wound frequently bleeds more than a deadly shot.

Like Brunner, Newsom liked to smoke a lot of pipe tobacco before pursuing wounded deer. He recommended waiting for at least two to three hours for the deer to "sicken and lie down," when shot in the paunch. They grow "stiff" as they rest and cool off. But he never explained how this "stiffening up" takes place or what it really means. He did, however, warn us about generalizing on the subject of wounded deer behavior:

"As to the effect of different shots on deer, I am strongly tempted to remain discreetly silent, for no matter what is said, it is wrong forty percent of the time. Deer vary greatly in vitality and ability to absorb lead, so that it is very dangerous to generalize on this subject. When you shoot a deer that refuses to be governed by the rules, put him down as one of the forty percent that are exceptions, and accept it as quite to be expected."

Indeed, the vitality of the white-tailed deer under wounded conditions is proverbial. They can carry an extraordinary

amount of lead and keep going for remarkable distances even when mortally
shot. Paul Brandreth, for example, a hunting companion of Newsom's, recalls in his
classic *Trails of Enchantment* (1930), how
one white-tailed buck in the Adirondacks
ran seventy-five yards straight uphill—and
a steep hill at that—before falling dead
from a bullet in its heart. He also noted
that a deer mortally hit with the first shot
seldom sticks to a runway, but often
crashes blindly in any direction before finally falling to the forest floor. I have experienced this situation on many occasions. He added that "when a blood trail
follows a runway you can be pretty sure
that although your quarry may be in a bad
way, he is, nevertheless, very likely to give
you a long chase."

Paul Brandreth will be remembered as
long as deer hunting survives in this country for this one liner: "If you are of the
right stamp, you will take pains to learn
where the vital spots are located on a
deer's anatomy, instead of blazing away
helter-skelter, and maiming several individuals before you happen, through a
stroke of graceless luck, to knock one
over."

By the 1940s deer biologists began to
pay lip service to the waiting game. Urban
C. Nelson, for example, a deer biologist
with the Michigan Department of Conservation, urged hunters not to continue the
chase of a deer badly injured "but to wait
at least a half hour before following the
trail, *thus giving the disabled victim a
chance to lie down and stiffen from shock
or loss of blood.*" He immediately added
this disclaimer, "it is probably best, however, to continue the chase if darkness is
approaching, snow is falling, or if the trail
must be followed on dry vegetation."

But will the deer stiffen from shock or
loss of blood? When will muscular action
become inhibited? Has anyone ever measured accurately all the physiological or ex-
traneous factors involved? Will the deer
experience an increase or a decrease in
temperature as a result of a gunshot
wound? An increase or a decrease in heart
rate? An increase or a decrease in respira-
tory movements? Does traumatic shock
contribute to and hasten death? None of
these questions have ever been determined
with any degree of accuracy. Yet, the myth
of the waiting game persists—based on
the nebulous notion that if given time,
wounded deer will "stiffen up," whatever
that means.

In a scientific paper on "Traumatology
in Wildlife Management" published in
1940, one wildlife researcher observed that
"a deeply penetrating and infected gunshot wound in the case of man is usually
accompanied by fever, inflammation and
weakness within a short time (usually
thirty-six to forty-eight hours) after injury." Should we wait thirty-six to forty-
eight hours before following wounded
deer?

NO! says Alex Cox, a deer hunter from
Texas. "Wait thirty minutes before proceeding. This is very necessary, for thirty
minutes will give a deer time to die, and if
not to die, it will give him time to hemor-
rhage internally or externally and to become sick, or perhaps get the blind staggers." *THE BLIND STAGGERS!* No,
Alex. I can understand pipefuls of tobacco and perhaps in a vague way "stiffening up," but the "blind staggers" borders on biological jibberish. Nevertheless,
for old Alex, thirty minutes was the magic
formula. Cox rightly pointed out one
curious fact, however, something I have
also experienced on several occasions:

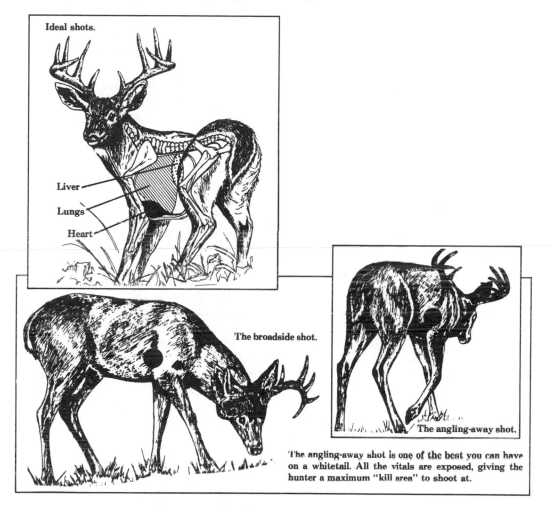

Ideal shots.

Liver

Lungs

Heart

The broadside shot.

The angling-away shot.

The angling-away shot is one of the best you can have on a whitetail. All the vitals are exposed, giving the hunter a maximum "kill area" to shoot at.

Wounded deer when being trailed frequently return to within a few hundred yards from where you first shot them.

Unlike Alex Cox, Larry Koller, one of the old masters from the Catskill Mountains, voiced the first major opposition to this long cherished idea of waiting in his classic deer book, *Shots at Whitetails* (1948). Since deer hunters in the Catskill Mountains kill a great majority of their deer in areas of high hunter density, Koller rightly argued that many unpleasant

scenes among hunters result from playing the waiting game: Hunters tagging deer shot by others.

"The best advice is to follow your deer at once, under these conditions, and finish it off as soon as possible. Better than this, make your hit a clean one, dropping your deer for good, and the trailing worry will be over." Koller, however, still recommended waiting "for an hour or more" for deer shot in the paunch *in the hope* that some other hunter is not ahead of you.

Type of Blood	Description
Lung Blood	Light red to pinkish, frothy with very small bubbles of air in it. Note: A fine spray of blood with bubbles may also be an indication of a wounded deer that has been running.
Chest Cavity Blood	Arrows which penetrate the chest cavity from the diaphragm forward, "not including lungs," will produce a moderately red blood with large air bubbles in it. This should not be confused with a lung hit.
Heart and Main Artery Blood	Crimson red blood usually found in larger quantities, can spurt out or gush. This spray effect subsides gradually as the system drains of blood.
Liver and Vein Blood	Tends to be a darker red color and may even resemble a brownish-red color at times.
Stomach (Rib Area)	Usually darker colored red (if any), color mixed with stomach fluids and brownish-green from undigested food particles.

Note: Watery, red blood usually indicates a flesh wound in a leg or ham.

The Ontario Bowhunters Association. *Bowhunting Notes:* 1980.

Koller was one of the first deer hunters to maintain that the most tangible evidence of a hit beyond blood manifests itself in tiny tufts of deer hair lying on the ground near the scene of action. "I believe that it is virtually impossible to hit a deer in any portion of its anatomy without cutting off a bit of hair." Many of us would agree. Several products aid today's deer hunter in this regard. One thinks of Moore's Original Hair Chart, the American Archery Company's "Trailing Tips" by Art Laha, as well as the "Big Game Recovery Guide" provided by the National Bowhunter Education Foundation—three basic items for the hunter's backpack that stress the importance of hair identification and tracking procedure.

Remember that a distinctive type of hair covers each part of a whitetail's body. The darker the hair, the higher the hit, serves the deer hunter as a general rule of thumb. More specifically, however, Art Laha's descriptions of body hair remain accurate and useful: (1) *Stomach hair*—coarse, hollow, brownish gray, tips are not as dark as hair from the spine area.

(2) *Navel hair*—white, coarse, hollow, curly, twisted. (3) *Hair from foreleg*—dark, short, medium coarse. (4) *Hair from between hind legs*—fine, white, silky, not hollow, curled tips. (5) *Tail hair*—long, coarse and wavy, black or grayish brown on top to pure white underneath. (6) *Hair from the spine area*—dark with black tips, long, coarse and hollow. (7) *Hair covering the heart area*—long dark guard hairs found only over the heart, graying with age. (8) *Brisket*—stiff and grayish black, curly and coarse. Koller would have been pleased to see this development of his original observation.

In 1950, noted deer biologist Bill Severinghaus of New York agreed with Larry Koller: When deer hunting in the southern tier and western sections of the Catskills, follow your deer as soon as you've stopped shooting. If you don't, be prepared to come upon somebody else dressing out your deer. After interviewing thousands of deer hunters at check stations, Severinghaus concluded that in areas of high hunting pressure, pursue wounded deer immediately. He also recommended immediate pursuit for deer bleeding freely in warm weather. "If a deer is bleeding freely in warm weather, it would seem advisable to push after him at once, since by pushing him the animal's heart action would be increased and death from loss of blood would be accelerated. Because of the warm weather, there would be no tendency for the deer to stiffen up if pursuit were delayed."

Severinghaus also made the interesting observation that deer often employ the trick of running with the wind for a considerable distance and then quartering back into the wind to a point of observation from which they can see and scent their trail. Consequently, search thoroughly for any patches of cover well to the right or left of the actual trail; the wounded deer may well have quartered back into them.

During the 1950s deer hunters in their attempt to solve the problem of wounded deer continued to debate the proposition of waiting before taking up the trail of the wounded animal. Francis Sell, that buckskin backwoodsman from the rural hills of Coquille, Oregon, emerged as the leading critic.

"When we consider the nature of wounds and the deer's reaction to them, the entire proposition of waiting is open to question. The initial shock of a wounding hit is not painful; it tends only to weaken the animal. Instinct causes it to seek the security of a thicket or other heavy cover in which to lie down. The wound then becomes painful, and this may cause the deer to get on its feet and move around. But if the wound is sufficiently severe and blood-loss is great, the downed animal seldom regains its feet. A wait of an hour

would be of no benefit under the circumstances. I have found it good practice to run out the first hundred yards of trail at once. This examination furnishes everything one needs to know for further trailing of a wounded deer, if such trailing proves necessary. The hunter will then know the nature of the wound, have track measurements, and be able to recognize individual characteristics of the prints."

After questioning the idea of waiting, Sell added several interesting opinions to the puzzle of wounded deer behavior: (1) Wounded deer will not continue along a trail used by the unwounded; (2) A mortal hit is indicated only when the flag goes down; (3) A change of pace betrays a hit; and (4) Uneven spacing in the prints in the trail can indicate (as Brunner suggested earlier) the deer's inability to run with a free stride.

Before leaving the trail of wounded deer overnight, Sell measured the exact length and width of both the hind and front hooves. He marked them on a hemlock branch he cut for that purpose. Before returning to his cabin, he carefully studied the individual prints as well. "Each is as individual as a fingerprint. A hoof chips and breaks in the course of normal use and this results in a variation of prints without end." Sell's advice: Gather all the information possible before resuming the track in the morning, if need be.

While tracking wounded deer, Frank Edminster, a professional wildlife biologist and author of *Hunting Whitetails* (1954), often observed the whitetail's amazing ability to run away after receiving a mortal wound. Indeed, many wounded deer initiate marathon tracking chores lasting from two to three days. Edminster urged hunters to draw detailed maps of

Maps of wounded deer behavior.

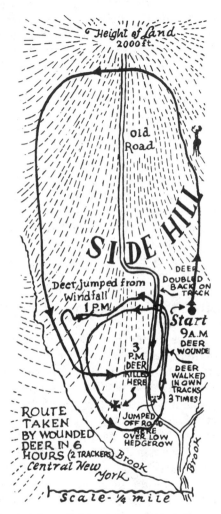

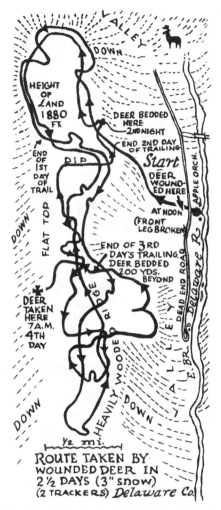

These maps of wounded deer behavior indicate the complex nature of the problem: (1) Deer will often double back and backtrack. (2) They will walk in their own tracks for considerable distances. (3) They will travel in a circular direction, frequently crossing their own trails.

These examples also suggest that wounded deer will stay in their home range unless pushed terribly hard. Note further that in both of these cases the trackers retrieved the deer quite close to where the animals were shot.

the trails of wounded deer, whether you recover the deer or not. In drawing maps himself, he noted that wounded deer frequently take a circuitous route when followed, trying to trick the hunter by devious maneuvers. This general circular

pattern of travel, Edminister believed, stays within the deer's home range. I have frequently found this same situation. "This means that your trail will not likely lead you very far from where you start."

With regard to the waiting game,

"Eddie," as he was known in deer camp, agreed with his friend Bill Severinghaus: "The weather and the hour often affect the decision of whether to track at once or wait. If the weather is very warm, the deer will not stiffen when it lies down as readily as in cold weather. It may be just as well to begin the pursuit at once as to wait."

Yet, other deer biologists insisted that we wait under all conditions. Arnold O. Haugen, for example, a wildlife research biologist with the Michigan Department of Conservation, maintained that "if hit, a delay will give the deer a chance to bleed out and/or stiffen so it won't be so apt to sneak away when you go after it." Haugen was perhaps the first biologist to attempt to define "stiffening up." "Stiffening is really just a stage of shock resulting from loss of blood and the using up of stored energy in the muscles and nerves." He did not elaborate.

Deer hunters, however, remained unconvinced about this idea of "stiffening up." Red Freeman, a professional guide from Maine, disagreed with Haugen. "The idea of waiting for a wounded deer to find a resting place before following it may be sound in theory, but I prefer to start trailing as soon as I have hit one. It will usually require considerable time to overtake the animal and time is something which is not too plentiful during the deer hunting season. Aside from humane reasons, I want to dispatch the wounded deer as soon as possible and before fever has progressed far enough to affect the meat. The time that is necessary for a wounded deer to 'stiffen up' so that it can be easily overtaken is usually so long that the meat will be full of fever-fighting anti-bodies and it will be undesirable, if not unfit for food."

Freeman added several important pieces of information to the detective work involved in tracking wounded deer: (1) When deer circle, cross and recross their own tracks leaving you with a complicated maze of tracks to untangle, circle the maze following the outside tracks until you find where the animal left the area instead of miring yourself down in all its twistings and turnings; (2) The longer a wounded deer remains with a group of deer, the less severe is its wound; and (3) Deer need water to alleviate the fever caused by wounds.

In 1954, Dr. Frederick Weston, a deer biologist with the Texas Game and Fish Commission, revived the idea of waiting: "When first hit, there is no pain and the animal will run his usual distance when disturbed, then slow down. When pain overtakes him, he is likely to move into the thickest cover at hand and lie down. If his wound is not serious, he may get up and move around trying to escape his pain but pain will keep him quiet if he is not disturbed. If he is seriously wounded, he will lie down, and if not disturbed, he will die from surgical shock, bleed to death, or hemorrhages will leave him too sick, weak, or sore to go anymore. He should not be disturbed, therefore, until his wounds have had time to take effect."

Weston advised hunters to avoid wounding deer by not taking chance shots at running deer. As a biologist, he observed that many body shots keep from bleeding because peristaltic action of the intestines often plugs the bullet holes with the entrails.

During the 1950s, deer biologists generally agreed that hunters wounded and failed to retrieve at least thirty percent of the legal harvest, but they disagreed amongst themselves with regard to the waiting game and its meaning and importance. Some deer biologists such as

Haugen and Weston believed in the notion of "stiffening up" and thus waiting. Following Edminster and Severinghaus, other biologists such as Harry Ruhl, the game chief of the Michigan Department of Conservation, rejected the old-time hunter's advice of waiting before pursuing. Writing in Walter Taylor's classic *The Deer of North America* (1956), Ruhl suggested that "once a deer is down it should be followed quickly. In many cases the animal is only stunned temporarily from shock but will recover within a few minutes. Take up the chase immediately rather than to take a chance that another hunter will down the wounded deer."

As the decade ended Ray Beck, a backwoods Pennsylvania trapper and briar patch philosopher, told readers of *Outdoor Life* to follow the trail immediately for a quarter of a mile or so and then decide to wait or not. "The deer ordinarily won't stop within that distance unless it's too weak to go further." Beck further added to our knowledge of myth and folklore the idea "that if a wounded deer wasn't chased it would walk twice as far as it had run and then lie down." Apparently, he based this peculiar notion on backwoods intuition.

In 1959, this gentlemanly advice came from our English neighbors across the Atlantic: "Consider a deer which is mortally wounded but has run away to die quietly in the nearest cover. If disturbed by searchers it will move on, in agony; whereas if left for fifteen minutes it will die peacefully. Surely the latter is the kinder and more humane action?" Fifteen minutes? Kinder and more humane?

During the 1960s, the idea of waiting before pursuing a downed deer ran into stiff opposition from the country's leading deer hunters. Tom Hayes, a well-known authority on hunting whitetails in Texas, viewed this idea as a myth we inherited from historical moose hunters of yesteryear. He insisted that the less experienced deer hunters, in particular, get on the trail at once. "Many veteran hunters, myself included, are quite skeptical as to the advisability of ever relaxing pressure on your wounded quarry . . . There is plenty of evidence that blood will flow more copiously and with less tendency to coagulate if a wounded animal is stimulated by fear and exertion." Push the deer, if you ever expect it to collapse from loss of blood.

Hayes added ten significant factors to our trail knowledge and woodcraft:

(1) The faster a deer is moving and the greater its fright, the less reaction it will display on being hit.

(2) A deer downed in the hindquarters and unable to travel will occasionally bleat.

(3) If your bullet passes through the animal, you will almost surely smell the odor of venison. (Tom, your sniffer is better than mine.)

(4) If a heavy, regular blood trail ends abruptly, your deer may well have bled out completely while running; you will probably find it dead within twenty-five yards.

(5) You will recover few deer when a light to moderate blood trail slowly peters out.

(6) A deer with a broken hind leg can run much faster than you can.

(7) When the blood trail plays out on a leg-shot deer, you will probably never see the deer again, unless you use a dog. Fourteen states and provinces today allow hunters to use dogs in their pursuit of wounded deer.

(8) Every whitetail you trail will increase your ability to trail the next one.

(9) Straight shooting and a powerful and properly loaded rifle can make up for a hell of a lot of ignorance about tracks and wounded deer sign.

(10) As you gain experience with wounded deer, you will also gain the desire to do all of your hunting *before* you shoot and learn to avoid leg-shots and gut-shots as you would your mother-in-law.

While thinking about the traditional "waiting pipe" before pursuing wounded deer, John Madson, a wildlife biologist and former assistant director of Conservation for the Winchester Division of the Olin Corporation, gave us this definition to consider: "Stiffening isn't usually the result of muscular damage, but a stage of shock resulting from loss of blood and the drain of nervous and physical energy." With this definition in mind and realizing that blood loss must be extensive if the hunter is to easily recover his animal, why would we want to wait? It would seem logical that the quicker we pursue the animal, the greater the blood loss and the greater the shock—thus hastening retrieval, not prolonging it. Why would we want to give the animal time to recover from blood loss and shock?

Under no circumstances would we want to do that, says Dutch Wambold, a renowned bow hunter from the hills of Pennsylvania. If you haven't read his pioneering ideas on blood volume and shock in his *Bowhunting for Deer* (1964), you have missed one of the greatest contributions to the subject. For he presents a fresh approach to clean kills and 100 percent recoveries based on scientific research and not on "me and Joe" tales—a point the outdoor writers, editors, and publishers of this country would do well to ponder, for the literature on the subject still remains saturated with nonsense.

Working with researchers at the School of Veterinary Medicine at the University of Pennsylvania and the Michigan Department of Conservation, Wambold came to favor immediate tracking or what he called a "hot pursuit" philosophy. He contended that a vitally hit deer bleeds freely internally and should be followed immediately without fear of lessening your chances of recovery. "I believe that if a deer is hit well enough to induce profuse bleeding, it will be able to run only a certain limited distance before collapsing from weakness and shock through blood loss. It seems to me this distance should not vary so greatly regardless of whether the deer is followed immediately or later on. There seems to be no good reason for waiting any specific time period before undertaking the trailing. Therefore, I favor immediate tracking."

Wambold believed that his "hot pursuit" philosophy applied for non-vital hits as well, since any wounded deer continues to weaken through continued movement. Movement keeps the wound actively bleeding, thus continuing the blood loss. Rest only permits coagulation and no further blood loss. In other words, by keeping the deer moving you more effectively compound the wound damage than by giving it a chance to rest.

"Any hit made in some part of the body where arteries or veins are small means loss of only a small volume of blood. However, by pushing deer in such cases, the bleeding will be aggravated. Were such a deer allowed to bed down, chances are that coagulation might close the wound and stop hemorrhaging. The deer could conserve its strength and recover enough to later travel very great distances and possibly never be found."

How much blood does a live white-tailed deer carry in its arterial system? What quantity of blood must a deer lose before it reaches a point of involuntary collapse? The answers to these two questions remain crucial, especially for the bow hunter.

We know from Wambold's findings and the research of other deer biologists that the average white-tailed deer of approximately 150 pounds in live weight carries at least eight pints of blood in its arterial system. For a bow hunter to easily recover a wounded deer, the blood loss must be extensive. A deer will have to lose at least thirty-five percent of its total blood vol-

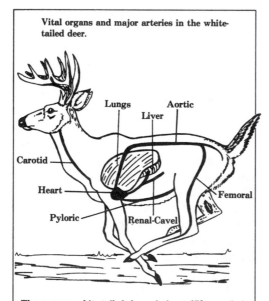

Vital organs and major arteries in the white-tailed deer.

The average white-tailed deer of about 150 pounds in weight carries approximately eight pints of blood in its arterial system. The blood loss must be extensive if the bow hunter is to easily recover a wounded deer. A deer will have to lose at least thirty-five percent of its total blood volume for rapid hunter-recovery to take place. That's a loss of at least 2¾ pints of blood in the case of a 150-pound deer. The quicker the blood loss, the sooner you will recover the animal. Deer biologists tell us that a running white-tailed deer has three times the heart rate per minute of a deer in the bedded position. Why would we want to wait and allow the deer to bed down after being wounded?

ume for rapid recovery to take place. That means a loss of at least 2¾ pints of blood in the case of a 150-pound buck. The quicker the blood loss, the sooner you will recover the animal. According to Professor Aaron Moen, a deer biologist at Cornell University, a running white-tailed deer has three times the heart rate per minute of a deer in the bedded position. Again we must ask the question: Why would we want to wait and allow the deer to bed down after being wounded?

Any shock the bow hunter hopes to inflict on a whitetail will only result through great and rapid loss of blood. Applying basic mathematics to his findings on wounded deer behavior, blood loss, and shock, Wambold presented us with this interesting and speculative scenario of a hard-hit 150-pound deer leaving a blood trail of 100 yards. Wambold's example is not necessarily a lung-shot deer, but a deer wounded to the extent of leaving a very well-defined blood trail indicative of arterial or other heavy bleeding with the arrow passing completely through the deer:

"This deer would have to lose fifty-two ounces, or about 3¼ pints of blood before collapse. Internal blood loss would have to extend to forty-one ounces, or about 2½ pints to stop the deer within the trail distance of 100 yards. In other words, the internal loss rate would have to be almost four times that of the external rate in order to down the deer. Average internal blood loss needed would be .41 ounces per yard; the eternal rate, .11 ounces per yard."

Since many of us wind up with lung-shot deer during the bow season, Wambold's detailed description of a lung-shot whitetail merits the thoughtful consideration of all of us:

White-tailed deer heart rates per minute for five activities throughout the year.

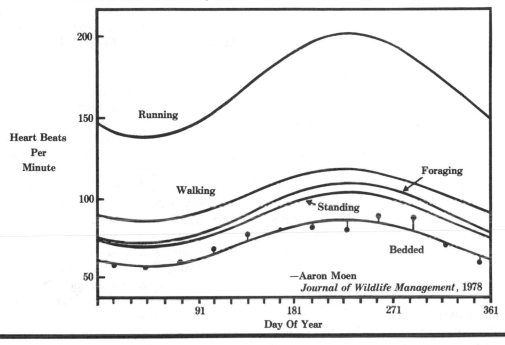

"This is one of the most effective hits for the bow hunter and it involves the largest target area. This also is the case, of course, with all big game. If the bow hunter will take the time to examine the lungs closely when he field-dresses his deer, he will find they have a spongy texture, containing countless tiny blood vessels. Supplied by a network of arteries and thousands of small blood vessels, the deer's blood supply is constantly circulated into and out of these two bellow-like organs. Oxygen taken from the air is added to the blood through the tiny cellular sponges; once charged with oxygen, the blood is then pumped to all parts of the body along the arterial route. Returned through the veinous system, the blood is again purified by fresh oxygen and sent on its way, the cycle being continuous with each breath of the animal.

"A broadhead arrow passing into or through a lung is definite assurance that the deer will fall within a relatively short distance. If a large artery is cut, death may be instantaneous in some cases. Usually the animal will travel until its lungs have filled through bleeding, eventually drowning. A deer that has run a considerable distance *before* an arrow strikes him may have become exhausted; then a lung hit could cause the animal to fall instantly. Overheated blood warms the air in the lungs but a sudden hole created, as when a shaft passes completely through the deer, allows cooler outer air to enter the lungs. This circumstance can induce lung collapse, asphyxiation, and quick death. The trail left by a deer hit in the lungs is frothy in pattern, pinkish-red in color, and notably sprayed to the sides of the animal's tracks because of the bellow-like action of the lungs. The hunter can usually expect to recover a deer hit this way within one hundred to one hundred and fifty yards."

If Wambold didn't destroy the myth of the waiting game, David O'Meara, a professor of Animal Pathology at the University of Maine, did. While examining post-mortem changes in eighty-five white-tailed deer in 1965, he demonstrated that *"stiffening" does not take place until after death;* that muscles in the legs for example, do not begin to stiffen until three to six hours after death. Such factors as physical condition and degree of exertion before death do not influence rigor mortis in white-tailed deer in any significant way. Yet, myths die hard.

As the 1960s ended, only a few select deer hunters from various parts of the country joined in the chorus and said "no" to the notion of waiting. Oregon's Francis Sell: "Don't wait around, get on the trail at once!" Chapman J. Milling, a South Carolina deer hunter and author of *Buckshot and Hounds:* "If dogs are to be used, the fresher the trail, the better the chance of finding him." Luther Anderson, author of *How to Hunt Whitetail Deer:* "The animal may get away if not quickly trailed. When hit, then, the deer should be trailed at once. It may drop shortly or it may be lost in heavy brush, but you will never know unless you follow shortly. Trail it at once. The longer you wait the fainter the trail sign will be." Wisconsin's George Mattis: "There are many pro and con arguments as to the feasibility of taking up the tracks immediately. From my experience and that of veteran hunters I have consulted, it is entirely practical to follow your quarry immediately, at least for a short distance. An animal is temporarily stunned by the impact of a bullet even

though the injury is not severe. If the hunter is quick enough to take advantage of this condition in the wounded animal, he might save himself a long chase."

During the 1970s, bow hunters and gun hunters argued about the waiting period. Bow hunters such as Fred Bear, M. R. James, Chuck Adams, and Russell Tinsley all clung tenaciously to the popular notion of waiting. But more and more gun hunters rejected the idea.

Ken Heuser, for example, a long-time deer hunter and author of *The Whitetail Deer Guide,* called the idea "pure bunk!" "My advice is to pursue and push immediately! Don't wait around for a deer to lie down and stiffen up. Pure bunk!

"Take advantage of all the shock your bullet has caused. When a deer recovers from his initial shock he may give you a long run. A lot has been said about a wounded deer lying down and bleeding to death. A deer is a tallowy animal whose body has a strong inclination to plug any leaks it may develop if given the time. A bullet does not cut flesh, it crushes and mutilates it. By smashing tissue it gives the blood vessels a chance to close off; the blood coagulates and tissue repair starts immediately. Tallow tends to close the entrance and exit holes of the bullet if the deer is quiet. You know very well that if you were wounded, the first instructions would be to lie down and become immobilized. Why? So there won't be an extra load on the heart causing it to beat harder and faster. The more action of the body, the more it bleeds. I have never heard of a medic saying, 'Walk out, soldier, the exercise will make you feel better!' The first-aid book says, 'Stop the bleeding, then treat for shock.'

"Allowing a deer to rest enables it to

recover at least somewhat from the initial shock and have a greater determination to get away from its pursuer. A rest may help the body to recover its blood pressure and the animal will regain its strength greatly. Even a gut-shot deer will become very sick right after the shot, but the sickness disappears with rest, and even though death is inevitable, the deer will travel a long way. It is a lot easier to approach a sick deer than one that is only concerned with eluding a pursuer. If there is no snow, the deer that stops bleeding is almost impossible to find. It's hard enough to follow a wounded animal, even if it continues to bleed. If you can, keep 'em bleeding! A deer has tremendous vitality and tenacity for life, but a body that keeps losing blood gets weaker every step. Ask any doctor."

Norman Strung, a veteran hunter and guide from Montana, labeled the waiting game, "a foolish decision," because he lost animals by doing so. "In the span of half an hour, blood will dry, become brown and be much harder to see. Other signs—tracks, disturbed leaves and grass—will be less obvious, too. A half-hour also gives the animal more time to cover ground and a chance both to get over the initial shock and doctor up its wounds, though it could easily die later. So rather than waiting, I always get right on the trail, slowly and methodically investigating every possibility."

On the other hand, Charley Dickey, that delightful outdoorsman from Florida, preferred to wait thirty minutes. "I'd rather let him bed with the *hope* that he'll weaken and stiffen." Hope? Indeed, the theory of waiting seems to be based on "hope." Ralph Norris, a guide from Maine and author of *The Science of Hunting the Whitetail Deer,* thinks so: "Your best hope is that he will lie down for fifteen or twenty minutes and weaken enough to stay down for good." "Hope" strikes me as a bit too metaphysical.

Robert Donovan, a deer hunter from Virginia and author of *Hunting Whitetail Deer,* also disagrees with the idea of waiting in hope that . . . . "Some hunters recommend waiting up to thirty minutes for the deer to bleed and stiffen up before getting on his trail. I don't. At least go check immediately the area where the animal was hit and the first few hundred yards of the trail. The shot will sometimes stun or temporarily disable the deer, thus providing the hunter with the opportunity for a quick, finishing shot. If this opportunity is by-passed, the alternative may be a long and arduous trailing job after the deer has recovered his senses and taken flight."

Wildlife photographer, Leonard Lee Rue III, also disagrees: "I always put quotation marks around the phrase 'stiffening up' because on the basis of my own experience as well as research I am not sure the term is accurate. A wounded deer does not really seem very stiff before death." Indeed, rigor mortis does not occur until after death.

According to John Weiss, a deer hunter from southeastern Ohio, immediate pursuit makes good sense: "The idea of promptly taking after a deer, rather than waiting on stand, and pressuring him into staying on the move, makes good sense. If the animal is never permitted to lie down but is forced to remain on his feet and always one jump ahead of an eager hunter, his heart will continue to frantically beat. A rapidly pumping heart maintains a high level of blood pressure, and consequently the wound never has a chance to close or become obstructed or plugged with a mixture of tallow and clotted blood. Further, the deer is never given the opportunity to rest and regain lost strength. If the weakened animal does fall, he probably won't be able to get up again. But even if he is able to stay on his feet he'll gradually slow to a stumbling walk, allowing the hunter to catch up and place a finishing round." Yes, a running deer has three times the heart rate per minute of a deer in the bedded position.

While the number of deer suffering from chronic gunshot or arrow wounds remains a matter of subjective speculation, it appears that traumatic injuries due to gunshot wounds are usually fatal and result in little chronic debilitation in the few deer that do survive them. In 1976, deer biologists at the University of Georgia collected 1002 white-tailed deer from the southeastern states for scientific purposes. Necropsy records of these deer indicated that seventy-six of them (7.6 percent) showed evidence of previous traumatic injury.

"Of these, 62 had a single injury, 11 were injured in two separate body regions, and 3 had injuries in three locations. Seventeen instances were recorded for superficial wounds involving skin and/or subcutis. Deep soft tissue injuries were found in 23 instances and skeletal injuries were most numerous with 53 observations. In-

juries were located most frequently in the legs and chest as compared to the abdomen, head, and neck. Five deer had lost a forelimb distal to the metacarpus. Shrapnel was recovered from 20 animals and was categorized as follows: buckshot (11), 22 caliber rimfire bullet (3), bullet fragments (2), birdshot (2), and arrowhead (2). In addition, three gunshot wounds without shrapnel and three wounds caused by arrowheads were observed."

The salient finding of this study demonstrates that only a small percentage of the deer examined (7.6 percent) showed evidence of previous injury. As Victor Nettles, a professor of Veterinary Medicine and principal researcher of the study, reports, "The few deer which survive hunter-inflicted injury do not become debilitated, as evidenced by the fact that deer in poor physical condition comprised only 6.6 percent of all injured animals. Thus long-term suffering resultant to traumatic injury probably affects very few white-tailed deer."

It seems ironic that as I write these very lines a white-tailed fawn approaches my corn feeder in front of my study window on this snowy April morning—the apparent victim of the previous gun hunting season. Traveling on three legs, this cripple circles the corn feeder hesitatingly for

Types of traumatic injuries and body regions affected in 76 injured white-tailed deer.

Region Injured	Type Of Injury			
	Superficial	Deep Soft Tissue	Skeletal	All Types
Head	0	2	5	7
Neck	2	1	0	3
Chest	4	7	13	24
Abdomen	1	9	0	10
Foreleg	5	2	17	24
Hindleg	5	2	15	22
Leg (Unspecified)	0	0	3	3

Victor Nettles, *et al*. "Observations on Injuries in White-tailed Deer," *Proceedings of the 30th Annual Conference Southeastern Association of Fish and Wildlife Agencies*, 1976.

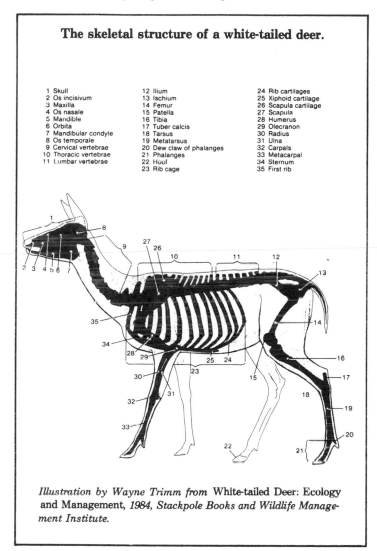

The skeletal structure of a white-tailed deer.

1 Skull
2 Os incisivum
3 Maxilla
4 Os nasale
5 Mandible
6 Orbita
7 Mandibular condyle
8 Os temporale
9 Cervical vertebrae
10 Thoracic vertebrae
11 Lumbar vertebrae

12 Ilium
13 Ischium
14 Femur
15 Patella
16 Tibia
17 Tuber calcis
18 Tarsus
19 Metatarsus
20 Dew claw of phalanges
21 Phalanges
22 Hoof
23 Rib cage

24 Rib cartilages
25 Xiphoid cartilage
26 Scapula cartilage
27 Scapula
28 Humerus
29 Olecranon
30 Radius
31 Ulna
32 Carpals
33 Metacarpal
34 Sternum
35 First rib

Illustration by Wayne Trimm from White-tailed Deer: Ecology and Management, *1984, Stackpole Books and Wildlife Management Institute.*

several minutes. This foreigner we have never seen before. The deer lacks the metatarsus of the right hind leg, yet the joint directly above it, formed by the tibia, tuber calcis, and the tarsus continues to flex when the deer takes off, but to no avail. The animal's physical condition indicates no observable signs of malnutri-tion. As the deer bounds away with only one hind leg, one wonders how the wound ever healed without medical treatment. Another example of Mother Nature working as a modern orthopedist?

The deer that I have personally lost while deer hunting during the past twenty-six years, I lost in many instances because I, too, followed the old theory of yesteryear. The scientific evidence, however, suggests to me that I pursue immediately but very quietly. My deer hunting journals indicate that wounded deer seldom lie down after running only a short distance. Those few that do may well begin to recover rather than "stiffen up," thereby stopping external bleeding and making tracking even more difficult. Why wait? The reasons generally given for waiting are based on "hope," if on anything; they are subject to so many disclaimers and qualifications that the very notion of waiting makes little or no sense. Does waiting provide a better opportunity for recovering wounded deer? I think not. If any scientific evidence exists to justify waiting, it escapes my attention.

In 1986, my colleague Al Hofacker, managing editor of *Deer & Deer Hunting* magazine, conducted a "Wounded Deer Survey" of the magazine's readership. Readers responded well to his survey and submitted a total of 1685 completed questionnaires, giving Hofacker a total of 2103 wounded deer. Did waiting affect the likelihood of recovering wounded deer?

"All evidence from the survey," Hofacker reports, "indicates that the length of the waiting period noticeably influences recovery rates of bow-shot deer, but in the opposite way the proponents of waiting have claimed for so many years."

Hofacker found that bow hunters recovered a noticeably higher percentage of the deer they wounded when they began trailing the deer either immediately or shortly after wounding a deer. The longer they waited, the higher the wounding rate, i.e., the higher the number of unrecovered

The myth of the waiting game.

Reasons for Waiting	Reasons for Not Waiting
1. Deer will lie down and "stiffen up."	1. It's snowing.
2. Hunter needs pipeful of tobacco.	2. It's raining.
3. Deer will get the "blind staggers."	3. You're in an area of high hunter density.
	4. Darkness is approaching and you can't hunt in the morning.
	5. Tracking takes place on dry vegetation.
	6. Deer bleeding freely in warm weather.
	7. Trailing wounded deer with dogs permitted in the area you hunt.
	8. Rigor mortis does not occur until three to six hours after death.
	9. A running deer has three times the heart rate of a bedded deer.
	10. Movement creates greater and more rapid blood loss, thus inhibiting coagulation.

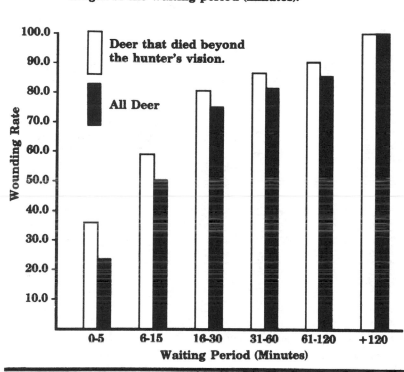

Wounding rates of bow-shot deer versus the length of the waiting period (minutes).

Reprinted from Al Hofacker, 1986. "On the Trail of Wounded Deer: The Philosophy of Waiting." *Deer & Deer Hunting* 10(2):80.

deer expressed as a percentage of the number of recovered deer.

Yes, myths die hard. Like so many other myths in history, the myth of the waiting game persists, based on a nebulous phrase in everyday language; in this case, the myth invents itself on the cherished phrase "stiffening up." Deer hunters, past and present, cling to this holy phrase with the hope of explaining the unknown. This hunting myth lies beyond reason and ripens as it spreads.

Chapter 21

Deer Hunting in the Uplands

In the winter, after the first snow, we frequently saw three or four Indians hunting deer in company, running like hounds on the fresh, exciting tracks. The escape of the deer from these noiseless, tireless hunters was said to be well-nigh impossible; they were followed to the death.
— John Muir, 1912

Iowa county lies within the Driftless Area of southwestern Wisconsin and is generally known as "The Uplands." Its rolling hills and lush, fertile valleys make it particularly beautiful when the oak leaves turn to the color of wine in October. When the autumn colors of the mixed hardwoods intermingle with majestic rock formations, The Uplands serve as a refuge for the hunter's spirit as well as a refuge for his quarry—the white-tailed deer; I cannot conceive of these beautiful bluffs, steep slopes, hidden valleys, and saturated meadows without deer.

This region not only presents one of the most picturesque arrays of landscapes in the state, but produces more deer than any other county in the Badger State. You do not need to climb the observation towers on Blue Mounds or stand on the Mississippi River bluffs at Wyalusing State Park to see the splendid views of valley bottoms, steep, forested bluffs, and cropped fields dotted with dramatic numbers of white-tailed deer; this picturesque landscape with its dynamic population of whitetails seems to be almost everywhere. You see it as you travel through the Wyoming Valley to view Taliesin, the magnificent home of world-famous architect, Frank Lloyd Wright; you experience it as you travel through the wooded hillsides of oak, birch, aspen, and black cherry to New Glarus for the annual performance of Schiller's drama of Swiss patriotism, *Wilhelm Tell.* The intimacy of these secluded valleys filled with fox-colored deer eating alfalfa during the summer rivets itself into the mind of the hunter and heightens anticipation.

Yet, this beautiful landscape was once devoid of white-tailed deer. According to Aldo Leopold's "Game Survey of Wisconsin" dated October 1, 1929, man originally exterminated them as early as 1870. The story of that extermination and how the deer herd eventually irrupted approximately 100 years later to the point where, in 1984, man again instituted a "deer shoot" to annihilate the beast, represents a classic case history of a deer explosion. That story underscores the difficulties of managing a public resource on private property and provides us with a great deal of information on crop damage and deer habits and movements on agricultural lands. Ultimately, it hints at the possible ramifications of overharvesting our yearling buck population and the possible benefits of land leasing and fee hunting. In many ways, it reveals a tangled set of responses to a contemporary predicament in an increasingly urbanized setting; it becomes a social comedy of tragic proportions including everything from legalized group bagging, road hunting, trespassing, and arguing with landowners to the appearance of gut piles on state highways. It involves a general public with emotional biases dealing with decisions of deer biology and matters of public policy of which it knows little or nothing.

Little or nothing is known of the deer herd in southern Wisconsin prior to 1823. In the summer of that year, William Hypolitus Keating (1799–1840), a geologist from the University of Pennsylvania, noted in his narrative of an expedition to the source of St. Peter's River that while traveling through southwestern Wisconsin his party only observed one deer. He attributed the absence of them to the killing of deer during all seasons of the year by the Indians due to their feeling that they were gradually losing the use of the land. After the Black Hawk War in 1832, a well-established belief took hold in the minds of many observers that a pronounced increase in the deer population took place as most of the Indians moved to reservations west of the Mississippi or to northern Wisconsin. One reporter described the situation as follows in an article in the *Prairie du Chien Patriot* dated December 6, 1848: "Since the Indians have left this part of the country, wild game has become plentiful. As their principal subsistence has been derived from hunting, notwithstanding the strong efforts made to permanently introduce agriculture among them, they have made game of all kinds very scarce in the neighborhood of the settlements, where they delighted to camp. Deer are now found in this vicinity in large numbers." McLeod in his *History of Wiskonsan* (1846) also believed that whitetails increased threefold with the withdrawal of the Indians.

Indeed, in spite of the Indians and mining developments, deer remained abundant in southwestern Wisconsin during the 1830s. Charles Fenno Hoffman (1806–1884), an author of some of the earliest articles ever penned on deer hunting, recalls seeing large herds of whitetails on the prairies in February of 1834. While exploring the mining country in the summer of 1837, William Rudolph Smith of Mineral Point writes in his *Observations on the Wisconsin Territory* (1838) that "deer are often seen sporting over the prairie, and in the groves and oak openings; they are frequently aroused out of the high grass, and as the rifle of the hunter has not yet sufficiently alarmed them in their secret lairs, they are in a measure less wild than in parts more densely settled; I have often seen them in my rambles, quietly gazing at the traveller, until he had passed by."

Deer continued to remain abundant

A few of the "Old Boys," mean and lean, who preceded the author by a few years. *Photo credit Wisconsin Historical Society*

during the 1840s. Mrs. Daniel Ruggles, who came to Ridgeway in 1841, summarizes the deer and deer hunting situation in The Uplands in the standard 1881 *History of Iowa County:* "The first years that we lived in (The Uplands), deer were very plentiful, and hunters from Mineral Point, Madison and Janesville used to come out here and stay weeks at a time. They generally came to have a big time; telling yarns and playing seven-up were the amusements of the evenings. At one time, there were seventeen dressed deer hanging in the trees near the house, the victims of those fun-loving Nimrods." Interestingly enough, she characterized deer hunting as early as 1841 as a form of recreation.

In a similar way, a young Swiss gentleman by the name of Theodore Rodolf, while exploring Iowa and Lafayette counties, noted in 1848 that "the country was full of game; prairie chickens, partridges, quails, ducks, geese, and deer were abundant. One evening while hunting . . . I counted more than fifty deer in a herd, but I could not get within shooting distance. Later in the season, when our cabbages in the garden were nearly full grown, they were almost all eaten up one night by a lot of deer which had jumped the fence, within a hundred feet of our dwelling, and regaled themselves at our expense. This was repeated several times." This statement might well represent the first official complaint of crop damage directed against the whitetail. Rodolf went on to point out that he could get mess pork at $40 a barrel and $4 for the hauling, but that venison was more palatable, and that venison could be gotten for the fun of hunting.

But John Muir, that wild man of the mountains and one of this country's greatest literary naturalists, viewed things differently. While admitting that deer were quite abundant in the Fountain Lake area near Portage, he suggested in his classic autobiography, *The Story of my Boyhood and Youth* (1913), that only the less industrious settlers of the south ever went deer hunting in the late 1840s. "Most of our neighbors brought some sort of gun from the old country, but seldom took time to hunt, even after the first hard work of fencing and clearing was over, except to shoot a duck or prairie chicken now and then that happened to come in their way. It was only the less industrious American settlers who left their work to go far a-hunting. Two or three of our neighbors went off every fall with their teams to the pine regions and cranberry marshes in the northern part of the State to hunt and gather berries. I well remember seeing their wagons loaded with game when they returned from a successful hunt. Their loads consisted usually of half a dozen deer or more, one or two black bears, and fifteen or twenty bushels of cranberries; all solidly frozen. Part of both the berries and meat was usually sold; the balance furnished their families with abundance of venison, bear grease, and pies."

Although Muir perceived deer hunting as an activity of subsistence rather than recreation, his account of how the Indians hunted deer hints at hunting for fun. "In winter, after the first snow, we frequently saw three or four Indians hunting deer in company, running like hounds on the fresh, exciting tracks. The escape of the deer from these noiseless, tireless hunters was said to be well-nigh impossible; they were followed to the death."

With the development of mining and pioneer farming, more and more deer were followed to their death. According to an article in the *Mineral Point Tribune* dated December 9, 1852, we read that a certain deerslayer by the name of Charles Desilva, of Dodgeville, killed twenty-three deer in six days. In another article in that paper dated January 10, 1885, we learn that two deer hunters on a three-day hunt during the winter of 1854–55 killed eleven deer within a few miles of Mineral Point.

While plentiful at first, the supply of white-tailed deer radically decreased especially during the severe winter of 1858. According to Paul Hunt, an early observer of this period, the snow of that winter "accumulated to such depths as to prevent the deer from finding food or moving about. As a result, many deer froze or starved to death, if they were not clubbed to death by the pioneers." One reporter bleakly noted in the *Black Earth Advertiser*, dated December 14, 1871, that four deer were still seen heading toward Avoca. These four deer might very well have been the last four that old-time deerslayers in The Uplands ever had the opportunity to blaze away at with their muzzleloading smoke pipes, for market hunting was taking its toll.

By the 1870s, the Indians, the miners, and the early pioneer farmers had virtually exterminated the white-tailed deer from the oak forests of southwestern Wisconsin. As a result, deer hunters such as David Cartwright were forced to travel north into the Chippewa Valley of northwestern Wisconsin in order to satisfy their desire to pursue whitetails in wild country. One century later the deer herd of the south exploded to a magnitude that would have surely satisfied this renowned deer-slayer's voracious appetite for hunting.

Cartwright, contrary to Muir's impressions of pioneer farmers, industriously cultivated his farm but spent every free moment pursuing whitetails for sport as well as the pot. Searching for a more virgin field for his hunting exploits, he came to southern Wisconsin in June of 1842 with $3 in his pocket. He immediately bought eighty acres of land in a heavily timbered section, known as Bark Woods. With the profits of the following winter's deer hunting and trapping, he paid for his land and soon added to his domain until it included 240 acres. This wild man of the woods hunted, fished, trapped, and guided and soon became known as the finest "professional deer-catcher" of his time. With the publication of his popular guide entitled *Natural History of Western Wild Animals* (1875), a book filled with practical knowledge far superior to the hypothetical and visionary trash of his day and ours, he instructed many a greenhorn hunter in the habits of the white-tailed deer and in the science and art of deer hunting.

Each winter Cartwright averaged about seventy-five deer. On one hunt, he recalls, "I caught thirteen deer in three days. I have quite a number of times caught five in a single day. Once I got six in one day, and that day at my first shot I killed two large bucks, and at my fourth shot I killed two fawns. Of the last fifteen tracks which I saw in that locality I killed fourteen deer. My farm work kept me busy during most of the year. But for five or six weeks during the fall and winter I deer hunted, and I would make 200 or 250 dollars in that time. By 1855 . . . the deer were very scarce."

Dressed in leather hunting shirts and trousers, wearing buckskin moccasins, these deerslayers pursued their quarry with their heavy rifle resting on one of their brawny shoulders; on the other hung a ball pouch riding next to the horn of an ancient buffalo filled with a pound of the best gunpowder the hunter could muster. With a butcher knife in scabbard and a tomahawk thrust through his girdle he still-hunted deer through the oak forests and prairie openings, occasionally glancing at the flint of his gun, its priming, and the leather cover of the lock. With excited pleasure some chased deer with hounds. In the summer months others fire hunted them with boat, gun, and lamp. Many used steel traps, while others preferred shooting deer by moonlight on platforms overlooking salt licks. Others cut birch saplings and stripped them of their branches except for two, which they twisted together forming a large noose at the end of a pole. With this primitive weapon in the stern of their lean skiff they "withed" deer while floating along the Wisconsin River: traveling through the rippling waters like an arrow, they approached their swimming quarry, placed the noose around the deer's neck and pulled them toward the skiff, putting an end to the encounter with a slash from their hunting knife. To facilitate "withing" deer, they fired the prairies and oak openings, forcing the deer into the rivers, lakes, and streams. Still others, ran deer to their death on horseback.

In 1881, Dr. Philo Hoy, a young medical doctor, described the deteriorating situation with regard to the vanishing southern deer herd: "Fifty years ago, this area was nearly in a state of nature, all the large animals were then abundant. Now, all has changed. The ax and plow, gun and dog, railway and telegraph have metamorphosed the face of nature. Most of the deer have been either exterminated, or have hid themselves away in the wilderness. In a short time, all of these will have disappeared from the state. There was a time when the deer, the antelope, the woodland caribou, the buffalo, and the wild turkey were abundant, but are now no longer to be found. All deer will soon be driven by civilization out of Wisconsin. The railroad and improved firearms will do the work, and thus we lose the primitive denizens of the forest and prairies." The very language used here—"will be driven out by civilization," "firearms will do the work"—reminds me of the 1984 Uplands Deer Shoot, but more on that later.

By the 1890s, then, the deer population in The Uplands was virtually wiped out. In his *History of Wisconsin Deer* (1946), Ernie Swift, the director of the Conservation Department during the late 1940s, compared the disappearing deer herd with a fading April snow bank. "As soon as the black prairie sod had been turned under and the mighty hardwoods burned away, the state's last big game animal was declared a public enemy for jumping stake-and-rider fences to nip off carrots and tender young wheat. Under the constant pressure of pioneer farming, the deer herds of southern Wisconsin faded away like an April snowbank."

Indeed, the deer seemed to vanish from The Uplands like the infamous Ghost of Ridgeway after one of his nocturnal raids on McKillip's Saloon—an infamous place in its own right on Old Military Road for deerslayers with a rather soiled and dented reputation. By 1890, the very sight of white-tailed deer remained a neighborhood newsmaker; reporters gathered to study the track. For thirty-six years, the deer season in Iowa County was closed. From 1907 to 1942, the guns remained silent in The Uplands during the somber days of November.

But today, almost 100 years later, the white-tailed deer is again a neighborhood newsmaker in The Uplands. In 1984, gun hunters killed 12,308 deer in Management Unit 70A. Bow hunters killed 931 deer and the automobile eliminated 534 deer for a grand total of 13,773 deer—making The Uplands the leading deer-producing area in the state. One might suspect that the deer were once again driven from civilization. Hardly! In February of 1985, Professor Lloyd Keith of the Department of Wildlife Ecology at the University of Wisconsin conducted a very extensive helicopter survey of Unit 70A. His $12,000 survey indicated that 8417 deer (26.8 deer/mi²) still roamed The Uplands. The observers in the helicopter noted high densities of deer concentrated in the track that a tornado took in the spring of 1984. Using the sex-age-kill method, the cornerstone of white-tailed deer management in Wisconsin, DNR officials originally estimated the preharvest 1984 population in Unit 70A at sixty-one deer per square mile of deer range. In evaluating this method in general and these figures in particular with his helicopter survey, Professor Keith concluded that it "underestimated preharvest densities by about twelve percent and post-harvest densities by about thirty-two percent. The latter may be of some consequence to managers considering population status relative to unit goals."

It seems incredible that in 1964 hunters killed 300 deer in this small area of deer range, and in 1984 they killed more than 13,000 of them. How do we explain this

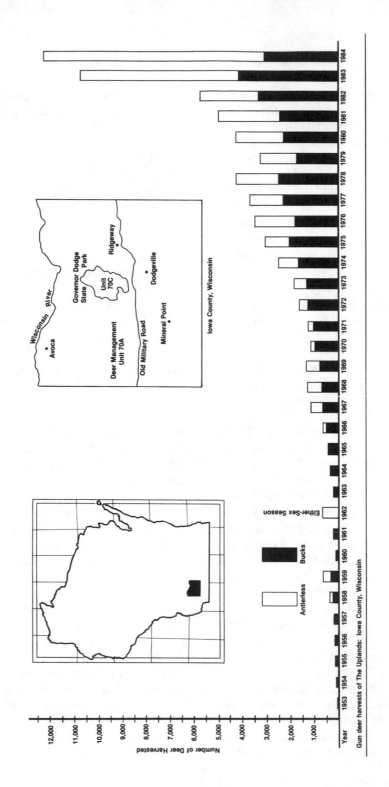

Gun deer harvests of The Uplands: Iowa County, Wisconsin

Iowa County, Wisconsin

Wisconsin River
Avoca
Governor Dodge State Park
Deer Management Unit 70A
Unit 70C
Old Military Road
Ridgeway
Dodgeville
Mineral Point

Number of Deer Harvested

12,000
11,000
10,000
9,000
8,000
7,000
6,000
5,000
4,000
3,000
2,000
1,000

Year

1953 1954 1955 1956 1957 1958 1959 1960 1961 1962 1963 1964 1965 1966 1967 1968 1969 1970 1971 1972 1973 1974 1975 1976 1977 1978 1979 1980 1981 1982 1983 1984

Antlerless   Bucks   Either-Sex Season

dramatic and remarkable comeback? No! The DNR did not truck them down from the north, as many local residents believed. As a matter of fact, many game managers during the 1960s were confronted with this type of dialogue:

"Say, you fellas musta dumped another load of deer out east of town this week. Took the wife out for a ride about sundown last night, deer all over. Counted sixteen in one bunch alone!

"Whatya mean, ya don't haul 'em down from up north? Them deer gotta come from somewhere.

"Why, I kin remember, 'bout thirty years back, if a man saw a deer down here, he bragged it up all winter. Always went north for deer season, weren't none 'round here. Now we got so many they're gettin' to be a nuisance.

"Cost my boy 200 dollars to fix up his car after he hit that buck last summer. Read in the paper where better'n 300 deer got hit by cars in this county last year.

"Now, if you guys ain't truckin' them deer in, where in 'ell they comin' from?"

In order to understand this dramatic comeback of the deer herd, we must consider several factors. First of all, during the 1930s the public gradually accepted hunting regulations and an increasingly effective warden force that led to a dramatic decline in the illegal kill. Secondly, during the 1940s the demand for marsh hay and pasture declined and many marshes and riverbottoms gradually grew back into hardwoods and brush.

Thirdly, and perhaps most important, a dynamic process of environmental change began to take place during the 1960s as a result of the Conservation Reserve Program of the Soil Bank, which President Eisenhower initiated in 1956. This program paid farmers and absentee land-

owners money not to plant agricultural crops on millions of acres across the country and encouraged the planting of millions of trees, shrubs, grasses, and legumes for erosion control and improved wildlife habitat.

Fourthly, as marginal farms failed, cattle no longer grazed the woodlots; as farm machinery got larger, farmers gradually stopped planting crops on hills and hillsides, thus creating ideal edge habitat for deer. As a result of these changes, the southern forest and the woody vegetation of non-agricultural lands grew rapidly, producing excellent food and cover for an ever-growing deer herd. In addition to this favorable alteration of the environment, the ensuing mild winters plus abundant food supplies allowed adult does to drop twin fawns each year, and even created a situation where more than thirty-eight percent of the doe fawns (at least in Governor Dodge State Park) breed in their first year.

Fifthly, in 1963 the Variable Quota Law went into effect, which promotes harvest in accordance with deer abundance and ensures against an overharvest of deer.

Sixthly, many absentee landowners began purchasing small blocks of land in The Uplands, which they posted. Everett Olsen, the long-time County Agent, recalls: "During the 1960s, people outside the area began to purchase the hill country for second homes or just land to own. Wyoming township experienced the greatest change, both in increased valuation and in loss of operating farms. Since then all of the townships north of Old Military Road have experienced an increase in absentee ownership. Some people have built buildings and most rent out farmland to neighboring farmers. Much concern has been expressed that these new owners have

Changes in Upland Habitat

These aerial photos illustrate the dramatic change in habitat that occurred in The Uplands between 1962 and 1976 as a result of the Conservation Reserve Program of the Soil Bank. They picture the area around Deershelter Rock, a majestic piece of stone extending sixty feet into the air and overlooking the beauty of Wisconsin's unglaciated southwest region. On top of this rock stands Alex Jordan's famous House on the Rock. If you study the fields in the center of the photos, you will see how the terrain changed almost beyond recognition.

contributed to an unreal value of farmland. It is priced above its true agricultural worth." This posted private property soon provided the whitetails with effective refuges.

And finally, the recent enactment of a $2000 fine for deer poaching adds further to the annual increases of deer.

As a result of these changes, the public encountered large numbers of deer and many controversial issues to deal with and discuss. Take deer-car collisions, for example, the worst imaginable way for deer and people to interact. In 1984, motorists killed 40,000 deer in the State of Wisconsin. Between July 1, 1983 and June 30, 1984, motorists killed 534 deer in Iowa County alone. The average claim runs from $407 to $503. The total cost in the state during a three-year period ran as high as $22.1 million. How much will people tolerate in terms of human injury and mortality, repair bills, and wasted venison lying along state highways?

How much crop damage will farmers tolerate in the fields of the wide valley of the Wisconsin River and in the fields beneath the steep, heavily wooded hillsides? In 1981, DNR researchers estimated that one deer in this area consumes one bushel of standing corn per year and ninety-two pounds of alfalfa per year—resulting in the average farm losing five to fifteen bushels of corn and 0.2 to 0.7 tons of alfalfa annually. According to a 1984 survey conducted by the Wisconsin Department of Agriculture and the University of Wisconsin's Department of Wildlife Ecology, deer damage between October 1983 and September 1984 amounted to $36.7 million. Corn and hay farmers sustained seventy-six percent of the figure. Yet, seven percent of the farmers in southwestern

Wisconsin indicated that we should increase the deer population; forty-two percent said that we should maintain the current population, and fifty-one percent (a slim majority), suggested that we decrease the population.

In 1984, the Department of Natural Resources decided to decrease the population by issuing 9172 antlerless permits resulting in a "deer shoot out," resembling a Ringling Brothers-Barnum & Bailey Circus: a form of pest control in which man seemingly attempted to annihilate the beast. We surely cannot dignify it with the word "hunt"; there was a great deal of *shooting* but not much *hunting!* Issuing antlerless permits via the radio for posted areas in which hunters have no place to hunt borders on the ridiculous; encouraging them to race to check stations after successfully shooting an antlerless deer for a bonus tag led to road hunting, indiscriminate shooting at running animals, trespassing, arguing with landowners, and the appearance of gut piles lying along state highways. The newly enacted, legalized group bagging resulted in gangs of hunters traveling the roads telling landowners, "We gotta get the job done!"

We encounter these kinds of problems when man tries to manage a public resource on private property. The comic and tragic atmosphere of such hunts denigrates the value the individual hunter places (or should place) on the natural resource itself.

To solve some of these problems, more and more farmers in The Uplands now entertain the idea of selling harvest rights of surplus deer on their property to offset crop damage. Justin Isherwood, a south-central farmer-literatus, clearly articulates this point of view:

"The Wisconsin deer hunt in its present

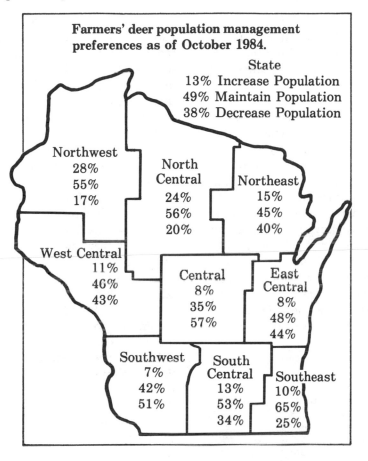

Farmers' deer population management preferences as of October 1984.

State
13% Increase Population
49% Maintain Population
38% Decrease Population

Northwest
28%
55%
17%

North Central
24%
56%
20%

Northeast
15%
45%
40%

West Central
11%
46%
43%

Central
8%
35%
57%

East Central
8%
48%
44%

Southwest
7%
42%
51%

South Central
13%
53%
34%

Southeast
10%
65%
25%

form is no longer the single satisfactory answer to the status of the whitetail in this state. I believe the DNR needs to recognize, in a sense of environmental bargain, that the deer herd is a product of the farm sector and current crop and management practices; that unless the farmer is willing to share his crops with this native herbivore the dispute will continue to grow. Beyond acceptance of these new attitudes lies the chance for farmers to benefit from a new economy. What I'm advocating is that farmers be allowed to sell harvest rights of surplus deer on their property. Indeed, promote white-tailed deer as a legitimate product of the Wisconsin farm."

While attempting to improve the nature of the hunt on farmlands, more and more deer hunters form clubs and lease land for hunting purposes. Although one fears the possible abuses of both deer and deer hunting under lease contracts and an agribusiness system, few alternatives currently present themselves for areas of private land with high densities of deer located near urbanized centers. In January of 1985, the Cooperative Extension Service of West Virginia University (817 Knapp Hall, Morgantown, WV 26506) issued an excellent legal guide for all landowners and hunters interested in setting up a lease for hunting purposes entitled *Real Property: Leasing Land for Hunting and Other Recreational Uses* (Publication #726).

The recovery of the whitetail in The Uplands from the brink of extinction to high densities of more than sixty deer per square mile in some areas remains one of the bright spots in our stewardship of this great animal. Another bright spot in The Uplands deer story revolves around the extensive research findings of deer biologists and managers between 1975 and 1985. During this period of time, six Master's Theses, one Ph.D. Dissertation (in progress), three DNR Technical Reports, and various articles in the scientific journals appeared on many facets of the southern

With topographic map, aerial photograph, and county soil survey in hand, Dr. Rob Wegner moved to The Uplands to live with the white-tailed deer; although once driven to the brink of extinction a century ago, they now circle his in-woods observation post at all times of the day. *Photo credit Maren Lea Wegner.*

deer herd — including food habits, habitat use, seasonal movements and home ranges, mortality and crippling losses, deer repellents and deer damage to corn and alfalfa, and so on. Their findings tell us that only five percent of the yearling bucks in the food-rich agricultural areas have spikes and that eighty-five to ninety-three percent of all bucks shot in The Uplands are yearlings. While admitting that the long-term effect on the herd's genetic fitness as a result of this severe exploitation of yearlings remains unclear, their research suggests that yearlings impregnate does when they achieve estrus, despite the fact that yearling bucks display less scent-marking behavior and lack a highly ritualized courtship performance.

With topographic map, aerial photograph, and county soil survey in hand, I moved to The Uplands to live with deer; although once driven to the brink of extinction a century ago, they now circle my in-woods observation tower at all times of the day. Indeed, I've reached the conclusion that 0900 to 1300 hours represent an excellent time of the day to hunt deer, for I continually experience this time period as a peak feeding activity especially when the deer remain undisturbed.

Unlike the deer of the northern timber, whitetails in The Uplands seem more tolerant of man, since they are forced to live in closer proximity to humans. Not only do their summer and winter ranges tend to overlap, but their home ranges in general seem smaller than those of the deer in the northern forests. The average home range approximates 402 acres for does and 506 acres for bucks. Although home ranges increase at the start of the bow season and triple in size during the opening days of the gun season, most deer in The Uplands remain nonmigratory. Scattered, small woodlot areas intermixed with agricultural fields allow the observant hunter to more readily pattern deer by locating natural bottlenecks—small places where habitat, terrain, and runways become constricted.

One of the most interesting research proposals currently being discussed with regard to whitetails in The Uplands revolves around the movements of deer on small blocks of private land in response to varying hunter densities within their home range during the small game, bow and arrow, and gun deer seasons. One University of Wisconsin researcher states the problem:

"The posting of private land creates small patches of different hunter densities and deer harvest rates within individual home ranges of deer. There is little information on the movements of deer in response to this variance. It is not known to what degree deer use small areas of light hunting pressure or how long deer might maintain altered movements resulting from high hunter densities. If altered movements occur, then harvest rates of deer in that area may be reduced. If mortality is reduced, then the deer population may increase. It is not known if deer will disperse from areas of this type into areas of higher harvest. Without an understanding of deer movements and the resulting population dynamics, proper harvest strategies and management cannot be attained."

Information on deer movements and deer densities during and after deer hunting season in situations of varying hunter densities is not only necessary for the management of these areas, but remains of great interest for the deer hunter and the landowner in agricultural areas.

The whitetail's fate and the future of deer hunting in areas such as The Uplands depend upon how well we understand the intricate details of these kinds of problems and on how well we deal with the paradox of managing a public resource on private property.

PART V

WHERE TO FIND
MORE INFORMATION

Chapter 22

Deer and Deer Hunting: An Annotated Bibliography Continued, 1838–1986

The whitetail deer, especially the trophy-grade male, is now firmly established as a cult object . . . The result has been a spate of books on deer hunting, during the last ten years or so, which has to be seen to be believed.
— John Wootters, 1983

A Note About the Bibliography

This bibliography represents a continuation of "The Deer Hunter's Four Hundred," a comprehensive, annotated list of more than 400 books published in the English language on the subject of deer and deer hunting found in *Deer & Deer Hunting,* Book 1 (Stackpole Books, 1984). I again annotate this list of 185 book titles with the hope that readers will seek out memorable titles that appeal to their interests. An asterisk (*) indicates that the book is out of print. It will either have to be located in a used-book store or you will need to have an out-of-print-book special-ist search for it. You will find a list of reputable book specialists in the field of outdoor literature in Chapter 24. Most of the books without an asterisk should be available through special order from your local bookstore. Privately printed titles may be difficult to locate, however, and could be another job for the out-of-print-book specialist. For an ongoing comprehensive review of books and information pertaining to white-tailed deer and deer hunting, read *Deer & Deer Hunting* magazine, Box 1117, Department 5B, Appleton, WI 54912, telephone (414) 734–0009.

When not roaming the back forty while hunting or scouting for deer, the author spends most of his time editing, writing, reading, and researching the white-tailed deer and the American deer hunting experience. *Photo credit Maren Lea Wegner*

Adams, Chuck. *The Complete Guide to Bowhunting Deer.* Illinois: DBI Books, Inc., 1984. 256 pp.

A basic how-to manual dealing primarily with equipment.

American Rifleman. *Deer Hunting.* Washington, D.C.: The National Rifle Association, n.d. 36 pp.

Reprints of articles on deer hunting from *The American Rifleman.* Includes several good ones by Francis E. Sell, who tells us that in interviewing twenty expert woodsmen he asked each of them how close they got to deer while hunting. All of them reported getting within ten feet or less of deer. In each instance they got that close by being on deer trails and by intensively studying deer trails.*

Arkava, Mort. *The Incipient Elk Hunter.* Missoula, Montana: Mountain Press Publishing Company, 1983. 112 pp.

This book, written by a professor at the University of Wyoming, emphasizes the idea that deer hunting is not merely a means of getting meat, but a way of life. Stresses the esthetic satisfaction of the deer hunting experience. Contains an excellent chapter entitled "The Legend of Elk Man."

Audubon, John James and John Bachman. "Cervus Virginianus." In Vol. 2 of *The Quadrupeds of North America.* New York: V. G. Audubon, 1851. pp. 220–239.

While most of us will never own a copy of this three-volume magnum opus, you will sometimes find it in the rare books collection of major university libraries. Your hunting efforts in locating a copy will pay great dividends, for like many of us, Audubon and Bachman believed that "no species of wild animals inhabiting North America, deserves to be regarded with more interest than the Common or Virginian Deer; its symmetrical form, graceful curving leap or bound, and its rushing speed, when flying before its pursuers, it passes like a meteor by the startled traveller in the forest, exciting admiration though he be ever so dull an observer."*

Australian Deer Association. *Australian Antlered Game Exhibition, 1981.* Melbourne: The Australian Deer Research Foundation Limited, 1982. 132 pp.

The keeping of antlered trophies as valued possessions has a very long history and this historically important book continues that tradition. This book is primarily a pictorial and statistical record of the most spectacular display of antlered trophies ever assembled in the deer's Australian history.

Bailey, James A., et al. *Readings in Wildlife Conservation.* Washington, D.C.: The Wildlife Society, 1974. 722 pp.

An excellent anthology containing some of the classic papers written on the subject. Provides the sportsman with a broad perspective of wildlife conservation. Available in paperback from the Wildlife Society.

TENTH ANNIVERSARY
APRIL 1987
$2.95
CDC00655
CANADA $3.95

Deer & Deer Hunting

PRACTICAL & COMPREHENSIVE INFORMATION FOR WHITE-TAILED DEER HUNTERS

Special Report

NEW
DISCOVERIES
ABOUT
BUCK RUBS

SIGNIFICANCE OF
DEER LICKS

TECHNIQUES FOR
LATE WINTER
SCOUTING

THE ART AND
SCIENCE OF
STAND HUNTING

HUNTING SOUTHERN WHITETAILS

0 72246 00655 04

For a fascinating mix of whitetail facts and deer hunting methods, read *Deer & Deer Hunting* magazine.

Baker, Ron. *The American Hunting Myth.* New York: Vantage Press Inc., 1985. 287 pp.

If you want to know how deeply ingrained the anti-deer-hunting sentiment is in this country read this vanity-published production, the most provocative indictment to appear. Strong on charges and accusations but very weak on substantial evidence and documentation.

Banwell, D. Bruce. *The Banwell Books.* New Zealand: The Halcyon Press, 1985. 608 pp.

This premier volume contains three of the most sought-after books on New Zealand deer and deer hunting: *Highland Stags of Otago, Wapiti in New Zealand,* and *Red Stags of the Rakaia,* all originally published by A. W. Reed in the 1960s. In them the author traces the history and origins of three major game animal herds and the development and spread of these herds since their introduction. A unique book in the history of deer hunting. An invaluable work of reference.

————. *Great New Zealand Deer Heads.* New Zealand: Halcyon Publishing Ltd., 1986. 176 pp.

An impressive record book and reference guide written by the leading authority on New Zealand deer herds. In it he examines the top eighty-five deer trophies taken in New Zealand. Will surely become a collector's item.

Bartlett, William W. "Big Game in Eau Claire County Seventy Years Ago." In *History, Tradition and Adventure in the Chippewa Valley.* Wisconsin: The Chippewa Printery, 1929. pp. 203–224.

This volume of regional history deals with the myths and legends of such locally renowned deerslayers as Charles Martin, David W. Cartwright, and Ivory Livermore, who hunted northwestern Wisconsin during the 1850s to the 1880s.*

Bass, Rick. *The Deer Pasture.* Texas: A and M University Press, 1985. 123 pp.

Of the more than six hundred books that exist on the subject of deer and deer hunting, *The Deer Pasture* has no counterpart; it's unique, original, fresh, and witty. It em-

phasizes traditions and values. In celebrating the habits of deer, the author reveals the close relationship between man, nature, and deer in the modern age. I have never read a better book that so deeply penetrates the depths of the universal bond that links together man, deer, family, and the deer hunting tradition. You will want to read this special book every year before leaving for deer camp.

Batten, John H. "Hunting the Whitetail Deer." In *The Forest and Plain.* New Jersey: National Sporting Fraternity Limited, 1984. pp. 43–68.

Traditional deer-hunting experiences centered on the shores of Lake Owen, near Cable, Wisconsin.

Batty, Joseph H. "White-tailed Deer." In *How to Hunt and Trap.* New York: Orange Judd Company, 1882. pp. 88–97.

One of the first accounts of deer hunting to actually use the word "scrape."*

Bauer, Erwin and Peggy Bauer. *Erwin Bauer's Horned and Antlered Game.* New York: Outdoor Life Books, 1987. 256 pp.

The third volume in Erwin Bauer's series covering all North American horned and antlered game. Includes chapters on elk, moose, caribou, whitetails, mule deer, blacktails, wild sheep, mountain goats, pronghorns, bison, and musk-oxen.

Beasom, Samuel L., and Sheila F. Roberson, eds. *Game Harvest Management.* Texas: Texas A and I University, 1985. 374 pp.

These proceedings of the Game Harvest Management Symposium, held in Texas in 1983, focus on the current knowledge about harvest quotas and the response of whitetails and other game to prescribed harvests. Deals with a wide variety of philosophies and approaches. Contains an excellent article on deer management and public opinion by Daniel Decker and his colleagues. A must for those interested in deer population and harvest strategies.

Beaufort, eighth duke of and Mowbray Morris. *Hunting.* England: Ashford Press Publishing, 1985. 385 pp.

This early vintage hunting book originally published in 1894, views deer hunting as "the most princely and royal chase of all chases." Contains an excellent discussion on the history and literature of hunting and a first-rate bibliography on hunting and hunters.

Bennett, Mike. *The Venison Hunters.* New Zealand: Reed, 1979. 216 pp.

Records how you could make a good living from deer hunting in New Zealand during the 1960s. Recalls the humor and hazards of what must have been one of the world's last great outdoor adventures: the deer wars of New Zealand.

Benson, Ragnar. "Deer." In *Survival Poaching.* Colorado: Paladin Press, 1980. pp. 145–169.

The memoirs of a self-confessed deer poacher. You've got to read this incredible farce to believe it. An indictment against "the greedy landowner for continuing his rampant posting" and a statement not only on how to poach, but why you should poach deer: so that lack of harvesting doesn't degrade their breeding quality!?! Views deer poaching as the only alternative open to the outstanding outdoorsman without considerable wealth. Would you believe that Benson is threatening to publish a second volume on the subject?

Bogardus, Adam H. "Wild Turkey and Deer Shooting." In *Field, Cover and Trap Shooting.* New York: Orange Judd Company, 1879. pp. 239–250.

Early deer shooting in Illinois with one of the champion wing shots of the world.*

Bond, Jim. *The Mule Deer: In Search of Big Heads.* Portland, Oregon: Privately printed, 1950. 125 pp.

A very unusual book on mule deer hunting in the western states. Combines the science of wildlife management with personal experiences. Rare and very expensive.*

Bowring, Dave. *Bowhunting for Whitetails.* Harrisburg: Stackpole Books, 1985. 304 pp.

Another standard-fare, run of the mill deer hunting manual, which proliferate like weeds and like weeds soon perish. Why we need more books of this sort remains anyone's guess.

Boyce, Mark S., and Larry D. Hayden-Wing. *North American Elk: Ecology, Behavior and Management.* The University of Wyoming, 1979. 294 pp.

This volume contains the edited proceedings of a symposium on elk ecology and management held at the University of Wyoming in April of 1978. Includes several interesting papers on movements and breeding behavior.*

Bradford, K. M. *Still Hunter's Handbook, or How to Sit, Sneak and Stalk.* California: Maynard P. Buehler, 1954. 30 pp.

A booklet of basic information written by a professional guide.*

Brander, Michael. *Deer Stalking in Britain.* England: The Sportsman's Press, 1986. 175 pp.

Brander, well known for his books on the history of sport, combines the old and the new with great imagination to produce a most interesting book on the history of deer stalking in Britain.

Bridges, Henry P. "Deer." In *The Woodmont Story.* New York: A. S. Barnes and Company, 1953. pp. 67–89.

Contains the classic anecdote on how buck fever afflicted the president of the Pittsburgh Steel Company while on a deer hunt at the Woodmont Rod and Gun Club in Hancock, Maryland. Describes how deer hunts were conducted at this elusive retreat, undoubtedly one of the finest hunting clubs in the country.*

Buchan, John. *John Macnab.* Great Britain: Hodder and Stoughton, 1941. 320 pp.

A well-known novel about deer poaching in the western Highlands of Scotland, written by an enthusiastic deer stalker but with a unique slant: three prominent public figures — a banker, a lawyer, and a cabinet minister — scheme and engage in the nefarious art of deer poaching. While the village poacher is frequently unforgiven, this rare case of poaching by gentry gets laughed off as an amiable eccentricity. Originally published in 1925.*

Burch, Monte. *Calling and Rattling Whitetail Bucks.* Outdoor World Press Inc, 1985. 32 pp.

————. *Pocket Guide to Field Dressing, Butchering and Cooking.* Outdoor World Press Inc, 1986. 80 pp.

Introductory pamphlets intended for the deer hunter's backpack.

Cadbury, Warder H. *Arthur Fitzwilliam Tait: Artist in the Adirondacks.* Associated University Presses, Inc., 1986. 344 pp.

This magnificent book dealing with one of the best-known and most prodigious nineteenth century painters of wildlife and sporting adventures contains some of the best and most romantic paintings of deer and deer hunting ever produced.

Cadieux, Charles L. *Pronghorn: North America's Unique Antelope.* Harrisburg: Stackpole Books, 1986. 254 pp.

A general introduction and practical guide.

Caractacus, ed. *The Autobiography of a Poacher.* England: John MacQueen, 1901. 255 pp.

Deer poachers, like pirates and indeed any others who live outside the pale of social convention, are interesting folk and Holcombe, the hero of this unique deer-poaching story is no exception. His deer-killing proclivities link him with the famous Robin Hood and the immortal William Shakespeare. Holcombe's deer poaching exploits culminate in him becoming a game warden, thus underscoring Kinglsey's idea that a game warden is only a poacher turned outside in and a poacher a game warden turned inside out. After playing both sides of the coin Holcombe concludes this fascinating book by proudly announcing to the reader that "if I had my time over again, I should certainly prefer poaching to gamekeeping. To see a deer at the head of a wood, to shoot him, to watch him tumble down, nobody can tell what a spree it is!" Penetrates into the mind of the deer poacher as few books do.*

Cartier, John O., ed. *20 Great Trophy Hunts.* New York: McKay, 1980. 269 pp.

This book of trophy hunts includes the personal accounts of how Jeff Brunk of Missouri, Harvey Olsen of Manitoba, and Dwight Green of Iowa shot their trophy whitetails. Green's buck still maintains the widest inside spread (30⅜ inches) ever recorded for a whitetail rack of the typical pattern.

————. *How to Get Your Deer.* New York: Outdoor Life Books, 1986. 284 pp.

A second edition of Cartier's 1976 book, entitled *The Modern Deer Hunter.* Undoubtedly given the new title to encourage sales.

Cartwright, David W. *Natural History of Western Wild Animals and Guide for Hunters, Trappers, and Sportsmen.* Ohio: Blade Printing and Paper Company, 1875. 280 pp.

The adventures of a nineteenth century Wisconsin deer hunter who became known as one of the finest "professional deer-catchers" of his time. With this popular guide, Cartwright instructed many a greenhorn hunter in the habits of the white-tailed deer and in the science and art of deer hunting. Filled with practical knowledge far superior to a great deal of the hypothetical and visionary trash of our day.*

Caughley, Graeme. *The Deer Wars: The Story of Deer in New Zealand.* New Zealand: Heinemann, 1983. 187 pp.

In a pleasing style and well-documented account, Caughley tells us what actually happened in the biggest control campaign waged against deer that the world has ever seen, a campaign that pitted government department against government department, deer hunters against the forest service, farmers against hunters, helicopters against helicopters, and private shooters against meat hunters. The author places these strange events into historic perspective, providing us with a great book on the politics of deer management.

Cochran, E. Winston. *Deer Tales and Pen Feathers.* Texas: The Taylor Company, 1975. 64 pp.

Poetry on deer and deer hunting written by a medical doctor and a wanderer of the deer forest who underscores one basic axiom of deer hunting: *"IF YOU'RE NOT GOING TO EAT IT, DON'T KILL IT!"**

Cox, Daniel J. *Whitetail Country*. Oshkosh, Wisconsin: Willow Creek Press, 1987.
Forthcoming.

Curtis, Capt. Paul A. "Deer Shooting." In *American Game Shooting*. New York: E. P. Dutton and Company, 1927. pp. 120–136.
Deer shooting during the 1920s with the one-time shooting editor of *Field & Stream,* who always emphasized the following moral: Never give up, for in deer hunting one never knows when his luck will change. Curtis frequently broke up deer camp card games by dropping a freshly killed deer right on the card table. While others played cards he gunned 'em down in the deer forest.*

Dam, Brian. *New York State Big Buck Club Record Book, 1984*. New York State Big Buck Club, 1984. 29 pp.
The third edition of New York's record typical and nontypical white-tailed bucks taken with bow and gun.

Davis, Goode P., Jr. *Man and Wildlife in Arizona: The American Exploration Period, 1824–1865*. Arizona: The Arizona Game and Fish Department, 1986. 231 pp.
In this unique blend of history and natural history the reader will find the early story of white-tailed deer and deer hunting in Arizona. Based on the accounts and words of the explorers and pioneers.

Decker, Daniel J. and Gary R. Goff, eds. *Valuing Wildlife: Economic and Social Perspectives*. Colorado: Westview Press, 1987. 424 pp.
This excellent human-dimensions reference volume includes four case studies dealing with deer and deer hunting: "Public Values and White-Tailed Deer Management in New York," "White-Tailed Deer in a Suburban Environment," "Landowners' Willingness to Tolerate White-Tailed Deer Damage in New York," and "Economic Values of White-Tailed Deer Hunting in an Eastern Wilderness Setting."

Dickey, Charley. *Opening Shots and Parting Lines*. New Jersey: Winchester Press, 1983. 208 pp.

————. *Movin' Along With Charley Dickey*. New Jersey: Winchester Press, 1985. 207 pp.
These two vintage volumes of outdoor humor and philosophy contain several marvelous tales on deer and deer hunting such as "What Is a Deer Hunter?" "Deer Mathematics," "On the Antlers of a Dilemma," and "All the Comforts of Deer Camp." Filled with generous portions of humor and nostalgia.

Dieter, William. *Hunter's Orange*. New York: Avon Books, 1983. 241 pp.
A pretentious, pulpy novel of a modern-day buffalo hunt that unconsciously becomes an antihunting novel. Literature of this kind goes a long way in destroying approval of American hunting by linking hunters with a boorish, unfeeling mentality.

Dobie, Duncan. *Georgia's Greatest Whitetails*. Georgia: Bucksnort Publishing, 1986. 440 pp.
Another state record book whose author reports that deer hunters killed over eighty percent of Georgia's record-book heads near major waterways in central, west-central, and south Georgia. Contains photos of many of the Peach State's finest record-book whitetails.

Donald, Garry. *Trophy Deer of Saskatchewan*. Saskatchewan: Privately printed, 1985. 304 pp.
As most trophy deer hunters know, Saskatchewan is number one for the most entries listed in the Boone and Crockett book. As of September 1985, 322 Boone and Crockett whitetails have been taken there over the years—thirty-one Boone and Crockett deer came from there in 1984. This volume contains pictures and information on 155 of them. It also contains a fascinating section entitled "Locked Horns."

Downes, Max. *The Forest Deer Project 1982*. Melbourne: The Australian Deer Association, 1983. 190 pp.
A report directed at Australian deer hunters and foresters, and dealing primarily with habitat management and the problems of deer and their place in forested country but of general interest to all deer hunters regardless of nationality.

Eaton, Randall L., ed. *The Human/Animal Connection*. Nevada: Sierra Nevada College Press, 1985. 90 pp.

High-power meditations and intellectualizing about the philosophy of hunting.

Eberle, Irmengarde. *Fawn in the Woods*. New York: Thomas Y. Crowell Company, 1962. 43 pp.

A story for children about a fawn.

Edwords, Clarence E. *Camp-Fires of a Naturalist*. New York: D. Appleton and Company, 1893. 304 pp.

The story of Lewis L. Dyche's expeditions after North American mammals, including mule deer and whitetails. Genuine descriptions of the life of a naturalist-hunter and the life of a hunting camp.*

Elman, Robert and David Seybold, eds. *Seasons of the Hunter*. New York: Alfred A. Knopf, 1985. 233 pp.

The best hunting anthology to come along in years. Broad enough to inform and entertain any literate reader, whether hunter or non-hunter. Contains an excellent mix of fiction, essays, and reporting by acclaimed novelists and short-story writers. Includes John Randolph's classic portrait on half-Indian white-tailed-deer-hunting expert Larry Benoit. Vance Bourjaily's foreword on the paradoxical nature of sport hunting in modern society is worth the price of the book alone.

Errington, Paul L. "Deer Hunt." In *The Red Gods Call*. Ames: Iowa State University Press, 1973. pp. 75–78.

An excellent description of a deer hunt by a distinguished professor of wildlife ecology.

Feather, Noel. *Battling Bucks: Antler Rattling Techniques that Work!* Wisconsin: Target Communications, 1985. 124 pp.

If you're hooked on rattling or just want to learn more about it, you'll want to read this practical guide, which strongly endorses antler rattling as a valuable tool in the white-tailed deer hunter's repertoire.

Fennessy, P. F. and K. R. Drew, eds. *Biology of Deer Production*. Wellington: The Royal Society of New Zealand, 1985. 482 pp.

In these proceedings of a 1983 International Conference of deer biologists, the general reader will find a vast amount of information on deer biology (especially information on antlers) and how man has used deer for food, medicine, and clothing for thousands of years. Of special interest for the white-tailed buck hunter is Larry Marchinton's article on whitetail territorality, in which he outlines how males establish breeding areas by marking and defending them against other males who do not exhibit subordinate postures. Marchinton notes that he has been unable to clearly demonstrate that does respond to scrapes by leaving their scent.

Fitz, Grancel. *How to Measure and Score Big-Game Trophies*. Indiana: Blue-J Inc. Publishers, 1977. 130 pp.

The standard work on the subject by an outstanding authority and a great historian of big-game hunting.

———. "Troubles with Whitetails." In *North American Head Hunting*. New York: Oxford University Press, 1957. pp. 20–46.

Like William Monypeny Newsom, Fitz believed that you can travel the world over in pursuit of trophies. Far back of beyond you may go, but one day you'll come back to follow the track of the white-tailed deer—the greatest prize of North American hunting. Fitz's hunting experiences led him to conclude that the real monarchs of the whitetail clan spend most of their time living on another planet.*

Fletcher, Nichola. *Venison: The Monarch of the Table*. Scotland. Privately printed, 1983. 63 pp.

This book provides the deer-camp cook with a marvelous array of venison recipes set forth in the European tradition of cookery. This classy book emphasizes the fact that venison is as versatile as any other red meat, but that we still suffer from the long-standing myth that heavy sauces with plenty of wine in them represent the only way to treat venison. Indeed, she dispels the many myths of venison cookery and emphasizes light, quick cooking rather than the rich, heavy cuisine of yesteryear. An excellent cookbook for the deer shack.

Forester, Frank. "Deer Hunting." In *Frank Forester's Field Sports*. New York: Stringer and Townsend, 1849. pp. 239–252.

A great essay on early American deer hunting, although critical in tone, by that bizarre nineteenth century philosopher of sporting ethics.*

Geist, Valerius. *Mountain Sheep and Man in the Northern Wilds*. Ithaca: Cornell University Press, 1975. 248 pp.

A great book by a natural storyteller. Popular science at its all-time best—beautifully written and very thought provoking. Provides exciting reading for anyone interested in the hunting of wild animals and man's relationship to one animal in particular: the wild sheep of the Canadian wilderness. When Geist writes of his cabin in the wilderness, we all think of our deer shacks, wherever they may be. "In the valley stood my cabin. How small it was in the distance. I raised the binoculars to take a closer look. Its tin roof was shining in the sun; a thin plume of whitish smoke drifted from its stove pipe; its irregular peeled logs seemed to be smiling. Oh, that irresistible tempting smile. How well I understood the men who wrote poems to their cabins, for, to them and to me, cabins are not just houses but living spirits with character and idiosyncrasies."

Geist, Valerius and Fritz R. Walther, eds. 2 vols. *The Behavior of Ungulates and its Relation to Management*. Switzerland: International Union for Conservation of Nature and Natural Resources, 1974. 940 pp.

These unique reference volumes contain fifty-six scientific papers on the social behavior, ecology, and management of all species of deer worldwide. Volume I contains Larry Marchinton's excellent paper on the marking behavior of white-tailed deer and its social function. Out of print and very scarce.*

Gilbert, Bil. "The Rites of Autumn." In *In God's Countries*. Lincoln: University of Nebraska Press, 1984. pp. 103–122.

A masterful narrative of deer hunting in Potter County, Pennsylvania—the so-called deer hunting mecca of America—told in gripping and graphic detail. Views the Potter County deer hunt as "one of the most enduringly popular pageants," in which hunters do in 7,500 whitetails annually. A must, in the event you missed this classic essay when it first appeared in *Sports Illustrated*.

Gillmore, Parker, "Virginian Deer." In *Prairie and Forest: A Description of the Game of North America with Personal Adventures in Their Pursuit*. New York: Harper and Brothers, 1874. pp. 106–129.

Early deer-shooting experiences with buckshot in the 1860s near Vincennes, Indiana. Based on a mixture of fact, fancy, and romance and written by a prolific author, soldier, and hunter who shot deer in all parts of the world.*

Gohdes, Clarence, ed. "Deer Hunting in the Yazoo Swamp." In *Hunting in the Old South*. Baton Rouge: Louisiana State University Press, 1967. pp. 120–124.

This splendid account of a deer hunt in the Mississippi bottomlands first appeared in the *Spirit of the Times* (6 April 1844), as a letter from a subscriber. The deer-hunting party consisted of ten Nimrods "mounted upon the *soberest* hacks the plantation could muster." After the initial Bang! Bang! of the first two barrels in quick succession, the deerslayer who had fired cried, "My liquor!" In five days of coursing, the party killed thirty-one deer. The narrator ends the tale by saying, "It is unnecessary for me to inform *you* how we finished the hunt,—it was highly satisfactory, I assure you. If I recollected the last toast I would give it, but do not."*

Goodwin, Fred and S. Stanley Hawbaker. *The Art of Deer and Bear Hunting*. Chambersburg, Pennsylvania: Privately printed, 1953. 19 pp.

A brief description of how to hunt big bucks by one of Maine's greatest trophy hunters.*

Gould, Stephen Jay. "The Misnamed, Mistreated and Misunderstood Irish Elk." *Ever Since Darwin: Reflections in Natural History*. New York: W.W. Norton and Company, 1977. pp. 79–90.

A great essay on antlers by a great popularizer of science.

Groves, Don. *Stalking Deer.* New York: Privately printed, 1986. 281 pp.

A privately printed self-help manual.

Haas, George H., ed. *Outdoor Life Deer Hunter's Yearbook, 1985.* New York: Outdoor Life Books, 1984. 181 pp.

————. *Outdoor Life Deer Hunter's Yearbook, 1986.* New York: Outdoor Life Books, 1985. 181 pp.

————. *Outdoor Life Deer Hunter's Yearbook, 1987.* New York: Outdoor Life Books, 1986. 181 pp.

Reprints from *Outdoor Life* and their *Deer and Big Game Annual.*

Haight, Austin D. "I Kill My First Deer." In *The Biography of a Sportsman.* New York: Thomas Y. Crowell Company, 1939. pp. 71–85.

After many years of hunting, Haight reached the conclusion that nothing could give him greater pleasure than bringing home a bloody, dirty boy with his first deer: the birth of a deer hunter who would never miss another deer season.*

Hallock, Charles. "Virginia Deer." In *The Sportsman's Gazetteer and General Guide.* New York: Forest and Stream Publishing Company, 1877. pp. 79–91.

Words of wisdom from the innovative editor of that great outdoor newspaper *Forest and Stream,* who rightly believed that "deer-stalking is simply man versus brute; and requires all the strength, craft and coolness of the man, before he can lay low the deer, who is possessed of a much keener sense of smell, immense speed, excessive nervous organization, and is ever on the alert to circumvent its human foe."*

Halls, Lowell K., ed. *White-tailed Deer: Ecology and Management.* Harrisburg: Stackpole Books, 1984. 870 pp.

There are twelve million deer hunters in this country. If they bought and read this book *en masse,* the sport of American deer hunting would be ensured and the white-tailed deer would be better for it. If you want to own your own library on the white-tailed deer, buy this splendid blue-chip deer book,

for this comprehensive and attractive volume literally consists of a library in itself. The bibliography of more than 2,300 items reads like a major university's card catalogue under the subject heading of *Odocoileus virginianus.* An incredible consolidation of information. A must for every deer enthusiast.

Hawker, Lieut. Col. P. *Instructions to Young Sportsmen, in All that Relates to Guns and Shooting.* Philadelphia: Lea and Blanchard, 1846. 340 pp.

This rustic volume by that great old sportsman Peter Hawker contains four fascinating articles on deer hunting written by various authors: "Deer Hunting" by J. J. Audubon, "Deer Hunting in Mississippi" by Harry W., "Fire-Hunting for Deer" by T. B. Thorpe, and "The Buck Ague" by George W. Kendall. Eric Parker once noted that much of Hawker's advice stands for us today as it stood for our great-grandfathers during the days of Waterloo.*

Helmer, Ron. *Stag Party.* New Zealand: Whitcombe and Tombs LTD, 1964. 180 pp.

This entertaining account of the doings of New Zealand's Deer Shooting Party Number Six, written by a Canadian deer hunter, recalls the life of Daniel Boone, Davy Crockett, and Henry David Thoreau all rolled into one unique volume. Reads like a dream where the big trout bite at every lure and the woods overflow with deer.*

Hoffman, Charles Fenno. *Wild Scenes in the Forest and Prairie.* New Jersey: Gregg Press, 1970. II Volumes. 576 pp.

A reprint of the rare and sought after 1839 edition of one of the oldest books on Adirondack deer hunting. Includes several stirring, spirited sketches. "The Dog and the Deer-Stalker," narrates the eternal debate between still hunting versus hounding. "Withing a Buck" describes the procedure for killing deer with willow twigs or birch saplings bound together to form a large noose and placed upon the end of a long pole. "A Sacondago Deer-Hunt" captures the essence of early Adirondack deer hunting at its all-time best.

Holden, Philip. *"The Deerstalkers."* New Zealand: Hodder and Stoughton Ltd., 1987. 350 pp.

A fifty-year history of New Zealand's deer and deer hunting written by New Zealand's most prolific and successful hunting writer.

————. *Fawn*. New Zealand: Hodder and Stoughton, 1986. 130 pp.

The first novel in Philip Holden's trilogy about the life of White Patch, a New Zealand red deer. Although this story turns placid, dramatic, joyous, and cruel, it is always realistic, especially the chapter on wounded-deer behavior and why man hunts. Characterizes the deer and deer-hunting scene in New Zealand where deer are continuously harassed by full-time meat shooters due to the insatiable demand for venison from countries such as Germany and the Netherlands.

————. *The Hunting Breed*. New Zealand: Hodder and Stoughton, 1979. 192 pp.

This volume documents the transition in Philip Holden from a deer hunter with the rifle to an adept and seasoned observer of the deer and deer hunting scene in New Zealand.

————. *White Patch*. New Zealand: Hodder and Stoughton, 1981. 144 pp.

The classic tale of a deer hunter and a deer set in the remote peaks and valleys of the South Island of New Zealand. Completes the trilogy begun with *Fawn* and *Stag*. Will appeal to readers of all ages.

Holland, Ray P. *Now Listen, Warden*. Vermont: The Countryman Press, 1946. 130 pp.

These sporting tales of law violators contain a rare combination of humor and punch, especially the deer-poaching tale entitled "Beer Bottle Caps." But as Joe Wilcox points out, "People of Italian descent may well be offended by Mr. Holland's ethnic slurs. He seems to imagine that Italians are the principal violators of game laws."*

Horner, Kent. *Art and Science of Whitetail Hunting*. Harrisburg: Stackpole Books, 1986. 190 pp.

This book, dedicated to deer hunters who sit in the tops of trees and wait, represents a rich blend of deer biology and personal hunting experience. Written by a biologist/deer hunter and field editor for the *Deer & Deer Hunting* magazine, it is intended for the scientifically trained as well as the good ol' boys. The author equates the discipline spent while sitting and studying in the laboratory to the same necessary discipline required to sit in a tree top studying, waiting, and trying to fool a white-tailed buck. Kent rightly argues that "deer hunting brings together a hodge podge section of people and personalities and levels them; in this sense deer hunting is a great equalizer."

Hornibrook, Isabel. *"Jacking for Deer."* In *Camp and Trail: A Story of the Maine Woods*. Boston: Lothrop Publishing Company, 1897. pp. 9–19.

A romantic and poetic description of living, glowing eyes in the night, of moonstruck deer and proud hunters trying to maintain at least a "rag of reputation" as deer hunters.*

Hull, Russell. *Trophy Bowhunting: The Supreme Challenge*. Kansas: Privately printed, 1984. 131 pp.

Deer stories and hunting techniques by a trophy bow hunter from Kansas.

James, M. R. *Successful Bowhunting*. Indiana: Blue-J Inc. Publishers, 1985. 239 pp.

General information on hunting big game by the editor/publisher of *Bowhunter Magazine*.

Johnson, Eldridge Reeves. *Buck Fever*. Philadelphia: Privately printed, 1911. 42 pp.

Bound in a dark green pigskin and illustrated with excellent black-and-white plates with printed overlays and watered silk endpapers, this three-hundred-dollar nostalgic deer-hunting volume describes the story of a deer hunt in California, philosophizes on why we hunt, and comments on that vicious malady buck fever that so paralyzes the emotions as to render the hunter foolishly harmless upon the sighting of a deer for the first time.*

Jones, Robert L. and Harold C. Hanson. *"White-tailed Deer and Their Mineral Environment."* In *Mineral Licks, Geophagy and*

Biogeochemistry of North American Ungulates. Ames: Iowa State University Press, 1985. pp. 133–180.

This unusual volume with the intimidating academic title explores the role of mineral licks in producing populations of large-bodied, highly fertile, and heavily antlered white-tailed deer. The authors examine data from numerous states, east and west of the Mississippi, relative to soil fertility and phenotypic development. Puts forth the general hypothesis that relates antler size to alkaline earth-rich habitats with adequate levels of calcium and magnesium.

Kimball, J. N. *An Essay at Deer Hunting.* New York: Meyer and Ninger, 1914. 26 pp.

A very droll story of an unsuccessful deer hunting trip in the hills of New Hampshire.*

King, William Ross. "American Deer." In *The Sportsman and Naturalist in Canada.* London: Hurst and Blackett Publisher, 1866. pp. 87–102.

An early account of Canadian deer hunting that emphasizes still hunting or stalking as the only sportsmanlike way of deer killing.*

Kirkland, Wallace W. *Shenshoo: The Story of a Moose.* Chicago: Thomas S. Rockwell Company, 1930. 64 pp.

The adventures of a moose, written for the young reader.

Krausman, Paul R. and Norman S. Smith, eds. *Deer in the Southwest: A Workshop.* Arizona: Arizona Cooperative Wildlife Research Unit, 1984. 131 pp.

The proceedings of a workshop developed to address the contemporary issues related to mule and white-tailed deer in the Southwest.

LaBarbera, Mark, ed. *Wisconsin Deer & Bear Record Book.* Minnesota: Privately printed, 1984. 248 pp.

Pictures, records, and various articles about Wisconsin deer and deer hunting written by various people.

Langbein, J. *North Staffordshire Deer Survey, 1983–1985.* Vol. 1, *Research and Development.* British Deer Society, 1985. 111 pp.

Embraces scientific studies in deer behavior and distribution and the education of the general public in all matters relating to deer.

Lawson, Larry E. *Trophy Bucks of Indiana.* Indiana: Privately printed, 1985. 189 pp.

Another volume in the ever growing literature of books dealing with pictures of record white-tailed bucks. Contains numerous photos and brief stories of some of the largest white-tailed bucks ever taken in the state of Indiana.

Lee, Ben Rogers. *Ben Lee's Formula for Deer Hunting.* Privately printed, 1986. 141 pp.

The personal style of a southern deer hunter.

Lewis, Gerald E. *My Big Buck: Outdoor Stories of Maine.* Maine: The Thorndike Press, 1978. 211 pp.

Hunting anecdotes, facetiae, and satire from Maine. The story entitled "My Big Buck" reminds one of Seton's "The Trail of the Sandhill Stag." Indeed, it is a very sophisticated deer-hunting yarn dressed up in overalls and filled with a fine sense of sportsmanship.*

Long, Jeff. *Outlaw: The True Story of Claude Dallas.* New York: William Morrow and Company, Inc., 1985. 239 pp.

No book better exemplifies the mind of the deer poacher than this one, which deals with a deer poacher who lives off the land, kills what he needs, and pitches his tent where he pleases. Vividly describes a Dodge City shootout between one mountain man, living the life of bygone times, and two dedicated game wardens representing twentieth century law and order. Chronicles the two-year manhunt that followed. One of the best books on the subject of deer poaching.

Low, James Jr. *Floating and Driving for Deer.* Geneva: The Continental Herald and Swiss Times, 1873. 62 pp.

The stirring and exciting events of fire-hunting whitetails in the Adirondacks. One of the most romantic narratives ever written on this subject. Provides us with an excellent example of how nineteenth century urban man confronted the wilderness while deer hunting. Rare and very expensive.*

McLellan, Isaac. *Poems of the Rod and Gun.* New York: Henry Thorpe, 1886. 271 pp.

Contains glowing lines on deer and deer hunting from that venerable poet-sportsman whose name was once a household word. Sporting lore at its all-time best. His liquid prose in such poems as "Deer Hunting in Maine," "Fire-Hunting Deer" and "Watching for Deer" quickens the pulse of the die-hard buck hunter and drives him back to the deer forest in tireless haste for one last glimpse of branching antlers.*

McMath, Neil. *Continuing the Story of Turtle Lake.* Michigan: Privately printed, n.d. 16 pp.

A portrait of the Turtle Lake Deer Hunting Club, a 27,000-acre private hunting club located in Michigan.*

McPhee, John. "North of the C.P. Line." In *Table of Contents.* New York: Farrar, Straus, Giroux, 1985. pp. 249–293.

In this story about a bush-pilot fish and game warden pursuing deer poachers in the sky, McPhee admits that he will believe anything about deer. "In my opinion they are rats with antlers, roaches with split hooves, denizens of the dark Primeval suburbs. Deer intensely suggest New Jersey. One of the densest concentrations of wild deer in the United States inhabits the part of New Jersey that I inhabit. Deer like people. They like to be near people. They like bean fields, head lettuce and anybody's apples. They like hibiscus, begonias, impatiens, azaleas, rhododendrons, boxwood and wandering jews. I once saw a buck with a big eight-point rocking-chair rack looking magnificent as he stood between two tractor-trailers in the Frito-Lay parking lot in New Brunswick, New Jersey. Deer use the sidewalks in the heart of Princeton."

Madson, John, et al. *The Outdoor Life Deer Hunter's Encyclopedia.* New York: Times Mirror Magazines, 1985. 788 pp.

This book might have been titled *The Outdoor Life Deer Hunter's Encyclopedia of Equipment,* for most of its 788 pages deal with equipment. If you are interested in equipment, you will want to look at this book.

Manierre, Franny. *The Story of the Clow Deer Hunt.* Michigan: Privately printed, 1938. 22 pp.

The Clow Deer Hunting Party of Michigan almost became an institution of that state, although their annual deer hunts actually took place at Bent's Camp in Vilas County, Wisconsin. This book documents the forty-year history of this group of ribald and boisterous characters. Yes, they hunted deer and got lots of them, but one of their cabins, called the "Robbers' Roost," indicated other activities occurred as well: empty toddy glasses, sticky spoons, deflated lemon halves and wet, smelly clothes were usually found scattered in all directions, mostly on the floor.*

Marburger, Rodney G. *The King of Deer.* Texas: Privately printed, 1983. 272 pp.

A fascinating blend of deer biology and deer-hunting techniques and anecdotes written by a professional biologist. Although it focuses specifically on Texas, the book represents an excellent, general, and simplified account of such deer management techniques as censusing, data collecting, and the aging of deer for the layman. Deals with scrapes and breeding activities, deer movements, and doe harvests, as well as the mystique of antler development and the economics of Texas deer hunting. A unique book.

Marcon, John G. *The Brush Cop.* Rice Lake, Wisconsin: Chronotype Publications, 1983. 269 pp.

A detailed narrative of the field experiences of a Wisconsin Conservation Warden (1940–1960), as he confronts backwoods deer poachers.

Maynard, Roger. *Advanced Bowhunting Guide.* New Jersey: Stoeger Publishing Company, 1984. 222 pp.

A general guide dealing primarily with equipment.

Mech, L. David. *The Wolf: The Ecology and Behavior of an Endangered Species.* Minneapolis: University of Minnesota Press, 1970. 384 pp.

This comprehensive survey of the ecology and habits of the wolf includes an excellent discussion of the wolf's encounter with white-tailed deer. It underscores the wolf's very low success rate when trying to hunt whitetails. According to Mech, you will find most wolf-killed deer during the winter months along frozen lakes, rivers, and beaver ponds.

Michmerhuizen, Lewey. *Grandpa Recalls Deer Hunting Stories.* Michigan: Lew Publishers, 1964.

This popular account of thirty-five years of Michigan deer-hunting experiences (1928–1963) captures the real essence of a northwoods deer camp.

Mighetto, Lisa, ed. "Deer." In *Muir Among the Animals: The Wildlife Writings of John Muir.* Sierra Club Books, 1986. pp. 20–24.

Muir believed that any glimpse into the life of a deer makes our own life much larger and better in every way. On deer Muir wrote, "Everywhere some species of deer seems to be at home, — on rough or smooth ground, lowlands or highlands, in swamps and barrens and the densest woods, in varying climates, hot or cold, over all the continent; maintaining glorious health, never making an awkward step. Standing, lying down, walking, feeding, running even for life, it is always invincibly graceful, and adds beauty and animation to every landscape, — a charming animal, and a great credit to nature."

Moen, Aaron N. *Wildlife Ecology: An Analytical Approach.* San Francisco: W.H. Freeman and Company, 1973. 458 pp.

Although carrying a very broad title, this volume is really a basic textbook on the biology and physiology of the white-tailed deer and provides us with a great deal of sound information on the whitetail's energy interactions with its environment, especially its metabolism and nutrition. In it the author puts forward a very aggressive push to computer simulation as a method of studying and analyzing deer populations. Contains excellent and very comprehensive reference lists.

————. *Deer Management at the Crane Memorial Reservation and Wildlife Refuge.* New York: CornerBrook Press, 1984. 89 pp.

A case study of deer dynamics in a populated area and in conflict resolution and decision making. Argues for controlled hunts such as the hunts at the Carey Arboretum in New York State, supported by a computer-based processing system.

Moen, Aaron N., and Ronald A. Moen. *Deer Management at the Bernheim Foundation Properties Clermont, Kentucky.* New York: CornerBrook Press, 1985. 52 pp.

A case study of the whitetail's carrying capacity on a natural area. Reaches one inescapable conclusion: "Since free-ranging deer are a public resource living on private land for the most part, cooperative efforts between the wildlife agencies responsible for the deer and landowners and tenants responsible for the land are not only encouraged, but are necessary if deer management is to proceed at the highest levels of professionalism currently possible."

Monson, Keith. *Remember: The Deer Do.* North Dakota: Privately printed, 1985. 135 pp.

A self-published booklet focusing in on deer drives for bow hunters. Written by a farmer from North Dakota.

Murphy, John Mortimer. "The Black-tailed and Virginia Deer and their Varieties." In *Sporting Adventures in the Far West.* London: Sampson Low, Marston, Searle and Rivington, 1879. pp. 275–309.

A fascinating account of hunting blacktails and whitetails in the western states during the 1870s. When a member of Murphy's deer hunting party killed a deer, the successful Nimrod not only received congratulations, but a dose of something stronger than tea was generally partaken of in honor of the special event; Murphy's boys usually relied on a homemade brew called "Stone Fence," a rich blend of old cider and snakeroot whiskey.*

Murray, Jeff. *For Big Bucks Only.* Minnesota: Morning Star Press, 1987.

Forthcoming.

Nagler, Forrest. *The Bow and Arrow for Big Game* and *Archery, an Engineering View.* Oregon: Frank Taylor and Son, Publishers, 1941. 70 pp. 77 pp.

These two books, published as one, contain the bow-hunting adventures of one of the pioneers of the sport.*

Nelson, Norm. *Mule Deer: How to Bring Home North America's Big Deer of the West*. Harrisburg: Stackpole Books, 1987. 192 pp.

Another how-to volume.

Nerl, Wilhelm. *Der Hirsch und sein Revier*. Germany: W. Ludwig Verlag, 1982. 387 pp.

A standard work on the biology and hunting of Germany's red deer that contains a fascinating chapter on deer in the mythology, legend, and medical science of the German nation.

Nesbitt, William H., ed. *Boone and Crockett Club's 18th Big Game Awards*. Virginia: The Boone and Crockett Club, 1984. 306 pp.

The official record book for the outstanding trophies take during 1980 to 1982. The first of the record books to deal with a single three-year period.

Nesbitt, William H., and Philip L. Wright. *Measuring and Scoring North American Big Game Trophies*. Virginia: The Boone and Crockett Club, 1985. 176 pp.

Contains all the score charts and procedures you need to measure your trophy deer, including tips for field evaluation.

Nesbitt, William H. and Jack Reneau, eds. *Boone and Crockett Club's 19th Big Game Awards*. Virginia: The Boone and Crockett Club, 1986. 410 pp.

This official record for the nineteenth awards entry period of 1983–1985 tells us the truth about the Ohio "Hole-in-the-Horn" buck. Contrary to antler collector Dick Idol's sensationalized claims, this buck is number two for the category, not the world's record.

New, Harry S. *The Story of Turtle Lake*. Michigan: Privately printed, 1923. 36 pp.

The story of the origin and development of the Turtle Lake Deer Hunting Club written by the one-time Postmaster General of the United States. In the many years of the Club's existence, the Turtle Lake rifles leveled many a white-tailed buck. The best head carried twenty-seven points and the heaviest buck weighed in at 263 pounds dressed.*

Nonte, George C. Jr., and Lee E. Jurras. "Handgunning for Deer." In *Handgun Hunting*. New York: Winchester Press, 1975. pp. 106–113.

Deer hunting as the handgunner would have it.

Nti, J. *The Deer Hunt Festival of the Effutus*. Cape Coast, 1955. 26 pp.

Describes the ceremonial festivities of the deer hunt for the Gold Coast people: the spectacle of catching live deer with bare hands, their war songs and war dances, and their popular music.*

Orman, Tony. *Reflections of a Deerstalker: The Essence of Hunting and a Plea for the Future of the Sport*. New Zealand: A.H. and A.W. Reed, 1979. 156 pp.

———, ed. *Memories of New Zealand Deerstalking: An Anthology*. New Zealand: Reed, 1981. 206 pp.

These two volumes capture the great moments in the hunting lives of leading New Zealand deer hunters. Orman is a deer hunter who thinks deeply about his sport; these volumes contain the reflections of a thinking and caring deer hunter. They will delight deer hunters of every generation and nationality.

Parker, Willie J. "The Deer Hunters." In *Game Warden: Chesapeake Assignment*. Maryland: Tidewater Publishers, 1983. pp. 100–109.

A brief and exciting description of Maryland's chronic jacklighting problem, written by one of this country's toughest game wardens.

Peach, Arthur Wallace. "Trailing in Deer Country." In *The Country Rod & Gun Book*. New York: Farrar and Rinehart, 1938. pp. 67–75.

Divides the American deer hunter into two classes: those who can "set" and those who "can't set." Believes this distinction outlines the whole psychology and philosophy of deer hunting.*

Peper, Eric and Jim Rikhoff, eds. *Hunting Moments of Truth*. New York: Winchester Press, 1973. 208 pp.

Every deer hunter at one time or other experiences that rare, mystical moment that vividly crystallizes everything that deer hunting means: the ultimate moment of truth. It might represent a magnificent shot and a downed trophy, an awesome kill or a nerve-wrecking wait, a failed stalk or a heartsickening cripple. Robert Elman's personal essay entitled "Success without Venison" beautifully captures the deer-hunting moment of truth for one hunter.

Perry, Oliver Hazard. *Hunting Expeditions of Oliver Hazard Perry of Cleveland.* Cleveland: Privately printed, 1899. 246 pp.

The daily adventures of a mid-nineteenth-century deerslayer in the deer forests of northern Michigan. His tales of how the deer "unfurled their white flags to the breeze" have to be read to be believed. With his primitive rifle belching out its staccato tones, Perry pursued the Old Hemlock Rangers with the vitality and intensity of Wagner's *The Flying Dutchman.**

Phillips, John C. *American Game Mammals and Birds: A Catalogue of Books, 1582 to 1925.* New York: Houghton Mifflin Company, 1930. 639 pp.

The most comprehensive bibliography of books dealing with the field sports, natural history, and conservation. Lists and annotates many of the deer books from the past but notes that American sporting literature conspicuously lacks attractive books on deer hunting and the natural history of the animal: "Little that ranks high in the realms of style and fine book-making." An essential research volume. Available as a reprint from Arno Press.

Plum, Dorothy A., ed. *Adirondack Bibliography.* New York: Adirondack Mountain Club, 1958. 345 pp.

————. *Adirondack Bibliography Supplement,* 1956–1965. New York: The Adirondack Museum, 1973. 198 pp.

Two indispensable bibliographies dealing with the great literature on deer and deer hunting in the Adirondacks. A "must" if you are searching for information on deer and deer hunting in that area.

Poortvliet, Rien. *Auf der Jagd: Ein Skizzenbuch.* Hamburg: Verlag Paul Parey, 1980.

A beautiful sketch book of romantic and impressionistic paintings depicting the hunted, especially deer and the metaphysics of the hunting experience, by that great European hunting painter. Captures the love of the animal and the essence of the chase in a way that few books do. Recalls the sprightly echoes of Johann Strauss' polka *Auf der Jagd.*

Potter, Arthur G., et al. *The 1907 Hunt of the Forest City Hunting Club in the Wilds of Northern Maine.* Maine: Privately printed, 1908. 111 pp.

Facetious stories, historical memories, and nostalgic photos of a deer-hunting club whose members hunted deer in different parts of the country, including Wisconsin, Minnesota, Canada, and the wilds of northern Maine. Very similar in substance and scope to Shaffmaster's *Hunting in the Land of Hiawatha,* 1904. Extremely rare.*

Pray, Leon L. *The Whitetail Deer Head Book for the Taxidermist.* New York: Modern Taxidermist magazine, 1944. 40 pp.

One of the earlier studies on mounting white-tailed deer heads. With regard to the perfect head, Pray writes that "however many times the gunner may fall short of taking the perfect buck head, he is not discouraged but goes to the forest each season with hope undimmed and determination unflagging."*

Ramsay, David. "Historian Ramsay on Deer-Hunting in South Carolina." In *A Southern Reader,* Willard Thorp, ed. New York: Alfred A. Knopf, 1955. pp. 227–229.

Perceives deer hunting in some respects as war in miniature and as a social diversion. Argues that while deer hunters die, deer hunting clubs are immortal.

Reimann, Lewis C. *The Game Warden and the Poachers.* Michigan: Northwoods Publishers, 1959. 196 pp.

A melange of historic anecdotes and episodes arranged in sketchy organization, dealing with Michigan deer poachers trying to outwit game wardens in the Upper Peninsula. Written by a well-known raconteur of early pioneer tales and regional folklore.

Filled with rough "he man" humor of deer poachers fighting their eternal battle with authority. Based on newspaper accounts, warden reports, interviews, patrols, court cases, and legal sentences.*

Reitz, Robert A. *The Mighty Buck: A Practical Guide to a Successful Deer Hunt.* Georgia: Gridiron Publishers, 1978. 115 pp.

A practical pocket guide for shooting white-tailed bucks in the deer forests of Georgia. I couldn't agree with the author more when he writes that "alcohol and gun powder do not mix. But it is always appropriate to serve wine with venison. Save just enough for a fitting toast to that MIGHTY BUCK."

Richey, David. *Hunting Fringeland Deer.* New York: Outdoor Life Books, 1987. 208 pp.

A guide to hunting whitetails in marginal areas such as farmland woodlots, small acres of fields under cultivation, and bits and pieces of sparse cover.

Riley, Perry G. *Bowhunting the Fake Scrape.* Indiana: Privately printed, 1985. 54 pp.

A short booklet on making mock scrapes.

Roberson, Sheila F., ed. *Deer-Proof Fencing.* Texas: Caesar Kleberg Wildlife Research Institute, 1985. 41 pp.

Discusses the contemporary question among landowners, hunters, and professionals of whether or not to construct deerproof fences. Raises the question of the wisdom of artificially restricting gene flow in a natural population.

Rogers, Robert, ed. *Great Whitetails of North America.* Vol. 2. Texas: Privately printed, 1981. 256 pp.

A revised edition of Volume 1, including pictures and stories of more than 100 trophy white-tailed bucks, edited and compiled by a Texas hunting guide.

———. *The Professional Guide to Whitetail.* Texas: Privately printed, 1984. 170 pp.

Photos and reprinted material on trophy hunting from various books and magazines.

———. *Legend of the Muy Grande.* Texas: Whitetail Publications, 1983. 160 pp.

Stories and photos of the Muy Grande Deer Contest in Texas, 1966–1983.

Roosevelt, Theodore, and George Bird Grinnell, eds. *American Big-Game Hunting.* New York: Forest and Stream Publishing Company, 1893. 345 pp.

A collection of unique hunting adventures in America by members of the Boone and Crockett Club.*

Rudge, A. J., ed. *The Capture and Handling of Deer.* London: Nature Conservancy Council, 1983. 273 pp.

A detailed manual on the physical capture, handling, and transportation of live deer. Filled with practical information on the use of drugs, weapons, projectile syringes, and techniques for physical and chemical capture. Although intended for the scientist, of general interest given the emotional subject matter.

Rue, Leonard Lee III, and William Owen. *Meet the Moose.* New York: Dodd, Mead and Company, 1985. 78 pp.

A great book for the young reader. I agree with the Wildlife Management Institute when they insist that this country should pass a law that *only* Leonard Lee Rue III be allowed to publish books on wildlife for children.

Salley, A. S. Jr. *The Happy Hunting Ground.* South Carolina: The State Company, 1926. 83 pp.

Personal experiences of deer hunting in the low-country of South Carolina.*

Schorger, A. W. "The White-tailed Deer in Early Wisconsin." In *Transactions of the Wisconsin Academy of Sciences,* vol. 42. Wisconsin Academy of Sciences, 1953. pp. 197–247.

A very exhaustive and detailed description of the white-tailed deer and the hunting of them in early Wisconsin between 1660 and 1900. Based primarily on newspaper accounts. Extremely thorough.*

Schuh, Dwight. *Bowhunting for Mule Deer.* Montana: Stoneydale Press, 1985. 175 pp.

A detailed guide for hunting open-country mule-deer bucks.

Seton, Ernest Thompson. "Moose Hunt." In *Trail of an Artist-Naturalist.* New York: Charles Scribner's Sons, 1948. pp. 259–275.

In this deer-hunting tale originally entitled "The Hunting of the Moose," the reader will recognize the quintessence of that later, classic tale, *The Trail of the Sandhill Stag.* In this earlier tale, Seton records the adventures of a 300-mile deer hunt on foot including nineteen days of heavy toil. Perpetuates the myth of the waiting game by suggesting that deer will "stiffen up" after being wounded. Adds to our knowledge of woodcraft the notion that the bluejay remains the deer's greatest tattletale who cries out in the forest: "Deer there—deer, deer, deer!"*

Shoemaker, Henry W. *Stories of Great Pennsylvania Hunters.* Pennsylvania: The Altoona Tribune Company, 1913. 54 pp.

The biographies of a dozen or more of Pennsylvania's greatest Nimrods. Undoubtedly, the first published effort to preserve a record of the lives and deeds of great hunters. Records how John Q. Dyce (1830–1904), poet, philosopher, and deerslayer, killed three deer with a single shot at 100 yards. A great companion piece to Shoemaker's *Pennsylvania Deer and Their Horns.* *

Smith, Edmund Ware. "Jeff Coongate's Perfect Crime." In *Strayed Shots and Frayed Lines,* John E. Howard, ed. New Jersey: Amwell Press, 1982. pp. 11–17.

The conflict between deer poachers and game wardens, between the law and the lawless, proved fertile ground for this master yarn spinner. This humorous gem deals with the theme of poaching deer and with Jeff Coongate—one of the most ingratiating rascals in outdoor literature, or as the author himself admits, "the greatest deer poacher ever this country heard tell of." Once again, we learn that "the way of the transgressor is hard, mighty hard." Originally published in the Derrydale edition of Smith's *Tall Tales and Short* (1938). Humorous, imaginative, immediate.

———. *The One-Eyed Poacher of Privilege.* New York: The Derrydale Press, 1941. 187 pp.

Hilarious tales of that lovable deer poacher with the one sparkling blue eye. Once again, Thomas Jefferson Coongate wouldn't shoot a deer "in season" unless by accident. In these delightful tales, Coongate prefers to get his venison illegally, although he was never known to kill more than he could eat or give to the poor. His violations of the game laws in Smith's beloved deer forests of Maine remind us of the legend of Robin Hood. Zack Bourne, Coongate's compadre in the crimes of deer poaching, deplores the fact that he cannot patent and sell his poaching equipment: "Dang shame a feller couldn't patint a rig like this. I'd call her the Zack Bourne Dead Shot Jacklightin' Frame. We'll test her out tonight on that old buck. Bet he'll dress two hundrid easy."*

———. *The Further Adventures of the One-Eyed Poacher.* New York: Crown Publishers, 1947. 219 pp.

The further adventures of Coongate whose chief occupation, when out of jail and sober, revolves around outwitting Tom Corn, the game warden, and playing Robin Hood to his neighbors. Captures in all their originality and vividness the figures of speech that abound between backwoods deer poachers and wardens. Refreshing.*

———. *The One-Eyed Poacher and the Maine Woods.* Fredrick Fell Publishers, Inc., 1955. 269 pp.

Violating the game laws merely represents for Coongate an assertion of human dignity and an emotional and instinctive response to the challenge of the deer forest. Deer poaching becomes an act of self-affirmation. Two types of hunts take place in this marvelous volume: the deer poacher pursues his quarry and the game warden pursues his victim. As one literary critic remarked: "Nature is on Jeff Coongate's side and the country doesn't stand a chance against poetic justice."

———. "My Game Warden Friends and Outlaw Companions." In *A Treasury of the Maine Woods.* Fredrick Fell Publishers, Inc., 1958. pp. 83–96.

In this article Smith reveals how he invented the character who was all deer poachers in one and another who was all game wardens. As Smith readily admits, "I am lucky in knowing the cream of these two opposing crops—one representing the law, the other holding out for a high protein diet, low meat bills, if any, and the mythical and nefarious 'summer hunting license.'" To the readers of his tales, both the poacher and the warden seem invincible; indeed, we look upon both of them with mutual admiration and respect—not knowing which to like most.

———. "Jake's Rangers Hunt the Whitetail." In *Upriver & Down*. New York: Holt, Rinehart, and Winston, 1965. pp. 132–148.

Read this classic tale as the open day approaches and your deer-hunting clan makes its way to rendezvous, for this famous tale of the annual gathering of the deer-hunting clan in the woods of Maine stands as a classic in the literature on deer and deer hunting. In this piece you will find remarkable similarities to life in your own deer camp. A universal characterization of the American deer camp.*

Smith, Ned. *Gone for the Day*. Pennsylvania: The Pennsylvania Game Commission, 1971.

The notebooks of that great white-tailed deer painter, written in the mountains and along the rivers of his native Pennsylvania. Originally published as his popular "Gone for the Day" column in the *Pennsylvania Game News*. "It would be less than honest," Ned tells us, "to maintain that all hunters are upright gentlemen, or even true sportsmen. But I'll bet that if all boys were taught the joys of deer hunting and an appreciation of the out-of-doors half our psychiatrists, social workers, policemen, and prison guards would be out of work when the next generation takes over."

Smith, Richard P. *Michigan Big Game Records*. Michigan: Commemorative Bucks of Michigan, Inc., 1986. 216 pp.

Using data compiled by the Commemorative Bucks of Michigan, Inc., Richard Smith has compiled a very informative book. One chapter in particular highlights this record book: "The Story of Bucky." When this story originally appeared in the *Deer & Deer Hunting* magazine it generated a tremendous volume of mail. It documents a very unique relationship between a white-tailed buck and a man named Bill Mattson. One of the best state record books.

Smith, W. McCombie. *The Romance of Poaching in the Highlands of Scotland*. Wales: Tideline Books, 1982. 164 pp.

Originally published in 1904, this reprint narrates the exciting, clandestine poaching exploits and adventures in the Highlands of Scotland of John Farquharson and Alexander Davidson, two men as far removed and superior to the ordinary run of deer poachers as one can imagine. The book ultimately raises the question "Is there not in all of us the sneaking regard for an imaginative daring thief?"

Speakman, Fred. *A Keeper's Tale*. Great Britain: G. Bell and Sons, 1962. 164 pp.

The memories of an old man looking back over a lifetime of service as a game keeper of deer in the Epping Forest of London. Deals with the period of 1870 to 1950. Focuses particularly on the deer that had to be defended from poachers but controlled to avoid crop damage to neighboring farms. Contains a fascinating chapter on dogs and deer.

Speltz, Merlin G. *Camp 17*. Minnesota: Privately printed, n.d. 27 pp.

An excellent, detailed, historic account of a Minnesota deer camp incorporated in 1956. Includes everything from tree planting and habitat improvement to land purchases and Pine County deer-kill statistics.

Stenlund, Milt. *Popple Leaves and Boot Oil*. Minnesota: Heritage North, 1985. 126 pp.

A unique and interesting narrative of the experiences of a wildlife biologist in northern Minnesota who works with wolves and whitetails.

Swendsen, David H. *Badge in the Wilderness*. Harrisburg: Stackpole Books, 1985. 191 pp.

The chapter entitled "Deer Week II," dealing with Billy Cooper and his folk-hero deer hunting adventures in Massachusetts, is itself worth the price of the book. If you want to learn more about deer hunters of the subculture, read this book.

Thompson, J. Maurice. *The Witchery of Archery*. North Carolina: The Archers Company, 1928. 259 pp.

Underscores the idea that there is no excellence in bow hunting without great labor. "The bowman, to be successful as a hunter, must learn to perfection the habits of his game. This necessity gives him opportunities to see many things, and note many habits peculiar to certain kinds of small game, overlooked by other sportsmen and naturalists." A great book. One of the prize possessions of my library. To read it is to hear the whistle of flying arrows and the hum of the bowstring. A lyric of exquisite purity. Available in paperback: Kim Fundingsland Productions, 1825 15½ St. S.W., Minot, ND 58701.

Thornberry, Russell. "The Ghost of the Fence Post Buck." In *Texas Hunter's Directory, 1982/83*. pp. 96–99.

An interesting account of a unique buck rub on a corner post of a fence line.*

Turberville, George. *Turberville's Book of Hunting, 1576*. London: Clarendon Press, 1908. 250 pp.

Among the earliest and most important English books on deer hunting. Originally entitled *Noble Arts of Venerie or Hunting*. This 1908 edition is reprinted page for page and line for line from the Bodleian copy of the black letter edition of 1576. In it the author suggests that the deer hunter can determine the size and general age of a buck by the size and figuration of the deer's droppings and that deer droppings differ in size and figuration in the morning from those made in the evening.*

Van Dyke, Theodore Strong. *The Still-Hunter*. Michigan: Gunnerman Press, 1987.

Finally, we have a reprint of this unsurpassed classic on all aspects of deer and deer hunting, a blue-chip deer book with no equal. Available from Gunnerman Press: Box 4292, Auburn Hills, MI 48057.

———. "Deer Hunting." In *Flirtation Camp: or, the Rifle, Rod and Gun in California*. New York: Fords, Howard, and Hulbert, 1881. pp. 240–254.

A whisper of that great classic on deer and deer hunting, *The Still-Hunter*, which followed one year later. Also contains two chapters entitled "Deer in the Open Hills" and "Tracking Deer on Bare Ground."*

Walsh, E. G. *The Poacher's Companion*. Great Britain: The Boydell Press, 1982. 265 pp.

An excellent anthology including some of the great English commentary on deer poachers and poaching. Includes a wealth of material on all aspects of poaching. "Those who have poached," the author writes, "can read about how others did it and think how much better they could do it themselves; those who have resisted the temptation can see that it is not always as exciting as tradition and song would have it."

Walsh, George Ethelbert. *White Tail: The Deer's Adventures*. Chicago: The John C. Winston Company, 1922. 135 pp.

One of the titles in the Twilight Animal Series, for children between the ages of four and ten.*

Walther, Fritz R. *Communication and Expression in Hoofed Mammals*. Bloomington: Indiana University Press, 1984. 423 pp.

An excellent general introduction to the study of animal communication and ungulate behavior. Especially useful for those interested in deer behavior and deer communication.

Wegner, Robert. *Deer & Deer Hunting*, Book 1. Harrisburg: Stackpole Books, 1984. 316 pp.

The Wildlife Management Institute notes that this book "takes a different trail than most books on the subject and offers new, interesting scenery." *Gray's Sporting Journal* calls it "an original book on the most overworked subject in the outdoor field." *Sporting Classics* classifies it as "first-rate, intelligent and literate. The best book on the subject in many years—has stimulated the sale of the better deer hunting books." I generally do not argue with these institutions. I call it volume one of a three-volume work.

Weiss, John. *Venison: From Field to Table*. New York: Outdoor Life Books, 1984. 365 pp.

According to statistics prepared by the Wildlife Management Institute, American deer hunters in the early 1980s harvested 128 million pounds of boneless venison annually. Using the equivalent price for ground beef, this amounts to a value of 185 million dollars in venison. It is not surprising to learn why so many deer hunters are enamored with venison. John Weiss tells us why in this detailed book of delicious recipes.

Wells, Hunter. *They Call Me Hunter.* Arizona: Ralph Tanner Associates, Inc., 1984. 224 pp.

A collection of the personal deer hunting experiences of Arizona guide Hunter Wells told with a down-home country writing style.

Whitehead, G. Kenneth. *Practical deer-stalking.* England: The British Deer Society, 1986. 192 pp.

A book full of detailed practical advice by that acknowledged authority on deer who has written nine books on various aspects of the subject. In this one he passes on his experiences of more than fifty years of deer stalking. Contains interesting material on wounded deer and their reaction to the shot.

Whyte, Jon, and E. J. Hart. *Carl Rungius: Painter of the Western Wilderness.* New Hampshire: Salem House, 1985. 184 pp.

Based on the hunting diaries of North America's renowned wildlife painter Carl Rungius, this volume depicts his fascinating life and powerful paintings of hunting big game.

Wilcox, Sidney W. *Deer Production in the United States, 1969–1973: Data Relating to Deer and Deer Hunters.* Arizona: Arizona State University, 1976. 77 pp.

An analysis and interpretation of data relating to deer and deer hunters including pre- and post-hunt estimates by species, bow and firearms hunter numbers, and the dollar value of the deer meat taken in all of the fifty states.*

Wixom, Hartt. *Elk and Elk Hunting.* Harrisburg: Stackpole Books, 1986. 287 pp.

A general, practical guide.

Wolfe, Oliver Howard. "Deer Hunting." In *Back Log and Pine Knot: A Chronicle of the Minnisink Hunting and Fishing Club.* Philadelphia: Privately printed. 34 pp.

Pleasant memories of a Pennsylvania deer hunting club. Reprinted in *Deer & Deer Hunting* 6 (1983): 38–47, under the title "The Minnisink Deer Camp."*

Wolff, Ed. *Elk Hunting in the Northern Rockies.* Montana: Stoneydale Press, 1984. 162 pp.

Information on hunting the premiere elk country of the northern Rocky Mountain states of Wyoming, Montana, and Idaho.

Wood, F. Dorothy. *The Deer Family.* New York: Harvey House Inc., 1969. 48 pp.

A book dealing with whitetails, elk, moose, caribou, and mule deer for grades K–2.*

Woodcock, E. N. *Fifty Years a Hunter and Trapper.* Ohio: A. R. Harding, 1913. 318 pp.

For fifty years E. N. Woodcock tramped the hills of Pennsylvania in pursuit of the white-tailed deer, especially in the Black Forest region of southeastern Potter County. This collection of articles that originally appeared in *Hunter-Trader-Trapper* records his fifty years of deer hunting experiences (1853–1903), and gives us an excellent portrait of one of the all-time giants of the Golden Age of American deer hunting. Thanks to *Fur-Fish-Game* the book still remains in print in an inexpensive paperback edition.

Wyoming Game and Fish Department. *The Mule Deer of Wyoming.* Wyoming: Game and Fish Department, 1985. 154 pp.

Not a treatise of how to hunt deer per se, but rather generalizations about the habits and weaknesses of mule deer. Within its covers, you will find information on the distribution of the mule deer throughout Wyoming, movements of the herds, estimated herd unit populations, and the latest harvest figures for each unit. By studying these statistics and bits of information, the shrewd hunter should be able to put together his own deer-hunting scenario.

Zumbo, Jim. *How to Plan Your Western Big Game Hunt.* Harrisburg: Stackpole Books, 1986. 95 pp.

A booklet on planning big-game hunts in eleven western states.

Chapter 23

The Deer Hunter's Checklist
Extraordinary Sources of Information

Today, the tiers of my books and reading materials are a presence as impor-
tant and comforting to my home as a full woodshed or a stocked freezer.
They are the doorway to some of the best hunting and fishing experiences
and most interesting sportsmen I've ever known. They can be enjoyed
without seasons, bag limits, or financial limitations. My favorite books
transport me to the field like a magic time capsule.
— Lamar Underwood, 1981

Master's Thesis and Ph.D. Dissertations

Aalgaard, Ronald Bruce. "Movements of the White-tailed Deer *(Odocoileus virginianus)* in the Prairie-Marsh Deer Range of South-central North Dakota." Master's thesis, North Dakota State University, 1973.

Altherr, Thomas Lawson. "'The Best of All Breathing': Hunting as a Mode of Environmental Perception in American Literature and Thought from James Fenimore Cooper to Norman Mailer." Ph.D. diss., Ohio State University, 1976.

Amidon, Paul H. "New York Deer Hunters: A Comparison of Deer Law Violators and Non-Violators." Master's thesis, Syracuse University, 1968.

Atkeson, Thomas Donnally. "Aspects of Social Communication in White-tailed Deer." Ph.D. diss., University of Georgia, 1983.

Autry, Donald C. "Movements of White-tailed Deer in Response to Hunting on Crab Orchard National Wildlife Refuge." Master's thesis, Southern Illinois University, 1967.

Baumgartner, David Michael. "Forest Resource Use and Management by Large Private Hunting and Fishing Clubs in Northern Lower Michigan." Ph.D. diss., Michigan State University, 1969.

Behrend, Donald Fraser. "Behavior of White-tailed Deer in an Adirondack Forest." Ph.D. diss., Syracuse University, 1966.

Berger, Michael. "Texas Hunters: Characteristics, Opinions and Facility Preferences." Ph.D. diss., Texas A and M University, 1974.

Bessey, Kenneth Michael. "Analysis of the Illegal Harvest of White-tailed Deer in Agro-Manitoba: Implications for Program Planning and Management." Master's thesis, University of Manitoba, 1983.

Brown, Bennett Andrew Jr. "The Annual Behavioral Cycle of Male White-tailed Deer." Masters thesis, Texas A and M University, 1971.

Cartwright, M. E. "An Ecological Study of White-tailed Deer in Northwestern Arkansas: Home Range, Activity and Habitat Utilization." Master's thesis, University of Arkansas, 1975.

Claggett, Richard T. "Populations, Movements, and Harvest of the Whitetail Deer on State Game Lands 176 (the Barrens), Pennsylvania." Master's thesis, Pennsylvania State University, 1976.

Curtis, Robert Lee Jr. "Climatic Factors Influencing Hunter Sightings of Deer on the Broad Run Research Area." Master's thesis, Virginia Polytechnic Institute and State University, 1971.

Decker, D. J. "The Influence of Internal Communication on the Development of the Bureau of Wildlife's Public Image in Relation to Deer Management in the Peripheral Adirondack Region of New York State." Master's thesis, Cornell University, 1976.

Duvendeck, Jerry Paul. "The Value and Prediction of Acorn Crops for Deer." Ph.D. diss., Michigan State University, 1964.

Fahlsing, Ray Duane. "Movement of White-tailed Deer in the Eastern Edwards Plateau in Response to Land Use Practices." Master's thesis, Texas A and M University, 1985.

Frodelius, Ronald B. "Determination of Anti-Hunt Organizations by Content Analysis of Their Literature." Master's thesis, Syracuse University, 1973.

Gibson, H. "Deer Hunting Clubs in Concordia Parish: The Role of Male Sodalities in the Maintenance of Social Values." Master's thesis, Louisiana State University, 1976.

Glover, Ronald L. "Characteristics of Deer Poachers and Poaching in Missouri." Master's thesis, University of Missouri-Columbia, 1982.

Gramlich, Francis James. "A Study of Factors Related to Low Deer Harvests in a Portion of Eastern Maine." Master's thesis, University of Maine, 1965.

Guynn, D. E. "Management of Deer Hunters on Private Land in Colorado." Ph.D. diss., Colorado State University, 1979.

Guyse, Keith DeLane. "Activity and Behavior of Unhunted White-tailed Deer Bucks During Rut in Southwest Alabama." Master's thesis, Auburn University, 1978.

Harmoning, Arlen Keith. "White-tailed Deer Dispersion and Habitat Utilization in Central North Dakota." Master's thesis, North Dakota State University, 1976.

Herron, John S. C. "Deer Harvest and Wounding Loss Associated with Bow Hunting White-tailed Deer." Master's thesis, University of Wisconsin-Madison, 1984.

Herriman, Kevin Ray. "Hunting Season Movements of Male White-tailed Deer on Davis Island." Master's thesis, Mississippi State University, 1983.

Hood, Ronald Earl. "Seasonal Variations in Home Range, Diel Movement and Activity Patterns of White-tailed Deer on the Rob and Bessie Welder Wildlife Refuge." Master's thesis, Texas A and M University, 1971.

Hosey, Arthur George Jr. "Activity Patterns and Notes on the Behavior of Male White-tailed Deer During Rut." Master's thesis, Auburn University, 1980.

Howard, Volney W. "Behavior of White-tailed Deer Within Three Northern Idaho Plant Associations." Ph.D. diss., University of Idaho, 1969.

Hygnstrom, Scott E. "Characteristics of Hunter-Collected Data on White-tailed Deer Movements and Environmental Conditions." Master's thesis, University of Wisconsin-Stevens Point, 1983.

Ishmael, William E. "White-tailed Deer Ecology and Management in Southern Wisconsin." Master's thesis, University of Wisconsin-Madison, 1984.

Ivey, Timothy. "Movement, Activity and Behavior of Female White-tailed Deer During the Rut." Master's thesis, Auburn University, 1980.

Kaminsky, Michael Arthur. "Analysis of the Spatial and Temporal Occurrence of Deer Spotlighting Violations in Virginia." Master's thesis, Virginia Polytechnic Institute and State University, 1974.

Kammermeyer, Kent Edward. "Movement-Ecology of White-tailed Deer in Relation to a Refuge and Hunted Area." Master's thesis, University of Georgia, 1975.

Kennedy, James Joseph III. "A Consumer Analysis Approach to Recreational Decisions: Deer Hunters as a Case Study." Ph.D.

diss., Virginia Polytechnic Institute and State University, 1970.

Kesel, James Alan. "Some of the Characteristics and Attitudes of Michigan Deer Hunting Violators." Master's thesis, Michigan State University, 1974.

Klessig, Lowell. "Hunting in Wisconsin: Initiation, Desertion, Activity Patterns and Attitudes as Influenced by Social Class and Residence." Master's thesis, University of Wisconsin, 1970.

Langenau, Edward E. Jr. "Non-Consumptive Uses of the Michigan Deer Herd." Ph.D. diss., Michigan State University, 1976.

Larson, Thomas Joseph. "Movement and Habitat Use of White-tailed Deer in South-central Wisconsin." Master's thesis, University of Wisconsin, 1974.

Lefes, William S. "The Sociology of Deer Hunting in Two Pennsylvania Counties, 1951." Master's thesis, Pennsylvania State College, 1953.

Lowe, T. M. "Characteristics and Attitudes of Mississippi Deer Hunters." Master's thesis, Mississippi State University, 1978.

Lubeck, Robert A. "Summer Flight Behavior of White-tailed Deer in Two Adirondack Forests." Master's thesis, Syracuse University, 1967.

McDowell, Robert L. "New Jersey Bowhunting Household Characteristics: Hunting Success, Game Utilization and Attitudes Toward Hunting." Master's thesis, Rutgers University, 1980.

McPhillips, Kelly Brian. "Characteristics and Success of South Dakota Archery Deer Hunters." Master's thesis, South Dakota State University, 1983.

Marchinton, Robert Larry. "Telemetric Study of White-tailed Deer Movement-Ecology and Ethology in the Southeast." Ph.D. diss., Auburn University, 1968.

Martin, Larry Kennedy. "Seasonal Movements of White-tailed Deer in North Dakota." Master's thesis, North Dakota State University, 1973.

Michael, Edwin Daryl. "Daily and Seasonal Activity Patterns of White-tailed Deer on the Welder Wildlife Refuge." Ph.D. diss., Texas A and M University, 1966.

Miller, Karl V. "Social and Biological Aspects of Signpost Communication in White-tailed Deer." Ph.D. diss., University of Georgia, 1985.

Moncrief, Lewis W. "An Analysis of Hunter Attitudes Toward the State of Michigan's Antlerless Deer Hunting Policy." Ph.D. diss., Michigan State University, 1970.

More, Thomas A. "Motivational Attitudes of Licensed Massachusetts Hunters." Master's thesis, University of Massachusetts, 1970.

Mott, Seth Evans. "Movements and Habitat Use by White-tailed Deer in a Bottomland Hardwood Area of Mississippi." Master's thesis, Mississippi State University, 1981.

Murphy, Robert K. "Deer Movements and Habitat Use of Irrigated Agricultural Lands in Central Wisconsin." Master's thesis, University of Wisconsin-Stevens Point, 1983.

Phillips, P. H. "The Economic Impact of the Louisiana Deer Hunter." Master's thesis, Louisiana State University, 1965.

Pledger, J. M. "Activity, Home Range, and Habitat Utilization of White-tailed Deer *(Odocoileus virginianus)* in Southeastern Arkansas." Master's thesis, University of Arkansas, 1975.

Progulske, Donald R. "Movements and Home Ranges of the White-tailed Deer *(Odocoileus virginianus)* in Central Missouri." Ph.D. diss., University of Missouri, 1956.

O'Brien, Thomas F. "Seasonal Movements and Mortality of White-tailed Deer in Wisconsin." Master's thesis, University of Wisconsin-Madison, 1976.

Schole, F. J. "Hunter Behavior, Attitudes, and Philosophies." Master's thesis, Colorado State University, 1973.

Shaw, Dale L. "The Hunting Controversy: Attitudes and Arguments." Ph.D. diss., Colorado State University, 1973.

Simon, Dennis Eugene, "Density, Migration and Mortality Patterns of White-tailed Deer Using a Sanctuary in Southeastern Minnesota." Master's thesis, University of Minnesota, 1986.

Smith, Frank Hubert Jr. "Daily and Seasonal Variations in Movements of White-tailed Deer on Eglin Air Force Base, Florida." Master's thesis, University of Georgia, 1970.

Sweeney, J. R. "The Effects of Harassment by Hunting Dogs on the Movement Patterns of White-tailed Deer on the Savannah River Plant, South Carolina." Master's thesis, University of Georgia, 1970.

Tucker, Randy Lee. "Home Range and Habitat Selection of White-tailed Deer in East Texas." Master's thesis, Austin State University, 1981.

Vilkitis, James R. "Characteristics of Big Game Violators and Extent of Their Activity in Idaho." Master's thesis, University of Idaho, 1968.

Vorderstrasse, Roger Ernest. "Hunting Deer with Bow and Arrow in the McDonald Forest, Oregon." Master's thesis, Oregon State College, 1955.

Welch, Joseph M. "A Study of Seasonal Movements of White-tailed Deer *(Odocoileus virginianus couesi)* in the Cave Creek Basin of the Chiricahua Mountains." Master's thesis, University of Arizona, 1960.

Whiteside, Richard W. "Evaluation of Hunter Utilization and Economic Characteristics of Deer Hunting on Selected Areas in Mississippi." Master's thesis, Mississippi State University, 1979.

Wiles, Gary Jr. "Movement and Use Patterns of White-tailed Deer Visiting Natural Licks." Master's thesis, Purdue University, 1951.

Wozencraft, Wallace Christopher. "Investigations Concerning a High Density White-tailed Deer Population in South Central Wisconsin." Master's thesis, University of Wisconsin-Madison, 1978.

Zagata, Michael DeForest. "Range and Movement of Iowa Deer in Relation to Pilot Knob State Park, Iowa." Ph.D. diss., Iowa State University, 1972.

Wildlife Monographs

Anderson, Allen E., Dean E. Medin, and David C. Bowden. *Growth and Morphometry of the Carcass, Selected Bones, Organs, and Glands of Mule Deer.* Wildlife Monograph no. 39. Washington, D.C.: The Wildlife Society, 1974. 122 pp.

Harper, James A., Joseph H. Harn, Wallace W. Bentley, and Charles F. Yocom. *The Status and Ecology of the Roosevelt Elk in California.* Wildlife Monograph no. 16. Washington, D.C.: The Wildlife Society, 1967. 49 pp.

Hirth, David H. *Social Behavior of White-tailed Deer in Relation to Habitat.* Wildlife Monograph no. 53. Washington, D.C.: The Wildlife Society, 1977. 55 pp.

Mackie, Richard J. *Range Ecology and Relations of Mule Deer, Elk, and Cattle in the Missouri River Breaks, Montana.* Wildlife Monograph no. 20. Washington, D.C.: The Wildlife Society, 1970. 79 pp.

Nelson, Michael E., and L. David Mech. *Deer Social Organization and Wolf Predation in Northeastern Minnesota.* Wildlife Monograph no. 77. Washington, D.C.: The Wildlife Society, 1981. 53 pp.

Peek, James M., David L. Urich, and Richard J. Mackie. *Moose Habitat Selection and Relationships to Forest Management in Northeastern Minnesota.* Wildlife Monograph no. 48. Washington, D.C.: The Wildlife Society, 1976. 65 pp.

Teer, James G., Jack W. Thomas, and Eugene A. Walker. *Ecology and Management of White-tailed Deer in the Llano Basin of Texas.* Wildlife Monograph no. 15. Washington, D.C.: The Wildlife Society, 1965. 62 pp.

Woolf, Alan, and John D. Harder. *Population Dynamics of a Captive White-tailed Deer Herd with Emphasis on Reproduction and Mortality.* Wildlife Monograph no. 67. Washington, D.C.: The Wildlife Society, 1979. 53 pp.

Technical Journals and Popular Magazines

Archery World. Winter Sports Publishing, Inc., 11812 Wayzata Blvd., Minnetonka, MN 55343. Eight issues annually.

Australian Deer. Australian Deer Association, P.O. Box 242, Camberwell 3124. Six issues annually.

Bow & Arrow Hunting. Gallant/Charger Publications, Inc., 34249 Camino Capistrano, Capistrano Beach, CA 92624. Six issues annually.

Bowhunter. Blue-J, Inc., 3808 S. Calhoun Street, Fort Wayne, IN 46807. Seven issues annually.

The Browse Line. Pennsylvania Deer Association, P.O. Box 864, Mt. Wolf, PA 17347. Six issues annually.

Bugle: The Quarterly Journal of the Rocky Mountain Elk Foundation. The Rocky Mountain Elk Foundation, Ltd., Route 3, Wilderness Plateau, Troy, MT 59935. Quarterly.

California Fish and Game. California Department of Fish and Game, 1416 Ninth Street, Sacramento, CA 95814. Quarterly.

Carnivore: Interfacing Biology, Anthropology and Environmental Studies. Sierra Nevada College Press, 800 College Drive, Incline Village, NV 89450-4269. Quarterly.

Cynegeticus: A Publication Devoted to the Interdisciplinary Study of Hunting. Box 315, Helena, MT 59624. Quarterly.

Deer & Deer Hunting. The Stump Sitters, Inc., P.O. Box 1117, Appleton, WI 54912. Six issues annually.

Deerhunters United. Deerhunters United, Inc., 3329 Ocmulgee E. Blvd., P.O. Box 66, Macon, GA 31202.

Deer: Journal of the British Deer Society. British Deer Society, Church Farm, Lower Basildon, Reading, Berkshire RG8 9NH. Quarterly.

The Deer Trail. Whitetails Unlimited, Inc., P.O. Box 422, Sturgeon Bay, WI 54235. Quarterly.

Gray's Sporting Journal. Gray's Sporting Journal, Inc., 205 Willow Street, South Hamilton, MA 01982. Quarterly.

Human Dimensions in Wildlife Newsletter. Yale School of Forestry and Environmental Studies, 205 Prospect Street, New Haven, CT 06511. Quarterly.

Jäger. Jahr-Verlag GmbH and Co., Burchardstrasse 14, 2000 Hamburg 1. Monthly.

Journal of the American Trophy Hunter. American Trophy Hunters Association, Inc. P.O. Box 16307, San Antonio, TX 78216. Six issues annually.

Journal of Environmental Education. Helen Dwight Reid Educational Foundation, 4000 Albemarle St., N.W., Washington D.C. 20016. Quarterly.

Journal of Leisure Research. National Recreation and Park Association, 3101 Park Center Drive, Alexandria, VA 22302. Quarterly.

Journal of Mammalogy. The American Society of Mammalogists, Department of Zoology, Brigham Young University, Provo, UT 84602. Quarterly.

Journal of Sport History. North American Society for Sport History, 101 White Building, Pennsylvania State University, University Park, PA 16802. Three issues annually.

Journal of Wildlife Management. The Wildlife Society, 5410 Grosvenor Lane, Bethesda, MD 20814. Quarterly.

Leisure Sciences: An Interdisciplinary Journal. Crane, Russak and Company, Inc., 3 East 44th Street, New York, NY 10017. Quarterly.

New Zealand Wildlife: The Journal for Hunters & Shooters. The New Zealand Deerstalkers' Association Incorporated, P.O. Box 6514, Wellington.

New York Fish and Game Journal. New York State Department of Environmental Conservation, Wildlife Resources Center, Delmar, NY 12054. Semiannually.

North American Whitetail. Game & Fish Publications, Inc. 2121 Newmarket Parkway, Suite 136, Marietta, GA 30067. Eight issues annually.

Pennsylvania Game News. Pennsylvania Game Commission, 8000 Derry St., Harrisburg, PA 17105-1567. Monthly.

Petersen's Hunting. Petersen's Hunting Magazine, P.O. Box 3353, Los Angeles, CA 90078. Monthly.

Proceedings of the Annual Conference of the Southeastern Association of Fish and Wildlife Agencies. An annual.

Proceedings of the Annual Conference of the Western Association of Fish and Wildlife Agencies. An annual.

The Professional Bowhunter Magazine. Professional Bowhunters Society, P.O. Box 5275, Charlotte, NC 28225. Quarterly.

Sporting Classics. Indigo Press, Inc., Highway 521, South Camden, SC 29020. Six issues annually.

Transactions of the North American Wildlife and Natural Resources Conference. Wildlife Management Institute, 1101 14th Street, N.W., Suite 725, Washington D.C. 20005. An annual.

Western Bowhunter. P.O. Box 511, Squaw Valley, CA 93646. Monthly.

"Whitetales": The Official Newsletter of the Minnesota Deer Hunters Association. Minnesota Deer Hunters Association, P.O. Box 413, Grand Rapids, MN 55744. Quarterly.

Wildlife Review. Office of Information Transfer, Editorial Section, U.S. Fish and Wildlife Service, 1025 Pennock Place, Fort Collins, CO 80524. Quarterly.

Wildlife Society Bulletin. The Wildlife Society, 5410 Grosvenor Lane, Bethesda, MD 20814. Quarterly.

Articles in Journals and Magazines

Allen, Glover M. "History of the Virginia Deer in New England: Part I." *The Game Breeder* 7(1929):203–204, 212–224.

———. "History of the Virginia Deer in New England: Part II." *The Game Breeder* 8(1929):235–236, 254, 256.

Applegate, James E. "Some Factors Associated With Attitudes Toward Deer Hunting in New Jersey Residents." *Transactions of the Thirty-Eighth North American Wildlife and Natural Resources Conference* 38(1973): 267–273.

———. "Deer and the People of New Jersey." *New Jersey Outdoors* 23 (February/March 1973):3–9.

———. "Attitudes Toward Deer Hunting in New Jersey: A Second Look." *Wildlife Society Bulletin* 3, no. 1 (1975):3–6.

———. "Attitudes toward Deer Hunting in New Jersey: A Decline in Opposition." *Wildlife Society Bulletin* 7, no. 2 (1979): 127–129.

———. "Attitudes Toward Deer Hunting in New Jersey: 1972–1982." *Wildlife Society Bulletin* 12, no. 1 (1984):19–22.

Brown, Perry J., Jacob E. Hautaluoma, and S. Morton McPhail. "Colorado Deer Hunting Experiences." *Transactions of the Forty-Second North American Wildlife and Natural Resources Conference* 42(1977): 216–225.

Burk, C. John. "The Kaibab Deer Incident: A Long-persisting Myth." *BioScience* 23, no. 2 (1973):113–114.

Burt, Charles J. "White-tailed Deer Hunter Attitudes in East-Central New York. *Wildlife Society Bulletin* 8, no. 2 (1980):142–149.

Clutton-Brock, T. H. "Red Deer and Man." *National Geographic* 170, no. 4 (1986):538–562.

Connolly, Guy. "Deer Hunting in Mendocino County, California." *Deer: Journal of the British Deer Society* 4, no. 8 (1979):438–442.

Decker, Daniel J., Tommy L. Brown, and William Sarbello. "Attitudes of Residents in the Peripheral Adirondacks Toward Illegally Killing Deer." *New York Fish and Game Journal* 28, no. 1 (1981):73–80.

Decker, Daniel J., Robert A. Smolka Jr., Nick Sanyal, and Tommy L. Brown. "Hunter Reaction to a Proposed Deer Management Initiative in Northern New York: Antecedents to Support or Opposition." *Transactions of the Fortieth North East Fish and Wildlife Conference* 40(1983):76–93.

Decker, Daniel J., George F. Mattfeld, and Tommy L. Brown. "Influence of Experience with Deer Damage on Farmers' Perception of Deer Population Trends." *New York Fish and Game Journal* 31, no. 1 (1984):38–44.

Elder, William H. "Primeval Deer Hunting Pressures Revealed by Remains from American Indian Middens." *Journal of Wildlife Management* 29, no. 2 (1965):366–370.

Etling, Kathy. "Can Science Produce a Race of Super Bucks?" *Outdoor Life* (January 1985):21–23, 46–47.

———. "The Deer Ph.Ds." *Outdoor Life* (June 1985):34–35, 94–96.

———. "Secrets of the Licking Branch." *Outdoor Life* (July 1986):51–53, 88, 90–91.

Fleming, Kay M. "Quality White-tailed Deer Management on an East Texas Hunting Club." *Proceedings of the Annual Conference of the Southeastern Association of Fish and Wildlife Agencies* 37(1983):118–126.

Fobes, Charles B. "Weather and the Kill of White-tailed Deer in Maine." *Journal of Wildlife Management* 9, no. 1 (1945):76–78.

Gafford, Charlotte. "The Deer Jackers." *Country Journal* (February 1978):72–81.

Geist, Valerius. "Neanderthal the Hunter." *Game News* (April 1983):3–9.

———. "The Paradox of the Great Irish Stags." *Natural History* 95, no. 3 (1986): 54–65.

Gladfelter, Lee. "The Compound Bow: Good News and Bad News." *Iowa Conservationist* (January 1983):20–22.

Gladfelter, H. Lee, James M. Kienzler, and Kenneth J. Koehler. "Effects of Compound Bow Use on Deer Hunter Success and Crippling Rates in Iowa." *Wildlife Society Bulletin* 11, no. 1 (1983):7–12.

Glover, Ronald L. "Detecting Lead in 'Arrow' Wounds in Deer Using Rhodizonic Acid." *Wildlife Society Bulletin* 9, no. 3 (1981):216–219.

Hale, Robert. "My Ten-Point Buck." *New Yorker* 20, no. 4 (1944):78, 81.

Glover, Ronald L., and Thomas S. Baskett. "Locations and Timing of Closed-Season Deer Poaching Incidents in Missouri." *Transactions, Missouri Academy of Science* 17(1983):87–93.

———. "Socioeconomic Profiles of Missouri Deer Poachers: Management Applications." *Transactions of the Forty-Ninth North American Wildlife and Natural Resources Conference* 49(1984):104–11.

Grau, Gerald A., and Brenda L. Grau. "Effects of Hunting on Hunter Effort and White-tailed Deer Behavior." *Ohio Journal of Science* 80, no. 4 (1980):150–56.

Greenhorn. "Deer Hunting in Michigan: Part I." *Forest and Stream* 7, no. 24 (1877):369–70.

———. "Deer Hunting in Michigan: Part II." *Forest and Stream* 7, no. 25 (1877):385–86.

Guynn, David C., T. M. Lowe, and H. A. Jacobson. "An Evaluation of Mississippi Game and Fish Commission I & E Programs with Reference to Deer Hunting." *Proceedings of the Annual Conference of the Southeastern Association of Fish and Wildlife Agencies* 32(1979):759–64.

Guynn, David C., Sarah P. Mott, William D. Cotton, and Harry A. Jacobson. "Cooperative Management of White-tailed Deer on Private Lands in Mississippi." *Wildlife Society Bulletin* 11, no. 3 (1983):211–14.

Hamilton, Joe. "Quality Bucks: Exploding the Myth." *South Carolina Wildlife* 31, no. 5 (1984):30–35.

Hansen, Lonnie P., Charles M. Nixon, and Forrest Loomis. "Factors Affecting Daily and Annual Harvest of White-tailed Deer in Illinois." *Wildlife Society Bulletin* 14, no. 4 (1986):368–76.

Haugen, Arnold O. "Deer Hunting: Indian Style." *Michigan Conservation* 15, no. 5 (1946):8–11.

———. "Palefaces 'Get Hep' to Hiawatha's Fun." *Michigan Conservation* 16, no. 10 (1947):6, 13.

———. "Bow 'N' Arrow Hunting: Good Conservation." *Transactions of the Thirteenth North American Wildlife Conference* 13(1948):459–64.

Hautaluoma, Jacob, and Perry J. Brown. "Attributes of the Deer Hunting Experience: A Cluster-Analytic Study." *Journal of Leisure Research* 10, no. 4 (1978):271–87.

Heberlein, Thomas A. "Stalking the Wild Deer Hunter." *Wisconsin Natural Resources* 1, no. 6 (1977):4–6.

———. "Hunter's Choice and Other Good Ideas." *Wisconsin Natural Resources* 2, no. 6 (1978):8–11.

Heberlein, Thomas, and John Trent. "Sure, The Game Managers Like It, But Just How Do Wisconsin Hunters Feel About Hunter's Choice?" *Wisconsin Sportsman* (November/December 1982):47–49.

Heberlein, Thomas A., John N. Trent, and Robert M. Baumgartner. "The Influence of Hunter Density on Firearm Deer Hunters' Satisfaction: A Field Experiment." *Transactions of the Forty-Seventh North American Wildlife and Natural Resources Conference* 47(1982):665–76.

Hendee, John C. "A Multiple-Satisfaction Approach to Game Management." *Wildlife Society Bulletin* 2, no. 3 (1974):104–13.

Hendee, John C., and Dale R. Potter. "Hunters and Hunting: Management Implications of Research." *Proceedings of the Southern States Recreation Research Applied Workshop,* U.S. Forest Service, General Technical Report SE-9 (1975):137–61.

Hill, Harry et al. "Michigan Deer Hunters' Perceptions and Attitudes towards Law Enforcement." *Proceedings of the Western Association of Fish and Wildlife Agencies* 59(1979):50–75.

Holsworth, William N. "Hunting Efficiency and White-tailed Deer Density." *Journal of Wildlife Management* 37, no. 3 (1973): 336–42.

Hope, Jack E. "Hunters: Useful Pruners of Nature or Just Killers?" *The Smithsonian* 4, no. 10 (1974):78–82.

Jackson, Robert. "Improving Ethical Behavior in Hunters." *Transactions of the North American Wildlife and Natural Resources Conference* 44(1979):306–18.

———. "Compound Intensity: The Wisconsin Bowhunter." *Wisconsin Natural Resources* (September/October 1983):12–16.

Jackson, Robert, and Robert Norton. "Deer Hunting is a Family Affair." *Wisconsin Natural Resources* (November/December 1979):10–15.

———. "The Last Hunt." *Wisconsin Natural Resources.* (November/December 1980): 5–10.

———. "'Phases': The Personal Evolution of the Sport Hunter." *Wisconsin Sportsman* 9, no. 6 (1980):17–20.

Jackson, Robert M., and Ray Anderson. "The Deer Hunting Experience." *Deer & Deer Hunting* 8, no. 4 (1985):8–18.

Jackson, Robert M., and Stephen E. Legans. "The Pull of the Bow." *Deer & Deer Hunting* 10, no. 2 (1986):16–26.

Jager, Ronald. "Deer Hunter's Journal." *Country Journal* (November 1980):86–99.

James, George A., Frank M. Johnson, and Frank B. Barick. "Relations Between Hunter Access and Deer Kill in North Carolina." *Transactions of the North American Wildlife and Natural Resources Conference* 29(1964): 454–63.

Kaminsky, Michael A., and Robert H. Giles Jr. "An Analysis of Deer Spotlighting in Virginia." *Proceedings of the Twenty-Eighth Annual Conference of the Southeastern Association of Game and Fish Commissioners* 28(1974):729–40.

Kellert, Stephen R. "Attitudes and Characteristics of Hunters and Anti-Hunters." *Transactions of the North American Wildlife and Natural Resources Conference* 43(1978): 412–23.

Kennedy, James J. "Attitudes and Behavior of Deer Hunters in a Maryland Forest." *Journal of Wildlife Management* 38, no. 1 (1974):1–8.

Klessig, Lowell L. "Hunting: Savage Instinct or Communion with Nature." *Wisconsin Academy Review* 20, no. 1 (1973):12–14.

Kohl, Larry. "Pere David's Deer Saved from Extinction." *National Geographic* 162, no. 4 (1982):478–85.

Kozicky, Edward L. "Tomorrow's Hunters — Gadgeteers or Sportsmen?" *Wildlife Society Bulletin* 5, no. 4 (1977):175–78.

Kuser, John. "Deer Roadkill Triples in 'Closed' Township." *New Jersey Outdoors* 10, no. 2 (1983):18–19.

Lampton, B. F. "Controversy in the 'Glades." *Florida Wildlife* 36, no. 4 (1982):12–19.

———. "The Everglades Deer Hunt." *Iowa Conservationist* 42, no. 2 (1983):15–17.

Langenau, Edward E., and Phyllis M. Mellon. "Characteristics and Behaviors of Michigan 12- to 18-Year-Old Hunters." *Journal of Wildlife Management* 44, no. 1 (1980): 69–78.

Langenau, Edward E., and J. M. Aldrich. "Immigration, Emigration, and Return Rates Among Firearm Deer Hunters in Northern Lower Michigan." *Journal of Wildlife Management* 45, no. 2 (1981): 314–22.

Langenau, Edward E., Richard J. Moran, James R. Terry, and David C. Cue. "Relationship Between Deer Kill and Ratings of the Hunt." *Journal of Wildlife Management* 45, no. 4 (1981):959–64.

Leopold, A. Starker. "The Essence of Hunting." *National Wildlife,* 10 (October/November 1972):38–40.

Loftin, Robert W. "The Morality of Hunting." *Environmental Ethics* 6, no. 3 (1984): 241–50.

Lyons, Gene. "Politics in the Woods." *Harper's* 257 (July 1978):27–36, 38.

Lyons, James R. "The New York State Bowhunter Education Program: Characteristics of Participants and Program Effectiveness." *Transactions of the North East Fish and Wildlife Conference* 37(1980):134–49.

McCullough, Dale R., and William J. Carmen. "Management Goals for Deer Hunter Satisfaction." *Wildlife Society Bulletin* 10, no. 1 (1982):49–52.

McKean, John W. "Deer Hunter Preferences." *Proceedings of the Forty-Seventh Annual Conference of the Western Association of State Game and Fish Commissioners* 47(1967):221–27.

Marsters, A. DeForest. "Some Characteristics of New York Hunters." *New York Fish and Game Journal* 25, no. 1 (1978):72–78.

Miller, Ronald R. "Congestion, Success and the Value of Colorado Deer Hunting Experiences." *Transactions of the North American Wildlife and Natural Resources Conference* 42(1977):129–36.

Murie, Olaus J. "Ethics in Wildlife Management." *Journal of Wildlife Management* 18, no. 3 (1954):289–93.

Nelson, Michael E. "Group Life Insurance for Deer." *Animal Kingdom* (November/December 1985):32–35.

Newsom, William Monypeny. "Dope for the Deer Hunter." *Field & Stream* (October 1926):18–19, 67, 90.

———. "The Common Bobcat a Deer Killer." *American Game* (April/May 1930):42, 50.

———. "Where Are the Big Bucks?" *Outdoor Life* (January 1932):30–31, 52.

———. "Buck Fever." *Outdoor Life* (September 1933):17–#.

———. "How Fast Can a Deer Run." *Outdoor Life* (June 1937):50–51, 109.

———. "When is an Elk a Moose?" *Outdoor Life* (August 1935):32–33, 51.

———. "Don't Let Our Deer Starve." *Outdoor Life* (March 1935):33, 48.

———. "Where Big Antlers Grow." *Field & Stream* (October 1936):3336–37, 3373–75.

———. "Winter Notes on the Moose." *Journal of Mammalogy* 18(1937):347–49.

———. "Mammals on Anticosti Island." *Journal of Mammalogy* 18(1937):435–42.

———. "Live Weight vs. Dressed Weight." *Outdoor Life* (September 1939):60.

———. "Deer Shots." *Pennsylvania Game News* (December 1940):8–11.

Oskison, John. "With Apache Deer-Hunters in Arizona." *Outing* 64(April/May 1914):65–78, 150–63.

Ozoga, John J. "White-tailed Deer." *Michigan Natural Resources* (September/October 1985):27–28, 30–33.

Packard, George V. "Ancient Extravaganza in the Black Forest." *Sports Illustrated* 45(October 4, 1976):80–83t.

Peterle, Tony J. "The Hunter—Who is He?" *Transactions of the North American Wildlife and Natural Resources Conference* 26(1961):254–66.

———. "Hunters, Hunting, Anti-Hunting." *Wildlife Society Bulletin* 5, no. 4 (1977):151–61.

Peterle, Tony J. and Joseph E. Scott. "Characteristics of Some Ohio Hunters and Non-Hunters." *Journal of Wildlife Management* 41, no. 3 (1977):386–99.

Phillips, John E. "The Big Bad Bucks Make Great Hunting!" *Hunters Deer Hunting* 6, no. 1 (1987):28–32, 74–75.

Porath, Wayne R., Steven L. Sheriff, Daniel J. Witter, and Oliver Torgerson. "Deer Hunters: A Traditional Constituency in a Time of Change." *Proceedings of the International Association of Fish and Wildlife Agencies* 79(1980):41–53.

Potter, Dale R., John C. Hendee, and Roger N. Clark. "Hunting Satisfaction: Game, Guns, or Nature?" *Transactions of the North American Wildlife and Natural Resources Conference* 38(1973):220–29.

Reznak, Robert. "Northern Wisconsin's Under-Hunted Trophy Bucks." *Wisconsin Sportsman* (January/February 1983):40–41, 66–67.

Roseberry, J. L., D. C. Autry, W. D. Klimstra, and L. A. Mehrhoff Jr. "A Controlled Deer Hunt on Crab Orchard National Wildlife Refuge." *Journal of Wildlife Management* 33, no. 4 (1969):791–95.

Roseberry, John L., and W. D. Klimstra. "Differential Vulnerability During a Controlled Deer Harvest." *Journal of Wildlife Management* 38, no. 3 (1974):499–507.

Sasser, Ray. "Doctor of Deer." *Sports Afield* (July 1983):59–60, 101–102.

Sawhill, Gary S., and Robert Winkel. "Methodology and Behavioral Aspects of the Illegal Deer Hunter." *Proceedings of the Annual Conference of the Southeastern Association of Game and Fish Commissioners* 28(1974):715–19.

Scanion, John J., and Michael R. Vaughan. "Social Groupings of White-tailed Deer in Shenandoah National Park, Virginia." *Proceedings of the Annual Conference of the Southeastern Association of Fish and Wildlife Agencies* 37(1983):146–60.

Severinghaus, C. W., and Robert W. Darrow. "The Philosophy of Deer Management." *New York Conservationist* 31, no. 2 (1976): 18–19.

Sexson, Keith, Bill Hlavachick, and Wayne Van Zwoll. "Kansas Deer — Resource on the Rebound." *Kansas Wildlife* 42, no. 6 (1985): 9–24.

Shafer, Elwood L., Paul H. Amidon, and C. W. Severinghaus. "A Comparison of Violators and Nonviolators of New York's Deer-Hunting Laws." *Journal of Wildlife Management* 36, no. 3 (1972):933–39.

Shaw, Dale L., and D. L. Gilbert. "Attitudes of College Students Toward Hunting." *Transactions of the North American Wildlife and Natural Resources Conference* 39(1974):157–62.

Shaw, William W. "A Survey of Hunting Opponents." *Wildlife Society Bulletin* 5, no. 1 (1977):19–24.

Sheehan, Joe. "Deer Hunting Past, Present and Future." *Outdoor California* (July/August 1983):1–6.

Shepard, Paul Jr. "A Theory of the Value of Hunting." *Transactions of the North American Wildlife Conference* 24(1959):504–12.

Skeen, Samuel L. "On the Horns of a Dilemma." *The Country Gentleman* 130, no. 4 (1980):42–43, 64–70.

Smith, Mason. "Lone Watch in a Gold-Fobbed Forest." *Sports Illustrated* (November 25, 1974):58t.

Stankey, George H., Robert C. Lucas, and Robert R. Ream. "Relationships Between Hunting Success and Satisfaction." *Transactions of the North American Wildlife and Natural Resources Conference* 38(1973): 235–42.

Sturgis, Harold. "Twenty Years at McDonald Forest." *Oregon Wildlife* (July 1977):3–6.

Sturgis, Harold, and David De Calesta. "The Mac Forest Deer Hunt: A Second Look." *Oregon Wildlife* (September 1981):3–8.

Tress, Arthur. "Deer Dances I Have Seen." *Dance Magazine* (September 1968):59–61, 84–85.

Trippensee, R. E. "Cooperative Deer Hunting." *American Wildlife* (November/December 1935):87, 92t.

Van Dyke, Theodore Strong. "Shooting Running Deer." *Forest and Stream* (February 14, 1878):26–27.

———. "Hunting the Virginia Deer." *Outing* (October 1902):20–30.

———. "The Tracking of Deer." *Collier's Outdoor America* (October 16, 1909):20.

——— "The Ambitious Deer Hunter." *Collier's Outdoor America* (November 2, 1912):36.

Van Etten, Robert C., D. F. Switzenberg, and Lee Eberhardt. "Controlled Deer Hunting in a Square-Mile Enclosure." *Journal of Wildlife Management* 29, no. 1 (1965):59–73.

Weber, Andrew, Frank B. Barick, and Jerry Wood. "Calibration of Deer Hunting Effort and Success." *Proceedings of the Twentieth Annual Conference of the Southeastern Association of Game and Fish Commissioners* 20(1966):181–88.

Wegner, Robert A. "The Stumpsitters: Leopold's Prophesy Fulfilled?" *Cynegeticus: A Publication Devoted to the Interdisciplinary Study of Hunting* 3, no. 4 (1979):1–7.

Wennergren, E. Boyd, Herbert H. Fullerton, and Jim C. Wrigley. "Quality Values and Determinants for Deer Hunting." *Journal of Wildlife Management* 41, no. 3 (1977):400–407.

Wheelwright, Jeff. "Deer Week." *Country Journal* (November 1976):54–5, 58–61.

Whiteside, Richard W., David C. Guynn, Jr., and Harry A. Jacobson. "Characteristics and Opinions of Mississippi Deer Hunters Using Public Areas." *Proceedings of the An-*

nual *Conference of the Southeastern Association of Fish and Wildlife Agencies* 35(1981):167–73.

———. "Characteristics and Expenditures of Deer Hunters Using Two Areas in Mississippi." *Wildlife Society Bulletin* 9, no. 3 (1981):226–29.

Winkler, Charles K. "Deer Management Plans for Private Lands in Texas." *Proceedings of the Annual Conference of the Southeastern Association of Fish and Wildlife Agencies* 37(1983):14–18.

Woolf, Alan, John L. Roseberry, and John Will. "Estimating Time of Death of Deer in Illinois." *Wildlife Society Bulletin* 11, no. 1 (1983):47–51.

Wright, Charles. "Deer and Deer-Hunting in Texas." *American Naturalist* 2(1869):466–76.

Young, Craig E. "Tree Rings and Kaibab North Deer Hunting Success, 1925–1975." *Journal of Arizona-Nevada Academy of Science* 14, no. 3 (1979):61–65.

Conservation Bulletins, University Publications, Extension Reports, Pittman-Robertson Reports, Proceedings of Symposiums and Miscellaneous Publications

Allen, Thomas J., and Jack I. Cromer. 1977. *White-tailed Deer in West Virginia*. West Virginia Department of Natural Resources, Bulletin no. 7.

Anderson, Donald D. 1964. *The Status of Deer in Kansas*. State Biological Survey of Kansas, Misc. Pub. no. 39.

Applegate, James, James R. Lyons, and Peter J. Plage. N.d. *Dynamic Aspects of the American Sport Hunting Population: An Analysis Based on the 1980 National Survey of Fishing, Hunting, and Wildlife-Associated Recreation*. The U.S. Fish and Wildlife Service, New Jersey.

Applegate, James E., and Ralph A. Otto. 1982. *Characteristics of First-Year Hunters in New Jersey*. New Jersey Agricultural Experiment Station, Publication no. R-12381-(1)-82.

Bailey, William Jr., George Schildman, and Phillip Agee. 1957. *Nebraska Deer*. Nebraska Game, Forestation and Parks Commission.

Banasiak, Chester F. 1961. *Deer in Maine*. Maine Department of Inland Fisheries and Game, Game Division Bulletin no. 6.

Bardwell, Flora, J. B. Low, and Ethelwyn B. Wilcox. 1968. *Venison: Field Care & Cooking*. Utah State Division of Fish and Game, Pub. no. 68-10.

Bartlett, Charles O. 1958. *A Study of Some Deer and Forest Relationships in Rondeau Provincial Park*. Ontario Department of Lands and Forest, Wildlife Series no. 7.

Beattie, Kirk H., ed. N.d. *Environmental Law Enforcement Theory and Principles: A Sourcebook*. College of Natural Resources, University of Wisconsin-Stevens Point, Vol. nos. 1 & 2, NR 440/640.

Beattie, Kirk and Richard Winstead. 1983. *Statistical Analysis of Wisconsin Hunting Accidents*. College of Natural Resources, University of Wisconsin-Stevens Point.

Bennett, C. L. Jr., L. A. Ryel, and L. J. Hawn. 1966. *A History of Michigan Deer Hunting*. Michigan Department of Conservation, Report no. 85.

Benson, Denis A., and Donald G. Dodds. 1977. *The Deer of Nova Scotia*. Department of Lands & Forests-Province of Nova Scotia.

Bevins, Malcolm I., et al. 1968. *Characteristics of Hunters and Fishermen in Six Northeastern States*. University of Vermont, Bulletin no. 656.

Biehn, Earl R. 1951. *Crop Damage by Wildlife in California, With Special Emphasis on Deer and Waterfowl*. California Department of Fish and Game, Game Bulletin no. 5.

Burke, David, et al. 1980. *New Jersey's White-tailed Deer*. New Jersey Division of Fish, Game and Wildlife, Deer Report no. 7.

Cahalane, Victor H. 1932. *Age Variation in the Teeth and Skull of the Whitetail Deer*. Cranbrook Institute of Science, Scientific Pub. no. 2.

Calhoun, John, and Forrest Loomis. N.d. *Prairie Whitetails*. Illinois Department of Conservation.

Caslick, James. 1982. *Venison: Boning, Freezing, & Cooking*. Cornell University, Miscellaneous Bulletin no. 99.

Craven, Scott. 1980. *Controlling Deer Damage in Wisconsin*. University of Wisconsin-Extension, no. G3083.

Craven, Scott, and Dennis Buege. 1979. *So You Got a Deer*. University of Wisconsin-Extension/Madison, no. G1598.

Cue, David C. 1978. *Firearm Deer Hunter Densities and Satisfaction: A Preliminary Report*. Michigan Pittman-Robertson Project W-117-R.

Cue, David C., and Edward E. Langenau. 1979. *Satisfaction and Deer Hunter Density*. Michigan Pittman-Robertson Project W-117-R, Michigan Department of Natural Resources, Wildlife Division Report no. 2848.

Davis, James R. 1979. *The White-tailed Deer in Alabama*. Alabama Department of Conservation and Natural Resources Special Report no. 8.

Davis, William C. 1967. *Values of Hunting and Fishing in Arizona in 1965*. University of Arizona.

Davison, Michael A. 1979. *Columbian White-tailed Deer Status and Potential on Off Refuge Habitat*. Washington State Department of Game.

Day, Benjamin W. Jr. 1964. *The White-tailed Deer in Vermont*. Vermont Fish and Game Department, Wildlife Bulletin no. 64–1.

DeLong, James W., Robert T. Wagner, and Robert M. Dimit. 1976. *Factors Associated With Varying Attitudes Among South Dakotans Toward Hunting, Hunters and Game Officials*. South Dakota State University, Report no. 6.

Dickinson, Nathaniel R., and Lawrence E. Garland. 1974. *The White-tailed Deer Resource of Vermont*. Vermont Fish and Game Department.

Doll, G. Fred, S. T. Mast, and Judy Denison. 1986. *Deer Hunter Perceptions and Preferences, Wyoming 1986*. University of Wyoming, Institute for Policy Research.

Donaldson, David, Carl Hunter, and T. H. Holder. 1951. *Arkansas' Deer Herd*. Arkansas Game and Fish Commission.

Dunn, Charlotte M. 1979. *Now It's Venison*. University of Wisconsin-Extension, no. B2095.

Erickson, Arnold B., et al. 1961. *The White-tailed Deer of Minnesota*. Minnesota Department of Conservation, Technical Bulletin no. 5.

Faunce, R. Frederick, Alan S. Kezis, and Gregory K. White. 1979. *Characteristics of Maine's Resident and Non-resident Hunters*. University of Maine at Orono, Bulletin no. 760.

Fitch, Vincent. 1970. *You, Too, Can Fillet Your Own Deer or Moose or Elk*. Delano, Minnesota.

Fitzhugh, E. Lee, and W. Paul Gorenzel. 1983. *How to Field Dress a Deer*. Cooperative Extension, Division of Agricultural Sciences, University of California, Leaflet no. 21364.

Foote, Leonard E. 1946. *Vermont's Wild Game Resource: A Study of the Vermont Hunter*. Vermont Fish and Game Service.

Forbes, Stanley E., et al. 1971. *The White-tailed Deer in Pennsylvania*. Pennsylvania Game Commission, Research Bulletin no. 170.

Garrett, James R. 1970. *Characteristics of Nevada Hunters*. University of Nevada-Reno, no. B22.

Giessman, Norbert F., and Eileen M. Dowd. 1983. *Deer in Missouri, 1983*. Missouri Department of Conservation.

———. 1984. *Deer in Missouri, 1984*. Missouri Department of Conservation.

Giessman, Norbert F., and Dean A. Murphy. 1982. *Missouri Deer Hunting*. Missouri Conservation Commission.

Gilbert, Alphonse H. 1977. *Vermont Hunters: Characteristics, Attitudes, and Levels of Participation*. University of Vermont, Misc. Pub. no. 92.

Gill, John D. 1956. *Review of Deer Yard Management*. Maine Department of Inland Fisheries and Game, Game Division Bulletin no. 5.

Guynn, David C. Jr., Thomas Michael Lowe, and Harry A. Jacobson. 1980. *Characteristics and Attitudes of Mississippi Deer Hunters*. Mississippi Department of Conservation, Project no. W-48-25, Job no. VII-C, Information Sheet no. 1300.

Hailey, Tommy L. 1979. *Basics of Brush Management for White-tailed Deer Production*.

Texas Parks and Wildlife Department, Booklet no. 7000–35.

Halls, Lowell K., and Thomas H. Ripley, eds. 1961. *Deer Browse Plants of Southern Forests*. Forest Service, U.S. Department of Agriculture.

Halls, Lowell K., ed. 1969. *White-tailed Deer in the Southern Forest Habitat: Proceedings of a Symposium at Nacogdoches, Texas*. Forest Service, U.S. Department of Agriculture.

Hansen, Christopher S. 1978. *Social Costs of Michigan's Deer Habitat Improvement Program*. Michigan Department of Natural Resources, Wildlife Division Report no. 2808.

Harlow, Richard F. 1959. *An Evaluation of White-tailed Deer Habitat in Florida*. Florida Game and Fresh Water Fish Commission, Technical Bulletin no. 5.

Harmel, Donnie E., and George W. Litton. 1981. *Deer Management in the Edwards Plateau of Texas*. Texas Parks and Wildlife Department, Booklet no. 7000–86.

Harris, L. H. 1981. *White-tailed Deer in New Zealand*. New Zealand Forest Service, New Zealand Wildlife.

Heberlein, Thomas A., and Bruce Laybourne. 1978. *The Wisconsin Deer Hunter: Social Characteristics, Attitudes, and Preferences for Proposed Hunting Season Changes*. University of Wisconsin-Madison, Working Paper no. 10.

Heeringa, Steven G. 1984. *American Public Attitudes Toward Hunting*. University of Michigan.

———. 1985. *1985 Sportsmen's Leadership Survey, Part 1: Sportsmen's Role in Grass Roots Information and Education Programs*. University of Michigan.

———. 1985. *1985 Sportsmen's Leadership Survey, Part II: Sportsmen's Views on the Major Issues and Problems Facing America's Hunters, Fishermen and Trappers*. University of Michigan.

———. 1985. *1985 Study of American Hunting Issues: A Comparison of Views Held by Sportsmen's Leaders, Wildlife Professionals and Outdoor Writers*. University of Michigan.

Hepburn, R. L. 1968. *Experimental Management of Mixed Conifer Swamps for Deer and Timber in Eastern Ontario*. Department of Lands and Forests, Section Report (Wildlife) no. 69.

Hosley, N. W. 1968. *Selected References on Management of White-tailed Deer, 1910 to 1966*. United States Department of the Interior, Special Scientific Report—Wildlife no. 112.

International Association of Fish and Wildlife Agencies. 1981. *Hunter Education in the United States and Canada With Recommendations for Improvement*. Fish and Wildlife Service, U.S. Department of the Interior.

Jacobson, Harry A. 1983. *Movements of Adult Male White-tailed Deer During the Deer Hunting Season in Mississippi*. Mississippi Department of Wildlife Conservation, Study XVI.

Jenkins, David H., and Ilo H. Bartlett. 1959. *Michigan Whitetails*. Michigan Department of Conservation.

Kabat, C., et al. 1962. *Deer-Forest Interrelationships in Forest Land Management*. Wisconsin Conservation Department.

Kabat, Cyril, Nicholas E. Collias, and Ralph C. Guettinger. 1953. *Some Winter Habits of White-tailed Deer and the Development of Census Methods in the Flag Yard of Northern Wisconsin*. Wisconsin Conservation Department, Technical Wildlife Bulletin no. 7.

Kellert, Stephen R. 1979. *Public Attitudes Toward Critical Wildlife and Natural Habitat Issues—Phase I*. United States Department of the Interior.

———. 1980. *Activities of the American Public Relating to Animals—Phase II*. United States Department of the Interior.

———. 1980. *Knowledge, Affection and Basic Attitudes Toward Animals in American Society—Phase III*. United States Department of the Interior.

———. 1981. *Trends in Animal Use and Perception in Twentieth Century—Phase IV*. United States Department of the Interior.

Kimball, Thomas L., and Allan G. Watkins. 1951. *The Kaibab North Cooperative Deer—Livestock Forage Relationship Study*. Arizona Game and Fish Commission and United States Forest Service.

Kittredge, Doug, et al. N.d. *How to Hunt Deer with Bow and Arrow.* Kittredge Bow Hut, Mammoth Lakes, California.

Klessig, Lowell L., and James B. Hale. 1972. *A Profile of Wisconsin Hunters.* Wisconsin Department of Natural Resources, Technical Bulletin no. 60.

Kogan, A. Alan. 1983. *Deer Herd Health Evaluation.* Oklahoma Department of Wildlife Conservation.

Kozicky, Ed, and John Madson. 1975. *Anti-Hunting: A Wasteful Issue.* Conservation Department, Winchester Group, Olin Corporation.

Krämer, August. N.d. *A Review of the Ecological Relationships Between Mule and White-tailed Deer.* Alberta Lands and Forests Department, Occasional Paper no. 3.

Krefting, Laurits W. 1964. *Research for Deer Management in the Great Lakes Region: A Contribution of the Great Lakes Deer Group.* The Great Lakes Deer Group.

Lang, E. M. 1957. *Deer of New Mexico.* New Mexico Department of Game and Fish, Bulletin no. 5.

Langenau, Edward E. Jr. 1979. *Human Dimensions in the Management of White-tailed Deer: A Review of Concepts and Literature.* Michigan Department of Natural Resources, Wildlife Division Report no. 2846.

———. 1980. *Deer Hunting Success: Skill or Luck?* Michigan Department of Natural Resources, Wildlife Division Report no. 2873.

———. 1985. *Evaluation of Michigan's 2-Deer Law.* Unpublished paper, Michigan Department of Natural Resources.

Langenau, E. E. Jr., G. E. Burgoyne Jr., and G. M. Bragdon. 1977. *Field Interviews of Firearm Deer Hunters Using Experimental Clearcuttings.* Michigan Department of Natural Resources, Wildlife Division Report no. 2776.

Langenau, Edward E. Jr., et al. 1980. *Effects of Deer Density on Hunting Quality: Management, Policy, and Theoretical Implications.* Michigan Department of Natural Resources, Wildlife Division Report no. 2866.

Langenau, Edward E. Jr., and Julie M. Aldrich. 1981. *Notes on the Accuracy of Field Biologists' Perception of Characteristics of Firearm Deer Hunters.* Michigan Pittman-Robertson Project W-117-R.

Lantz, D. E. 1908. *Deer Farming in the United States.* U.S. Department of Agriculture, Farmers' Bulletin no. 330.

Laramie, Henry A. Jr., and David L. White. 1964. *Some Observations Concerning Hunting Pressure and Harvest on White-tailed Deer.* New Hampshire Fish and Game Department, Technical Circular no. 20.

Latham, Roger M. no. 1950. *Pennsylvania's Deer Problem.* Special Issue no. 1. *Pennsylvania Game News.* Pennsylvania Game Commission.

Laub, Kenneth. 1975. *Wildlife Conservation in Ohio: The Role of Hunting and Trapping.* Ohio Department of Natural Resources, Pub. no. 273.

Leopold, A. Starker, et al. 1951. *The Jawbone Deer Herd.* California Department of Natural Resources, Game Bulletin no. 4.

Lindzey, James S. 1950. *The White-tailed Deer in Oklahoma: Management and Production.* Pittman-Robertson Project no. 37 R, Oklahoma Game and Fish Department.

Longhurst, William M., A. Starker Leopold, and Raymond F. Dasmann. 1952. *A Survey of California Deer Herds: Their Ranges and Management Problems.* California Department of Fish and Game, Game Bulletin no. 6.

McAninch, Jay B., Mark R. Ellingwood, and Raymond J. Winchcombe. 1983. *Deer Damage Control in New York Agriculture.* New York State Department of Agriculture and Markets.

McCaffery, Keith R., and William A. Creed. 1969. *Significance of Forest Openings to Deer in Northern Wisconsin.* Wisconsin Department of Natural Resources, Technical Bulletin no. 44.

McCulloch, Clay Y., and Philip J. Urness. 1973. *Deer Nutrition in Arizona Chaparral and Desert Habitats.* Arizona Game and Fish Department, Special Report no. 3.

McDowell, Robert. 1980. *The Rate of Non-Reporting Legal Bow and Arrow Deer Kills in New Jersey.* Transactions of the Northeast Wildlife Conference 57:129–133.

McDowell, Robert, ed. 1974. *New Jersey's White-tailed Deer, 1973–1974.* New Jersey Division of Fish, Game and Shellfisheries, Report no. 1.

———. 1976. *New Jersey's White-tailed Deer, 1975–1976.* New Jersey Division of Fish, Game and Shellfisheries, Report no. 3.

———. 1977. *New Jersey's White-tailed Deer, 1976–1977.* New Jersey Division of Fish, Game and Shellfisheries, Report no. 4.

———. 1978. *New Jersey's White-tailed Deer, 1977–1978.* New Jersey Division of Fish, Game and Shellfisheries, Report no. 5.

McGuiness, Dan. N.d. *Bowhunting the Bay State.* Massachusetts Division of Fisheries and Wildlife, Publication no. 12620-44-500-12-81-C.R.

Madson, John, and Ed Kozicky. *For the Young Hunter.* Conservation Department, Olin Corporation.

———. 1971. *Game, Gunners and Biology.* Winchester Press.

Mann, Kurt C. S., ed. 1952. *The Deer of California—A Guide for the California Hunter.* Associated Sport Publications, Ltd.

Marriott, N. G., et al. 1980. *Deer Processing for the Sportsman.* Extension Division Virginia Polytechnic Institute and State University, Publication no. 877.

Masters, Raymond, ed. 1978. *Deer Trapping, Marking and Telemetry Techniques.* State University College of Environmental Science and Forestry.

Melnyk, Michael J. 1978. *Factors Associated With Wildlife Law Violation in Alberta.* Alberta Recreation, Parks and Wildlife-Fish and Wildlife Division.

———. 1977. *Hunter Attitudes Toward Alberta's Wildlife Laws and Wildlife Officers.* Alberta Recreation, Parks and Wildlife-Fish and Wildlife Division.

Moore, George C. 1977. *The Louisiana Deer Story.* Louisiana Department of Wildlife and Fisheries, Wildlife Education Bulletin no. 108.

Mustard, Eldie W., and Vernon Wright. 1963. *Food Habits of Iowa Deer.* Iowa State Conservation Commission.

New Jersey Division of Fish, Game and Wildlife. 1981. *A Study of the New Jersey Deer Herd.* Project no. W-45-R-17.

Northeast-Southeast Deer Study Group Meeting, September 6–8, 1977. Northeast-Southeast Deer Study Group Proceedings.

Park, Barry C., and Bessie B. Day. 1942. *A Simplified Method for Determining the Condition of White-tailed Deer Herds in Relation to Available Forage.* United States Department of Agriculture, Technical Bulletin no. 840.

Pearce, John. 1937. *The Effects of Deer Browsing on Certain Western Adirondack Forest Types.* Roosevelt Wildlife Forest Experiment Station at the New York State College of Forestry, Syracuse, New York. Roosevelt Wildlife Bulletin, Volume 7, no. 1.

Peery, Charles, and Joe Coggin. 1978. *Virginia's White-tailed Deer.* Virginia Commission of Game and Inland Fisheries.

Perkins, Jim R. 1979. *Supplemental Feeding.* Texas Parks and Wildlife Department, Booklet no. 7000–33.

Pils, Charles M., Mark A. Martin, and James R. March. 1981. *Foods of Deer in Southern Wisconsin.* Wisconsin Department of Natural Resources, Report no. 112.

Pils, Charles M. 1981. *The White-tailed Deer in Governor Dodge State Park.* Wisconsin Department of Natural Resources, Report no. 109.

Pomerantz, Gerri Ann. 1977. *Young People's Attitudes Toward Wildlife.* Michigan Department of Natural Resources, Wildlife Division Report no. 2781.

Porath, Wayne R., Daniel J. Witter, and Steven L. Sheriff. 1980. *Deer Hunter Information Survey.* Missouri Department of Conservation, Study no. XLIII.

Rice, William W., ed. N.d. *What About Bowhunting?* New York State Field Archers Association.

Richardson, Arthur H., and Lyle E. Petersen. 1974. *History and Management of South Dakota Deer.* South Dakota Department of Game, Fish and Parks, Bulletin no. 5.

Rogers, Lynn L., Jack J. Mooty, and Deanna Dawson. 1981. *Foods of White-tailed Deer in the Upper Great Lakes Region—A Review.*

U.S. Department of Agriculture-Forest Service, General Technical Report no. NC-65.

Rossman, George, and Allen Rossman. 1959. *Whitetail Country. Grand Rapids Herald-Review,* Grand Rapids, Minnesota.

Russo, John P. 1970. *The Kaibab North Deer Herd: Its History, Problems and Management.* Arizona Game and Fish Department, Wildlife Bulletin no. 7.

Safari Club International. N.d. *Profile: The Issue Is Hunting.* Safari Club International Conservation Fund.

Schole, Bernhard J. 1973. *A Literature Review on Characteristics of Hunters.* Colorado Division of Wildlife, Wildlife Research Section and Cooperative Wildlife Research Unit, Special Report no. 33.

Sexson, Keith. 1984. *Deer Population Dynamics and Harvest Trends—Annual Report, 1983.* Kansas Fish and Game Commission.

———. 1985. *Deer Population Dynamics and Harvest Trends—Annual Report, 1984.* Kansas Fish and Game Commission.

Shaw, Samuel P., and P. LeRoy Wilson Jr. 1951. *The Management of White-tailed Deer in Massachusetts.* Massachusetts Division of Fisheries and Game, Bulletin no. 13.

Shaw, William W. 1975. *Attitudes Toward Hunting: A Study of Some Social and Psychological Determinants.* Michigan Department of Natural Resources, Wildlife Division Report no. 2740.

Shaw, William W., and Ervin H. Zube, eds. 1980. *Wildlife Values.* University of Arizona-School of Renewable Natural Resources, Institutional Series Report no. 1.

Shissler, Bryon P. 1985. *White-tailed Deer Biology and Management in Pennsylvania: Wildlife Management on Private Lands.* Wildlife Managers.

Silver, Helenette, and N. F. Colovos. 1957. *Nutritive Evaluation of Some Forage Rations of Deer.* New Hampshire Fish and Game Department, Technical Circular no. 15.

Solee, Barbara, and Phyllis Solee. 1977. *Venison Recipes: Family Tested.* Sunny Isle Enterprises, Crookston, Minnesota.

Southeast Deer Study Group Meeting, February 26–29, 1984, Abstracts. Southeast Deer Study Group.

Southeast Deer Study Group Meeting, February 17–20, 1985, Abstracts. Southeast Deer Study Group.

Southeast Deer Study Group Meeting, March 2–5, 1986, Abstracts. Southeast Deer Study Group.

Spencer, Gary E. 1983. *Pineywoods Deer Management.* Texas Parks and Wildlife Department, Bulletin no. 7000–88.

Stanton, Don C. 1963. *A History of the White-tailed Deer in Maine.* Maine Department of Inland Fisheries and Game, Game Division Bulletin no. 8.

Stoll, Robert J., and Gregory L. Mountz. 1983. *Rural Landowner Attitudes Toward Deer and Deer Populations in Ohio.* Ohio Department of Natural Resources, Division of Wildlife, Ohio Fish and Wildlife Report no. 10.

Strode, Donald D. 1954. *The Ocala Deer Herd.* Florida Game and Fresh Water Fish Commission, Game Pub. no. 1.

Synatzske, David R. 1981. *Effects of Baiting on White-tailed Deer Hunting Success.* Texas Pittman-Robertson Project, Job no. 37.

Tebaldi, Angela F., and Diana Kocornik. 1981. *Sybille Controlled Deer Hunt.* Wyoming Pittman-Robertson Project 3-R-26, Work Plan no. 3, Job no. 2W.

Teer, James G. 1965. *Texas Deer Herd Management: Problems and Principles.* Texas Parks and Wildlife Department, Bulletin no. 44.

Transactions of the Second Meeting of the Northeastern Deer Study Group, August 24–26, 1966. Northeastern Deer Study Group.

Transactions of the Fifth Meeting of the Northeastern Deer Study Group, September 9–11, 1969. Northeastern Deer Study Group.

United States Department of the Interior. 1970. *1970 National Survey of Fishing and Hunting.* Resource Publication no. 95.

United States Department of the Interior. 1982. *1980 National Survey of Fishing, Hunting, and Wildlife-Associated Recreation.*

University of Wisconsin-Stevens Point, College of Natural Resources. 1974. *Hunting: Sport or Sin?* University of Wisconsin-Stevens Point.

Vaske, Jerry J., et al. 1984. *The Maryland Deer Hunter: Social Characteristics, Behaviors* and Preferences for Alternative Hunting Regulations. Maryland Wildlife Administration, Pittman-Robertson Project.

Wadsworth, William H., ed. 1975. *Bowhunting Deer: National Bowhunter Education Manual.* National Bowhunter Education Foundation.

Watson, Marvon H., Gale C. Jamsen, and Lewis W. Moncrief. 1972. *The Michigan Deer Hunter.* Michigan Department of Natural Resources, Research and Development Report no. 259.

Weis, Norman D. 1969. *All About the White-tailed Deer.* Denlinger's, Middleburg, Virginia.

Weishuhn, Larry L., Robert L. Cook, and W. Fielding Harwell. 1979. *An Annotated Bibliography of Texas White-tailed Deer Research and Selected Articles From Other States.* Texas Parks and Wildlife Department, Booklet no. 7000–52.

Wennergren, E. Boyd. 1977. *Demand Estimates and Resource Values for Resident Deer Hunting in Utah.* Utah State University, Bulletin 469.

Westover, Alton J. 1971. *The Use of a Hemlock-Hardwood Winter Yard by White-tailed Deer in Northern Michigan.* Occasional Papers of The Huron Mountain Wildlife Foundation, no. 1.

White-tailed Deer in the Midwest: A Symposium, Presented at the 30th Midwest Fish and Wildlife Conference, Columbus, Ohio, December 9, 1968. U.S. Department of Agriculture-Forest Service, Research Paper no. NC-39.

The White-tailed Deer: Its Problems and Potentials, Proceedings of the Wildlife Conference, June 29–30, 1966. Texas A and M University.

Yantis, James H., et al. 1983. *Deer Management in the Post Oak Belt.* Texas Parks and Wildlife Department, Bulletin no. 7000–96.

Deer Movements, Activity Patterns and Home Ranges

Adams, Lowell and Stanley D. Davis. "The Internal Anatomy of Home Range." *Journal of Mammalogy* 48, no. 4 (1967):529–36.

Alexander, Bobby G. "Movements of Deer in Northeast Texas." *Journal of Wildlife Management* 32, no. 3 (1968):618–20.

Altmann, Margaret. "The Flight Distance in Free-Ranging Big Game." *Journal of Wildlife Management* 22, no. 2 (1958):207–209.

Anderson, D. John. "The Home Range: A New Non-parametric Estimation Technique." *Ecology* 63, no. 1 (1982):103–12.

Ashcraft, Gordon C. Jr. "Deer Movements of the McCloud Flats Herds." *California Fish and Game* 47, no. 2 (1961):145–52.

Balding, Terry A. "Radio-tracking a White-tailed Deer." *The Ohio Journal of Science* 67, no. 6 (1967):382–84.

Barkalow, Frederick S. Jr., and Walter E. Keller. "Escape Behavior of the White-tailed Deer." *Journal of Wildlife Management* 14, no. 2 (1950):246–47.

Behrend, Donald F. and Robert A. Lubeck. "Summer Flight Behavior of White-tailed Deer in Two Adirondack Forests." *Journal of Wildlife Management* 32, no. 3 (1968):615–18.

Bryant, Harold C. "The Range of an Individual Deer." *Journal of Mammalogy* 5, no. 3 (1924):201–202.

Bunnell, F. L., and A. S. Harestad. "Dispersal and Dispersion of Black-tailed Deer: Models and Observations." *Journal of Mammalogy* 64, no. 2 (1983):201–209.

Burt, William Henry. "Territoriality and Home Range Concepts as Applied to Mammals." *Journal of Mammalogy* 24, no. 3 (1943):346–52.

Carlsen, J. C., and Robert E. Farmes. "Movements of White-tailed Deer Tagged in Minnesota." *Journal of Wildlife Management* 21, no. 4 (1957):397–401.

Dasmann, Raymand F. "Factors Influencing Movement of Non-migratory Deer." *Proceedings of the Thirty-third Annual Conference of the Western Association of State Game and Fish Commissioners* 33(1953):112–16.

De Young, Charles A. "Possibilities of Discerning Behavior Patterns of Deer Through Use of Radio Telemetry." *Proceedings of the First Welder Wildlife Foundation Symposium* 1(1979):242–48.

Dickey, Charley. "When Do Deer Move? Exploring the Mystery." *North American Whitetail* 2, no. 3 (1983):44–53.

Dickinson, Tony G., and Gerald W. Garner. "Home Range Use and Movements of Desert Mule Deer in Southwestern Texas." *Proceedings of the Annual Conference of the Southeastern Association of Fish and Wildlife Agencies* 33(1979):267–78.

Diehl, Scott R. "Houdini the Whitetail." *Wisconsin Natural Resources* (November/December 1983):25–29.

Downing, Robert L. et al. "Seasonal Changes in Movements of White-tailed Deer." In *White-tailed Deer in the Southern Forest Habitat, Proceedings of the Symposium at Nacogdoches, Texas* (1969):19–24.

Downing, Robert L., and Burd S. McGinnes. "Movement Patterns of White-tailed Deer in a Virginia Enclosure." *Proceedings of the Annual Conference of the Southeastern Association of Game and Fish Commissioners* 29(1975):454–59.

Drolet, Charles A. "Distribution and Movements of White-tailed Deer in Southern New Brunswick in Relation to Environmental Factors." *The Canadian Field-Naturalist* 90, no. 2 (1976):123–36.

Eberhardt, Lester E., Eric E. Hanson, and Larry L. Cadwell. "Movement and Activity Patterns of Mule Deer in the Sagebrush-Steppe Region." *Journal of Mammalogy* 65, no. 3 (1984):404–409.

Eckstein, Ronald G., et al. "Snowmobile Effects on Movements of White-tailed Deer: A Case-study." *Environmental Conservation* 6, no. 1 (1979):45–52.

Ellisor, John E. "Mobility of White-tailed Deer in South Texas." *Journal of Wildlife Management* 33, no. 1 (1969):220–22.

Gladfelter, H. Lee. *Movement and Home Range of Deer as Determined by Radio Telemetry.* Pittman-Robertson Report, Federal Aid Project no. W-115-R, Phase B. Study no. 1 (1978). Iowa.

Glazener, W. C. "Homing Instinct of White-tailed Deer." *Texas Game and Fish* 6, no. 8 (1948):5, 17.

Hahn, Henry C. Jr., and Walter P. Taylor. "Deer Movements in the Edwards Plateau." *Texas Game and Fish.* (November 1950):4–9, 31.

Hamerstrom, F. N. Jr., and James Blake. "Winter Movements and Winter Foods of White-tailed Deer in Central Wisconsin." *Journal of Mammalogy* 20, no. 2 (1939): 206–15.

Hamilton, Rex. "Factors Affecting Dispersal of Deer Released in Indiana." *Journal of Wildlife Management* 26, no. 1 (1962): 79–85.

Harlow, Richard F., and William F. Oliver Jr. "Natural Factors Affecting Deer Movement." *Quarterly Journal of the Florida Academy of Sciences.* 30, no. 3 (1967): 221–26.

Hawkins, R. E., and G. G. Montgomery. "Movements of Translocated Deer as Determined by Telemetry." *Journal of Wildlife Management* 33, no. 1 (1969):196–203.

Hawkins, R. E., W. D. Klimstra, and D. C. Autry. "Dispersal of Deer From Crab Orchard National Wildlife Refuge." *Journal of Wildlife Management* 35, no. 2 (1971): 216–20.

Heezen, Keith L., and John R. Tester. "Evaluation of Radio-Tracking by Triangulation with Special Reference to Deer Movements." *Journal of Wildlife Management* 31, no. 1 (1967):124–41.

Henry, Byron A. M. "Habitat Use and Home Range of White-tailed Deer in Point Pelee National Park, Ontario." *Canadian Field Naturalist* 89, no. 2 (1975):179–81.

Horner, Kent. "Home Range of the White-tailed Deer." *Deer & Deer Hunting* 6, no. 6 (1983):54–58.

Hoskinson, Reed L., and L. David Mech. "White-tailed Deer Migration and its Role in Wolf Predation." *Journal of Wildlife Management* 40, no. 3 (1976):429–41.

Hyngstrom, Scott. "The Effect of Environmental Conditions on Deer Movements." *Deer & Deer Hunting* 6, no. 1 (1982):22–29.

———. "Deer on the Move." *Deer & Deer Hunting* 6, no. 3 (1983):50–57.

———. "Daily Activity Patterns of Deer." *Deer & Deer Hunting* 7, no. 4 (1984):44–45.

Inglis, Jack M., et al. "Home Range of White-tailed Deer in Texas Coastal Prairie Brushland." *Journal of Mammalogy* 60, no. 2 (1979):377–89.

Ishmael, William E., and Stephen DeStefano. "Opening Day Buck Movements." *Deer & Deer Hunting* 7, no. 3 (1984):28–32.

Ishmael, William E., and Orrin J. Rongstad. "Economics of an Urban Deer-Removal Program." *Wildlife Society Bulletin* 12, no. 4 (1984):394–98.

Ivey, Tim L., and M. Keith Causey. "Movements and Activity Patterns of Female White-tailed Deer During Rut." *Proceedings of the Annual Conference of the Southeastern Association of Fish and Wildlife Agencies* 35(1981):149–66.

Jackson, Rodney M., Marshall White, and Frederick F. Knowlton. "Activity Patterns of Young White-tailed Deer Fawns in South Texas." *Ecology* 53, no. 2 (1972):262–70.

Jeter, Lewis K., and Robert L. Marchinton. "Preliminary Report of Telemetric Study of Deer Movements and Behavior on the Eglin Field Reservation in Northwestern Florida." *Proceeding of the Annual Conference of the Southeastern Association of Game and Fish Commissioners* 18(1964):140–52.

Jewell, P. A. "The Concept of Home Range in Mammals." *Symposium of the Zoological Society of London* 18(1966):85–109.

Kammermeyer, K. E., and R. L. Marchinton. "Notes on Dispersal of Male White-tailed Deer." *Journal of Mammalogy* 57, no. 4 (1976):776–78.

———. "The Dynamic Aspects of Deer Populations Utilizing a Refuge." *Proceedings of the Annual Conference of the Southeastern Association of Game and Fish Commissioners* 29(1976):466–75.

Kroll, James C. "Buck Sanctuaries: Trophy Hunting's Great Discovery. Part I." *North American Whitetail* 4, no. 3 (1985):34–38, 75.

———. "Buck Sanctuaries: Trophy Hunting's Great Discovery. Part II." *North American Whitetail* 4, no. 4 (1985):8–14.

———. "Buck Sanctuaries: Trophy Hunting's Great Discovery. Part III." *North American Whitetail* 4, no. 5 (1985):44–51.

Kucera, Emil. "Deer Flushing Distance as Related to Observer's Mode of Travel." *Wildlife Society Bulletin* 4, no. 3 (1976):128–129.

Larson, Thomas J., Orrin J. Rongstad, and Frank W. Terbilcox. "Movement and Habitat Use of White-tailed Deer in Southcentral Wisconsin." *Journal of Wildlife Management* 42, no. 1 (1978):113–17.

McCullough, Dale R. "Relationship of Weather to Migratory Movements of Black-tailed Deer." *Ecology* 45, no. 2 (1964): 249–56.

Marchinton, Robert L., and Lewis K. Jeter. "Telemetric Study of Deer Movement-Ecology in the Southeast." *Proceedings of the Annual Conference of the Southeastern Association of Game and Fish Commissioners* 20(1966):189–206.

———. "Radio-Telemetic Study of White-tailed Deer Movement and Behavior." *Journal of the Alabama Academy of Science* 38(1967):327–28.

Marshall, A. D., and R. W. Whittington. "A Telemetric Study of Deer Home Ranges and Behavior of Deer During Managed Hunts." *Proceedings of the Annual Conference of the Southeastern Association of Game and Fish Commissioners* 22(1968):30–46.

Michael, Edwin D. "Movements of White-tailed Deer on the Welder Wildlife Refuge." *Journal of Wildlife Management* 29, no. 1 (1965):44–52.

———. "Activity Patterns of White-tailed Deer in South Texas." *Texas Journal of Science* 21, no. 4 (1970):417–28.

Montgomery, G. G. "Nocturnal Movements and Activity Rhythms of White-tailed Deer." *Journal of Wildlife Management* 27, no. 3 (1963):422–27.

Morris, David. "Deer Movements." *Georgia Sportsman.* (November 1980):19–25, 56.

Nelson, Michael E. "Home Range Location of White-tailed Deer." U.S.D.A. Forest Service Research Paper NC-173 (1979). St. Paul, Minnesota.

Nelson, Michael E., and L. David Mech. "Home-Range Formation and Dispersal of Deer in Northeastern Minnesota." *Journal of Mammalogy* 65, no. 4 (1984):567–75.

Ockenfels, Richard A., and John A. Bissonette. "Estimates of White-tailed Deer Activity Levels in Oklahoma." *Proceedings of the Annual Conference of the Southeastern*

Association of Fish and Wildlife Agencies 36(1982):445–53.

Oklahoma Wildlife. "Homing Deer Finds Way Back to Refuge." Oklahoma Wildlife 14, no. 2 (1958):15.

Pilcher, Brian K., and Glen E. Wampler. "Hunting Season Movements of White-tailed Deer on Fort Sill Military Reservation, Oklahoma." Proceedings of the Annual Conference of the Southeastern Association of Fish and Wildlife Agencies 35(1981): 142–48.

Progulske, Donald R., and Thomas S. Baskett. "Mobility of Missouri Deer and Their Harassment by Dogs." Journal of Wildlife Management 22, no. 2 (1958):184–92.

Robinette, W. Leslie. "Mule Deer Home Range and Dispersal in Utah." Journal of Wildlife Management 30, no. 2 (1966):335–49.

Rongstad, Orrin J., and John R. Tester. "Movements and Habitat Use of White-tailed Deer in Minnesota." Journal of Wildlife Management 33, no. 2 (1969):366–79.

Russell, Carl Parcher. "Seasonal Migration of Mule Deer." Ecological Monographs 2, no. 1 (1932):3–46.

Sanderson, Glen C. "The Study of Mammal Movements—A Review." Journal of Wildlife Management 30, no. 1 (1966):215–35.

Schatz, Lyndon. "Trapping and Transplanting: Spreading Deer Around." Texas Parks and Wildlife. (January 1983):8–11.

Schemnitz, Sanford D. "Marine Island-Mainland Movements of White-tailed Deer." Journal of Mammalogy 56, no. 2 (1975): 535–37.

Severinghaus, C. W. "Fall Movements of Adirondack Deer." New York State Conservationist 7, no. 2 (1952):6–7.

Siglin, Roger J. Movements and Capture Techniques: A Literature Review of Mule Deer. Denver: Colorado Department of Game, Fish and Parks, 1965. 38 pp.

Sparrowe, Rollin D., and Paul F. Springer. "Seasonal Activity Patterns of White-tailed Deer in Eastern South Dakota." Journal of Wildlife Management 34, no. 2 (1970): 420–31.

Staines, Brian W. "A Review of Factors Affecting Deer Dispersion and Their Relevance to Management." Mammal Review 4, no. 3 (1974):79–91.

Sweeney, John R., R. Larry Marchinton, and James M. Sweeney. "Responses of Radio-Monitored White-tailed Deer Chased by Hunting Dogs." Journal of Wildlife Management 35, no. 4 (1971):707–16.

Tester, John R., and Donald B. Siniff. "Aspects of Animal Movement and Home Range Data Obtained by Telemetry." North American Wildlife Conference 30(1965): 379–92.

Thomas, Jack Ward, James G. Teer, and E. A. Walker. "Mobility and Home Range of White-tailed Deer on the Edwards Plateau in Texas." Journal of Wildlife Management 28, no. 3 (1964):463–72.

Tierson, William C. et al. "Seasonal Movements and Home Ranges of White-tailed Deer in the Adirondacks." Journal of Wildlife Management 49, no. 3 (1985):760–69.

Verme, Louis J. "Movements of White-tailed Deer in Upper Michigan." Journal of Wildlife Management 37, no. 4 (1973):545–52.

Weeks, Harmon P. Jr. "Characteristics of Mineral Licks and Behavior of Visiting White-tailed Deer in Southern Indiana." The American Midland Naturalist 100, no. 2 (1978):384–95.

Wiles, Gary J., and Harmon P. Weeks Jr. "Movements and Use Patterns of White-tailed Deer Visiting Natural Licks." Journal of Wildlife Management 50, no. 3 (1986): 487–96.

Zagata, Michael D., and Arnold O. Haugen. "Winter Movement and Home Range of White-tailed Deer at Pilot Knob State Park, Iowa." Proceedings of the Iowa Academy of Science 79, no. 2 (1973):74–78.

———. "White-tailed Deer Movement at Pilot Knob State Park, Iowa." Proceedings of the Iowa Academy of Science 81(1974):76–82.

Zwickel, Fred, Gardiner Jones, and Homer Brent. Movement of Columbian Black-tailed Deer in the Willapa Hills Area, Washington. The Murrelet 34, no. 3 (1953):41–46.

Rubs, Scrapes, and Breeding Behavior

Atkeson, Thomas D., and R. Larry Marchinton. "Forehead Glands in White-tailed

Deer." *Journal of Mammalogy* 63, no. 4 (1982):613–17.

Altieri, R., and D. Müller-Schwarze. "Seasonal Changes in Flehmen to Constant Urine Stimuli." *Journal of Chemical Ecology* 6, no. 5 (1980):905–909.

Barrette, Cyrille. "Scent-Marking in Captive Muntjacs, Muntiacus Reevesi." *Animal Behaviour* 25, no. 3 (1977):536–41.

Brown, Bennett A., and David H. Hirth. "Breeding Behavior in White-tailed Deer." *Proceedings of the First Welder Wildlife Foundation Symposium* 1(1979):83–95.

Brownlee, Robert G., and Robert M. Silverstein. "Isolation, Identification and Function of the Chief Component of the Male Tarsal Scent in Black-tailed Deer." *Nature* 221 (January 18, 1969):284–85.

Cheatum, E. L., and Glenn H. Morton. "Breeding Season of White-tailed Deer in New York." *Journal of Wildlife Management* 10, no. 3 (1946):249–63.

Cowan, McT., and Valerius Geist. "Aggressive Behavior in Deer of the Genus Odocoileus." *Journal of Mammalogy* 42, no. 4 (1961): 522–26.

de Vos, Antoon. "Rubbing of Conifers by White-tailed Deer in Successive Years." *Journal of Mammalogy* 48, no. 1 (1967): 146–47.

de Vos, A., P. Brokx, and V. Geist. "A Review of Social Behavior of the North American Cervids during the Reproductive Period." *The American Midland Naturalist* 77, no. 2 (1967):390–417.

Espmark, Yngve. "Rutting Behaviour in Reindeer (Rangifer tarandus L.)." *Animal Behaviour* 12, no. 1 (1964):159–63.

———. "Studies in Dominance-Subordination Relationship in a Group of Semi-Domestic Reindeer (Rangifer tarandus L.)." *Animal Behaviour* 12, no. 4 (1964):420–26.

Forand, Kenneth J., R. Larry Marchinton, and Karl V. Miller. "Influence of Dominance Rank on the Antler Cycle of White-tailed Deer." *Journal of Mammalogy* 66, no. 1 (1985):58–62.

Geist, Valerius. "How Deer Communicate—The Dominance Game." *Deer & Deer Hunting* 9, no. 6 (1986):34–43.

Graf, William. "Territorialism in Deer." *Journal of Mammalogy* 37, no. 2 (1956):165–70.

Haugen, Arnold O. "Breeding Records of Captive White-tailed Deer in Alabama." *Journal of Mammalogy* 40, no. 1 (1959):108–13.

Hawkins, R. E., and W. D. Klimstra. "A Preliminary Study of the Social Organization of White-tailed Deer." *Journal of Wildlife Management* 34, no. 2 (1970):407–19.

Henderson, Jane, Richard Altieri, and D. Müller-Schwarze. "The Annual Cycle of Flehmen in Black-tailed Deer (Odocoileus hemionus columbianus)." *Journal of Chemical Ecology* 6, no. 3 (1980):537–47.

Hershkovitz, Philip. "The Metatarsal Glands in White-tailed Deer and Related Forms of the Neotropical Region." *Mammalia* 22, no. 4 (1958):537–46.

Hiller, Ilo. "Whitetail Body Language." *Texas Parks & Wildlife.* (December 1980):28–31.

Hoffman, Roger A., and Paul F. Robinson. "Changes in Some Endocrine Glands of White-tailed Deer as Affected by Season, Sex and Age." *Journal of Mammalogy* 47, no. 2 (1966):266–80.

Jacobson, Harry A. *Effects of Delayed Breeding on Reproductive Performance of Female White-tailed Deer and Their Offspring.* Pittman-Robertson Report, Federal Aid in Wildlife Restoration Project W-48-27, 28, 29, 30 (1984). Mississippi.

Kile, Terry L., and R. Larry Marchinton. "White-tailed Deer Rubs and Scrapes: Spatial, Temporal and Physical Characteristics and Social Role." *The American Midland Naturalist* 97, no. 2 (1977):257–66.

Klein, Earl H. "Phenology of Breeding and Antler Growth in White-tailed Deer in Honduras." *Journal of Wildlife Management* 46, no. 3 (1982):826–29.

Kucera, Thomas E. "Social Behavior and Breeding System of the Desert Mule Deer." *Journal of Mammalogy* 59, no. 3 (1978): 463–76.

Marchinton, R. Larry, and W. Gerald Moore. "Auto-Erotic Behavior in Male White-tailed Deer." *Journal of Mammalogy* 52, no. 3 (1971):616–17.

Marchinton, R. L., and T. D. Atkeson. "Plasticity of Sociospatial Behaviour of White-tailed Deer and the Concept of Facultative Territoriality." In *Biology of Deer Production,* edited by Fennessy, P. F., and K. R. Drew. Wellington: The Royal Society of New Zealand, 1985. pp. 375–77.

Miller, Karl V., et al. "Variations in Density and Chemical Composition of White-tailed Deer Antlers." *Journal of Mammalogy* 66, no. 4 (1985):693–701.

Miller, Karl V., R. Larry Marchinton, and Victor F. Nettles. "The Growth Rate of Hooves of White-tailed Deer." *Journal of Wildlife Diseases* 22, no. 1 (1986):129–31.

Miller, Karl V., and R. Larry Marchinton. "New Discoveries About Antler Rubs." *Deer & Deer Hunting* 10, no. 3 (1987):28–31.

Moen, Aaron N. "Buck Rubs." *Deer & Deer Hunting* 10, no. 1 (1986):54–60.

Müller-Schwarze, Dietland. "Complexity and Relative Specificity in a Mammalian Pheromone." *Nature* 223 (August 2, 1969):525–26.

———. "Pheromones in Black-tailed Deer (Odocoileus Hemionus Columbianus)." *Animal Behaviour* 19, no. 1 (1971):141–52.

———. "Responses of Young Black-tailed Deer to Predator Odors." *Journal of Mammalogy* 53, no. 2 (1972):393–94.

———. "Social Significance of Forehead Rubbing in Black-tailed Deer (Odocoileus Hemionus Columbianus)." *Animal Behaviour* 20, no. 4 (1972):788–97.

———. "A Note on the Use of the Antorbital Gland in Marking by Eld's Deer." *Applied Animal Ethology* 1(1975):301–303.

———. "Complex Mammalian Behavior and Pheromone Bioassay in the Field." In *Chemical Signals in Vertebrates,* edited by Müller-Schwarze, D., and M. M. Mozelli. New York: Plenum, 1976. pp. 413–33.

———. "Chemical Signals in Alarm Behavior of Deer." In *Chemical Signals in Vertebrates,* edited by Müller-Schwarze, D., and M. M. Mozelli. New York: Plenum, 1979. pp. 39–51.

———. "Experimental Modulation of Behavior of Free-ranging Mammals by Semiochemicals." In *Chemical Signals in Vertebrates,* edited by Müller-Schwarze, D., and M. M. Mozelli. New York: Plenum, 1982. pp. 235–44.

Müller-Schwarze, Dietland, and Christine Müller-Schwarze. "Olfactory Imprinting in a Precocial Mammal." *Nature* 229 (January 1, 1971):55–56.

———. "Subspecies Specificity of Response to a Mammalian Social Odor." *Journal of Chemical Ecology* 1, no. 1 (1975):125–31.

Müller-Schwarze, Dietland, et al. "Mammalian Pheromone: Identification of Active Component in the Subauricular Scent of the Male Pronghorn." *Science* 183 (March 1, 1974):860–62.

———. "Response to a Mammalian Pheromone and Its Geometric Isomer." *Journal of Chemical Ecology* 2, no. 3 (1976):389–98.

———. "Osmetrichia: Specialized Scent Hair in Black-tailed Deer." *Journal of Ultrastructure Research* 59(1977):223–30.

———. "The Caudal Gland in Reindeer (Rangifer tarandus L.): Its Behavioral Role, Histology and Chemistry." *Journal of Chemical Ecology* 3, no. 5 (1977):591–601.

———. "The 'Deer Lactone': Source, Chiral Properties, and Responses by Black-tailed Deer." *Journal of Chemical Ecology* 4, no. 2 (1978):247–56.

———. "Responses of Reindeer to Interdigital Secretions of Conspecifics." *Journal of Chemical Ecology* 4, no. 3 (1978):325–35.

Nielsen, David G., Michael J. Dunlap, and Karl V. Miller. "Pre-rut Rubbing by White-tailed Bucks: Nursery Damage, Social Role, and Management Options." *Wildlife Society Bulletin* 10, no. 4 (1982):341–48.

Ozoga, John J. "Marks of Excellence." *Wisconsin Sportsman.* (September/October 1985):40–42.

———. "The Social Role of Buck Rubs and Scrapes." *Wisconsin Sportsman.* (September/October 1986):23–27, 82–86.

Ozoga, John J., Louis J. Verme, and Craig S. Bienz. "Parturition Behavior and Territoriality in White-tailed Deer: Impact on Neonatal Mortality." *Journal of Wildlife Management* 46, no. 1 (1982):1–11.

Payne, R. L., E. E. Provost, and D. F. Urbston. "Delineation of the Period of Rut and Breeding Season of a White-tailed Deer Population." *Proceedings of the Twentieth Annual Conference of Southeastern Asso-*

ciation of Game and Fish Commissioners 20(1966):130–39.

Quay, W. B. "Histology and Cytochemistry of Skin Gland Areas in the Caribou, Rangifer." *Journal of Mammalogy* 36, no. 2 (1955): 187–201.

———. "Microscopic Structure and Variation in the Cutaneous Glands of the Deer, Odocoileus Virginianus." *Journal of Mammalogy* 40, no. 1 (1959):114–28.

———. "Geographic Variation in the Metatarsal 'Gland' of the White-tailed Deer (Odocoileus Virginianus)." *Journal of Mammalogy* 52, no. 1 (1971):1–11.

Quay, W. B., and Dietland Müller-Schwarze. "Functional Histology of Integumentary Glandular Regions in Black-tailed Deer (Odocoileus Hemionus Columbianus)." *Journal of Mammalogy* 51, no. 4 (1970): 675–94.

———. "Relations of Age and Sex to Integumentary Glandular Regions in Rocky Mountain Mule Deer." *Journal of Mammalogy* 52, no. 4 (1971):670–85.

Richardson, Larry W., et al. "Acoustics of White-tailed Deer (Odocoileus Virginianus)." *Journal of Mammalogy* 64, no. 2 (1983):245–52.

Pruitt, William O. "Rutting Behavior of the White-tailed Deer (Odocoileus Virginianus)." *Journal of Mammalogy* 35, no. 1 (1954):129–30.

Rue, Leonard Lee III. "Forehead Scent Gland in White-tailed Deer." *Deer & Deer Hunting* 6, no. 6 (1983):22–27.

Sawyer, Timothy G., R. Larry Marchinton, and C. Wayne Berisford. "Scraping Behavior in Female White-tailed Deer." *Journal of Mammalogy* 63, no. 4 (1982):696–97.

Severinghaus, C. W. "Some Observations on the Breeding Behavior of Deer." *New York Fish and Game Journal* 2, no. 2 (1955): 239–41.

Thiessen, Del, and Maureen Rice. "Mammalian Scent Gland Marking and Social Behavior." *Psychological Bulletin* 83, no. 4 (1976):505–39.

Thomas, Jack Ward, R. M. Robinson, and R. G. Marburger. "Social Behavior in a White-tailed Deer Herd Containing Hypogonadal Males." *Journal of Mammalogy* 46, no. 2 (1965):314–27.

Verme, Louis J., and John J. Ozoga. "Sex Ratio of White-tailed Deer and the Estrus Cycle." *Journal of Wildlife Management* 45, no. 3 (1981):710–15.

Volkman, N. J., K. F. Zemanek, and D. Müller-Schwarze. "Antorbital and Forehead Secretions of Black-tailed Deer (Odocoileus Hemionus Columbianus): Their Role in Age-Class Recognition." *Animal Behaviour* 26, no. 4 (1978):1098–1106.

Warren, R. J., et al. "Reproductive Behaviour of Captive White-tailed Deer." *Animal Behaviour* 26, no. 1 (1978):179–83.

Wootters, John. "Reading Scrapes Can Help Tell a Successful Hunting Story." *Petersen's Hunting.* (November 1980):18, 20.

Crippling Losses and Wounded Deer Behavior

Anonymous. "Cripple Kill." *Wyoming Wildlife.* (1952):12–15.

Causey, Keith, et al. "Bowhunting White-tailed Deer with SCC-Treated Arrows." *Wildlife Society Bulletin* 6, no. 3 (1978):142–45.

Costley, Richard J. "Crippling Losses Among Mule Deer in Utah." *Thirteenth North American Wildlife Conference* 13(1948): 451–58.

Creed, William A., and John F. Kubisiak. "Experimental Deer Hunt at Sandhill." *Wisconsin Conservation Bulletin* 38, no. 4 (1973): 24–26.

Croft, Robert L. "A Survey of Georgia Bow Hunters." *Proceedings of the Southeastern Association of Game and Fish Commissioners* 17(1963):155–63.

Dahlberg, B. L., and Ralph C. Guettinger. *The White-tailed Deer in Wisconsin.* Wisconsin: Conservation Department (1956). P. 219.

DeBoer, Stanley G. "Waste in the Woods." *Wisconsin Conservation Bulletin* 22, no. 10 (1957):10–15.

———. "Less Waste in the Woods." *Wisconsin Conservation Bulletin* 23, no. 10 (1958): 13–17.

Dechert, James A. "The Effects of Over Population and Hunting on the Fort Knox Herd." *Proceedings of the Southeastern Association* of Game and Fish Commissioners 21(1968):15–23.

Downing, Robert L. "Comparison of Crippling Losses of White-tailed Deer Caused by Archery, Buckshot, and Shotgun Slugs." *Proceedings of the Southeastern Association of Game and Fish Commissioners* 25(1972):77–82.

Etten, Robert C., et al. "Controlled Deer Hunting in a Square Mile Enclosure." *Journal of Wildlife Management* 29, no. 1 (1965):59–73.

Garland, Lawrence E. *Bow Hunting for Deer in Vermont: Some Characteristics of the Hunter, the Hunt and the Harvest.* Montpelier: Vermont Fish and Game Department, 1972. 19 pp.

Gladfelter, H. Lee. "Crippling Loss." *Deer in Iowa.* Iowa Research Bulletins, 1970–1979.

Gladfelter, H. Lee, et al. "Effects of Compound Bow Use on Hunter Success and Crippling Rates in Iowa." *Wildlife Society Bulletin* 11, no. 1 (1983):7–12.

Gladfelter, H. Lee, and James M. Kienzler. "Effects of the Compound Bow on the Success and Crippling Rates in Iowa." In *Proceedings of the Midwest Bowhunting Conference,* Kirk Beattie and Bruce Moss, eds. Stevens Point, 1983. pp. 215–19.

Gore, Horace G., and Glenn A. Boydston. "Archery Wounding Loss in Texas." Unpublished paper presented at the 10th Annual Meeting of the Southeast Deer Study Group, February 22–25, 1987. 16 pp.

Hardin, J. W., and J. L. Roseberry. "Estimates of Unreported Loss Resulting from a Special Deer Hunt on Crab Orchard National Wildlife Refuge." *Proceedings of the Twenty-Ninth Annual Conference of the Southeastern Association of Game and Fish Commissioners* 29(1975):460–66.

Hart, Ray D. "Antelope Crippling Loss and Movement Study, 1959." Pittman-Robertson Report, (1960). South Dakota.

Herron, John S. C. "Deer Harvest and Wounding Loss Associated with Bow Hunting White-tailed Deer." Master's theses, University of Wisconsin-Madison, 1984. 36 pp.

Hofacker, Al. "On the Trail of Wounded Deer: The Philosophy of Waiting." *Deer & Deer Hunting* 10, no. 2 (1986):65–85, 104.

Hunter, Gilbert W. "Crippling Loss." *Big Game Kill.* Colorado State Game and Fish Commission 2(1945):10–11.

Kelker, George A. "Let's Reduce the Crippling Loss on Deer Hunting." *Utah Fish & Game Bulletin.* (September 1955):2–3, 6–7, 12.

Krefting, Laurits W. "Mortality." *Research for Deer Management in the Great Lakes Region.* (1964):27–31.

Landwehr, Thomas J. "Archery Deer Hunter Survey: 1982 Season." Unpublished Report. Minnesota Department of Natural Resources, 1983. 19 pp.

Langenau, Edward E. Jr. "Factors Associated with Hunter Retrieval of Deer Hit by Arrows and Shotgun Slugs." Unpublished paper, 1985.

Leopold, Aldo. *Game Management.* New York: Charles Scribner's Sons, 1961. pp. 188–90.

Lohfeld, Michael. "Determination of the Extent and Importance of Cripple Loss and Illegal Kill During the Fall Deer Seasons." Pittman-Robertson Report, (1978). New Jersey Division of Fish and Game. 26 pp.

Losch, Thomas A., and David E. Samuel. "Unretrieved Deer Left by Hunters: A Literature Review." *Proceedings of the Northeast Fish and Wildlife Conference* (1976):17–34.

McCaffery, Keith R. "On 'Crippling' Sematics: An Opinion." In *Proceedings of the Midwest Bowhunting Conference,* Kirk Beattie and Bruce Moss, eds. Stevens Point, 1983. pp. 213–14.

McCaffery, Keith R., and Frank P. Haberland. "Archery Hunting Impacts on Wisconsin Deer." In *Proceedings of the Midwest Bowhunting Conference,* Kirk Beattie and Bruce Moss, eds. Stevens Point, 1983. pp. 131–45.

McPhillips, Kelly Brian. "Characteristics and Success of South Dakota Archery Deer Hunters." Master's thesis, South Dakota State University, 1983. 49 pp.

McPhillips, Kelly B., et al. "Nonreporting, Success, and Wounding by South Dakota Deer Bowhunters—1981." *Wildlife Society Bulletin* 13, no. 4 (1985):395–98.

Moen, Aaron N. "Crippling Loss . . . How Much of a Problem." *Deer & Deer Hunting* 10, no. 3 (1987):32–35.

Nelson, Urban L. "Losses of Crippled Deer." *The Conservation Volunteer* 43(1944):34–35.

Robinette, W. Leslie. "Deer Mortality from Gunshot Wounds." *Wildlife Leaflet* 295. Washington D.C.: U.S.D.I. Fish and Wildlife Service, 1947. 8 pp.

Robinette, W. Leslie, N. V. Hancock, and D. A. Jones. "Hunting Mortality." In *The Oak Creek Mule Deer Herd in Utah*. Publication no. 77-15. Salt Lake City: Utah Division of Wildlife, 1977. pp. 81–91.

Sanders, Roy Dale. "Results of a Study of the Harvesting of Whitetail Deer in the Chequamegon National Forest." *Fourth North American Wildlife Conference* 4(1939):549–53.

Schofield, R. D. "Waste in the Woods." *Michigan Conservation*. (November/December 1958):22–24.

———. "Determining Hunting Season Waste of Deer by Following Fox Trails." *Journal of Wildlife Management* 24, no. 3 (1960): 342–44.

Severinghaus, C. W. "Effectiveness of Archery in Controlling Deer Abundance on the Howland Island Game Management." *New York Fish and Game Journal*. (July 1963): 186–93.

Sheriff, Steven, Kurt Haroldson, and Norb Giessman. *Survey of Archery Hunters of Deer and Turkey in Missouri, 1980*. Special Report, Missouri Department of Conservation, 1983. 12 pp.

Stapley, H. D. "Deer Illegal Kill and Wounding Loss." Pittman-Robertson Report (1971). Salt Lake City, Utah. 7 pp.

Stormer, Fred, et al. "Hunter-Inflicted Wounding of White-tailed Deer." *The Wildlife Society Bulletin* 7, no. 1 (1979):10–16.

Strode, Donald D. "Deer Losses." *The Ocala Deer Herd*. Game Publication no. 1. Tallahassee: Florida Game and Fresh Water Fish Commission, 1954. Pp. 28–31.

Swank, Wendell G. "Mortality." *The Mule Deer in Arizona Chaparral and an Analysis of other Important Deer Herds*. Wildlife Bulletin no. 3. Phoenix: Arizona Game and Fish Department, 1958. Pp. 78–79.

Tully, Robert J., and Paul F. Gilbert. "Mortality Factors Affecting Deer and Elk Herds:

Determination of Hunting Loss." Pittman-Robertson Report (1957). Colorado Fish and Game Department. 23 pp.

Wallmo, Olof C. "Crippling Loss and Illegal Kill during Hunting Season." In *Mule and Black-tailed Deer of North America*. Lincoln, Nebraska: University of Nebraska Press, 1981. pp. 308–11.

Weeks, Harmon P., et al. 1974. "Unrecovered Losses of White-tailed Deer on the Crane Naval Ammunition Depot." *Thirty-Sixth Midwest Wildlife Conference*. Mimeo. 15 pp.

Wegner, Robert A. "Crippling Losses and the Future of American Deer Hunting." *Deer & Deer Hunting* 5, no. 1 (1981):18–27.

Welch, Robert D. "Progress on Mule Deer Crippling Loss Study in New Mexico." *Proceedings of the Western Association of State Game and Fish Commissioners* (1971). Colorado. pp. 415–27.

———. "Illegal Kill and Crippling Loss of Deer during Regulated Hunting Seasons." Pittman-Robertson Report (1974). New Mexico.

Whitlock, S. C., and Lee Eberhardt. "Large-Scale Dead Deer Survey: Methods, Results and Management Implications." *Twenty-First North American Wildlife Conference* 21(1956):555–66.

Wisconsin Department of Natural Resources. "The Archery-Deer Crippling Controversy." Unpublished manuscript, n.d. Wisconsin.

———. "Deer Crippling Losses — Bow Versus Gun." Unpublished manuscript, 1968. Wisconsin.

Worsham, Daniel. 1977. "A Survey of Unrecovered Deer Hunting Losses at Land Between the Lakes, 1977." Tennessee. Mimeo. 30 pp.

The Human Dimensions of Hunting

Amory, Cleveland. *Man Kind? Our Incredible War on Wildlife*. New York: Harper & Row, 1974. 372 pp.

Anderson, J. K. *Hunting in the Ancient World*. Berkeley: University of California Press, 1985. 192 pp.

Ardrey, Robert. *The Hunting Hypothesis: A Personal Conclusion Concerning the Evolu-

tionary Nature of Man. New York: Atheneum, 1976. 242 pp.

―――. *The Territorial Imperative: A Personal Inquiry into the Animal Origins of Property and Nations*. New York: Dell Publishing, 1966. 390 pp.

Audubon, Marie R. *Audubon and His Journals*. Vols. 1 and 2. Gloucester: Peter Smith, 1972. 1086 pp.

B. B., ed. *The Shooting Man's Bedside Book*. New York: Charles Scribner's Sons, 1948. 479 pp.

Bourjaily, Vance. *The Unnatural Enemy*. New York: Dial Press, 1963. 181 pp.

Brander, Michael. *Hunting & Shooting: From Earliest Times to the Present Day*. New York: G. P. Putnam's Sons, 1971. 255 pp.

―――. *The Hunting Instinct: The Development of Field Sports over the Ages*. Edinburgh: Oliver and Boyd, 1964. 176 pp.

Brokaw, Howard P., ed. *Wildlife and America: Contributions to an Understanding of American Wildlife and its Conservation*. Washington: U.S. Government Printing Office, 1978. 532 pp.

Butler, Alfred Joshua. *Sport in Classic Times*. Los Altos, Calif.: William Kaufmann, Inc., 1975. 213 pp.

Capstick, Peter Hathaway. *Death in the Silent Places*. New York: St. Martin's Press, 1981. 258 pp.

Caras, Roger A. *Death as a Way of Life*. Boston: Little, Brown and Company, 1970. 173 pp.

Chalmers, Patrick. *The History of Hunting*. Philadelphia: J. B. Lippincott Company, 1936. 384 pp.

Clark, Stephen R. L. *The Moral Status of Animals*. Oxford: Oxford University Press, 1984. 221 pp.

―――. *The Nature of the Beast: Are Animals Moral?* Oxford: Oxford University Press, 1984. 127 pp.

Coon, Carleton S. *The Hunting Peoples*. Boston: Little, Brown and Company, 1971. 413 pp.

Dickey, James. *Deliverance*. New York: Dell Publishing, 1970. 236 pp.

Durant, Mary, and Michael Harwood. *On the Road with John James Audubon*. New York: Dodd, Mead and Company, 1980. 638 pp.

Eaton, Randall L. *Zen and the Art of Hunting: A Personal Search for Environmental Values*. Nevada: Carnivore Press, 1987. 137 pp.

Evans, George Bird. *Men Who Shot and Wrote About It*. Pioneer Press of West Virginia, 1983. 203 pp.

Fox, Michael W. *Returning to Eden: Animal Rights and Human Responsibility*. New York: Viking Press, 1980. 281 pp.

Frazer, Sir James George. *The Golden Bough: A Study in Magic and Religion*. New York: Macmillan Publishing Co., 1922. 864 pp.

Fromm, Erich. "Man the Hunter: The Anthropological Adam." In *The Anatomy of Human Destructiveness*. New York: Holt, Rinehart, Winston, 1973. pp. 129–44.

Groos, Karl. *The Play of Animals*. New York: Arno Press, 1976. 341 pp.

Hemingway, Ernest. *Green Hills of Africa*. New York: Charles Scribner's Sons, 1935. 295 pp.

Herscovici, Alan. *Second Nature: The Animal-Rights Controversy*. Montreal: CBC Enterprises, 1985. 254 pp.

Hinman, Bob. *The Golden Age of Shotgunning*. New York: Winchester Press, 1975. 175 pp.

Huizinga, Johan. *Homo Ludens: A Study of the Play Element in Culture*. Boston: Beacon Press, 1955. 220 pp.

Humphrey, William. *Home From the Hill*. New York: Dell Publishing, 1984. 312 pp.

―――. *Open Season*. New York: Delacorte Press, 1986. 323 pp.

Krutch, Joseph Wood. *The Great Chain of Life*. Boston: Houghton Mifflin Company, 1956. 227 pp.

Lee, Richard B., and Irven DeVore, eds. *Man the Hunter*. New York: Aldine Publishing Company, 1979. 415 pp.

Leopold, Aldo. *A Sand County Almanac*. New York: Ballantine Books, 1966. 295 pp.

Leopold, Luna B., ed. *Round River: From the Journals of Aldo Leopold*. New York: Oxford University Press, 1953. 173 pp.

Lindsey, Alton A., ed. *The Bicentennial of John James Audubon.* Bloomington: Indiana University Press, 1985. 175 pp.

Lorenz, Konrad. *On Aggression.* New York: Bantam Books, 1967. 306 pp.

McCoy, J. J. *In Defense of Animals.* New York: Seabury Press, 1978. 192 pp.

McGuane, Thomas. *The Sporting Club.* New York: Farrar, Straus and Giroux, 1968. 220 pp.

Messenger, Christian K. *Sport and the Spirit of Play in American Fiction: Hawthorne to Faulkner.* New York: Columbia University Press, 1981. 369 pp.

Moore, Patrick, ed. *Against Hunting: A Symposium.* London: Victor Gollancz Ltd., 1965. 159 pp.

Neihardt, John G. *Black Elk Speaks.* New York: Washington Square Press, 1959. 238 pp.

Ortega y Gasset, Jose. *Meditations on Hunting.* New York: Charles Scribner's Sons, 1985. 132 pp.

Petchenik, Jordan B., and Thomas A. Heberlein. "Aggression and Hunting: Personality and Social Differences Between Wildlife Photographers and Hunters." Unpublished paper presented at the First National Symposium on Social Science Resource Management, Corvallis, Oregon, May 12–16, 1986. 24 pp.

Phillips, John C., and Lewis Webb Hill, eds. *Classics of the American Shooting Field: A Mixed Bag for the Kindly Sportsman, 1783-1926.* Boston: Houghton Mifflin Company, 1930. 214 pp.

Regan, Tom. *The Case for Animal Rights.* Berkeley: University of California Press, 1983. 425 pp.

———. *All That Dwell Therein: Essays on Animal Rights and Environmental Ethics.* Berkeley: University of California Press, 1982. 249 pp.

Regan, Tom, and Peter Singer, eds. *Animal Rights and Human Obligations.* Englewood Cliffs: Prentice-Hall, Inc., 1976. 250 pp.

Ruffer, Jonathan Garnier. *The Big Shots: Edwardian Shooting Parties.* New York: Arco Publishing Company, 1977. 144 pp.

Ringer, Alexander Lothar. "The Chase: Historical and Analytical Bibliography of a Musical Genre." Ph.D. diss., Columbia University, 1955. 431 pp.

Salt, Henry S. *Animals' Rights: Considered in Relation to Social Progress.* Clarks Summit: Society for Animal Rights, Inc. 1980. 232 pp.

Schullery, Paul. "Introduction." In *Theodore Roosevelt: Wilderness Writings.* Salt Lake City: Peregrine Smith Books, 1986. 292 pp.

Serpell, James. *In the Company of Animals.* Oxford: Basil Blackwell, 1986. 215 pp.

Shepard, Paul. *Nature and Madness.* San Francisco: Sierra Club Books, 1982. 178 pp.

———. *The Tender Carnivore and the Sacred Game.* New York: Charles Scribner's Sons, 1973. 302 pp.

Singer, Peter. *Animal Liberation: A New Ethics for Our Treatment of Animals.* New York: Avon Books, 1975. 297 pp.

Singer, Peter, ed. *In Defense of Animals.* New York: Basil Blackwell Inc., 1985. 224 pp.

———. *Practical Ethics.* Cambridge: Cambridge University Press, 1980. 237 pp.

Thomas, Keith. *Man and the Natural World: A History of the Modern Sensibility.* New York: Pantheon Books, 1983. 427 pp.

Thomas, Richard H. *The Politics of Hunting.* England: Gower Publishing Company Limited, 1983. 313 pp.

Tober, James A. *Who Owns the Wildlife? The Political Economy of Conservation in Nineteenth-Century America.* Westport, Connecticut: Greenwood Press, 1981. 330 pp.

Trefethen, James B. *Crusade for Wildlife: Highlights in Conservation Progress.* Harrisburg: Stackpole Books, 1961. 377 pp.

———. *An American Crusade for Wildlife.* New York: Winchester Press, 1975. 409 pp.

Turgenieff, Ivan. *Memoirs of a Sportsman.* New York: Charles Scribner's Sons, 1927. 347 pp.

Verney, Peter. *Homo Tyrannicus: A History of Man's War Against Animals.* London: Mills and Boon Limited, 1979. 187 pp.

Waterman, Charles F. *Hunting in America.* New York: Holt, Rinehart and Winston, 1973. 250 pp.

Wilson, Edward O. *Biophilia*. Cambridge, Massachusetts: Harvard University Press, 1984. 157 pp.

————. *On Human Nature*. Toronto: Bantam Books, 1982. 272 pp.

————. *Sociobiology*. Cambridge, Massachusetts: Belknap Press, 1980. 366 pp.

Chapter 24

Booksellers Who Specialize in Out-of-Print Outdoor Literature

In response to a cultural crisis, an underground network of secondhand booksellers specializing in outdoor and natural history subjects has sprung up. Although such booksellers do not produce new titles, they do help ensure that the best from the golden years of outdoor recreation and research will not be lost.

—George Reiger, 1981

Kenneth Anderson Books
38 Silver Street
Auburn, MA 01501
(617) 832-3524

Angler's and Shooter's Bookshelf
Goshen, CT 06756
(203) 491-2500

Judith Bowman Books
Pound Ridge Road
Bedford, NY 10506
(914) 234-7543

Seymour Brecher
The Woodland Gallery
Box 987
Monticello, NY 12701

Callahan & Company Booksellers
Box 505
Peterborough, NH 03458
(603) 924-3726

Gamebag
Box 838
Twin Lakes, WI 53181
(414) 279-5478

Gary L. Estabrook—Books
Box 61453
Vancouver, WA 98666
(206) 699-5454

Colonel J. Furniss
Old Police House
Strathpeffer
Ross-shire
Great Britain

Grayling Books
Lyvennet, Crosby Ravensworth, Penrith
Cumbria CA10 3JP
Great Britain

Gunnerman Books
P.O. Box 4292
Auburn Hills, MI 48057
(313) 879-2779

Donald E. Hahn
Natural History Books
Box 1004
Cottonwood, AZ
86326
(602) 634-5016

E. Chalmers Hallam
9 Post Office Lane, St. Ives
Ringwood, Hants BH24 2PG
Great Britain

Morris Heller
Box 46
Swan Lake, NY 12783
(914) 583-5879

Henderson & Park
Fifth and Main
Greenwood, MO 64034
(816) 537-6388

Patricia Ledlie — Bookseller
Box 46B
Buckfield, ME 04220
(207) 336-2969

Melvin Marcher Bookseller
6204 N. Vermont
Oklahoma City, OK 73112
(405) 946-6270

Piece of Time
Jack Ragonese
North Stonington, CT 06359
(203) 535-1375

Pisces and Capricorn Books
514 Linden Ave.
Albion, MI 49224
(517) 629-3267

Ray Riling Arms Books Co.
6844 Gorsten St.
P.O. Box 18925
Philadelphia, PA 19119
(215) 438-2456

Lou Razek
Highwood Farms Books
P.O. Box 1246
Traverse City, MI 49684
(616) 271-3898

Trophy Room Books
Box 3041
Aqoura, CA 91301
(818) 889-2469

University Microfilms International
Dissertation Copies
P.O. Box 1764
Ann Arbor, MI 48106
(To order by phone and credit card, call
(800) 521-3042, toll free.)

John Valle
550 Mohawk Rd.
West Hempstead, NY 11552
(516) 887-3342

Watkins Natural History Books
Rebecca and Larry C. Watkins
R.D. #1
Belden Corners Rd.
Dolgeville, NY 13329-9526
(518) 568-2280

R. E. and G. B. Way, A.B.A.
Brettons
Burrough Green, Newmarket, Suffolk
CB8 9NA
Great Britain

Index